SOUL

Without the support of these special companies this book would not have been possible. As always our huge thanks go to the people who believed in this project and said "yes"!

BARNEYS
NEWYORK

EMPORIO ARMANI

Paul Smith

In support of

i-D

SOUL

300 of i-D's best loved international contributors and collaborators share their ideas and thoughts on contemporary values.

Edited by Tricia Jones

TASCHEN

soul i-D

Introduction 9. Foreword 11

family future positive

Orion Best 18. Zoe Bedeaux 19. Judy Blame 19. Moira Bogue 20. Koto Bolofo 21. Mark Borthwick and Maria Cornejo 22. Paul Burston 24. Jake and Dinos Chapman 24. Donald Christie 25. Lena Corner 26. Giannie Couji 26. Joe Casely-Hayford 27. David Davies 28. Sophie Dahl 28. Fiona Dallanegra 28. Kevin Davies 29. Soraya Dayani 30. Tony and Janey Elliott 31. Luther Enninful 32. Edward Enninful 32. Jason Evans 36. Fabrizio Ferri 37. Kathryn Flett 38. Christine Fortune 38. Caryn Franklin 39. Susanna Glaser 40. Jane How 40. Adam Howe 41. Rick Haylor 41. Kayt Jones 42. Dylan Jones 44. Matt Jones 45. Terry Jones 46. Tricia Jones 47. Charlotte Knight 50. Nick Knight 051. Helmut Lang 56. James Lavelle 58. Ralph Lauren 58. Mark Lebon 60. Angel Lopez 64. Mark Mattock 65. Eamonn J McCabe 66. Cameron McVey and Neneh Cherry 68. Pat McGrath 69. Michel Momy 69. Donald Milne 70. Dennis Morris 70. Jeremy Murch 72. Paolo Roversi 73. Amber Rowlands 74. Stefan Ruiz 77. Derrick Santini 78. Elfie Semotan 82. James Sleaford 84. Julie Sleaford 84. Raf Simons 84. Talvin Singh 85. David Sims 86. Francesca Sorrenti 90. Mario Sorrenti and Mary Frey 91. Vanina Sorrenti 92. Paul Smith 92. Bernard Sumner 93. Beth Summers 93. Sølve Sundsbø 94. Philip Treacy 95. Juergen Teller 96. Wolfgang Tillmans 98. Oliviero Toscani 100. Ellen Von Unwerth 102. Donatella Versace 102. Alek Wek 103. Veronica Webb 103. Max Vadukul 104. Paul Wetherell 106. Melanie Ward 107. Jonathan Worth 108. Patti Wilson 109.

beyond price

Giorgio Armani 126. Mark Anthony 126. Fabien Baron 127. Caroline Baker 127. Antonio Berardi 128. Vanessa Beecroft 128. Judy Blame 128. Moira Bogue 130. Hardy Blechman 130. Victoria Bartlett 131. Koto Bolofo 132. Zowie Broach and Brian Kirkby (Boudicca) 136. Gemma Booth 136. Matt Brooke 137. Paul Burston 137. Danny Burrows 137. Terry Burgess 138. BJ Cunningham 138. Hussein Chalayan 139. Rowan Chernin 140. Bethan Cole 140. Susan Corrigan 141. Giannie Couji 142. Fiona Dallanegra 142. Ann Demeulemeester 143. Robin Derrick 144. Larry Dunstan 145. Alessandro Dell'Acqua 145. Jason Evans 146. Sean Ellis 146. Alberta Ferretti 148. Caryn Franklin 148. Simon Foxton 148. Manuela Gherardi 149. Malcolm Garrett 149. Johnny Giunta 150. Nick Griffiths 151. Mauricio Guillen 152. Georgina Goodman 153. Rick Haylor 153. Frank Horvat 154. Wichy Hassan 154. Jane How 155. Henrik Halvarsson 156. Marc Jacobs 158. Adam Howe 158. Paul Hunwick 159. Liz Johnson-Artur 159. Matt Jones 160. Kayt Jones 162. Terry Jones 164. Tricia Jones 166. Donna Karan 167. Calvin Klein 167. Nick Knight 168. Hiroshi Kutomi 169. David LaChapelle 170. Kate Law 172. Mark Lebon 174. Helmut Lang 176. Grace Lam 177. James Lavelle 177. Merryn Leslie 177. Duc Liao 178. Angel Lopez 180. Meg Matthews 181. Julien Macdonald 181. Paul Mittleman 181. Avril Mair 181. Maison Martin Margiela 182. Stella McCartney 184. Kylie Minogue and William Baker 185. Issey Miyake 186. Michel Momy 187. Eddie Monsoon 188. Kate Moss 189. Dennis Morris 190. Clare Moyle 191. Kostas Murkudis 192. Miuccia Prada 192. Tobias Peggs 193. John Pearson 194. Terry Richardson 195. Paolo Roversi 196. Amber Rowlands 197. Inacio Ribeiro and Suzanne Clements 197. Stefan Ruiz 198. Marcus Ross 198. Derrick Santini 199. Sarah 200. Peter Saville 201. Elfie Semotan 202. Alix Sharkey 203. Nigel Shafran 204. David Sims 206. Jil Sander 207. Talvin Singh 208. Franca Soncini 208. Paul Smith 208. Eugene Souleiman 209. Vanina Sorrenti 210. Beth Summers 210. Guido Torlonia 211. Rossella Tarabini 211. Atsuro Tayama 211. Alexi Tan 212. Naoki Takizawa 212. Takemoto Takahiko 213. Marcia Taylor 213. Juergen Teller 214. Inez Van Lamsweerde and Vinoodh Matadin 216. Ellen Von Unwerth 218. Tim Walker 220. Glenn Waldron 221.

learn and pass it on

Ron Arad 238. Hilary Alexander 238. Giorgio Armani 239. Eloise Alemany 240. Paul Archer 241. Marie-Claude Beaud 242. Zoe Bedeaux 243. Mark Borthwick 244. Anette Aurell 246. Neil Barrett 247. Veronique Branquinho 248. Gemma Booth 248. Neville Brody 249. Antonio Berardi 252. Richard Buckley 252. Jeff Burton 252. Martha Camarillo 254. Nick Compton 254. Maurizio Cattelan 255. Natascha Chadha 256. Hussein Chalayan 257. Tim Chave 258. Suzy Crabtree 259. Donald Christie 260. His Holiness the Dalai Lama 262. Kevin Davies 264. Fiona Dallanegra 265. Peter de Potter 266. Fred Dechnik 267. Uwe Doll 268. Thomas Degen 269. Larry Dunstan 270. Pete Drinkell 272. Tracey Emin 273. Edward Enninful 274. Jason Evans 275. Kevin Ellis 276. Lorenzo Fluxá 276. Simon Foxton 276. Caryn Franklin 277. Tom Ford 277. Stephen Gan and Tobias Schweitzer 278. Kate Garner 279. Didier Grumbach 280. Laura Genninger 281. Liz Hancock 282. Matthew E. Hawker 282. Amanda Harlech 283. Steve Harris 283. Jake Gavin 284. Amanda Gowing 285. Mark Hooper 286. Desiree Heiss 286. Marc Jacobs 287. Takashi Homma 287. Matt Jones 288. Terry Jones 290. Gabriela Just 291. Tricia Jones 292. Nick Knight 294. Hiroshi Kutomi 299. Calvin Klein 299. Joerg Koch 300. Julien Macdonald 300. Karen Leong 301. Duc Liao 301. Maison Martin Margiela 302. Mark Mattock 304. Craig McDean 306. Iain McKell 308. Michel Mallard 309. Shawn Mortensen 310. Alasdair McLellan 312. Colin McDowell 312. Ravi Naidoo 313. Raffaello Napoleone 314. Nadia Narain 315. Helmut Newton 316. Bianca Pilet 317. Jessica Ogden 318. Miuccia Prada 318. Jane Peverley 319. Tesh Patel 319. Clarice Pecori-Giraldi 320. Shannon Plumb 320. Vava Ribeiro 322. Terry Richardson 324. Mischa Richter 326. Carlo Rivetti 327. Oriana Reich 328. Anita Roddick 328. Myriam Roehri 330. Renzo Rosso 331. Gilles Rosier 331. Paolo Roversi 332. Amber Rowlands 333. Kris Ruhs 334. Derrick Santini 337. Sarah 337. Stephan Schneider 338. Jicky Schnee 338. Paul Smith 338. Shambhala 339. Venetia Scott 340. Irene Silvagni 341. Raf Simons 342. Robert Triefus and Caleb Negron 343. Francesca Sorrenti 344. Vanina Sorrenti 344. Stephen Sprouse 346. Angelika Taschen 346. Marcia Taylor 347. Wolfgang Tillmans 348. Juergen Teller 350. Max Vadukul 352. Willy Vanderperre and Olivier Rizzo 353. Milan Vukmirovic 354. Ellen Von Unwerth 356. Iain R. Webb 358. Jules Wright 358. Vivienne Westwood 358. Patti Wilson 359. Paul Wetherell 359.

not in our name

Miguel Adrover 373. Joe Casely-Hayford 374. Hussein Chalayan 375. Peter de Potter 375. Tracey Emin 376. Sophia Kokosalaki 377. Terry Jones 377. Mark Lebon 378. Ali Mahdavi 379. Antonio Marras 380. Alexander McQueen 381. Shawn Mortensen 382. Keiron O'Connor 384. Nathalie Ours 384. Maryvonne Numata 385. Carlo and Sabina Rivetti 386. Dominique Renson 387. Kris Ruhs 388. Mischa Richter 389. Bob and Roberta Smith 389. Raf Simons 390. Paul Smith 391. Jun Takahashi 392. Dries Van Noten 393. Matthias Vriens 394. Ellen Von Unwerth 396.

make poverty history

Dennis Morris 401. Giorgio Armani 402. David Bailey 402. Johnny Borrell 403. Judy Blame 403. Orion Best 404. Rose Bakery 405. Koto Bolofo 406. Bono 408. Gemma Booth 410. Neville Brody 411. Boudicca (Zowie Broach and Brian Kirkby) 412. Joe Cohen 412. Joe Casely-Hayford 413. Larry Dunstan 414. Uwe Doll 415. Olafur Eliasson 416. Jason Evans 417. Tracey Emin 418. Caryn Franklin 419. Sheryl Garratt 420. Bob Geldof 422. Katharine Hamnett 424. Terry Jones 424. Tricia Jones 425. Nick Knight 426. Jessica Landon 428. Mark Lebon 429. Wangari Maathai 430. Matt Jones 432. Chris Martin 433. Alexander McQueen 435. Renzo Rosso 436. Yoko Ono 437. Anita Roddick 437. Khamis Ally Pandu 437. Kris Ruhs 438. Peter Saville 440. Dr. Vandana Shiva 441. Paul Smith 442. Marcia Taylor 442. Tennekoon 443. Wolfgang Tillmans 444. Dries Van Noten 446. Patrick Vieira 447. Marcus Tomlinson 454.

safe+sound

Chidi Achara 460. Giorgio Armani 461. Christopher Bailey 462. Ben Benoliel 462. Clare Bennett 463. Claire Badhams 464. Debbie Bragg and Sarah Bentley 464. Orion Best 465. Sam Bleakley 466. Neville Brody 468. Gemma Booth 469. Veronique Branquinho 469. Jota Castro 470. Lauren Cochrane 472. Hussein Chalayan 473. Stuart Cohen 474. Francisco Costa 477. Fraser Cooke 478. Maria Cornejo 479. Eduardo Costantini 480. Nicki Cotter 481. Giorgio De Mitri 482. Joanna Dudderidge 484. Dolce & Gabbana 486. Alber Elbaz 487. Edward Enninful 488. Chantelle Fiddy 490. Simon Foxton 491. John Galliano 492. Antony Genn 494. Katia Gomiashvili 495. Georgina Goodman and BJ Cunningham 496. Kim Gordon 498. Bethany Hamilton 499. Gemma Hogan 500. Ian 501. Steve Harris 502. Hannah Jones 502. Stephen Jones 503. Kayt Jones 504. Dylan Jones 506. Matt Jones 507. Terry Jones 508. Tricia Jones 510. Takashi Kamei 512. Kaws 513. Ben Kei 514. Hyun Jung Kim 515. Kirby Koh 516. Sophia Kokosalaki 517. Nick Knight 518. Helmut Lang 519. David LaChapelle 522. Tyrone Lebon 524. Drieke Leenknegt 526. Rufus May 527. Mary McCartney 528. Ryan McGinley 529. Alexander McQueen 530. Francesca McCarthy 531. Dani Kiwi Meier 531. Shawn Mortensen 532. Jo Metson Scott 534. Nadia Narain 538. Erin O'Connor 539. Nathalie Ours 540. Manuela Pavesi 542. Javier Peres 542. Gareth Pugh 543. Millie Robson 544. Kris Ruhs 546. Sabisha 547. Jeremy Scott 547. Peter Saville 548. Collier Schorr 550. Alix Sharkey 551. Wing Shya 552. Raf Simons 554. Matthew Stone 555. Paul Smith 556. Paul D. Smith 558. Jean Touitou 558. Sam Taylor-Wood 559. Marcus Tomlinson 560. Kris Van Assche 561. Kevin Trageser 561. Walter Van Beirendonck 562. Willy Vanderperre 563. Francesco Vezzoli 564. Julian Vogel 566. Ellen Von Unwerth 567. Ben Watts 568. Kevin Wong 570. Yohji Yamamoto 571. Michiko Yamamoto 572. Italo Zucchelli 573.

Biographies 575. Index 598.

Swallows in Heart Tree. Kenya 2005. Photography by Tricia Jones.

introduction

Soul i-D is a selection of work collected over the past ten years. Separate projects originally published independently by i-D with the approval and ok of its founding creative director and editor-in-chief Terry Jones who, luckily for me, has also been for zillions of years my lifetime partner! Undoubtedly without Terry's inspiration and guidance I would never have had such a wide, varied and extraordinary selection of contributors and collaborators to call upon. This book is divided into chapters, the headings of which are the names of the originals Family Future Positive, Beyond Price, Learn and Pass it On and Safe+Sound, but we have also included two sections which appeared in the magazine itself when we felt particularly moved to enter a more political debate.

The realisation that something, which began as a whispered idea to Terry about three to four years ago, has actually become a reality owes everything to Benedikt Taschen's huge trust and confidence in us and also to everyone in the small team who have worked so incredibly hard to put it together. I cannot thank any of you sufficiently or apologise to your partners enough for the many late nights home and dinners missed! It would have been impossible to do it without you.

I have had over the years an idiosyncratic and sometime ambiguous link to the fashion world, often more boys' style than girls and certainly happiest in jeans and classic Converse or Superga white trainers. For this reason I am more often defined by my footwear than anything else! However, the friendships and talents represented through this book will, I think, show a different side of a creative industry too often represented as shallow and myopic. Neither Terry nor I are particularly comfortable in the media spotlight, but I have become increasingly aware of the extraordinary responsibility that being an independent voice within the publishing world carries. Unencumbered by financial suits and strategy gurus we have, within the constraints always of a limited budget, been free in a different way to explore ideas and beliefs that are important to both of us. As I have said to friends and collaborators many times, realising that hugely successful and serious companies choose us to carry their advertising campaigns because they feel that we can, in some small way, influence the way someone buys a bag or a pair of shoes, made me realise that this also allows us to "use" this influence – however small that may be, to think about other things that affect all of our lives – if you like a slightly alternative view of an increasingly consumer led contemporary society.

The important thing to understand is that each chapter of the book at once marks a moment in time and has therefore been left largely untouched (apart from rearranging contributors in alphabetical order) but yet, I hope, carries a timeless message from those who contributed. Looking back on these pieces over the past few months, revisiting things I thought I already knew so well, has given me personally the hugest pleasure. Many is the evening when Matthew Hawker has sat patiently at his computer with me looking over his shoulder as we moved and rearranged for the umpteenth time, to fit just one more "must-have" piece in. There is also a real excitement that we will hopefully reach a much wider audience with this book and Taschen's distribution skills, than we were ever able to do simply as i-D.

If those of you who pick this up, feel at least some of the energy, love and passion that's gone into putting the book together then it will be totally worthwhile. It's a small present from us to you which we send out into the world with the utmost humility and once again my very hugest thanks to everyone who has agreed to be part of it.

Tricia Jones
February 2008

Ripple. Wales 2003. Photography by Tricia Jones.

foreword

"For in one soul are contained the hopes and feelings of all mankind"
Kahlil Gibran

I first came across these books, now compiled as Soul i-D, in February 2002. February 1st actually. I remember the specific date because I have a copy of a card, written fervently that evening to Tricia, thanking her for a gift rich in hope, broad in original expression and unified in the similarities that make up that greatness which is the human spirit. I only ever keep a copy of my pen and ink correspondence when it is vital for me, at a later date, to refer back and somehow glean faith or spiritual solace from the experience that prompted the writing. I have several that relate to the progression of this project and all say more or less the same thing. That as a reader, I have been overwhelmed by the depth and generosity of the stories shared within these pages, the courage and innovative images that gently scream volumes about our human condition.

We are living in confusing times. We have no definitive enemy, no clear nemesis to focus our energies. It is no longer 1939. We are surrounded by uncertainty, whether it be economic implosion, corporate dictation on how we live, lack of trust in our governing leaders or sheer apathy in the face of ever escalating global issues. It's difficult to keep track, to find home or to begin again from an explicit starting point – we're constantly in a state of catch-up. It's not too hard to feel overwhelmed.

Where I find hope, juice if you like, is that even during these times, there are those who are willing and committed, compelled perhaps, despite situation or social background, to drop the mask and share candidly what they think, feel and have had to overcome – dedicated to honoring their truth, sharing their wisdom and in doing so, creating a bond that is beyond the frenetic minefield that is modern life. In revealing themselves, they collectively invite us all to do likewise. To pause, to centre ourselves and to ask ourselves those questions that define our very essence, our individual souls.

Much has been made of this being the 'Age of Aquarius'. A period of time that some say began around the year 2000. It is an age in which the pursuit of wealth and power at any cost and man's desecration of our planet's resources will finally come to a head. An introspective time when, as one global race, we will be forced through the consequences of our previous actions to take stock, heed the bigger picture and shift to a more rewarding and holistic consciousness. If we were to find our world reduced to the bare essentials, then wouldn't the greatest fear be to discover that as a race, we really weren't equipped with the necessary basics to seed a new beginning?

Within these pages, you will be taken on a journey that clearly validates that we do indeed have all the gifts and virtues imperative to forge a better future. My hope is that you will be enthused with faith, relieved to find that you are not alone and inspired to confront any problem, no matter how daunting. The human spirit is a glorious thing, and at its best, capable of transcending the most critical obstacles. In attempting this however, it is paramount that we engage our creative spirit and embrace our common integrity – examples of which are evident on every page of this book.

And so with this in mind, I am eternally grateful to Tricia and Terry, the ever grafting i-D team and to all those brave and brilliant people who have whole-heartedly contributed to this volume.

Welcome to Soul i-D

John Pearson
22nd February 2008

This book is dedicated to all of our children and
grandchildren and the hope that we can all take responsibility
for the world and the values they will inherit.

My big personal thanks must also go to:
Gemma Hogan, Karen Leong, Matthew Hawker and Ben
Kei from the i-D team for their huge dedication in putting
this book together – I definitely could not have done it
without you.
John Pearson our outside, unbiased pair of eyes who has
proved such a brilliant support.
Benedikt Taschen for believing and trusting us with this
project – it's been a very great honour.
Simone Philippi from TASCHEN for guiding it so
sympathetically, but professionally once it left our hands.
And finally Renzo Rosso the Head of the Diesel group and two
key members of his team Antonella Viero and Fed Tan who
have supported us from the very beginning of this project.

FUTURE POSITIVE

family

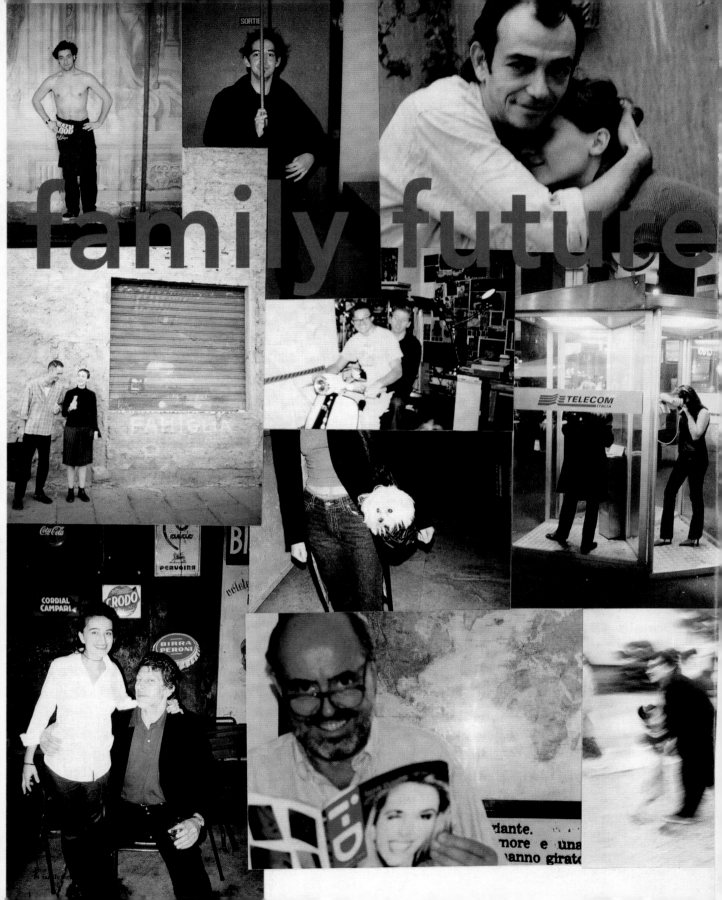

family future

positive

15

family future positive

The concept initially was mine to make a special issue of i-D which would be a celebration of family in its broadest sense. The challenge to come up with a title and a message that was neither preachy nor sentimental and allowed everyone to interpret the brief in as free a way as they wanted was taken up by the editorial team, hence 'Family Future Positive'.

To everyone we asked the same question: what does family mean to you?

So to all of you who have taken up the challenge and made it as personal or brilliantly idiosyncratic as you've wanted, my biggest thanks. It's been a complete pleasure to see the results coming in, and for any who have missed our as-usual-yesterday deadline, this project is still a work in progress. We are planning exhibitions around this theme in Paris, London, Milan and New York to date, so please keep the images and words coming in – the more the magical!

Tricia Jones 1998

This is a strange time to be talking about family. And Family Future Positive? Stranger still. After all, the traditional family unit seems an anachronism today, a statistical anomaly in the face of recent revelations that three million children now live in one-parent families, there will soon be more step-families than nuclear families, one third of all births currently take place outside wedlock and almost half of all new marriages are doomed to failure. You'd be forgiven for viewing this as a shocking vision of societal collapse. Certainly Tony Blair does – so much so that in October, the Government published a Green Paper promising to protect breadwinning dad, homemaking mum and their two point four kids. Now nobody would see anything wrong with explicitly encouraging modern marriage and the stability that it should supply; indeed most parents would appreciate hard policy and a helping hand instead of the more usually prescriptive governmental rhetoric. But New Labour need to acknowledge what a recent ICM poll for *The Observer* newspaper proved: surprising public tolerance to these supposedly unorthodox family set-ups. No-one seemed to have a problem negotiating diverse relationships – 80 per cent of those questioned disagreed with the statement that unmarried couples were worse parents, 68 per cent said single parents were just as able to bring up their children successfully. In short, general recognition that the family is in no worse state than before, just taking different forms. Adapting, changing – but, above all, surviving. Still, you might find it strange for this magazine to be talking about family. We don't think so. From the outset of i-D, it has been founder Terry Jones' intention to promote the ethic of respect for individuality while also recognising the strength of collaboration – fundamental principles for any family, whether based on biology or not. And while you know i-D's influential status as international fashion industry bible, you may not know that it initially started as a stapled fanzine from Terry's upstairs room. When I first arrived here some six years ago, it was apparent that I hadn't just acquired a job but had instead been adopted into an extended family that spanned cultures and continents, a talented multi-generational tribe united by a love of life and each other. That i-D family is now scattered to the corners of the earth, its global importance defying its humble origins – even though the magazine itself has never ceased to be defined by the beliefs developed during those early days in a West Hampstead home. Like the biological family it closely resembles, i-D has changed –

growing from precocious child to awkward adolescent into the charming if cheeky maverick that it is today. Likewise, those who have overseen this change: now as grown up as the magazine itself, they are shaping the futures of fashion, music, art, literature, television and technology – you can find i-D family members in any field where convention is being flouted. So Tricia Jones' idea for this special issue made perfect sense to us: bringing the family born 18 years ago back within the fold, joining them together with more recent additions in a celebration of global alliance that goes further than blood ties. We asked for personal interpretations of Family and contributions, pointed and poignant, came pouring in from the worldwi-De creative community. From those at the summit of their careers and those just starting out, from the culturally significant and the internationally renown, from editors and TV producers, from artists and authors, from stylists and photographers and pop stars. Mothers, fathers, sisters and brothers; friends, colleagues, sons and daughters – it soon seemed everyone had something to say about family. The experience has been an encouraging and uplifting one for us; proof that the i-D family, though unconventional by current governmental standards, shares the same love and stability of the best biological groupings.

Forms of family are changing at the close of the 20th Century; feelings of family are not. How positive is that?

Avril Mair

PS – Having just read Avril's introduction, I should like to add one thing. If anybody with any access at all to the wheels of power is listening and if Tony Blair and the Labour Party genuinely want to help Britain's families, biological or not, my suggestion is make child development a compulsory part of the national curriculum. Equip today's teenagers to be tomorrow's parents through education – because it's only through education that negative patterns are broken down. Give a map to guide us through the minefield and mysteries of taking on the responsibility of another human being.

Family *n, pl –lies* 1 a social group consisting of parents and their offspring. 2 one's wife or husband and one's children. 3 one's children. 4 a group descending from a common ancestor. 5 all the people living together in one household. 6 any group of related objects or beings: a family of chemicals. 7 *Biol* one of the groups into which an order is divided, containing one of more genera: the cat family. – *adj* 8 of or suitable for a family or any of its members: films for a family audience. 9 *in the family way* Informal: pregnant.

Bez and his boys.

Orion Best

The family, the cosmic, transcends our realms of humanity.
Your mother
    father
    sister
    brother
    stranger
    lover
    friend
    and enemy
The birds
The bees
The flowers
The trees
All interstellar entities
Everything that lives and breathes.
We are all family.

Zoe Bedeaux

Me bottle feeding Mabel, plus part of my family: Dave Baby, Isaac, John Maybury, Emily Dollar, Naima Jade, Felix, Sharlene, Linda, Cameron McVey, Glen Luchford, Mark Lebon, Camilla Arthur, Marlon, Jenny Howarth, Christopher Nemeth, Kiepo and Tyson McVey Cherry.

Family is forever. My family goes beyond blood ties – friendship, love and spirit rule the day. I'm so lucky in that I have real warmth from my tribe. I'd stop the bullet and I think they would too. My godchildren (Isaac and Tyson) are my hope for the future.

Judy Blame

My new family.

Coming from a 'broken' family, I never believed it possible to find myself in a lasting and creative relationship. Not until I met and fell in love with Trevor. We are very different in our characters and approach to life, but have in common a strong desire to make it work. We try to find time to talk through any problems (not always successfully). With Trevor came Ava, his 11-year old daughter, and though she doesn't live with us, Trevor's responsibility and emotional involvement with her brings a deeper dimension into our relationship.

I think the key to keeping our family positive has something to do with learning to let go; tolerating differences and overcoming the need for people to be like you.

Louis, our newborn son, I'm sure will have much to teach me on this subject.

Moira Bogue

I found these photographs in an antique shop in South Africa and ended up using them in a short film I made called *The Land Is White, The Seed Is Black*, which was shown at the Berlin Festival and then internationally.

It tells the story of my father, Professor Makhaola Dublin Paul Bolofo, who was born in Basutoland in 1918. A history teacher, he was forced to flee his country some 30 years ago, unfairly accused of Communist infiltration by the Apartheid government.

His family house was destroyed, his father's land confiscated, even his car had to be abandoned. But after Nelson Mandela was elected to presidency, he returned in 1994 to find his people, his rights and what was remaining from his past.

Photographs courtesy of Koto Bolofo African Archive collection.

Koto Bolofo

Family means love
and complete whole.

Mark, Maria, Bibi and Joe Borthwick – forever.

Mark Borthwick and Maria Cornejo

Family is what you make of it. Choose your relations as carefully as you choose your friends. And try to forgive your parents – the chances are, they didn't do it on purpose.

Paul Burston

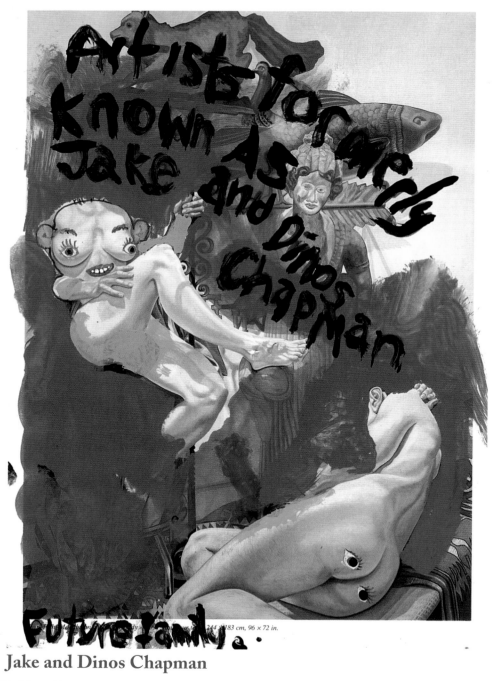

244 × 183 cm, 96 × 72 in.

Jake and Dinos Chapman

Family is life.

Donald Christie

Nepal, 1995.

Fast forward into the not too distant future and drop into your local maternity ward. Consider the possibilities. In one bed lies an 80-year-old woman. It's 'thaw day' and she's just produced her first baby from an egg she had frozen decades earlier. Another happy mother opted for the cloning technique. The girl she cradles in her arms is, to all intents and purposes, her identical twin. And in the rest of the ward, doting parents gaze lovingly at their 'perfect' children. Designer specimens whose genetic make-up was altered at the embryonic stage to create a new breed of high achievers; babies made to order who have been tampered with to fit their parents' very specific requirements. Gone is the era where a quick count – ten fingers, ten toes – was enough to announce the arrival of a normal, healthy baby. If it sounds like an implausible sci-fi nightmare, think back to 1978 and the alarm which greeted the birth of Louise Brown, the first test tube baby. Nowadays IVF treatment is seen as a perfectly ordinary option for parents wanting to start a family. In fact, probably the only thing which won't exist in the above scenario is the maternity ward itself, cast aside along with the rest of the NHS. Although currently we are staring into an abyss of ignorance, genetics is set to become one of the dominant sciences of the 21st century. The implications of this are both powerful and frightening. A designer baby service is already in operation at a hospital in Saudi Arabia where, for around £10,000, a doctor will create a baby of whichever sex their parent requires. In China, where family size is restricted, people are opting for IVF methods so doctors can pick between embryos, selecting the healthiest one and discarding the rest. Choosing carefully from the estimated 70,000 genes that make up a human, it's possible that in a brave new world parents will be able to pick their baby type. It's a process of unnatural selection where offspring could be granted an IQ of 180 or installed with the gene for footballing genius, turning it into a receptacle for the hopes of pushy parents. Make your child taller, happier, faster and stronger; take the service to its logical conclusion by fashioning its physical features in the same way as you'd pick the clothes it would wear. Choose its eye colour, prevent it from ever going bald and avoid discrimination by changing its skin colour or sexual orientation.

Aside from the obvious benefit of screening out inheritable diseases, the possibilities for 'improvement' are endless. But to what result? The blanding out of endearing 'faults' to create a population of overachievers.

Or worse, a race of Übermensch created with the vision of Hitler's fascist politics. Andrew Niccol's sci-fi dystopia, *Gattaca*, creates an imagined future of a designer race. Stretching today's DNA-bending possibilities, a neat dividing line is drawn up between the genetically perfect 'valids' and the flawed 'in-valids'. As it says in the film, "they've got discrimination down to a science". What's more scary is that genetic discrimination is already in evidence here and in the States, with companies refusing to insure people who have hereditary disease. As usual, it boils down to the marketplace. Those who can afford it pump a load of money into bringing their young Frankensteins into the world and hope they live up to expectations. Those who can't, condemn their unborn to a genetic underclass forever.

Lena Corner

Family: it's a shield. Family: it's a target of love – trust, respect, loyalty, happiness, protection and integrity. Famille: une armure. Famille: c'est une cible d'amour – de confiance, de respect, de loyauté, de bonheur, de protection et d'integrité.

Giannie Couji

Gunter Grass
MERVYN PEAKE
Umberto Eco · Scott Heron
CHRISTIAN BERARD · anton chekov
FELA · FLAUBERT · CONSTANTINE BRANCUSI
JORGE LUISE · J.E. CASELY-HAYFORD · SUN ra
HALWILNER · BORGE · CHINUA ACHEBE · Eric newby · W.h. Auden
BALTHUS Marc CHAGALL · Michel Foucault · Eric newby
William Cobbett · PABLO NERUDA · marcel Proust · Gertrude Stein
Gilbert & GEORGE · Lee · DICK HEBDIGE · Ezra Pound · Gertrude Stein
Martin Luther king · Lee · Odilon Redon · Trish & Terry Jones · Egon Schiele
Travis · U Roy · Samuel Foss · Henri Gaudier Brzeska · Leila Arab · Buddy & Vivienne
Walker evans · NELSON MANDELA · Caroline Baker · Glen P Gould · ARSHILE GORKY
Laura Nyro · Douglas Coupland · Ray Petri · Joseph Beuys · Maxim gorky · I Roy
Dorothea Tanning · Schoenberg · Seydou Keita · Nick Cave · Boccioni · J.D. SALINGER
Joe henderson · BALZAC · Wole Soyinka · Don van Vliet · Sara · COLETTE · photek
Ludwig Wittgenstein · Mr Myers · Voltech Havel · John Coltrane · Herman Hesse
Angela Davis · Roland barthes · Arvo Part · Anselm Kiefer · nicolette · attra blues · Balzac
Muhammad Ali · Jimi Hendrix · James Baldwin · Christian Boltanski · Bertrand Russell
Bertold Brecht · Miles Davis · BASQUIAT · Rotimi Fani-kayode · ALICE Coltrane
Samuel Beckett · Cinty · Mania · Leroy · Nick Cave · Pere Ubu · ZOLA
Terry Riley · Roland Kirk · Charlie Mapa · ALICE · André Walker · David Thomas
Tom Jenkinson · Joanne · Margret + Giles · CHOPIN · Ronnie foster
Desmond Tutu · Luke Vibert · K.Peter + Beverly · Hasegawa · Bunty Mathias
Bruce Nauman · Ashley · GUS + Sarah Medeski · Miura · Jeff Jessop · GIDE
Martin Shaw · Viktor Frankl · Giselle Pragen · Martin + hood · Yokota · Eusebio · Pete
Walter Rooney · IBSEN · Pharoh Sanders · charlie Gillett · Doug Carn
Freya Stark · Jean Cocteau · Idris Muhammad · William Blake · Mozart
Gladys CASELY-Hayford · EDWARD SAID · Oscar wilde · George Orwell · Ben Okri
OSKAR KOKOSCHKA · Zannia Bhim · 2000 money · Chaucer
David Bradshaw · Wild man Fisher · SCORSESE · BOCCACCIO
MAX Beerbohm · JONI MITCHELL · Christopher Isherwood
Ingmar Bergman · LOIS · Karen Binns · Georgia O'Keeffe
EDITH SHWELL · Sue · MARCEL DUCHAMP · Willa Cather
Saul Williams · STEVE Williamson · Samuel Coleridge-Taylor · Paul Butler
Knudert + Dorfmeister · EISENSTEIN · Cut Chemist · Stacey M
Langston Hughes · Ottoline morrell · Leigh Bowen
Elizabeth Suter · Liz Ford R.I.P · Steve Reich
UMA BIM HASAAN · DIX · Poulenc
Michael Clark · MOUSSORGSKY
DIAGHILEV · Thos De Quincey
Maupassant
Pound
Jarrerson

JCH family
past present future
X

Joe Casely-Hayford

I'm from the suburbs. And the first thing I did was get out. I moved to London when I was 19. Berlin at 21 and New York by 22. I didn't get a job until I was 24, and even then it was something as nefarious as editing *Mixmag*. I asked my wife to marry me on holiday in America and tied the knot in 24 hours. In a Las Vegas drive-thru. I'm not sure that I care too much what anyone else thinks and, as my wife will confirm, I won't do anything I don't want to. I'm an awkward little fucker and I can't imagine ever fitting in with the norm. Hopefully however by next June I will be the proud father of the puking, shitting, screaming bag of fun that will be our first child. Plus married and mortgaged. Wanting children has been the strangest thing. All this effort to do something different, new, to live life with ideas of personal choice and freedom and then to find myself programmed like some animal. Not in some rampant seed-spreading physical way, but mentally; wired for responsibility and serious adulthood. And nor do we do this with some warped, romantic vision of parenthood. We know about the sleepless nights, the haemorrhaging bank balance, the end of social life as we know it. I know all the statistics about young married fathers working the longest hours in Britain, about the dangers and disappointments that absence means. And God, what brain-meltingly dull baby bores we will become. Pushchairs, stair guards, playgroups, schools, whether the baby-sitter is smoking. THOMAS THE TANK ENGINE. But I can't explain it. This life in handbrake turnaround. And that lack of a rational explanation is the most chilling thing of all. Write it down on paper and you've got to be insane.

You seen the way babies eat? You like the idea of wiping someone else's arse? Thought not. It's not rational. Not clever, given what it's doing to my poor wife's career. And not even remotely cool. And yet we are going out of our minds with excitement.

We're going to have a baby. A family. And, of course, we feel like we'll be the first people on the planet to do so. We know we're falling for all that hokey shit about the wonder of life, the magic of birth. And is even this the biggest con of all? Some biological programme giving us the thrill of it all now, only to renege later with a demanding child? I've tried, I can't explain it. It's not a thought, it's a feeling. Just spare me the suburbs.

David Davies

Family is anyone who is there for you in your hour of need, or anyone you are there for even when you're not needed.

Fiona Dallanegra

A history: Making shepherd's pie for my little brothers and sister, with them talking about stuff and my sister, who's 14, calling my brother a fat poof all through supper. Maureen, who helped bring me up with stoic calm. Making up country and western songs with my mum. The smell of my father's hands, tobacco and his suede jacket. My mother kissing me goodnight before she went out when I was little, her scent filling the room with expectations. Loathing Christmas. Arguments. Giggling with my sister all night in her bed. My grandmother saying 'Life is not a bowl of cherries' with quiet despair in her Kentucky sloe gin voice. My wise aunts. Tough women. All my stepfathers. Joy. Huge all-encompassing enduring tiger-like love for each and every bloody one of them.

Sophie Dahl

My daughter on a tractor, Dublin, September 1998.

Family has the ability to be the most fulfilling experience in one's life and the most annoying. That's what makes it so unique.

Kevin Davies

My family, Killiney Beach, Dublin, September 1998.

Friends are often closer than family.

Soraya Dayani

Photography by Frederike Helwig.

Family is the ultimate unit – a true love
experience never to be severed – the meaning of
life – a rollercoaster that never lets you get off –
forever learning – always be there.

Tony and Janey Elliott

Janey, Rufus, Lawrence, Bruce and Tony.

The women in my life hold everything together.

Luther Enninful

When I was spotted by superstylist and i-D contributing fashion editor Simon Foxton on my way to college at the age of 16, I had no idea that this chance encounter on the Metropolitan line would change my life forever. But two weeks later I found myself in the most serene house in Richmond, modelling for a strange and influential magazine called i-D. This was the first time I met Nick Knight and Charlotte, surrogate parents to many a fashion orphan. After modelling for a year while acting as Simon Foxton's assistant (or taste bud, as I prefer to say), i-D's then fashion editor Beth Summers commissioned me to shoot a story with photographer Jason Evans.

Despite an early apprenticeship at the knee of my dressmaker mother, this was my first real work as a stylist.

A year later, following a meeting with i-D's maverick creative director Terry Jones, I was appointed the magazine's fashion editor, aged just 18. Fast forward eight years later and I'm still here. Now, though, I am surrounded by my own fashion family – and, in true i-D tradition, am trying to find fresh faces to add to the family tree.

Edward Enninful

MRS GRACE ENNINFUL
'FASHION GURU'

LUTHER ENNINFUL
"NEW KID ON THE BLOCK"

Pepa
"future DIVA"
Neice darling

ZOE BEDEAUX MOON SHANTI
♡ ☾ ☮
'TE AMO ATI'

Rein's the most important things in the family are Peps + heels to walk all over me

Rohan - b4 fashion

Naomi
Halloween '98

Patti Wilson
"10"

Giannie Couji
" Boy I know you better watch out → Da thing.

GRETA FAT SUPERSTYLIST'

JANE HOW.
IN MY FAVOURITE PLACE

Darling it's all about Boy! hanging out!

PAT MCGRATH:

♡ LOVE ♡ UNCONDITIONAL ♡

M BOADI PEACE OUT FOR THE YEAR 2000 xxx.

Neil Shart - Bad boys.

SIMON FORTON MOTHER

TO EDWARD
NICK, CHARLOTTE, EMILY, ELLA AND x CAZUM ♡ BIG LOVE x NOV 1998 x0

Flaming Tiger ... Serving Darwin ...

Beth Summers GODESS ♡

EDWARD YOU'RE A ☆
Tricia- biglove + hugs ♡ TERRY
Edward- your office mum! x

BIG ♡ fiti x

THANKS FOR HOLDING MY HAND - Marcus.

TO EDWARD, THE MOST GENIUS style Master ever, Big thank YOU for my time as your assistant- will treasure it always. i-D rules much ♡ Ⓜ

Jeslyn Lewis New girl on the block! xx

EDWARD YOU'RE LIKE THE SISTER I NEVER HAD DON'T MAKE ME BLUSH! TOBY.
DO YOU WANT EXTRA CHILLIES ED? MARCIA x
No messing with my boys... LOVE Kate

35

My sister Catherine.

Everyone is my family.

Jason Evans

Family is any network of feeling that allows the transmission of love.

Fabrizio Ferri

Sting holding the foot of his youngest daughter, taken from *La Famiglia di Sting a Monastero*, a book published to raise funds for the Paediatric Aids Foundation.

To me, family has little to do with sharing a twisted candy cane of DNA. Maybe it's a little unusual, but when I think about the idea of family I don't think about the people to whom I am related at all, perhaps because we are not much of a family, being small and scattered. Fragmented in so many senses of the word. My parents divorced 25 years ago and seven years after that my mother went back to her native Australia, with the man who became both my stepfather and my 17-year-old half brother's father. My stepfather is dead now, but we were never close. And then, just a couple of months ago, my father – also Australian – decided to go home too. My family, then, such as it is, spans 12,000 miles and light years in terms of lifestyles. We don't tend to bother with birthdays (I'm not sure I've ever sent my brother a card for his, or he one for mine) or Christmases and we only speak occasionally. Mostly we just get on with our lives. This doesn't mean I don't love my family – I do. I just don't need them, or even expect them to be in my life in the same way I need and expect my friends to be around. My friends are my family. And, although I have a lot of friends, there is one small group that probably fits the familial bill better than any other. It's appropriate to be writing about family for i-D, because it was while working on this magazine, aged 20, in the early 1980s, that I found a family, all of whom have watched each other's lives loop-the-loop ever since. We got our first professional breaks working on the magazine during an extraordinarily creative period in publishing; a period when we were allowed (in fact positively encouraged) to make up the rules as we went along, learning on the job, never drawing demarcation lines between work and play, because all of it was research (or at least that was our excuse!). Some of us fell in (and out) of love with each other, acquiring complicated lives and haphazard (albeit largely successful careers) en route. And, somehow, all of us stayed friends. It is so easy to be nostalgic about the period of your life when you first find your niche, first discover that there's a place of belongingness in a world which might have seemed, until then, as though it always happened somewhere around the next corner, a place you could never quite reach at quite the right time. Back then, for the i-D family though, it felt as if the world was happening right where we were (ah, the arrogance of youth!) and it was this sense of working and

playing right in the middle of a media playground newly-fixated on a peculiarly creative youth culture that made it so damn thrilling, so much bloody fun. In the early 1980s, youth culture had yet to be appropriated by multinational corporations, manufactured and packaged for the delectation of young people from Peking to Penge, via Paris and Peoria. Just 15 years ago, being young was still a well-kept secret, talked about in coded whispers via tip sheets. i-D and *The Face* (there were no other magazines like i-D and *The Face*) may have been available in WH Smith, but they were still the bush telegraph of an essentially underground urban culture, and so, via their pages, we contributors whispered to those members of our family tribe whom we didn't know, but whom we felt sure we'd recognise if we ever met them. This was, then, a kind of conspiracy, constructed in words and pictures and sent out to those who got the jokes, who spoke the same language, and though we worked very hard, it didn't ever feel quite like work – or at least not in the same way that every job (however much fun) I've ever had since has felt like work.

I guess that comes down to the people – colleagues who became friends, lovers, siblings, soulmates… the kind of people you know will still be around when you lose your hair/teeth/head/limbs and, eventually, your life;
the people who remind you that, whatever life hurls your way, in a family there can be an emotional continuity of a kind that will never be understood by those who don't share the same experiences and reference points. After nearly 20 years, the i-D family is sprawling, generational. I don't know many of the members of the current family – in fact, we could pass each other on the street and not even know we were related – but when I do meet an i-D second cousin once removed, I see the branches and roots of this particular family tree extending, still reaching for the sky, still digging deep, still kindred spirits, 'til i-Death do us part.

Kathryn Flett

My family are a source of inspiration, encouragement and continued support. I try to treat them with the respect and honesty that they have always shown me.

Me and Edward Enninful.

Christine Fortune

Back in 1983...

It was in its creative infancy when I became part of the family in 1982. To outsiders, a montage of black and white documentary stills, reporting the visual exotica of urban club and street scenes, held together with staples and magenta ink; i-D magazine was a problem child, kicking and screaming against traditional publishing restraints. To the rest of the fellowship, and me, i-D was the solution. From the start, we were on our own. No newsagent would stack a landscape fanzine and never before had a publication devoted its pages to the thoughts and images of unknowns. We grouped in clannish conspiracy – these outlandish strangers were simply tomorrow's stars in preview but only the initiated were in on the buzz. Members lived all over the place – Steve in York, Thomas in Munich, Paul in Montreal: our concept of family was – and still is – boundary free. It was also unfettered by a hierarchical requirement for qualification and status. Love of life was the only prerequisite for membership to this small but growing band. Art students, shop assistants and Cha Cha's regulars then, we thought we knew it all. And when the time came to birth another issue, we packed noisily into a bedroom studio, nestled in a family house, to cavort with typewritten copy, spray mount and scalpel. The card and art of our computer illiterate generation would – under the paternal direction of Terry – ripen from messy, raw and unsophisticated organ into a living, breathing body of words, pictures, ideas and dreams. And like all families, we had our disagreements. Tempers would fray. Difference was occasionally hard to celebrate. The hide and seek application of text, the black on black sheets, or photography obscured or flavoured with fluorescent luminosity, unhinged even the boldest writers and image-makers. Does an old filing cabinet still bear the scars of a punch, landed by one disgruntled lensman after learning that his photographic subjects had been accidentally decapitated? Other times we were thrown our of our spiritual home – ejected by Terry's wife Trish, in her attempt to reclaim house and husband. We would always return. Terry had a vision

and we were his devotees, sacrificing all hours, all efforts. There were no financial incentives as mainstream advertisers had yet to acknowledge the power of 'youth culture', or understand fully the meaning of street credibility, but from all corners in cities big and small came encouragement. The magazine consumed energy and time like an insatiable newborn. And, as it grew, The Slits, Marine Girls, Jah Wobble and Killing Joke offered lullabies from the turntable at the top of the house. During the mad panic to put it to bed, with the printer on stand-by anticipating our handiwork, nights sometimes merged into day, so we slept under tables nestling amongst bills, doubts, fag butts like exhausted guardians of a future potentate. We even delivered it ourselves – freshly printed and 75 pence per copy – from a battered Saab to the Great Gear Market in the Kings Road, or packed it off lovingly to Aflecks Palace down Manchester way. i-D celebrated bloodless ties and the family adopted anyone who cared enough to join; fostering developing talent with a nurturing eye. Identity – in a mainstream society that had begun to prioritise opposition to change and innovation – became an intuitive means of expression. Ours was a quest for individuality, for experimentation, and we developed a manifesto for bold statement. Mostly it would be said with the body, or on the body – in an environment where the ear-splitting synthesised pulse obscured audible communication, clothes and hair and make-up verbalised dreams. We had photographers recording those with something to say and the straight-up (a documentary picture of the woman in the street, or man on the dancefloor) spawned a multitude of imitations. We clubbed, drank, danced and worked together. A large family of people bound together by the beat. We took i-D across the pond. In a cramped New York hotel room, we took turns with the mattress and shared clothes, fags and money. In Canada, we imbibed more chemicals than truly necessary. In Japan, we adorned T-shirts. Unconvention was always the norm; a typical day for this fashion editor involved lending my BOY mohair jumper to another unknown singer called Madonna for a cover shoot, then teaching Terry and Tricia's daughter to cartwheel in their front room. We've all grown older now and covered our tattoos with Rifat Ozbek and Issey Miyake. And like proud parents, we've watched i-D develop from sulky adolescent to perfect-bound maverick about town, learning plenty from the protégé that now inspires us.

Some of us have children of our own and post-punk arrogance has given way to pre-millennial contemplation. We've buried friends and we've come far enough to know we don't know so much.

We are broadcasters, authors, art directors, magazine editors, events organisers, external assessors, a shoe designer, even a Cabinet PR. And like the magazine, bound and glued, where concepts, feelings, questions and thoughts are gathered and stuck between pages, where individuals are in unison and, at times, in opposition, we have survived the test of time. Like the magazine, we are still together – relationships cemented and friendships held firm – with people sticking to each other over the years. That is the i-D family.

Caryn Franklin

Sometimes, when I look in the mirror, I try to find him. I trace my eyebrows, ponder the shape of my nose, smile a fake grin to see the contours of my cheeks. Did his do this? I feel I want to find him in me, maybe because that's the only place I'll ever get to know my father properly. My father died when I was seven. Old enough to understand that he's not coming back. Too young to fathom the consequences. I knew him. But only as any other seven-year-old knows their father. My father didn't die from a car accident. Or a terrible disease. He was 75 years old. Many men die at that age, don't they? Tragic, maybe, I don't know. He'd had one helluva life, glittering career, adventures. And not many men at that age can boast of fathering two children with a (second) wife 36 years his junior. But a sudden blood clot got the better of him.

I was the last to see him alive. He said he'd return in half an hour and switch off the reading light (I kept Donald Duck comics under my pillow). I got bored waiting – switched it off myself. When I woke up the next day my life seemed colder, irrevocably incomplete.

That first day everything was out of balance – made me dizzy. I went to school and everybody wanted to know if it was true. My teacher patted my soft young blonde hair with tears in her eyes. I was special. Then the awful guilt set in. And it never went away. Daddy's little girl wants Daddy's approval. And it just ain't there. Whatever I do, nearly 20 years on, is accompanied by an asterisk at the back of my mind – 'What would he think? Would he want this?' I remember the kindergarten ladies mistakenly telling me my granddad had come to collect me. But with modern medical technology (think Viagra) and the gradual cultural delay of the mother-baby moment, my situation could become the norm. The nuclear family has already ceased to exist. But the future may bring a new kind of ageing parent, leaving behind increasing numbers of bewildered offspring. Children who will always blame: 'They must have known they only had a few years left.' And who will always be looking for something unattainable. You try to pad them out through other people. But it's tricky. Asking questions is emotionally taboo and reading his letters feels too sneaky. The person becomes a patchwork of secondhand stories, photographs and your own limited memories. The things I remember for sure are tiny little filmic episodes – seeing him pour orange juice on his cornflakes by mistake, getting told off when I interrupted him watching the news and laughing at him when he entertained us with bizarre monkey-faces. But he was also a public figure in my birth country, Norway. He arrived in Scandinavia, one of the few German Jews to escape the Holocaust (most of his – no – my family wasn't so lucky), when he was 24. Music was his life – first as a virtuoso violinist and later an inspirational conductor. When he left his position as the country's 'chief of culture', the newspaper headline said simply '[he] is gone – what now?' Knowing that he was well-loved, makes me love him. And it drives me to know more. It's like a part of yourself you're continually chasing, questioning and pondering. He's a jigsaw that'll never end. The pieces keep turning up, but there's some that are always going to be gathering dust under the sofa. At home I'm surrounded by my father. Our stairs are lined with caricatures of his famous friends, including a few of himself. Pewter plates and other paraphernalia are inscribed with copius thank you's for his outstanding achievements and work. He has a medal he was given from King Olav V. A huge oil portrait sits in the living room, while downstairs a photograph makes it look like he's playing the violin for us while we eat breakfast. But these things don't bring me any closer to him. My father was married before he met my mother and had two daughters, my half-sisters, who are both over 60. We're rarely in contact, yet when I'm with them I feel there must really be something of his person in both of them and myself. Especially because they knew him properly, as adults. And there's the flicker of a realisation that my father isn't just a picture postcard memory borrowed secondhand, but a real flesh and blood part of an extended, confusing family. But it isn't enough. And I go back to the mirror. I never lose the hope that, one day, I will find him.

Susanna Glaser

THE FAMILY THAT GAVE BIRTH TO ME MUCH RESPECT.

THE FAMILY THAT HELPS ME GIVE BIRTH

THE ONLY FAMILY I'VE GIVEN BIRTH TO SO FAR.

Jane How

Family means a world of chaotic regimentation, running at times like a badly-oiled machine, single-handedly relieving you of any selfish notions you previously entertained, rendering you hopelessly devoted and in a strange state of bliss.

Adam Howe

Adam and son.
Photography by Takay.

From the moment of conception, you're on a rollercoaster ride going through every human emotion possible. Who needs drugs with kids?
"Family means being together, caring for one another, loving and sharing with one another, teaching one another and sometimes not liking one another." Molly (9)
"You must never run away from home. Family means you stay together, see." Darcy (4)

Darcy and Molly visit the dentist.

Rick Haylor

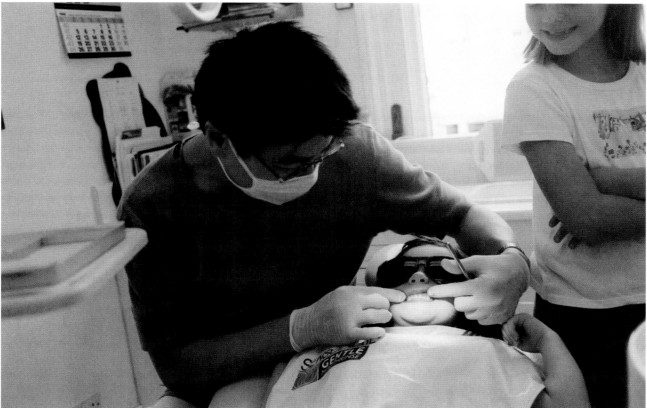

The origin of the word family is in the Latin *familia*, a household. It's also the root of the less formal word *familiar*. I wanted to capture something of how people in displaced, foreign locations, people on the move, in transit, create from friendships and objects the familiar. These households in Paris, London and New York express the transient nature of contemporary life, which tends to be nomadic: a Pole living in London, a Manchurian in New York, a Brixtonite in Paris. I believed that if asked to select items from home that were precious, the objects would be at once totally unique and *universally familiar*. Photography helps create this universal familiarity. It is as if photography were invented at just the moment when our lives became more fragmented so as to help us keep all the pieces together.

Kayt Jones

Left to right: Titti, Erik and Raymond, who have been living together for three years.

Paris
A list of words all starting with CO, which is the prefix giving the sense of sharing something with somebody: Co-operate, conversation, conviviality, cordiality, conviction, contribute, community, consideration, combat, co-existence. Erik Halley

Titti Kwan, stylist. Personal items: my cat, Little Boy; a headpiece Erik made especially for me; pictures of my friends; my whole life on a piece paper by a fortune teller Master Chan; toiletry bag.

Erik Halley, plumes and accessories designer. Personal items: a mini Polaroid camera and pix of my boyfriend Bertrand; my toy chick, a present from my dear friend Marion; a sketch of me surrounded by birds from Leo; NY K2 Rollerblades; Sony minidisc.

Raymond Cole, PR for Patrick Cox. Personal items: photos of life-long friends; cuttings of Arsenal winning the championship; wooden box; golden pipe; ashtray.

Left to right: Adam, Helen, Stephen and Mikolai, who have been living together for one year.

London
I'm not trying to be retroactive, but I think that a certain balance between the old and the new should be respected. In all this rushing for a better, brighter future, are we not forgetting about the knowledge that can be drawn from the traditional family? After all, the family is the base of the society and the future we're so eagerly leaping into. Mikolai Berg

Adam Hindle, personal objects: typewriter; CD Walkman; CDs including Spiritualised *Purephase*, New Order *Republic*, The Smiths *Strangeways* and Stevie Wonder *Innervision*; lightshade from Morocco, a gift from Mikolai.

Helen Smith, aspiring soap star. Personal objects: Adam, Stephen and Mikolai!

Stephen Poskitt, model. Personal objects: wooden carvings from Japan; leather jacket from Oxfam; ashtray from Oxfam; table from second hand shop.

Mikolai Berg, model. Personal objects: picture of me and my mum; family photos dating back to the 1800s; Duran Duran single 'I Don't Want Your Love' ; '50s soda-siphon; antique painting of Mary and Jesus, family heirloom; signet ring, family heirloom; Nikon FM2 camera.

New York
I can tell you what family means in just one word.
Love. Karen Elson

Karen Elson, model. Personal objects: My friends have nicknamed me Tinkerbell and I sometimes feel like a fairy so that's why I bought this book on fairies; also a book of spells; kaleidoscope from boyfriend; collection of postcards; my soft toy FoFo that I've had since I was two; my pink teddy Luna; silver star frame with a photo of me and my twin sister Kate aged three.

Maggie Rizer, model. Personal objects: $1 bill with coins attached to it sent to me by my eight-year-old sister when I explained that the reason I was in New York and not at home was to earn some money; seashell from Mexico brought back by my boyfriend Jorge so that I can hear the ocean at all times; prayer from St Francis that my grandmother used to keep in her wallet, which was given to me when she died; Edward the teddy bear, gift from grandparents; my giant photo album with favourite photos of family and friends; watch, a twentieth birthday present from my parents.

Erin O'Connor, model. Personal objects: framed Polaroid of me and my boyfriend Steven; necklace that Steven gave me; fairy wand that my parents gave me; family photo album; Elmo from Sesame Street, another present from my parents; blessed Rosary beads from first Holy Communion when I was seven, which travel with me everywhere.

Left to right: Karen, Maggie and Erin, who have been living together since September 1998.

With best man Robin Derrick on my wedding day.

She wasn't the first person to say it, she wasn't even the second, but someone was listening when Marlene Dietrich said "It's the friends that you can call at 4am that matter." Knowing that the Blue Angel had a rather rapacious habit of calling on many people at four o'clock in the morning – particularly if they were young, libidinous and male – perhaps it's not so surprising that she was so open about her insecurities. Friendship is a tricky business. A very tricky business indeed. Like a love affair, say, the new REM album or anything you're unlucky enough to find on Channel 5, a friendship won't stand up to scrutiny. While it's true that we can spend our lives discussing life, death, sex, work, politics, God and the inexplicable penchant that estate agents have for square-toed shoes, what we rarely talk about is our relationships with each other. And if we do, we're doomed. Cynics might say this is largely because most friendships have such tenuous foundations that any close analysis would cause them to crumble, while the truth of the matter is that after a while explanations become unnecessary. Received wisdom dictates that a friendship is based on two defining principles. Firstly, to like and dislike the same things. Secondly, and more pertinently, a friend is someone who knows all about you, yet still likes you. Well, maybe. True friendships are based on far more delicate and abstruse things than that, as shared interests and a modicum of loyalty are the lynchpins of any relationship. An acquaintance once said to me, without any obvious ulterior motive, that your friends might not necessarily be the best people suited for the job, they just happened to get there first. Perhaps,

but then people do move in and out of our lives with alarming speed, through no fault of their own, or indeed ours. I think perhaps it wrong to have such high expectations of friendship. Often they just fade, and sometimes with good reason. Feeling aggravated that people have manoeuvred themselves out of your life is as selfish and myopic as not realising that you've done the same thing to other people on more occasions than you can hope to remember.

They say that a friendship should be nurtured, but a good friendship, an honest friendship, is one that can be left to simmer. A good friendship – and the good ones always have their own particular shorthand – takes time. One of the crushingly disappointing things about growing up is discovering that friendships, while they can certainly be cultivated, can never, ever be forced. Nudge it and it might nudge back. Push it and it falls over. Have low expectations, I say. Be realistic. Expect nothing and love in hope. Who knows, you might be surprised. As for Marlene, she was right, of course. But in her day they didn't have answering machines.

Dylan Jones

Photography by Kevin Davies.

Biological or non-biological, family is the best thing in the world.

Matt Jones

Creative, supportive, unconditional, unstoppable – with love.

Terry Jones

Matt and Jicky's engagement day, 10 June 1998. This page is dedicated to Amanda.

Wales – the view we've shared with all the people we love.

Tricia Jones

This page is dedicated to my parents.

My mum, my daughter, my grandma – four generations. Photographed at home by Oliviero Toscani, 1974.

A letter from my mum

My name is Myra Cohen and I am 75 years old. From 1968 to 1985, I worked as an Art Therapist at Hill End Hospital in St Albans, a psychiatric hospital with 500 patients. I worked with a colleague and friend Patricia Ball, and when she retired in 1978 I took on her role as head of department. I continued to see her, probably about once a fortnight on a regular basis. Around 1995, after I retired, I noticed a slow deterioration in her behaviour. She was then starting to show signs of early Alzheimer's. Whilst working at the hospital, in addition to colour we used poetry for our patients to express feelings, and on 1 November 1972 *The Guardian* newspaper gave their work a very good write-up. Patricia Ball has also published four books of her own poetry. I mention this only to give you some insight into the type of person she is. When it was evident that she could no longer cope with day-to-day living – and being an only child herself and childless – I managed to get Patricia her own room in a very good nursing home close to where I live. The home itself has been upgraded to BUPA status. It's really very good, in an open and attractive position in Hertfordshire. The staff are attentive and helpful, but they cannot put life back into a mind that ceased to function and this is my cry! I go and visit Pat every Wednesday but I cannot take more than 30 to 45 minutes. I've watched new clients come in – mostly they are stroppy and abusive and unwilling to accept what is happening to them. After two weeks, I see them, eyes vague, by then mostly quiet; they just sit, and sit and sit – or sleep, curled up in their chair. What are we calling life? Not this! By all means, nursing homes, good ones, are invaluable for the elderly that have clear minds and are able to communicate. These people, some of whom held important roles in their working lives, are just waiting to die. They also have the added indignity of being incontinent.

I love Pat – she still knows me. Her eyes are still as blue and her smile as gentle, but nothing else of her remains. Take on the responsibility of saying without mind, life is meaningless and offer to us death with dignity. We owe it to each other.

Myra Cohen, studied Sculpture at Regent Street Poly 1954-56, then Painting at St Martins School of Art 1956-58. Art Therapist 1968-85. At present my mum is retired. She attends regular meetings of U3A (University of the 3rd Age) and swims 30 minutes daily. Makes great soups too! 1923-2005

My dad, Monty; the best grandpa 1920-2005.

An article published in the Observer Newspaper, 29.01.06

She didn't deserve it and she thought she had covered herself against it. On 3 October last year, my mother finally defied the doctors and, although they had declared 'all her vital organs working' and released her from intensive care, she died in the night, alone in a ward where she could not speak and had not the strength to call for a nurse if she needed one.

But it should have been so different. We had all been told: 'I have done my living will, darling. It's with my doctor.'

Painter, sculptor, potter, swimmer and member of numerous groups, at 82, my mum was ageing brilliantly, an inspiration to us all. Her joie de vivre was famous. As with all wonderful Jewish matriarchs, she could also drive you nuts, but that was all part of the mix.

On 15 June 2005, she was admitted to hospital with a minor stomach complaint only to discover a condition that required emergency surgery. Three months and three separate stays in hospital later, a second operation was deemed necessary and it was from this that she never recovered.

Fully conscious, but unable to communicate other than by an imperceptible nod or shake of the head, my kindly and smiling mum's face became Edvard Munch's *Scream*. There was nothing I could do to fulfil her wishes.

The last two weeks of her life were a living hell for all of us and somehow we, as a society, need to take more responsibility for how we deal with the end of the journey. We have to allow people some choice and the ability to demand death with dignity if that is their wish. It's no longer good enough for doctors to continue to save lives at all costs, with no thought for the quality of life that they are saving us for. This is not just a question that concerns the elderly – it can happen at any age – a car crash, a motorbike accident, a stroke.

We need to decide where we stand on this most contentious of issues and campaign for a change in the law. Why did the living will signed and witnessed correctly mean nothing to the doctors when I took it into the hospital? Why should I have had to beg and plead, sobbing, when she thought she'd had it sorted? How can we treat our pets with more humanity than our parents? Or, God forbid, our children?

We demand respect and choice in many other areas of our lives, so how can we ignore this most important of experiences just because it will be hard to monitor, hard to legislate for? There has to be a humane and intelligent way forward and we should all be committed to finding it, if for no other reason than it could be us or our loved ones next.

For me, families
are warm
memories that
carry you
through life.

Charlotte Knight

However different we are on the outside,
we are all one human family.

Nick Knight

Styling by Simon Foxton and Jonathan Kaye.
Hair by Johnnie Sapong at Streeters for Aveda Salon at Harvey Nichols.
Make-up by Julie Jacobs and
Hina Dohi at Streeters.
Model: Lee Cole at Ordinary People.
Computer: Steve Seal at Seal Digital.
Special thanks to Rohan, Rhonda, Donna, Audrey, Ebbie, Deborah, Johnnie, Jennifer and their
friends and families.

Leslie with youngest daughter Wealthy.

My immediate family are people
I met though life. They are from different
parts of the world but it feels like we
are all of the same kind. This family
is one of the most important things for me.

then there are people whom I have
met sometimes only for seconds, minutes
or hours but immediately feel comfortable
with. this is my extended family
based on the principles of TRUST
and RESPECT for each other and
the desire one day to spend some
more time together. Louise is one
of them.

Helmut Lang

Photography by Juergen Teller.

Family means foundation.

James Lavelle

The importance of family has always
been a driving force in my life and in
Polo Ralph Lauren. My wife Ricky and
our three children have inspired me in
building my company. As my family
grew, so did Polo Ralph Lauren with
brand extensions into womenswear,
infants' and children's apparel, and the
home business. The Polo lifestyle is
about quality of life, and the most
important element of that is the family.

Ralph Lauren

Mark Lebon

House and home.

He came up around this
time here I am at Clarke's
2nd time today. I've recently
been looking under my nose for the
answer and I suppose Clarke's as
home it's not only the reliability
of the place being open and the
good food it's also the people especially
Roland and Jonne. We are
family without too much baggage
not much of a past not much
secundary plenty of practical
boundaries. At this point of
my life today now this is
my most familiar spot where
I feel safe cared for and
able to care for myself. My
home studio frightens me I
do not feel confident of any
family work or home. Even
when I'm with my 4 year
old Frank I do not feel like
the home is complete physically

At spiritually. It's as much
to do with people as it is to do
with things. The ingredients
are needed but in terms
of consistency or reliability
Clarke's comes first. I complete.
As a teenager coming from divorced
parents I wanted to love the whole
world. When I realised Loyolls
me all my teenage dreams. I've
wanted the whole world to
love me. I want the whole
world to be one big happy
family. I think the world
is one big happy family.
In all family's there are
problems and friction. Growing
is a slow and sometimes
painful process. Being born
and dying are two fine
examples of this. & the
whole earth family lives and
dies and suffers its pains
the teaching and humbling
spirit

friendships grow
and friends are
an essential refuge.
Friends come and
go with life they
flow. and so does
family. Though
mum and dad
and those before
are always
part of me.
As are the
memories of
friends.

what actual
happens to that
sperm and egg.
Where do they
go.
Change
is change.
makes things.
Gonna
happen"

Secure in security.

Flesh and blood.

To my Darling
MUM
I feel terribly homesick
But i think i can just keep
It in. I hope you like
My writing i teke a
Long time, I redly am
missing i be seeing you
in ten Days. Lots of love
James

Love and tears.

My brother-in-law and nephew.

The word family makes me think of a place where you can stop for a meal and leave without having to talk. Family means a place where you can watch a football game without women asking you to explain the game or without anyone trying to change the channel. Family means huge special occasions saturated with drunkenness, bad jokes and bad outfits.

Angel Lopez

Family is where I came from and where I'm going.

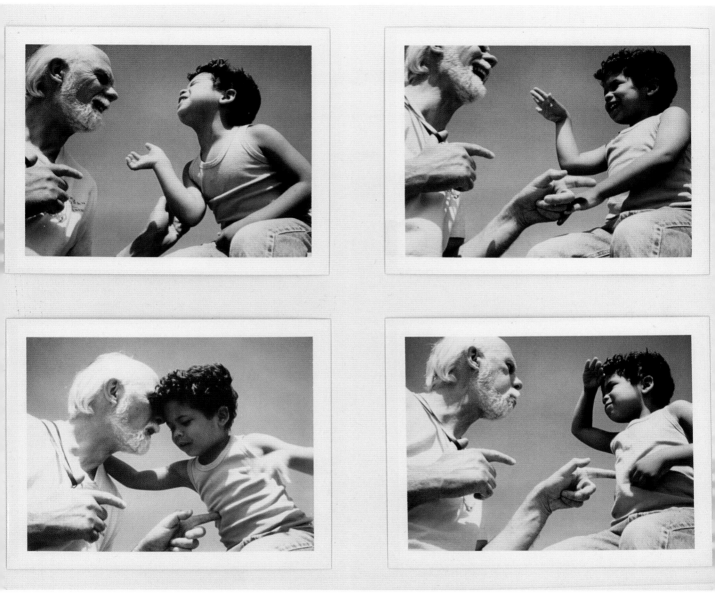

My father David and my son Wyatt.

Mark Mattock

To me, these shots represent a family portrait of a culture still surviving; as strong now as it was in its emergence during the early '50s. The people I photographed here have one binding connection – the music of the 1950s and a belief that the music and the culture would never die. Like one giant extended family, they come together to share the music, dance and dress of the rock 'n' roll era, to celebrate. For three years I became part of that family: travelling around England to weekend bashes, meeting, talking and documenting their way of life.

During that time, I was always welcomed into this family and made to feel at home. They wanted to share their joy. I met couples who had changed their names to that of their idol, who had christened their son 'Malcolm Elvis' after Elvis Presley, a man they had never met but meant so much to them. They tattooed themselves with the names of Buddy Holly, Eddie Cochran and Jerry Lee Lewis. They were in that era and never wanted to leave. To photograph such people, you do not need to direct them in front of the camera. I remembered i-D's philosophy from the first issues, of taking 'straight-ups'. The rule was to shoot only two frames of the portrait and I felt it was right also for this project. Their laughter and love of rock 'n' roll came across so clearly to me that I realised I had a very special subject. They were a huge family that all knew and respected each other because they understood each other. "We're not weekend Teds," one man told me. "This is our life."

Eamonn J. McCabe

At home in London, 1998.

Cameron McVey and Neneh Cherry

Photography by Mark Lebon.

Unconditional love.

Pat McGrath

Intimacy
+ affection
+ respect
= family.

Michel Momy

Family means support and friendship.

Mairi and Harry Milne, London 1994.

Donald Milne

Goldie's like the Grand Wizard – he just sprinkles magic dust on everyone and gets them moving. It even rubbed off on me. Sam Pattinson was the first one to realise that I should work with Goldie. Sam reckons that we're similar, that we both break boundaries – which I hope is true. I've worked with a lot of people – Marley, Sex Pistols, Marianne Faithful, Supergrass, Oasis, Tricky, Simply Red – and Goldie is up there with all of them in terms of having real power. When you're with him, there's a presence.

And all those connected with Goldie's Metalheadz set-up have got their own power too – it's not like he's the pied piper with everyone dancing to his tune, he's more like the figurehead of the family.

Everyone involved, everyone I've photographed and worked with for this project, is very supportive. Everything gels.

For me, the whole drum'n'bass scene is like black punk. If you turn the music up, it hurts you – but in a positive way. It can pound you into questioning yourself, it makes you aware if you're sliding and not doing anything with your life. It thumps you, just like punk did.

When it hits you, it hits your mind, body and soul. I saw a girl at the Metalheadz Sunday Session and she had an orgasm in the club. There was this break in the music and then the bass came crashing back in and she was like 'aaaahhh!!!' – she got it, she was sprinkled with that magic dust.

With many thanks to Sahra Mirreh at Metalheadz and Sam Pattinson, my associate.

Dennis Morris

MC Fats, Nadia Hatem, Darren at Eskimo, Lee at Urban Security, DJ Bailey, DJ Ink, Troy at Eskimo Noise, DJ Loxy, DJ Clarky, Source Direct, MC GQ, Lemon D, Jo Hines, MC Justiyc, Sahra Mirreh, MC Moose, Goldie, Adam F, Sci-Clone, DJ Marly Marl, J Majik, Matrix, KT Edminston, A-Sides, Randall, Digital, Spirit, Source Direct, Kemistry and Storm.

Family means Christmas dinner.

Jeremy Murch

At home with brother Bill, his wife Sarah, Hannah and Samuel.

Villa Teresa, Marina di Ravenna, Italia. 22 Agosto, 1998.

Marco, Nadia, Chiara, Alessandro, Beba, Silvia, Manuela, Tina, Giambattista, Franco, Tea,
Anna, Francesco, Romano, Stella, Matteo, Antonio, Maria, Stanislas, Carlo, Zia Antonietta,
Lucia, Irene, Nonna Teresa, Caterina, Franca, Francesca, Zio Carlo, Giuseppe, Laetitia.

Paolo Roversi

My brother left home when he was 15 to live on site. We've never really been big on contact but always seem to know roughly what each other is up to. The day I found out he was going to be a dad, I thought it was the most ridiculous and irresponsible thing I had ever heard. Never mind the fact that he's only 18. But when I spoke to Mum about it, she said he was over the moon, really excited and proud. So who am I to judge Tom's decision? He's not in the most ideal situation but despite that is just getting on with it, which seems to be the attitude of all these other young dads that I met.

Amber Rowlands

Styling by Beki Lamb. Assisted by Alice Eden Schofield. Concept by Simonez.

Tom, 20 and Amy May, four months.

Mike, 30, Luke, 10 and David, 13.

Baby J, 25 and Luke, 7.

My cousin Kenji with his son Kyle and neighbour in New Mexico.

Family means blood.

Stefan Ruiz

Dogs have always been a part of family life and, in many cases, a direct substitute for a partner or family.

If you decide to get a puppy, you are unwittingly buying into a rather large family – in this case, Bull Terrier Bonnie's family. So now you have ten individuals, couples and indeed families that become one very large extended family, spread all over the shop but linked through this litter of puppies. It's the beginning of a mad family tree and, with eight bitches, in a few years it's going to be huge!

Lilly White Shadow, aka Lilly, and me.

Derrick Santini

Dad Spary's Bully One Time Magic Storm, aka Storm, and Mr and Mrs Del Spary.

Afro Tokyo Girl, aka Onushi, and Afro and Yoshiko.

Hoxton's L'il Snapper, aka Amy, and Anthony Oliver.

Local Crunchy Girl, aka Crunchy, and Mash.

McQueen's Juicy Good Time Girl, aka Juice, and Alexander McQueen.

England's Hope And Glory, aka Mouse, and Katy England.

Family (life) is an idea I do not like very much, though I am living it…

Seven positions to happiness… a house to live in.

Children and family.

A ball to play with.

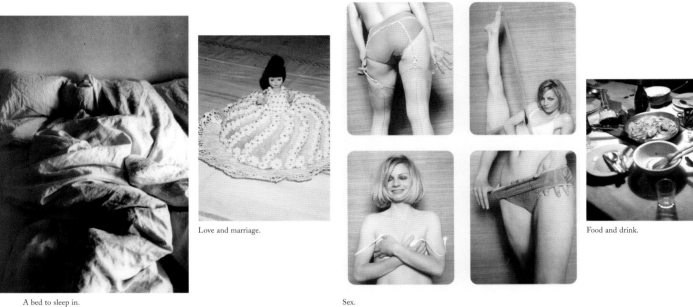

A bed to sleep in.

Love and marriage.

Sex.

Food and drink.

…wonderfully and painfully all the time.

Elfie Semotan

Support, warmth, love and guidance, Sunday roasts, fried breakfasts and the occasional Chinese burn from my sister – well, not everything's perfect!

James Sleaford

Family is anywhere you feel you belong.

Julie Sleaford

Wishful thinking – my parents thought I would be a famous footballer!

Raf Simons

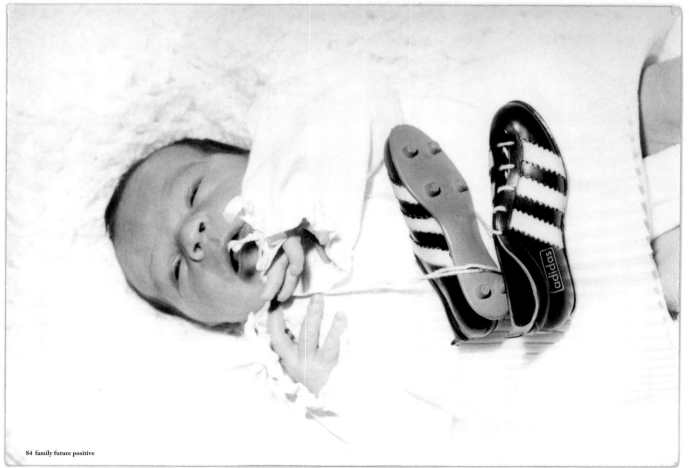

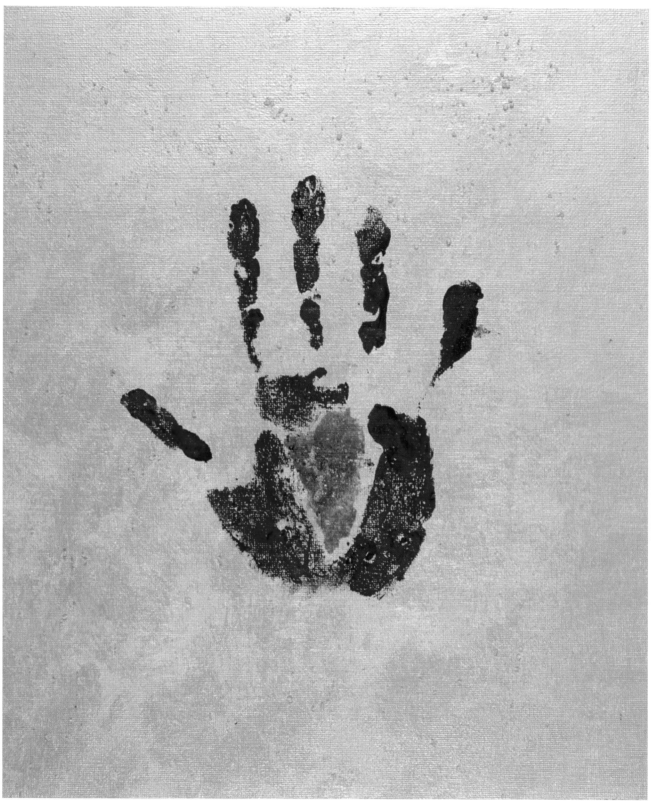

India in the palm of my hand.

Talvin Singh

My Mum.

My Dad.

David Sims

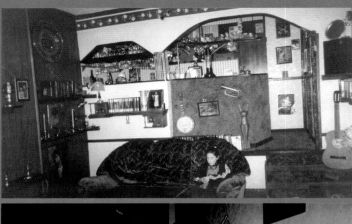

Me and my mum's family.

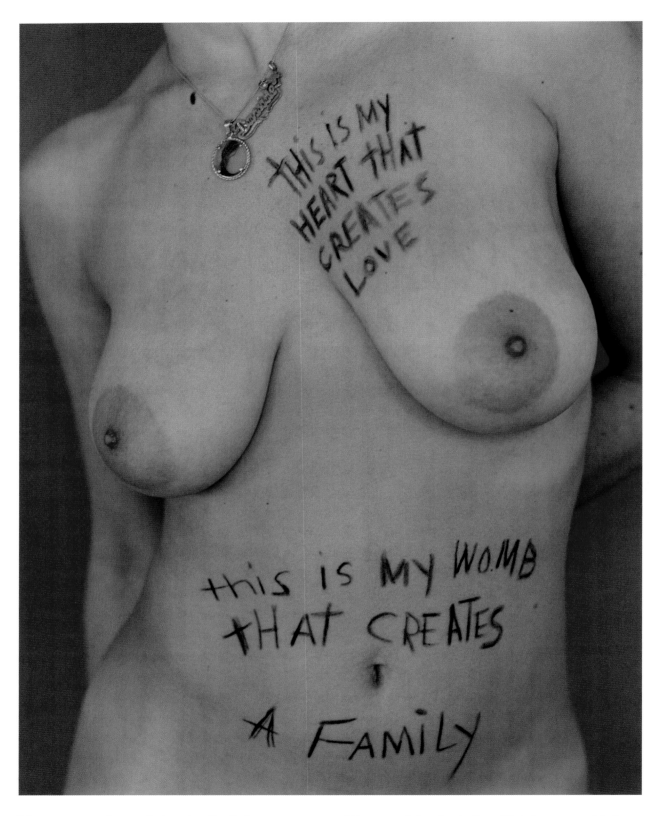

I have come to the conclusion that family is past, present and future, and the physicality of it is in your total being.

Francesca Sorrenti

Overdue, November 1998.

It's definitely today… if not today, tomorrow.

Mario Sorrenti and Mary Frey

In memory of my brother Davide.

Family is joy and family is pain.

Vanina Sorrenti

Internet pen friend's and extended family

Paul Smith

Paul Smith

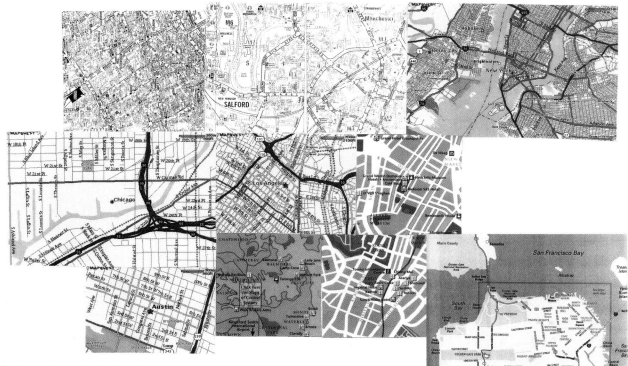

A family of clubs that have been relevant to my past and groups...

Manchester: Haçienda, Russel Club, Kitchen. London: Spectrum, Taboo, Heaven. Soho: Venus, Black Hole, Groucho. New York: Funhouse, Paradise Garage, Danceteria. Chicago: Metro. LA: Powertools. Ibiza: Amnesia, Ku, Manhattan. Amsterdam: Roxy. Dallas: Stark. Austin: Backstreet. Sydney: Fondue Here. Tokyo: Lexington & Queens. Liverpool: Erics, Quadrant Park.

Bernard Sumner

My family means to me:-
Love, cuddles, Playing,
Kisses, fighting, helping eachother,
touching, being horrible, and making up,
Presents.

(Eden age 6)

Beth Summers

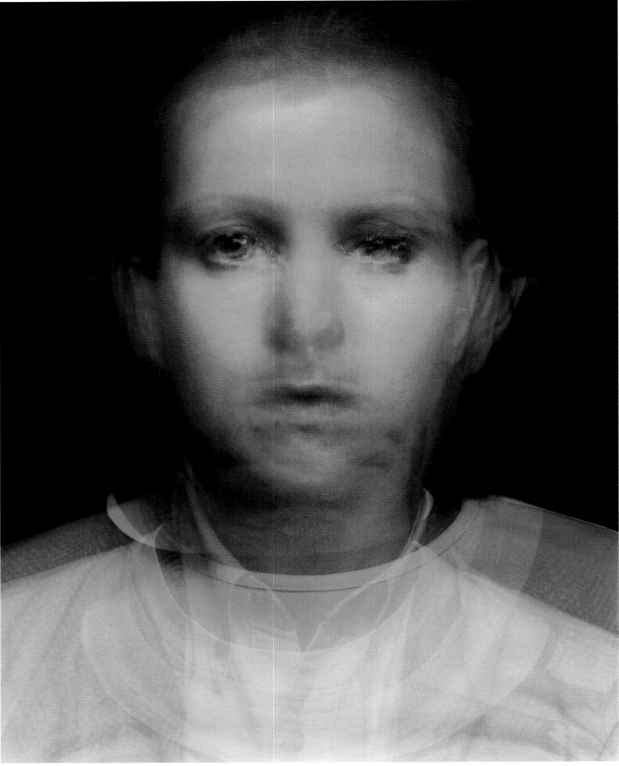

All my London family.

Your family is the people that, when merged into one, become yourself.

Sølve Sundsbø

Me and Mr Piggy.

Family Future Positive is friendship, loyalty and trust.

Philip Treacy

Photography by Sandro Hyams.

The first year.

Juergen Teller

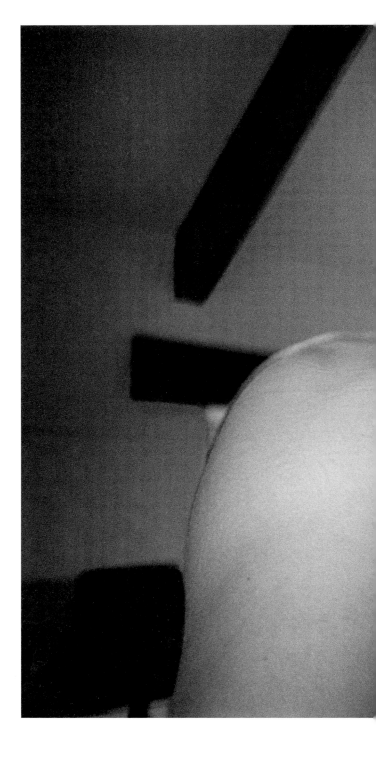

Daniel, Jochen and Christopher.

Wolfgang Tillmans

Monika and Vito.

Livorno is a place in Italy far removed from the 'art-city' or the fashionable location. I know it well – I live only a few miles away. As a project initially for the Biennale di Firenze and later a book, my idea was to represent Livorno by the faces of its inhabitants: the hard, smiling, young, old, rich and poor faces of the Livornese.

Cities that speak to us of their roots are rare, but this is exactly the possibility that the social fabric of Livorno offers.

Casting Livorno became a kind of anthropological atlas: men, women and children photographed at the close of the 20th Century; a detailed catalogue of the protagonists of a city which records a portrait of time.

Oliviero Toscani

My angels, Paris 1990.

Family to me means warmth and strength.

Ellen Von Unwerth

Whatever else is going on, ultimately my family is my absolute priority. You need something to keep you in touch with reality and for me that's my children. I realise more and more that the most important thing is to be a mother. Nothing can make you look better than feeling good about yourself and knowing your family is happy and safe. I talk openly to my children about anything I do, about everything I see. I want them to be prepared for life. It's better if they know what life's about.

Donatella Versace

Family means two things to me. There is the family which I was born into. My immediate family that I have grown with, love and care for. Then there are those that I have met along the way which are close friends. They are just like family. In the end family is what you make of it.

Alek Wek

On a basic level, family is the innate desire to protect another person physically and spiritually.

It means wanting as much, if not more, for them as you want for yourself.

Every day I strive to have the selflessness, strength and joy my mother shares with her friends and family, loving us so deep and so strong we can feel her love around us like a force field every breathing moment of our lives.

Veronica Webb

To be a successful father, there's one absolute rule: when you have a kid, don't look at it for the first two years!

My children Alex and Eloise, age nine, on holiday at Virgin Gorda.

Max Vadukul

My mum and dad.

Family is a six letter word that means the world to me.

Paul Wetherell

Family. Mum, Dad, Brother, Nanny, Best
Friends, Dogs; Long Summer Holidays;
Dancing on my Dad's Feet; Happy, Happy
Happy; Still a Happy Family; Safe.

Melanie Ward

Photography by Anthony Ward.

The football family David Beckham, Michael Owen and Rio Ferdinand of the England Football Squad.

My family are the only constants in my life.

Jonathan Worth

My dad, aunt and my uncle.
Photography by Jonathan Worth.

My chihuahua Chino.

It's a dog's life.

Patti Wilson

Bare
your
soul

BARNEYS
NEWYORK

SCREAM

This is only a boy. This is a boy who is showing courage, anger, hate...
this boy is showing us a feeling. This boy is equivalent of everything real.
This is a real picture of real life.

Faust89, 19, Burgas

TRUE LOVE

Soon after developing this photo, I was walking down the street thinking about it, when I saw a familiar face. At the moment I couldn't quite place it, but then I looked down at his knuckles (he was standing, holding his bike).

Boogie, 39, Brooklyn

FATHER & SON

Father feeding his son.

Shalabuddin Siregar, 29, Yogyakarta

IS THERE ANYBODY OUT THERE?

Humanity regretfully presents the history of shelter dogs...anytime, anywhere.

Fib, 28, Istanbul

LAST ONE

Breakfast 9:00AM. "Eat my darling and I'll be the happiest mum in this world!".

Sisters, 23, Daugavpils

DIALOGUE

Is it normal that a kid stops to talk to a man coming out of a manhole? Maybe it's just because he's made of bronze. Anyway, it's better than not even speaking to our neighbours, as usually happens.

Sara Munari, 36, Lecco

PROUD

Bulgarian Veteran Woman.

Daemonia, 24, Sofia

URBAN PRINCESS

"I hope my prince will arrive, on bus number 45, late in the afternoon." Lots of princesses find their man in transition places, but sometimes time and destiny cross a couple of feet away.

Joel Pereira, 29, Caldas Da Rainha

Do you feel it?

When the light is just right and this life we're living reveals a small truth. We don't know what will make history, but we know it when we see it. It has soul. And it lives in a photo long after the moment has passed. It shines on forever if you're lucky enough to catch it before it disappears. Send us yours.

www.makehistory.eu

for life

beyond
price

Photography by Derrick Santini

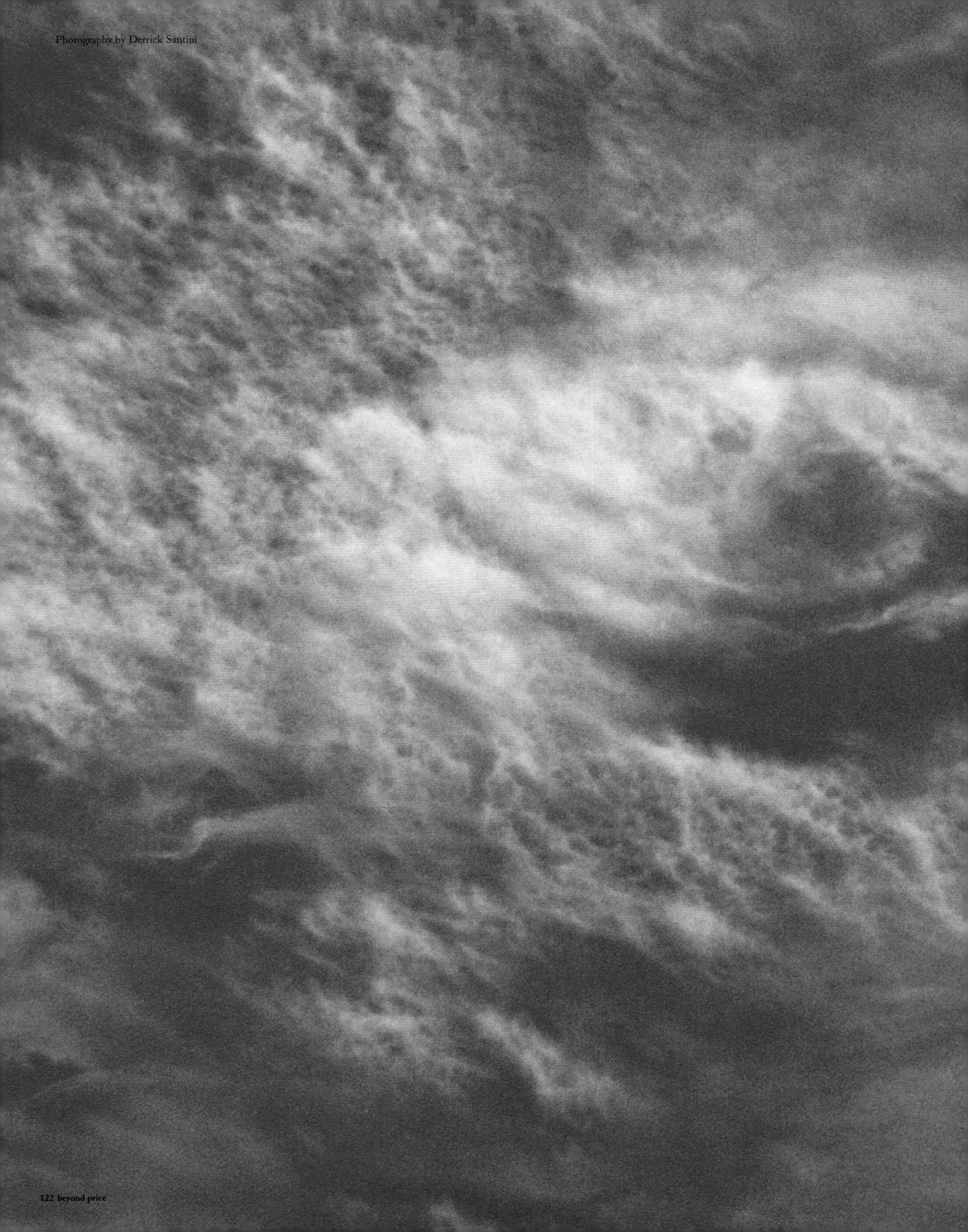

Our deepest fear is not that we are inadequate. Our deepest fear is that we are powerful beyond measure. It is our light, not our darkness, that most frightens us. We ask ourselves: "Who am I to be brilliant, gorgeous, talented, fabulous?" Actually, who are you not to be? You are a child of God. Your playing small doesn't serve the world. There's nothing enlightened about shrinking so that other people won't feel insecure around you. We were all meant to shine, as children do. We were born to make manifest the glory of God that is within us. It's not just in some of us; it's in everyone. And as we let our own light shine, we unconsciously give other people permission to do the same. As we are liberated from our own fear, our presence automatically liberates others.

Taken from Nelson Mandela's Inauguration Speech in 1994, quoting Marianne Williamson's *A Return to Love: Reflections on the Principles of a Course in Miracles.*

beyond price

The idea for Beyond Price came as a result of two things, thoughts in the half-waking hours one fitfully sleeping night. It was the sight on my desk of a special book initiated by Caryn on my 50th birthday – a file made up of words, memories and pictures, secretly organised amongst my dearest friends – one of my most prized possessions, and Kayt's photo shoot for Family Future Positive. She had asked different people who live together and regarded each other as family to bring their most personal and loved possessions to the studio with them. It was then that I realised how many things we all have in our lives that are often completely priceless to us, but that money has not bought. It seemed that if we could only make a record of these things, think about them, appreciate them and share them in the international melting pot that is i-D, this could be an anthology – a record worth having. If you like, a non-materialistic look at the end of the 20th Century. When so much around us concentrates on the commercial and the constant acquisition of more, the freedom to think beyond these things feels both a privilege and also almost an obligation. So to all of you who have once again made a special book possible, our huge thanks. Everyone was given the same brief – what in your life is beyond price? What things do you have in your life now that money can't buy? (Wish lists were not allowed!) My Dad, who's the cynic of the family, remarked cryptically: "That's going to be a very slim volume." Well Dad, I love you loads but I'm pleased to say we've proved you wrong!

Tricia Jones 1999

For me, it has to be the magical combination of the sun and the sea. The sun because it energises and uplifts the spirit. The sea because it represents real freedom, but with an underlying sense of mystery. Together they inspire and invigorate.

Giorgio Armani

My other half...a solid bond. Beyond words...there is no explanation that would really do justice.

Mark Anthony

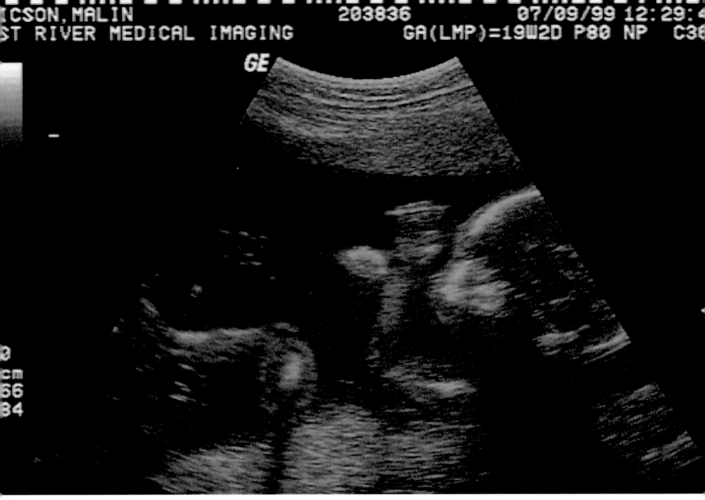

GE

0
cm
66
34

Eva Baron, 07/09/99, 19 weeks and 2 days.

Fabien Baron

What truly matters, what I value most. Number one: my body and my health – this is my engine and keeping it in peak condition is my priority. Above all else, my daughter – having given her life, I feel a powerful responsibility for her present, her future, her life. Tangentially, my ability to earn a living and keep us all in the way we have got accustomed with a roof over our heads, fuel for our rockets and spare parts for the robots.

Elodene and I in our for-the-moment fave outfits, tight and stretchy.

Caroline Baker

Photography by John Rowley.

Left: Vanessa Beecroft, Coronado CA, 1999. Above: Mom and Dad, Italy, summer 1968.

Humility and charity are the two things my father Joe has inspired in me. That, coupled with a father's love and understanding, is priceless.

Antonio Berardi

Vanessa Beecroft

After years of abuse and mayhem caused by too much drink and too many drugs, I finally dragged my tired old butt into rehab. What a revelation! When once I thought my addictions were because of my character defects and weaknesses, I now know I have an incurable disease, affecting one in ten people. In treatment I was detoxed and educated, with intensive counselling and group therapy, to recognise the signals that trigger my addiction. Learning to focus my energy and behaviour to 'Just say no!' I now know how to have some control over my life, in a way I never thought possible.

After the initial paranoia of 'Will I lose my creativity? Can I socialise? What will happen without mind-altering substances?' etc etc, I can now put my hand on my heart and say I'm enjoying being sober more than being out of it. After almost 20 years of chaos (some of it bloody good fun!) I now have peace of mind and a natural energy to live in the real world with no more escape or delusion. It's hard work, but by keeping it simple and taking it one day at a time, I will win. I'm not going to preach, each to their own, but if anybody feels you can't control your intake of drink and drugs, seek help, you can't do it alone! Willpower is not enough. Let your soul rest and your spirit soar.

Art and style director, recovering addict.

Judy Blame

CLEAN
HAPPY
LIFE

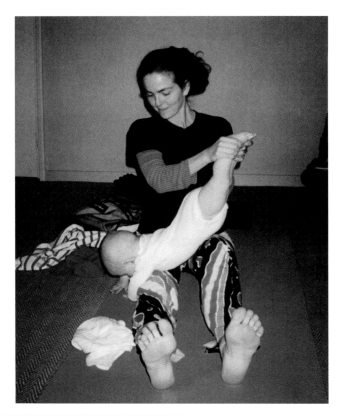

I had been practising yoga for six years before Louis was conceived so my body was already in good shape (ie. my internal organs) and the connection of breath to relaxation also well established. I joined Francoise Freedman's class at Biomedical Trust once a week and practised at home most days. Yoga during pregnancy helps to open up the hips and pelvis but, most importantly, it uses breathing and relaxation as a way of tapping a deep source of energy which calms and nourishes mind, emotions and helps to earth the body. After Louis was born, I found the most powerful thing about baby yoga, but the most difficult to do, was the relaxation. To really relax you have to let go… of your thoughts, emotional preoccupations, perceived responsibilities, and (most of all) worries about your baby!

The results were extraordinary. I saw babies calm down completely after seemingly being very distraught by the simple act of the mother relaxing.

And I have experienced the same thing happening with Louis on many occasions. We always try to find reasons why a baby is crying – constipation, teething, tired, hungry, bored – but I am convinced that ultimately the baby is just reflecting its mother's emotions. When you nourish your own body and soul, and allow the baby to be themselves for just ten minutes without fussing over them, the baby will be calm and content. And a calm and happy baby is truly beyond price.

Moira Bogue

Only ten years ago we all drank tap water. Today, bottled water is the norm. As a litre of drinking water now costs more than a litre of petrol, I start to realise how far away the closest fresh water flows. With oxygen now being bottled and consumed in Japanese cities as the only fresh air accessible, I start to realise how far away from the city I want to be… Drink your urine and mind your breath.

Hardy Blechman

In Memory Of… There is no value
that can substitute the loss of a life
and friendship.

Victoria Bartlett

Robben Island

interrogation strip chained naked violence overthrow truth masters cooperate threat Communism sensitive government torture will unity academic testicles confess wall fire games philosophy history pain comrade anger shit-filled raped Motherland memory castrated toilet escorted urinate kill no clothes no food lost bastard guard blankets statement we solitary patriotism years fingerprinted abused files mental denied mosquitoes fleas lice personal wife pen letter Damn-it dogs hate cold guilty medicine die terminated cell no love proud world weapon doubt freedom rule sewage starvation odor banging duty kicking cursing trial sea swim breasts song censorship lesson search detention wife vomit warden sodomy blood exile sleep rotten work stomach barbarism smuggled they underfed tuberculosis pellagra blindness control lies repressive fight ancestors us one intellectual discipline invaders miracle revolution homesickness toothbrush sex touch nature lunatic disappointment order release air crawl calm hallway segregated slaves justify stale complaint decaying you everyday me country domination diarrhea liberty exercise unauthorized razor eat vile ransacking thinking fear endless path silence when birthright GOD life Beyond Price

by Koto Bolofo

Robben Island, near the coast of Cape Town,
South Africa, where Nelson Mandela was
imprisoned for almost 20 years.

Koto Bolofo

Lime quarry where Nelson Mandela
and other prisoners worked.

Nelson Mandela's prison key for his cell.
Visitors' waiting room.
Mandela's plate, spoon and cup.
The blankets in his cell.

Printed by Peter Guest at The Image.

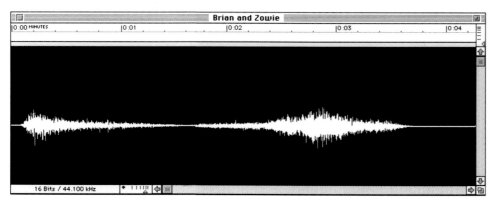

A sound graph of our breath.

Zowie Broach and Brian Kirkby

Spending the best years of my childhood in East Africa taught me that you can't buy happiness. Without TV and other childhood distractions I learnt the value of daydreams, creativity and imagination. My experience opened my eyes to the wider world, helped me to keep my feet on the ground and head firmly in the clouds.

Gemma Booth

beyond price

It costs £16 to get into Portman Road, the home of Ipswich Town. Or £32 if I buy my dad's ticket too, which is only fair seeing as he bought me a fair few when my pocket money wouldn't stretch beyond a copy of *Shoot!* and a quarter of Midget Gems. Sure, 32 quid ain't cheap. You can go to the pictures for less and not give a toss about who wins. But for me, the joy I share with my dad and my best mates when the Town scores, goes well beyond the previous content of my wallet. It's all our pasts, presents and futures rolled into one fantastic, explosive moment. Blue Army!

Matt Brooke

Health, love, a good memory and a sense of humour are all priceless to me.

Paul Burston

My job is beyond price: I have fashioned myself a career within the sports that I am a participant in. For me, these extreme and board sports are a tonic to the mind, body and soul, giving inspiration and drive to the other facets of my life. It's about the thrill, the closeness I feel to the environment, the sense of achievement and the opportunity to hang out with like-minded people. The clarity of thought and purity of soul you get when sitting waist deep in the ocean on your board, using the kinetic energy of the wave to propel yourself towards the beach, is incomparable and irreplaceable. Riding boards becomes a raison d'être, going beyond the realms of a sport and infusing every aspect of life. It's the very substance that feeds existence. I have created my life around these sports,

writing and shooting pictures of them for the sole purpose of earning enough cash so that I can carry on riding myself. It's a sentiment others share. There was an old chap who used to surf at the same beach as I in the States, who would turn up whenever there was a swell with his longboard strapped to the roof of his Porsche. Apparently he was a surgeon in Palm Beach and I always imagined his patients being trollied to the operating theatre only to find a notice hung on the door: "Gone surfing". For him and me, as with most participants of these sports, they are truly beyond price. Money can't buy you happiness.

Danny Burrows

I've spent hours pouring over coral pink lingerie from the '30s, mammoth cartoon-sized cami-knickers made from flimsy satin,

renounced perhaps by a Radio City Rockette or chic Bette Davis lookalike. My favourite pair of shoes originally belonged to an intrepid land army girl who no doubt battled on the home front when the Second World War kicked in. I love the way the blakies on the toe make me feel like Miss Jean Brodie when I walk. I'm a sucker for that evacuee look too and I've bought some beautiful double-breasted princess coats with velvet collars that have somehow made a pilgrimage to the dustiest flea-pits imaginable and emerged in my hot hands. Just when I think I've found all the '50s print dresses I could possibly want that make me look like I'm going on a hike with the Famous Five, I'll unearth a suitcase full at a market and snap up another. Ever since I can remember, I've been mesmerised by books and clothes. Books spin stories that relive prosaic normality and clothes can communicate their own poetic histories too. My wardrobe is full of other people's cast-offs peppered with designer moments. It's taken a long time to mutate to where it is now and I'm looking forward to the next 30 years of plot development. Its value to me goes way beyond price. Most of my treasures I've picked up for pennies. I can remember exactly where, when and why I bought everything stuffed in my cupboards – it's like a three-dimensional scrapbook of my world so far. Everything I buy is an ongoing wardrobe possibility, so I'm more often than not wearing something I bought several years ago. But that's the point. My affection for '50s swimsuits is eternal. At 14, I imagined my puppy fat would miraculously disappear into the huge girdles that were derigeur when Diana Dors was the toast of Cannes, and I've still got piles of frilly skirts and matching sun bonnets stored away in anticipation of a smart beach picnic. When I was a bit older, I realised that bias cut '30s dresses gave practically everybody a svelte silhouette and I voraciously hoovered up everything I could find that struck me as even vaguely along the lines of a Jean Harlow look. Most of my finds were hand-made which fired my fantasies further – fairy-sized stitches on embroidered collars or mother of pearl buttons fixed to hand-sewn button-holes are labours of love that I relish. Before I started my first job as Lulu Guinness' assistant, I spent a miserable few months learning to type. I was unemployed. I had no money, but every Friday I went to Portobello Market to cheer myself up and that's where I bought a balloon print dress that was at least 60 years old then. Somebody had sewn a blue frill onto the hem to make it a little longer and despite its patches, it made my heart melt with joy. It was on a £5 bargain rail. I've worn it to luxury weddings and New Year's Eve parties since then. It's spread a discernible amount of happiness into my life and I imagine that whoever it was made for would approve whole-heartedly. When Vivienne Westwood invented the mini-crini, I discovered the grand echelon of designer fashion and gravitated towards the creators who spun elegant worlds of fantasy. To this day, it's the seasonal collections that floor you with a positive narrative that I drool over. Even though I was at University, I spent every penny I had on Westwood's Crini collection, including the extra-large boater that came with a veil. I imagined myself at Henley Regatta and wore it to Solaris on a Sunday instead. My Mum wore it to my brother's wedding in Gretna Green. When Browns started stocking Stephen Sprouse for the first time, I saved up and bought hot pink drainpipes and I thought I looked like Debbie Harry. A stripy mohair jumper from the same collection fuelled post-punk daydreams and for a while I resembled an extra from *The Great Rock And Roll Swindle* (or so I imagined). And now when I decide to throw on a Sex T-shirt, I always remember the time we bought a black leather mast to go with the Cambridge Rapist muslin shirt to create an extra-special party outfit. I can't help wondering what it must have been like to be a youth when clothes could be an arrestable offence. I attempt to jettison superfluous wardrobe stock simply for the space, but I always live to regret it so I don't try too hard. I really wanted to wear this knitted '50s cheerleader jumper the other day. I got it from Camden Market and it reminded me of the square outfit Sandy wears in Grease. But to my horror, I realised I must have sent it to a charity. I just really, really hope it's gone to a good home – if you find it, it looks excellent with a ra-ra skirt and tap shoes.

Terry Burgess

I lost my arm.
I lost my left arm.
I lost my left arm from my left life.
I lost my left arm to a motorcycle crash.
It wasn't even a good crash.

I lost my left arm to find myself.
I lost my left arm and found I could improve.
I lost my left arm and started to feel my heart.
I lost my left arm and married my wife.
She is my education.

I lost my left arm to change.
I lost my left arm and learnt pain,
I lost my left arm but it wasn't my right.
I lost my left arm pretending to be someone else.
Someone else's left arm.

I lost my left arm and lost my vanity
And lost my blame
And lost my bigotry
And lost my anger
And lost nothing.

I lost my left arm
It was Beyond Price.
I would lose my right arm.
If I could gain half as much again.
Half as much again.

BJ Cunningham

Childhood is priceless.

Istanbul street scene photographed by Andreas Kokkino.

Hussein Chalayan

Laugh (larf) vb: to express or manifest emotion, especially mirth or amusement, typically by expelling air from the lungs in short bursts to produce an inarticulate voiced noise, with the mouth open. Laughter is good. It's universal and free. Laughter can happen, whether or not you are in a state of happiness or unhappiness, both a different barrel of jollies altogether. You can be really pissed-off, wet, tired, realise you've lost your front door keys, left your wallet somewhere you can't remember, you get an obscene phone call from an ex who tells you she's banging one of your mates, and then the grand finale, the dog shit. Oh, mercy! You slip, slide and twist your best trainers. What else is there left to do in this situation? In a manifest state of hell, laughter is the voice of heroes.

Rowan Chernin

Björk once said that she didn't take drugs because her emotions were acute enough anyway. I know how she feels.

Without spilling forth some of the more ruptured and short circuiting transmissions between my synapses, I feel with a severity and an intensity which is almost unbearable. When I'm happy, it's like flying. When I'm sad and paranoid, it stings. Like walking through Ian Sinclair's premillennial London in impenetrable smog, it is utterly desolate, totally devoid. Like Sonic Youth's 'Tunic (Song For Karen)', "I feel like I'm disappearing, getting smaller every day." There is no middle ground. I lurch between ecstasy and a self-hatred that's almost as intolerable as having your fingernails ripped out with pliers. But don't worry. I'm not gonna lose it. You don't have to be my therapist. I'm together. It's all under control. This isn't self-obsession. All the people I love best, the 'kindred spirits', are twisted inside too. They might not say anything. But I know they veer on a knife edge between stability and feeling too much as well. Everyone talks about emotions now. The culture of the confessional has devalued the blistering excruciation of feeling itself. The flaccid gush of 'someone else's trauma', unless they're dying or living in Kosovo, doesn't seem to mean anything anymore. So if you don't care about me, that's absolutely fine. Quite a few of my friends have been to bleak emotional places. Lost it on drugs. Or felt too deeply, thought too much. I love them more than they will ever know. One of them once wrote me this letter, which I shall always keep. In it he said: 'Whatever people think, I know it can never be worse than the thoughts I have about myself at times'. People who experience things very sharply will always feel like outsiders. It's like being on an island in close proximity to the mainland and waving back at the rest of the world as you drift further out to sea. Yet there are bittersweet blessings in this isolation. An appreciation of happiness and placidity that only comes from visiting emotional wastes that are totally derelict and rotten and inhumane. These days, searing pain can be numbered into blank acceptance so easily with a little 20mg green and white pill called fluorexetine.

But, and this will sound like cringeworthy psychobabble, learning to live with the way you feel is one of the bravest and most fulfilling things you will ever do.

So this is the story of how I came to love and accept my emotions. They are, ha ha, truly priceless. How, instead of knowing I was different, or at least not 'normal' and worrying what people might think, getting to a point where I would never compromise being myself, however radical it might be. The times of unreal happiness. The instants on the edge of the abyss. The moments of crippling shyness, panic and social awkwardness. During my teenage years I externalised my intemperate nature. I was a Revolutionary Communist and a separatist feminist (although I still had boyfriends) who liked Talking Heads and John Hughes films, wore see-through plastic dresses to festivals and had fights with boys… just because. My behaviour was very extreme but I didn't know why. A counsellor my best friend knew told me I should take Holly and Crabapple Bach Flower remedies to 'cure' my angry and hateful temperament. In my twenties, I managed to assimilate a bit more into society on the outside, but internally my emotions seemed more excessive than ever, resulting in periods of severe reclusion and inexorable mental torment. Feeling too much began to suffocate my existence, a slow searing garotte that ripped into the flesh and squeezed out every last breath of vitality. All that remained was writing. Without indulging you in the miserable details, I got through it. Now, I look forward to growing older and becoming more idiosyncratic, more eccentric. At this exact moment, I am sitting in my room listening to New Order's 'Technique' (sample lyric: 'My life ain't no holiday, I've been to the point of no return') with only my crazy feelings and this computer for company. Scary, huh? You know what, though? It's fine. I am completely calm. And calm is a very rare state for us extreme types. Amongst people, it is almost impossible for me to feel like this. I am rigid with panic. Ironically, in an era where 'chill out', 'ambient' and 'slacker' have had a kind of totemic resonance, 'calm' the calm that you had when you were eight or nine and were completely at ease with your body and feelings, has to be re-learned via 'relaxation techniques', tai chi and yoga. Peace and calm is something to aspire to. Accepting the harshness of your sentimental existence is the first step. One of my ex-boyfriends once said that going out with me was like being on drugs. I take that as a compliment. I'm not gonna apologise for the way I am: whether it's plunged into melancholy, so paranoid I can't leave the house, mashed up on the dancefloor at a garage night or cackling (probably too loudly) at my flatmate's acerbic humour. Because maybe, just maybe, this extremity is part of the deal when you write or you paint or do other vaguely creative stuff. I'm not suggesting we should all wallow in moroseness like 14-year old goths. Merely go with the acuteness. Feel sensitive, vulnerable, thin-skinned. Or rapturously euphoric. Don't repress it. Don't hate yourself for it. I guess this piece is a paean to everyone else I know who's emotionally 'out there'. Go boldly. Rock hard. And don't be afraid to feel…

Bethan Cole

It takes 25 years to get the 'all clear' after cancer – until then, you're in remission.
I should know: I'm the girl in the photograph wearing an ash-blonde wig to hide my shiny five-year-old bald head.

Embarrassing brown home-crafted crocheted ties keep it fastened under my chin. In a state of distress on my very first Class Portrait day, I hurled this Orphan Annie mess out the nursery window to pose with the other kindergarteners, a fuzzy-pated alien in their midst. About a year later, I discovered diagrams in our medical book which unravelled the mystery of the wig and the foot-long scar across my abdomen marking the surgeon's removal of The Lump. Keen not to blight my future psychological development, my mother spoke of my 'lump' rather than assign a deadly word she thought I wouldn't understand. Indeed, it was a whopping great case of terminal Lump, a malignancy that ought to have taken me out of action and six feet under within three months. Everyone in charge of Lumps told my mother to go coffin-shopping, sharpish, rather than worry about school places. Let's just say she found the diagnosis as malign as anything inside me when she decided to hand me over for emergency surgery and two years' worth of radiation and chemotherapy. No child had ever been given such radical treatment, but it worked. The scalpels, the drugs, the endless hospital stays, the drip-feed, the down-the-throat and up-the-arse barium rations, the anaesthetic that kicked in when the nurse asked me to count backwards from 100; they all worked. My mother, who always had problems taking orders or tolerating bullshit explanations from so-called authority figures, was never happier to prove a few idiots wrong. She liked being able to come to the rescue. Everybody likes a cancer story to end happily, but such a close brush with death transforms the life that follows, sometimes casting a shadow like those found on some of my more ominous X-rays. Every year, I went for a sleepless week of tests, feeling utterly alone as I struck poses for radioactive cameras and waited in grey early-morning light for my parents to turn up after shifts at work. At school, I placed a surly wall between myself and the stupidly cruel kids who called me Kojak and left me out of games. Yearly tests faded into biannual check-ups and then into the strange purgatory of long-term remission, years where I waited in vain for my tits to arrive while my mum compulsively pushed the idea of sending me to study medicine at one of America's finest universities to repay my debt to society. Victim culture awards its virtual medals to survivors like me, but I'm not interested in collecting any of them. The real victims of cancer are not people who have an ability to write about it or the privilege of a sympathetic publisher. However, today's 'cancer columnist' can't be blamed for their output: there's advantages to providing your GP with a report card millions can read in an age where one in three of us will die of one cancer or another and the treatment methodologies, save a few very expensive wee gadgets, haven't changed much over the last 25 years. The numbers also suggest an emerging 'cancer underclass' – the cash – and the time-poor more likely to succumb to disease than their wealthier counterparts. Landmark cases like mine raised the hopes and expectations placed on doctors, governments, hospitals, insurers, pharmaceuticals and all manner of research scientists. Growing up to see others die endlessly often makes me so angry or guilty I forget how lucky I actually am. My family found this out the hard way at home, in America, where health care is privatised and insurance companies rule the wards. My aunt Elaine, our corner's Grace Kelly look alike, spent the best part of a summer wondering why her health was failing her, only to discover – after tests for every aliment from Lupus to Hepatitis C – she'd been marked as another one of cancer's victims. Two weeks after her terminal diagnosis – secondary level cancer, possibly originating in her ovaries – she received a letter from the GP she'd been hassling for months, asking why she'd never followed up last year's dodgy smear test. Despite a lifetime of niggling irregularities, they'd never bothered to send her those results. Calmly, she phoned the office and told them where to go. Her little sister – my mum – tried once again to mobilise the Cancer Police, marching into the oak-panelled offices of lawyers and specialists and the corridors of the Mayo Clinic, but this time it was too late. Sure, there was light chemotherapy, but only to dull the pain and slow my aunt's decline. Sitting by a lake, trying to have a picnic on a windy autumn afternoon, the two sisters watched the breeze take lock upon lock of Elaine's hair away with it, each golden strand a broken promise. My aunt died on her 56th birthday, a very dignified exit I wasn't home to witness. Five thousand miles away, I sat alone in my flat squeezing back tears before bedtime, lonely, guilty and misunderstood, hit with a 'ton of bricks' which colleagues and even my closest friends found alienating. For the first time in my entire life, cured and out of remission, I didn't feel like survival was all it was cracked up to be. Of course, this doesn't have to be a depressing story with a downbeat ending. Like the child in a hospital ward, reading Grimm's fairy tales while the other patients slept, it took me nearly two years to recover from another illness – and this time it wasn't even mine. Loss has its own lessons, near-loss just as many. Reminding myself that apparent setbacks often sharpen my already well-developed survival skills, my experience and hard-won knowledge seem less like crosses I have to bear in a world that doesn't always change as fast as I'd like it to. Death, no matter the cause, shares out its costs among the living; our resilience under this pressure is one of life's more priceless qualities. Knowing this makes me one of the lucky ones, keeping faith in a future where I cease to be one of the only ones.

Susan Corrigan

Learn from the past. Immerse myself in the present.

Diamond Rock, Martinique. Right: With my grandmother, Anna Couji.

Giannie Couji

My nan, Ethel Irene Dallanegra, photographed by Ben Bannister, on one of her daily visits to Chapel Market, Islington, 28.9.99.

Fiona Dallanegra

MEMORIES

ARE BEYOND

PRICE

NOBODY CAN

TAKE THEM AWAY

FROM YOU

EACH MOMENT

YOU LIVE

IN AN

INTENSE WAY

WILL BECOME

A MEMORY

WE HAVE

THE ABILITY

TO CREATE

MEMORIES

Ann Demeulemeester

Beyond price are my friends and I realised they are all on my fridge.

Robin Derrick

Lochie-Lou, Stefan and Grandad.

Larry Dunstan

The only thing beyond price is love:

the love that I feel for the people near me and the love they give me.

Alessandro Dell'Acqua

145

I simply cannot evaluate the importance of MUSIC IN MY LIFE. I collect across the board, regardless of genre, preferring the elusive quality I like to think of as SOUL. This definition has to do with integrity. Were I forced, at gunpoint perhaps, to compile a list of my favourite SOUL MUSIC, I would decline, have to take the bullet, unless the ALL KNOWING SUPER BEING could define that word 'favourite'. The qualitative list is a vile control mechanism designed by evil feudalists and one simply should not have to qualify or compare in this life. However I would be intrigued to discover, for example, how it is that certain and various music can make me well up with emotion that is somewhere at the cusp of pathos and joy, and invariably ends in tears. For the Beyond Price project I have chosen to make a portrait of Rob and Sean, collectively known as Autechre, who have made an invaluable contribution to the quality of my life. I must confess to not always understanding or even enjoying everything that they do, but then nobody said this was gonna be a picnic. I have been to see them play live three times and each time, by some strange coincidence, have missed the performance, which is probably just as well – the prospect is just too exciting. I would like to take this opportunity to share with you a gorgeous Autechre moment: a damp and foggy Autumn morning in Norfolk through fields between Winterton and Martham. Having viewed the seal colony at Horsey, I cycled back to my mother's house with Autechre on my Walkman feeding my head. I look to my left and there in the stubble at the very edge of visibility (remember there is a thick fog) a hare is running parallel with me. For a wonderful moment I am the hare and the hare is Autechre and the feeling is absolutely beyond price. "This is what it is about," I think, wiping away a tear.

Jason Evans

The beauty of youth is beyond price.

This page: Me and sister Kate. Opposite page, from left to right: Nick Knight, Karen Elson, Eugene Souleiman, Erin O'Connor, Brett Anderson, Sharleen Spiteri, Alexander McQueen, Edward Enninful, John Galliano, Kubrick, Stella McCartney, Terry Jones, Shalom, Simon Foxton.

Sean Ellis

My sons have their own
passion, and they are
my passion above all.

Alberta Ferretti

The Hug
Skin on skin.
Arms wrapped tight,
and time stands still.
Problems, cares melt away.
Fleetingly and forever.
Her smell.
Her brave heart flat against mine.
Her little body, so big and strong,
so vulnerable.
It's only a hug,
a momentary gesture.
But from daughter to mother
it means the world to me.

Caryn Franklin

A man goes into a pet shop and says to the shopkeeper: "I'd
like to buy a wasp please." The shopkeeper looks bemused and
says: "I'm sorry, we don't sell wasps." "Well, you've got one in
the window," replies the man.

Simon Foxton

Things I believe in and that can be achieved without money: experience, tolerance, strong will, sense of morality. I can lose love or a job, but what I have gained in all these years is a wealth I'll always bring with me.

Manuela Gherardi

For almost 20 years I have owned a (not particularly classic) American car from the late '60s. It was only the third car I ever purchased and I'll probably never part with it. Since you ask, it is a 1969 Plymouth Sport Fury. It is a two-door 'coupe'. It was a metallic aquatic green when it left the factory, but now it is red. It has the obligatory black vinyl interior so prevalent in the '60s. It has a 318 cubic inch V8 engine (5.3 litres in Eurospeak), which is quite potent enough for London streets, although performance purists know that a 440ci would suit it better. There is, of course, no substitute for inches. Driving it has given me the most consistent level of pleasure throughout my adult life. It both fires me with enthusiasm and relieves all mental stress, as the worries of professional life simply fade away in its presence. Whether driving fast, or slow, or being parked, or even broken down by the roadside, I always love it. It is truly beyond price. You could say that it's only a car and money can certainly buy plenty of those, but what I'm trying to get

at is how to express for you the feelings that are liberated when visiting this fount of automotive euphoria, feelings that encompass both a visual appreciation and an emotive state. Simply looking at it and admiring it, as I have from every conceivable angle, is great but driving it is… well, just better than that. Actually, if I'm being honest, it need not have been this particular car. There have been, and will continue to be, others that do almost the same thing for me, and I do currently own three more of similar vintage. However, in iconographic terms this one sums it up, especially as it has been a part of my life for so long. Those who know me, can't fail to know it too. In short: it's big, it's powerful, it's fast, it's beautiful, its styling says pure '60s, and culturally that's where I come from. You might say it's wilfully pretentious, or simply unnecessarily excessive in these days of conspicuous conservation, but when I'm at the wheel the world stands still, and that's all I need to know.

Malcolm Garrett

Patrick versus brain tumour. Patrick wins.

My friend Patrick was diagnosed this past December with a golf ball - sized tumour attached to the meninges surrounding his brain. The laceration and stitching is a result of a radically invasive surgical procedure called a craniotomy. Blindness and death were strong possibilities. Fortunately, the tumour was removed and aside from a large headache, Patrick is doing well. The photo was taken three days after the surgery. It's not until someone, either family or friend, becomes gravely ill that you realise how important they are to you and your life. That's something you can't put a price on. Life is beyond price.

Johnny Giunta

This is a picture of Scarlet with her mother. It is a change of life to become a family man, a change that comes without cons. All I can do is thank Heidi for her love and our Scarlet. You cannot put a price on love, or the beauty and miracle of life in all forms.

Nick Griffiths

Photography by Jeremy Murch.

The things which in silence are expressed.

Mauricio Guillén

Ideas are just there, behind the curtain of perception.
Ideas are clear, when they allow themselves to be seen.
Ideas belong to themselves, to their place in the sky.
Ideas can be cherished and channelled, but can never be had.
Ideas are for everyone and nobody.
The gift of charming them down is beyond price.

Georgina Goodman

The last time I saw
my mother.
(Mother's Day, 1998).

Rick Haylor

Thirty years ago, when I acquired a little house and three hectares of terraces in Provence, the old almond tree was the tallest on the ground. Since that time, many pines, oaks and even several younger almond trees have grown much higher, while the old fellow has shrunk. Every fall, in order to keep him alive, I have to saw off the ailing branches to give way to some smaller but healthier ones, which I then tie to a rock on the ground in order to bend them in the right direction. So every spring the tree blossoms again, and every summer its fruits turn out bigger, and even seem tastier, than those of its younger neighbours. And everytime I look at it, I wonder whether the old thing will outlive me.

Frank Horvat

It's very simple. It's the one word "love".

Wichy Hassan

Money can't buy… a sense of humour in times of disorder and chaos.

Jane How

Photography by Paolo Roversi.

Spirit of Christmas.

Henrik Halvarsson

This photograph represents the warmth I feel from the guy I love. No price could ever be put on how this makes me feel.

Marc Jacobs

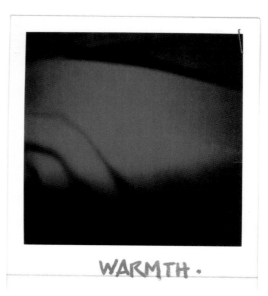

WARMTH.

Beyond Price? Vision!

Adam Howe

1. You're in Istanbul, you've been arrested (rightly or wrongly) and it's 4am in your home town back in the UK. How many people if you called them would catch a plane, bail you out and be happy to do so?
a. 0 b. 1-2 c. 3-4 d. 5+

2. A colleague/acquaintance/ family member deliberately says or does something to hurt your feelings. Do you:
a. Take revenge b. Accept it c. Ignore it d. Show them extra kindness

3. You're in a restaurant with a friend, you both order fish. The wine list arrives and they want to order red. Do you:
a. Insist on ordering two half bottles (red for them, white for you) b. Say nothing c. Kindly advise them to choose a fine white d. Find a red wine that goes rather well with fish

4. Personal identity should be based on one's…
a. Status b. Sexuality
c. Nationality d. Own choice

5. Which of these brands could you not live without?
a. Coca Cola b. Helmut Lang
c. Apple Mac d. None of the above

6. Which of the following pieces of design do you regard as the finest?
a. The Spice Girl shoe b. The Vivienne Westwood corset
c. Hussein Chalayan's paper dress
d. The banana

If you answered 'd' to most or all of the above questions, I would say you have a good understanding of the value of things 'beyond price'. If your answers were all 'b's and 'c's, you're probably on your way to getting there. If, however, your answers were all 'a's, it's perhaps time to take another look at yourself and your world.

Paul Hunwick

Knowledge is priceless.

Portrait: Einar.

Liz Johnson-Artur

Priceless moments.

Matt Jones

New York.

Milan.

Wales.

New York.

It's the simple things that are beyond price.

Kayt Jones

Waking…

Walking…

Daydreaming…

…it's a bowl of cherries with a priceless woman. **Terry Jones**

Things in my life that are
beyond price...

love. loyalty. laughter.
L. to be loved by the people
I love.

instinct. intuition.
to find simple answers
I. when I've had complicated
questions.

family. friendship. faith.
to possess beautiful presents
F. that were made with time
and love not money.

to have faith and find
myself not forgotten.

energy + enthusiasm.
to know that good health is
E. one of life's real luxuries.

to walk with my feet on the
grass but my head in the clouds!

Tricia Jones

166 beyond price

Spending time with my family.

Donna Karan

Photography by Fabrizio Ferri.

You can't buy style. It's a point of view that's inherent – you have to know what you believe in and have the confidence to stick to it, no matter what.

Calvin Klein

Nick Knight's picture was unable to appear on this page due to export restrictions. It was part of the Beyond Price exhibition in Paris.

The freedom to choose your own sexuality is something that is beyond price. With cosmetic surgery it is possible, whereas before it wasn't. There are people who are not clear about their sexuality, it's something they've been stuck with and it's made them exceedingly unhappy, exceedingly disoriented and exceedingly frustrated. If people can actually do something about that, it gives them the freedom to finally allow their physicality and sexuality to meet. I wanted to do a picture of Natasha to hold it up and say to people this is what it looks like. It's not a horror show going on below the waistline. It looks, to all intents and purposes, like any girl's bits. One of the things photography can do is take us to places we've never been before. We had no knowledge or concept of what it would look like and I thought as a society it was important to have a vision of it. We all have genitals. It's not meant to titillate, it's not meant to subvert, it's not shocking, it's not vulgar, it's not coarse, it's not underhand. It's just saying these are what they look like.

"My surgeon has done a very good job and I'm very lucky sexual surgery's around. I love her and I think she's handsome. You can't buy this kind of freedom, there is no price. The freedom to go into a ladies sauna, a changing room or to lie on a beach. All the normal things that natural born women take for granted. Next time I step into a shower I can wash myself and feel what my brain was telling me to feel. Before I had to wash something that was totally alien to me". Natasha nee David.

Nick Knight

Yoko and Hiroshi.

The emotion which makes me warm.

Hiroshi Kutomi

This is a picture
of my boyfriend,
who could not
be bought.

David LaChapelle

My grandfather, Christopher Law, was a Communist, spending his whole life fighting for socialist causes. He remained politically active until his recent death. On several occasions he visited the Soviet Union, and attended Moscow's World Peace Conference in 1977. Back in 1950, Picasso came to this country to attend The World Peace Conference in Sheffield. As appointed minder, my grandfather met him off the train to protect him from crowds of reporters.

Picasso, even then worth millions, scorned the trappings of wealth – he dressed and lived simply. The two men struck up a friendship. My grandfather would collect Picasso each morning and take him for a bacon sandwich at the local café.

Picasso was amongst many leading figures lending their support at the conference. Also in attendance were Dr Hewlett Johnson (Red Dean of Canterbury), Aneurin Bevan (the Labour minister credited with establishing the National Health Service in Britain), W. Gallagher

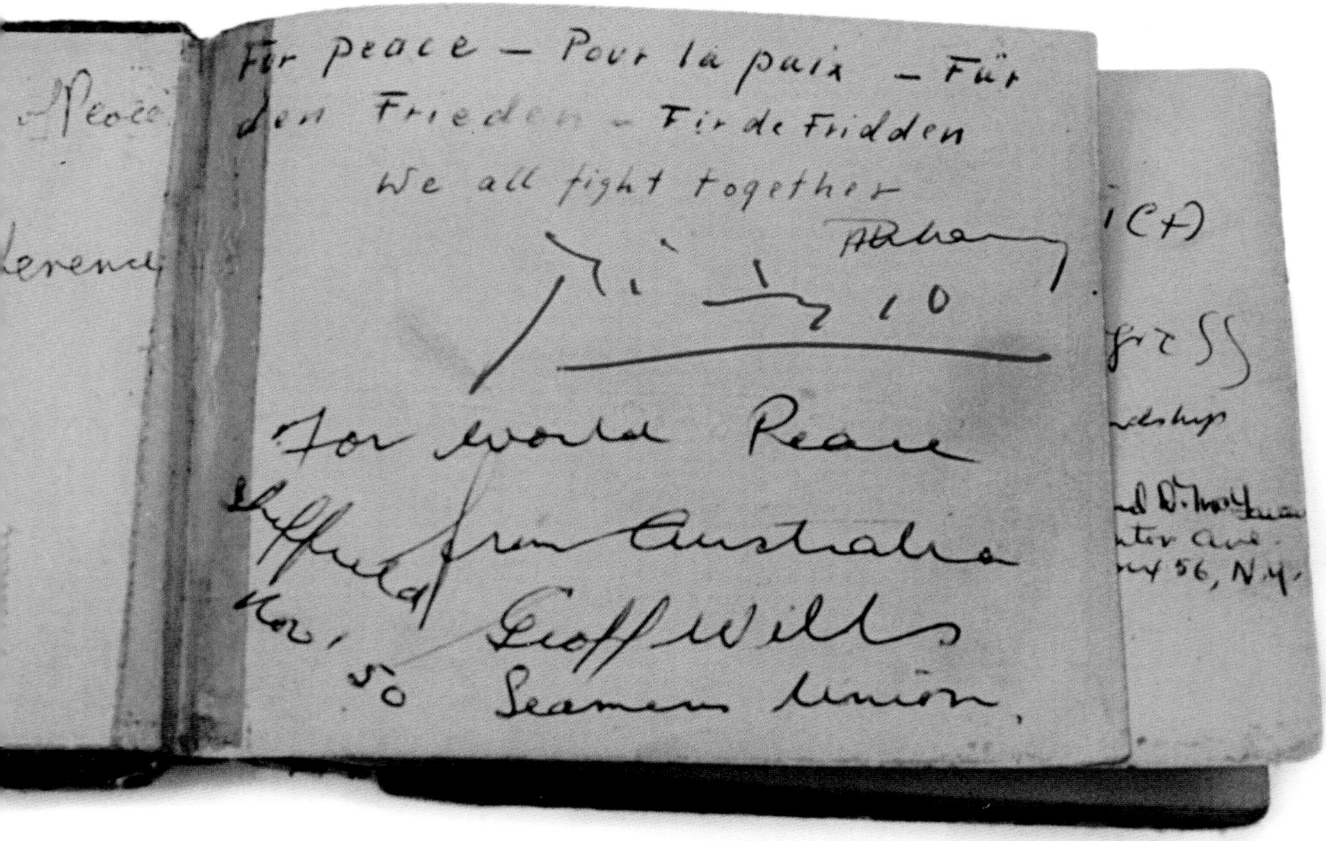

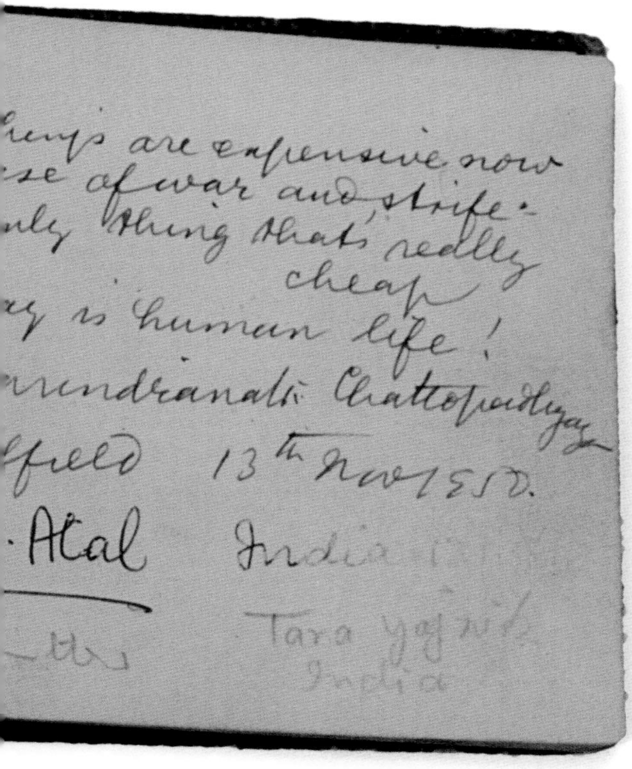

For peace — Pour la paix — Für
den Frieden — Fir de Fridden
We all fight together

For World Peace
Sheffield from Australia
Nov, 50
Geoff Wills
Seamen Union.

things are expensive now
...se of war and strife.
...ly thing that's really
cheap
...y is human life!
...rundianath Chattopadhyay
...field 13th Nov 1850.
...Atal India
...ths
Tara Yaju
India

(communist MP) and Harry Pollitt (then leader of the British Communist Party). Many people from Third World countries had difficulty affording their fare to the conference. Various methods of raising money included Picasso drawing the symbolic dove of peace in crayon on card, which was auctioned on the spot for £50! The last time I saw my grandfather was on a visit earlier this year. He presented my father and I with this book, explaining how precious it was to him and how it needed looking after. The book is full of signatures of those who attended that conference in Sheffield, including Picasso's, alongside poems about peace and other inscriptions. The book documents not only the important event, but it also represents much of what my grandfather stood and tirelessly fought for.

Kate Law

Living in the moment.

Adapted from *Fucked But Up*, commissioned by the Nemeth Gallery, Tokyo.

Mark Lebon

Privacy.

Helmut Lang

Photography by Elfie Semotan.

Past memories are priceless.

Hong Kong International Airport closed down in July 1998. Since leaving home at the age of 13, it has been a strong link for me between England and Hong Kong. These pictures are dedicated to mommy, grandma and Hing, my nanny.

Grace Lam

My daughter, Lyla Blue Lavelle.

James Lavelle

Acting on instinct, questioning nothing. Crazy clothing from crazy places in the middle of nowhere. Charity shop bargains, hand-made hand-me-downs, forgotten silhouettes – all still relevant. Personal interpretation is Beyond Price, individuality, self expression. For me, charity shops are havens of magic waiting to happen. I love the rush of finding something interesting, something new. I can remember all my charity shop buys; they are a point of memory reference that pull me back to the very day of purchase, to the shop, the crazy old ladies behind the counter, the place. A record of my travels. I can remember the very first charity shop that I went into when I was 14 and I can remember how mad I went and the huge pile of clothing that I bought (much to my mum's horror). I still have a beautiful embroidered top from that day. Charity shopping and my Grandmother's wardrobe are why I'm involved in fashion today. It's essential to my well being that I get into a charity shop regularly, miles away from catwalks and all that is 'fashion'. It is my little Beyond Price that will be part of who I am and my creative expression until the day I die.

Right: An Opportunity (charity) shop in Hillston, near Mt Bootheragandra and the Lachlan river, NSW, Australia.

Merryn Leslie

Precious images left from a peaceful time. These pictures are the only 'souvenirs' that my family saved from the Cambodian war: the only link from the past. All these icons I've been wearing for the last 20 years. Faith belongs to the pure heart.

Duc Liao

Solitude and tranquility are beyond price.

Angel Lopez

"I love the Rollers" 1973 – with my two sisters, Lesley and Bevley, photographed outside our home in Merthyr Tydfil, South Wales.

The only thing money cannot buy is youth and childhood memories.

Julien Macdonald

Health is beyond price.

Paul Mittleman

"I have sometimes dreamt that when the Day Of Judgement dawns and the great conquerors and lawyers and statesmen come to receive their rewards – their crowns, their laurels, their names carved indelibly upon imperishable marble – the Almighty will turn to Peter and will say, not without a certain envy when he sees us coming with our books under our arms, 'Look, these need no reward. We have nothing to give them. They have loved reading'."

Virginia Woolf, *The Common Reader*.

Avril Mair

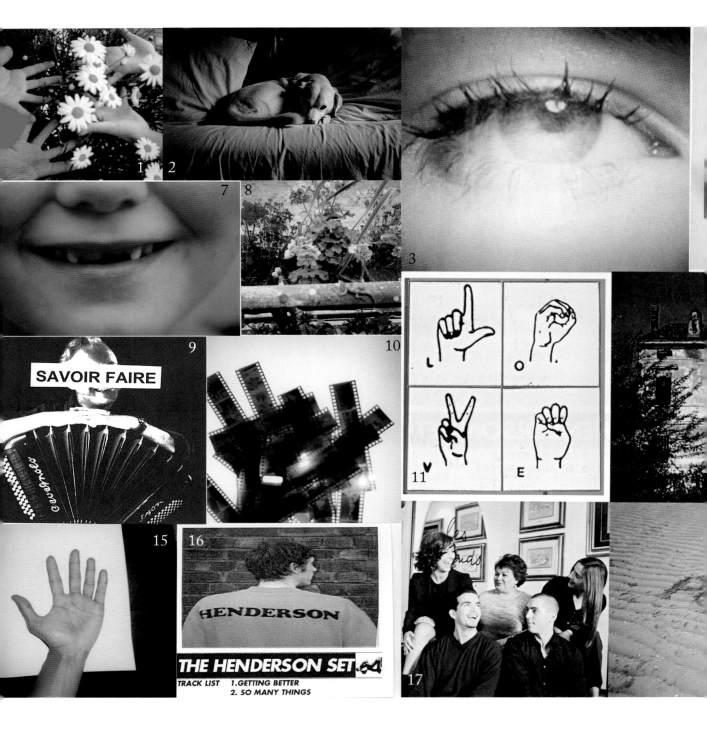

1. Annie: Chef Comptable
2. Art: Commercial Department
3. Isabelle: Commercial Department
4. Jenny: President
5. Kasha: Chef de Studio
6. Marie-France: Accounts Department
7. Didier: Directeur Général
8. Eduardo: Press Department
9. Axel: Directeur Commercial

10. Catherine: Press Department
11. Martin: Designer
12. Nina: Bureau de Style
13. Patrick: Directeur Communication
14. Sandrine: Chef d'Atelier
15. Fabrice: Atelier
16. Harley: Bureau de Style
17. Tiziana: Commercial Department
18. Virginie: Commercial Department

cœur

4

5

6

12

14

Oliver Óg Scallon
March 14th 1974 — December 17th 1991

18

13

Maison Martin Margiela

True love.

Stella McCartney

Photograph by Paul McCartney
(his foot is on the left) of Linda McCartney.

Diamonds are a girl's best friend.

Photography by Jules Kulpinski.

Delicate, timeless, involved, boundless. Friends give meaning to emotion, shared experiences become a physical part of me, they teach me about the world and myself. I have laughed and cried with Willie, we are partners in crime, he understands me when I don't and he's my favourite handbag. Our hearts ache for friendship.

Kylie Minogue

My friendship with Kylie is unconditional. The melting of two souls into one. She brightens up my life more than any diamante I glue onto her tiara and she gives me confidence, love and respect. I feel honoured and grateful when she dances through my life… I have been, and ever shall be, her friend.

William Baker

The English actress Tilda Swinton gave me this more than ten years ago. Since then, it has been my good luck charm and I always wear it. To me, it is exactly something that is beyond price.

Photography by Yuriko Takagi.

Issey Miyake

L'amour! Bien sur.

Michel and Myriam's thumbprints, 14 February 1994.

Michel Momy

No amount of money can buy what takes
a lifetime of dedication to achieve.

My Taekwon-do instructor, Mr Leroy Small, 5th Dan, Kings Cross Taekwon-do.

Eddie Monsoon

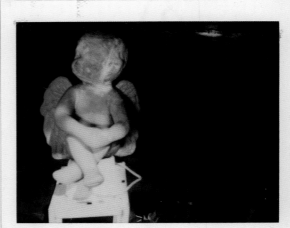

The natural physical world and the unseen world, along with the love that binds them… Life itself is beyond price.

Kate Moss

Innocence and Freedom, Hackney, London.

Innocence has become beyond price. Every day we see images of young children with guns, forced by escalating conflicts worldwide to grow up quickly, fighting for their freedom and, in doing so, losing their innocence. Children no longer play with toy guns innocently. The games they now play reflect their everyday existence; robbed of innocence, play has a new and menacing meaning.

Dennis Morris

We were somewhere where probably no-one had ever been before. There was no evidence anywhere that man existed. I was on expedition in the wilderness of Southern Chile's Pacific coastline, ten of us, travelling by canoes around the thousands of tiny forested islands and lagunas, tracking uncharted territory. All we had with us was the bare minimum for survival. It rained and was cold too. When we were wet, it was hard to get dry. I slept on the beaches under the canoe. I would keep my clothes on in my sleeping bag, hoping that by morning time I might have dried even just the slightest bit. The food tasted bad but, when you'd been on the move all day, sitting down to a campfire meal was beautiful. The one time of day we could stop and look around at the wonder of where we were, I saw seals and penguins and mink and dolphins. None of them had seen humans before and they were curious about us. I canoed through a mile-long school of giant jelly fish, I canoed through the rapids.

I saw the sunrise over the Andes and the sunset over the Pacific. I saw the water glow at night with phosphorate funghi and bathed under a 20-metre waterfall. I learnt how to build a tree bed and stayed dry from then on.

I made friends that I missed dearly for months afterwards, people who were strangers three months previously. We suffered and struggled but every minute of the way was truly an experience I will always treasure. Rest in peace José, your skills in survival were an inspiration.

Clare and José in Chile, 1997.

Clare Moyle

Watching raw intuition, which is part
of every child, is an especially fulfilling
and invaluable experience. People say:
"There is a child in every man." I hope
my child stays and grows.

Kostas Murkudis

Fortunately or
unfortunately, nearly all
the things that really
matter in life are
priceless.

Miuccia Prada

Adrenaline. The raw rush. The effect of hyper-speedy chemicals screaming around your body when you're pumped up to the max. I love that feeling.

I'm addicted to it. I'm constantly on a search for the next full-on fix. Snowboarding through deep off-piste powder, bungee jumping from incredible drops, paragliding off steep mountain faces. Whatever, whenever, wherever, with whoever – if there's a rush at the end of it, I want it. Now. And two or three times in a row if possible. But while the adrenaline rush is a wonderful, life-enhancing feeling, the one thing better is the enormous sense of satisfaction in the immediate aftermath. It's the adrenaline addicts' parallel to a post coital cigarette. After the rush, as your heartbeat slowly steadies from Gabba-speed, this amazing aura of purified achievement washes through your bloodstream, totally replenishing your body and soul. You feel like you've done something really worthwhile, that you're really worthwhile. That awesome sense of achievement is, to me, beyond price. And for every extra inch you've pushed yourself, the rewards come back double. I remember my first bungee jump, from Chelsea Bridge in London. Bungee is a pretty mad rush. It all happens so quickly. You turn up, pay your money, get into a rickety old cage attached to a crane, get your legs tied to a rope and start the ascent. This all takes seconds. There's no time to bottle out. The Chelsea Bridge jump, as far as city jumps go, affords some staggering views. As the crane raises higher, the whole of London seems to spread out mile by mile as your visual horizon gains ever more distance. For a few moments, the fear of the inevitable disappears completely and a serene silence overcomes you – as if the wonderful eye-feast presented is draining all the power from your other senses. Then some hairy-arsed Australian (they're always Australians and mostly hairy arsed) bellows in your ear: "Stand up, mate. Put your hands on the rail!" and he opens the cage door in front of you. This is the precise moment of mammoth rush with a bungee. The moment the serenity is shattered by the internal scream of a billion years worth of evolutionary instinct. Don't jump! Not from this height! It's not like some ten-foot wall where you might sprain an ankle, and it's not like skydiving where the ground is so far away it doesn't seem to matter if you jump from the plane because you'll surely never hit terra firma. The height of a bungee is scarily tangible. You've been here before. On the roof of your office block, or on the cliff tops along Cornwall's beaches. And you know that if you jump you die. Black and white. And the Australian counts down: "Three, two, one… bungee!" And you leap… totally shitting your system as… the elastic stretches, slowing you down from the hyper speed of gravitational acceleration to absolute zero, and then safely plays with you like a human yoyo as you bounce over the river Thames shouting and swearing that, yes, you've fucking done it! You've pushed yourself that extra inch and got double the rewards. The last jump I did was fantastic. I'd moved house that weekend, not really slept for a couple of days between building beds, wardrobes and hanging calico curtains, desperate to get that Wallpaper*-approved look in my living space. I had to get the removal van I'd hired back to the depot by 8:00 in the morning. I needed to pop into the office on the way, just to sort our some shit before everything got underway for another week. And I had to do a bungee at 9:30. It was a press-blag. "Hi, we're from XYZ cable TV channel and we're letting journalists do a free bungee jump in return for some coverage in your magazine," the PR had said on the phone the week before. "Yeah, sure, no problem," I'd said. 'Yeah, right, as if' I thought. So I turned up, bang on time, got strapped in, got to 200ft, rushed, leaped, screamed, got on the tube and got back to work at about 10:10, just as everyone else was rolling in. "How was your weekend?", they asked. 'How was my morning?!?' I thought. Fuck. I did nothing but sit at my desk, mentally wired for the whole day.

The other week I was stood at the top of a skyscraper. A mate of mine had just moved into a luxury loft-style high-rise (lucky sod). I'd been researching a feature on BASE-jumping at the time (where mad bastards leap from fixed objects like skyscrapers and cliffs, pulling a parachute at the last moment to break the fall). I'd become a bit obsessed by the sport, fascinated and curious by the rush you must get when, say, you jump off the World Trade Centre and bear down on New York, or step off the cliff top at the Yosemite National Park and fly past the rock face at 120 miles per hour. And now I wanted to jump off that tower block. The urge was enormous. Worse than that, irrationally, I actually wanted to do it without a chute. I reasoned that the rush of plummeting from such a height would be so great that anything else I did in life would never compare, would always be second best – so I might as well end it all there. There'd be no better way of going out. But then I thought about how I would feel after I made the leap, after I'd seen the pavement scream towards me, after I'd reached terminal velocity, pulled the chute, flown towards the sun and landed a mile downwind to the deafening sound of inner elation. And that persuaded me to BASE-jump properly, safely, to capture the moment and then enjoy it for as long as possible. If I could keep my life going for infinity I would remember the rush for ever. I would always enjoy the magic feeling of raw, pure, utterly complete achievement. And, of course, I'd have more time to try and find something even madder…

Tobias Peggs

It was the spring of 1973. I was almost eight years old and took a special father/son trip with my dad to Torquay. My parents had divorced three years previously and at that time, divorce was still, like me, in its infancy. I felt ashamed and not like the other kids at school as my father's home was two hours away and I lived with my mum and two elder sisters.

We, my father and I, travelled on a bus, then nine hours to the place where I saw my first palm tree. I was excited by the adventure, the old bus, the sing songs, the jovial banter that the seated travellers parried to and fro, all looking forward to their weekend's break.

We arrived at the B&B, a mock Tudor detached, atop of a hill, with its very own palm on the front lawn. We were shown our rooms and I remember feeling pleased that we had two single beds side by side (like the army) and our very own sink. This was great, just dad and me.

The next morning was beautiful. The sun shone, the air smelt salty and the seagulls sang as they fought to pick up treasures, nicked from the decks of the dawn's incoming fleet. Today we were going to visit a boat and then make our way to the famous model village. Running around the boat, proud in my captain's hat, I noticed my father wheezing heavily. I was used to this, he'd had chronic asthma since being 18 months old. He'd stop, shoulders rounded, rest one hand on a rail and with the other, deftly search out his inhaler and take a couple of puffs. Moments later, and with caution, he'd resume his explanations of Port/Starboard/Bow and Stern. The day passed quickly and I was aware of how special this time was. Just dad and me.

Making our way back at dusk, we had to conquer the steep hill. I'd be constantly checking over my shoulder, roles somehow reversed, as I egged him on. I didn't know where we were, reliant on his adult status to show me the way. Half way up and he stopped. Looking deathly grey his fight for breath took on a new intensity. The only words I heard were "Go and get help". I didn't hesitate, I ran, not knowing where we were or which way to go. I remember all the houses looking the same and being somehow in a dream, basked in orange street lights. Minutes passed, seeming like hours and panic rose and fell as I'd chance upon a clue. As I began to feel despair and with the added worry that I too would be lost, I came upon that familiar tree. Amazed and relieved, I ran straight into the smoky bar and shouted that my dad needed help. The boozed up troops were quick to react.

How they found him, I do not know but they carried him in, sat him by the bar and poured him a pint. I remember that night, being scared to close my eyes, listening and watching as he breathed heavily in his sleep. I also remember watching the up and down of his ribcage, his skin so smooth and questioning why it caused him so much pain when it looked so beautiful. The next day we returned to Sheffield and my fear was assuaged with the duty of taking my cap around to collect for our driver. At the station, I was the one who had to pull the large suitcase up the stairs as he once more struggled with his lungs. Three years later, during the hottest summer of the 20th century, he was dead.

Now I am a father myself, of three beautiful children, two sons and a daughter. They mean the world to me, their existence is Beyond Price. Whenever possible, I take them away, each on their own and get to know them more. They are fascinating, funny, caring and bright.

I believe that weekend spent with my father was a defining moment in the way I approach parenthood. I believe that the lessons of life can be harsh and seem cruel but good will always prevail.

So thank you dear dad, you taught me to be responsible, you taught me to trust and cherish life, you taught me in your absence to be a better dad, a fairer man. And thus, lessons taught through experience are indeed Beyond Price. P.S. Marley, my 4 year old daughter tells me you speak to her all the time.

In appreciation of Graham Arthur Pearson, 11/11/30 – 08/07/76.

John Pearson

Recovery.

Terry Richardson

In this immensity, my thought is drowned.
And I enjoy my sinking in this sea."

Giacomo Leopardi, The Infinite, 1819.

Paolo Roversi

A tree I used to climb as a child.

Amber Rowlands

Hector.

Inacio Ribeiro and Suzanne Clements

My brother.

Stefan Ruiz

Stevland Morris, although blind from birth, sure has vision. Better known as Stevie Wonder, or Little Stevie Wonder as he was nicknamed by Motown when he landed his first record deal as a teenager, his pseudonym could not be more appropriate because he makes music that is a true revelation, inspiring both fans and musicians alike for over 30 years. I cannot remember hearing his music for the first time, like I cannot remember first distinguishing colour, but since then his music has been a constant source of pleasure. Throughout my changeable whims as a pedantic boy and teenager, Stevie Wonder records were always amongst my favourites. For me, all other music must first be judged by his brilliance in order to be validated, and I thank him for funking up my life.

Marcus Ross

In the words of Bob Marley, "If you knew what life was worth, you would look for yours on earth", and to Shakespeare, "Life is but a dream within a dream". So to dream is also beyond price.

Sky Eye, Italy, November 1998.

Derrick Santini

What's beyond price? First you think of love, friendship, family, health, the beauty of nature. But, unfortunately, there's also hate, stupidity, indifference, egoism… you meet these every day and can't change them. I think these two images, taken by Jeff Mermelstein in the streets of New York City, are a good representation of the world around us. It's true that for me, what is beyond price is just the person who will be always here when you need it, or someone who will help you when you didn't expect it. But is there an image which can show that? Often, we don't even realise what's happening when it's so wonderful!

Sarah

Photography by Jeff Mermelstein.

My mother before she was my mother.

Peter Saville

Photography by Harold Foley, 1939.

Close relationship.

Elfie Semotan

Sit and do nothing? You must be joking

When I was still a kid, back in the late '60s and early '70s, there was a kind of joke question that often popped up in tv comedy shows. One character would ask another 'ok bigshot – so what's the key to the universe?' Or perhaps 'tell me, oh great one, what is the meaning of life?' Anyway, it was always the same question, a kind of cosmic jape, a way of debagging the pompous and mystical.

Essentially, it was meant to satirise the oldest question we know: 'who am I, and what is the point of all this?'

The assumption, of course, was that even the smartest smartarse would be dumbstruck by this unanswerable question. And underlying that assumption, I believe, was another: that it was futile and meaningless to quest after universal spiritual truths which were clearly beyond our comprehension. The suggestion being that if you really insisted on posing big, stupid questions about the meaning of existence, then there was a perfectly serviceable state church with a big book full of slick answers and a neat, circular argument. Meanwhile, we would all be better off acknowledging our lowly place in the scheme of things and getting on with the business of living normal, mundane lives.

Funny, but you don't hear that joke much anymore.

I think there are several reasons for this. Certainly mainstream society isn't so threatened by mysticism as it was back then, when the cultural upheavals of the hippy era were still fairly fresh and vivid. And the last twenty years has seen an explosion of information, products and status brands in the developed world, making rampant consumers of us all. There are more things to watch, listen to, wear and buy than ever before: we all live in a nintendo sony sega disney mcdonalds apple airwalk nike levi's diesel calvin stella absolut frenzy of consumption, and just the basics. Not much time to ponder the imponderable when you're ticking off that shopping list.

Thirty years ago, when I was a kid, most working people could only dream of owning colour tvs, new cars, computers and property, air travel and foreign holidays were only for the rich. Now everybody expects a millionaire lifestyle as a basic right. Yet despite our relative luxury, freedom and privilege, this lifestyle remains essentially unsatisfactory.

The main problem, I think, is that we try to construct an identity out of our patterns of consumption. We say this is me, this is my boyfriend, this is my look, these are my nike trainers, these silver and blue ones. In fact we go further and we say, this '80s look is really me, those trainers are so you, darren's haircut is so darren. We say, I am totally unique because I am very fashionable and cutting edge, and I only smoke this brand, and only like this kind of cheese, or underwear, or furniture. I drink vodka and grapefruit, because I'm me and nobody else. Then we meet someone else who smokes the same brand and drinks the same drink, and we're either delighted because like us, they are totally unique and original, or we feel angry that they have copied us. We try to establish ourselves, our originality in this way, them expend lots of energy maintaining our uniqueness, teaching it, updating it. Phew! How exhausting!

But no matter how hard we try, we can never get enough of whatever it is we think we need: money, clothes, drugs, food, holidays, fame, property, status. We might get some, but it doesn't bring lasting happiness or security, so we go looking for more and more. Or we might look for a relationship, a girlfriend or boyfriend, someone to love, someone who will make us whole. And that may be nice for a while, but eventually our relationship brings its own problems, and may even become a complete pain in the arse. Eventually, try as we might to avoid it, we are confronted with the stark fact of our heroic, ironic, but ultimately neurotic and unsatisfactory existence.

Which is why so many of us have that old joke question, or a version of it, echoing in the back of our minds. 'Yeah,' we say, feeling very cheated about the lack of reward for all the effort we keep putting in, 'just who am I and what is the point of all this?' And since we've all become so accustomed to having our needs, desires and interests continually serviced, we notice a curious lack of response in this area. And we would really like to know the answer.

When I was a little kid, about six or seven, I learned this funny trick. I would go somewhere to be on my own, like the bathroom, and sit very quietly and just look at my right forearm. Then I would ask myself 'who am I?'

At first nothing would happen, but as I kept staring at my skinny little arm and asking this question, eventually it started to look very strange, almost alien, as if it were no longer a part of me. Then this kind of creepy feeling would come over me, and I would just kind of wallow in it until it seemed natural. Even at that age, I realised that I wasn't my name, that 'alexander' was just a convenient tag for this consciousness and this body which were somehow united and yet not the same thing.

Eventually, I must have worn the trick out, or maybe those tv shows convinced me that the question was a stupid one, because at some point I decided that I knew who I was, namely someone called Alexander who was totally totally unique and only liked this kind of music and these clothes, and had this kind of haircut and only smoked this brand.

Looking back at that trick now, I think it was a kind of homegrown kiddy meditation technique. I had intuitively learned to sit and do nothing, while reflecting on the mystery of being. Which, of course, is nothing particularly special. In fact, it may be quite common for little kids to discover this sensation. When my daughter was about six she told me one day that she had been asking herself the same question. It doesn't surprise me. After all, kids have far less experience in construction and defending their egos than adults, and so are probably more aware of the tenuous, illusory nature of identity.

Anyway, when I was asked by i-D to write about something beyond price, I knew this would be my subject matter, because until we address this joke question and start working on the answer, all issues of wealth and value are totally meaningless. If you want to know more about meditation, my advice is to find a teacher from the tibetan buddhist tradition, but you may prefer someone from another tradition who is more your style. If you chose a tibetan buddhist teacher, make sure they are from one of the four main schools: nyingmapa, kagyupa, gelug or sakya. Alternatively you might choose a zen or theravadin buddhist teacher, if you think this is more your style.

Finally, I would like to leave you with a quote from a tibetan buddhist teacher called chogyam trungpa. He is dead now, and the book this is taken from is currently out of print, but I think it is an appropriate way to end:

'I would like to plant one basic seed in your mind: I feel that it is absolutely important to make the practice of meditation your source of breath, your source of basic intelligence. Please think about that. You could sit down and do nothing, just sit and do nothing. Stop acting, stop speeding. Sit and do nothing. You should take pride in the fact that you have learned a very valuable message: you actually can survive beautifully by doing nothing.'

Alix Sharkey

Camping trip, Snowdonia, 1999.

Nigel Shafran

Mountain rescue by friend. I was stuck on a ledge after having had a nasty fall.

David Sims

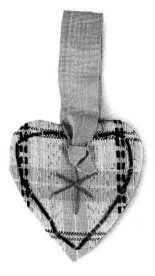

Ein Herz aus Stoff ist kein Herz aus Gold. Für mich jedoch ist diese kleine Sentimentalität mehr als Gold wert. Dabei weiß ich nicht einmal, wer es gemacht hat. Ich weiß nur, daß es eines Morgens, als ich für ein paar Tage auf einer kleinen Mittelmeerinsel ausspannte, neben meinem Frühstücksgedeck lag. Ich habe nie heraus gefunden, wer es mir geschenkt hat. Das Herz aus Stoff und Pappe ist Gold wert.

A heart of fabric isn't a heart of gold. But for me this little sentimentality is worth more than gold. Although I don't even know who made it. The only thing I know is that one morning, when I stayed to relax for a couple of days on an island in the Mediterranean, it lay beside my breakfast place. I never found out who made that present to me. This heart of fabric and cardboard is worth gold.

Jil Sander

Music is beyond price. Its value can't be quantified. It is omnipresent, an internal and external force. By making music, you bond both these forces, catching a moment yet going beyond time. I couldn't exist without it.

Talvin Singh

A picture of the earth taken from the moon: black, deep black and into this black, a blue sphere, suspended, as transparent as glass… We must love this blue sphere where our past and our future lie. We treat her wrong, we hate, we kill; there are men with a medieval mentality still believing the earth is flat. We all have to love our earth, so fragile, so lone.

Franca Soncini

Continued Health and Happiness

Paul Smith

Photography by KM Aboud.

My mother Sheila, 1961.
My father Salih, who recently passed away, 1961.
Right, Nyasa.

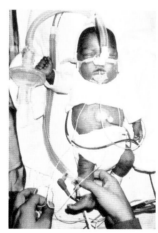

My god-daughter Nyasa.

Life is beyond price

Nyasa was born after a gestation of 22 weeks and six days weighing just 1lb 2oz, an experience her parents, Auriol and Ayo, describe as "beyond comprehension". To help others in a similar situation they produced a book, *Beyond*, from which these baby photographs are taken. If you would like to help babies like Nyasa, send donations (cheques payable to UCLH Special Trustees Neo-Natal Research Fund) to The Senior Nurse (Ref NG), Neo-Natal Unit, Unversity College London Hospital, Huntley Street, London WC1E 6AU.

Eugene Souleiman

Boy: "You wanna take a picture?"
Vanina: "Yes."
Boy: "Take this!"

Vanina Sorrenti

Eden's gappy grin is to me beyond price; to
Eden it's worth about £4.50.

Beth Summers

It didn't take me long to realise that the most invaluable thing in my life is serenity. When I am in my country house in Umbria, relaxing on the veranda with a book, I soon find myself totally captured by the landscape. I forget about my reading and I stare at the valley for hours, feeling totally happy and fulfilled. I find my interior balance and energy through this vision. I don't need to travel anymore, I can have whatever I need just contemplating the astonishing Valle del Tevere. My feeling is hard to describe; serenity needs to be experienced, it goes beyond words and it's beyond price.

Guido Torlonia

What's beyond price? The emotion raised by Jeff Buckley singing *Alleluia*. Waking up to see my dog Ciccia looking at me with 'those eyes'. Coherence, sincerity, honesty.

Rossella Tarabini

My liberty.

Atsuro Tayama

26

27

My Liberty

211

When I was a child I used to make many different things. One of my special pieces was a silver doll which I carved with a penknife. A good luck charm which is beyond price.

Naoki Takizawa

Alexi Tan

My father, Peter, who passed away, 17 May 1999.

During the summer holidays at junior school, I used to stay at my uncle's place to eat ice-cream with my cousins.

The house was situated in Kobe, near Osaka; an area which got totally destroyed during the January 1995 big earthquake in West Japan. Today that area is rebuilt with a highway. I wish I could visit my uncle's house and maybe live there; instead I have my memory.

Takemoto Takahiko

My taste of childhood: Spacedust, cola pips, cola chews, cola cubes, spearmint chews, cider apples, rosie apples, alphabet letters, Parma Violets, Bazuka Joes, Banjos, Treats, Bubbalicious, Wham bars, Fruit Salads, Refreshers, Black Jacks, bonbons, Army and Navy, cola bottles, Curly Wurlies, coconut flakes, Popeyes, Kof Kofs, flying saucers, Caramacs, Quirks, Jazzies, traffic lollies, posh lollies, toffee apples, burger bites, fish and chips, twisters, Salt'n'Shakes, bag of bones, sweet peanuts, Pacers, Texan, bloodsuckers, toffee cushions, puffs, KP Crisps, Refreshers, Gold Rush, Drumsticks, Toffos, Pacers, United, 54321, Wagon Wheels, Lovehearts, jawbreakers, gobstoppers, bubblegum lollies, candy bracelets, candy floss, Texans and Paynes Poppets.
Left to right: Me, Terina, Patrick and Devon.

Marcia Taylor

Lola Teller, Italy, Summer 1999.

Juergen Teller

For Inez, having Vinoodh is beyond price; for
Vinoodh, having Inez is beyond price.

Photographs courtesy of Matthew Marks Gallery, New York.

Inez Van Lamsweerde and Vinoodh Matadin

Things money can't buy are love
(I mean true love), trust, friendship, freedom.

Rebecca and Christian Fourteau.

Ellen Von Unwerth

A happy childhood is beyond price.

Tim Walker

Nearly every defining experience of my life comes with the mumbled disclaimer: "Well, maybe you had to be there". Retelling the story just doesn't work. The simple facts are never enough. In the pub or the flat or the restaurant, the best of my stories fall apart, hideously reconstructing themselves as the schmaltziest moments from American daytime soaps. It's impossible for me to explain how, as a 14-year-old, the campfire burning of a Bucks Fizz record could have seemed so symbolically important – a bold gesture on a level with all the best symbolic burnings in history. Impossible to explain how me and my best mate came together over a projectile sneeze across a crowded bar. Or how the image of my great-grandmother's denture tablets is still one of my clearest memories. None of these moments are captured in photographs. The snap of the camera feels like a betrayal of the memory. Suddenly I'm no longer having a laugh in a foreign country, I'm 'Having a laugh! Budapest 1993.' Flicking through a photo album, the things I'd rather remember become swamped, pushed out by a single shot of feigned surprise and Christmas Day smiles (and I've forgotten who these people are anyway). But one day, the details of the story become blurred. I start things and forget halfway through how they ended, restoring elaborate reconstructions of how things should have ended: "And then the waiter brought in a hippopotamus' head!" It's then that I realise why people take photographs. A selective memory is better than none at all.

Glenn Waldron

Love of life...

...is always beyond price

CHiC
КРАСОТА

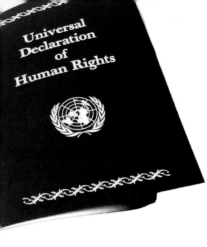

Preamble

Whereas recognition of the inherent dignity and of the equal and inalienable rights of all members of the human family is the foundation of freedom, justice and peace in the world,

Whereas disregard and contempt for human rights have resulted in barbarous acts which have outraged the conscience of mankind, and the advent of a world in which human beings shall enjoy freedom of speech and belief and freedom from fear and want has been proclaimed as the highest aspiration of the common people,

Whereas it is essential, if man is not to be compelled to have recourse, as a last resort, to rebellion against tyranny and oppression, that human rights should be protected by the rule of law,

Whereas it is essential to promote the development of friendly relations between nations,

Whereas the peoples of the United Nations have in the Charter reaffirmed their faith in fundamental human rights, in the dignity and worth of the human person and in the equal rights of men and women and have deter-

equal before the law and are en
y discrimination to equal protection
e entitled to equal protection again
tion in violation of this Declaratio
r incitement to such discrimination.

Article 8

ne has the right to an effective reme
tent national tribunals for acts violati
al rights granted him by the constitu

Article 9

e shall be subjected to arbitrary arre
exile.

Article 10

one is entitled in full equality to a f
aring by an independent and impartia
e determination of his rights and obli
y criminal charge against him.

Universal Declara
of Human Righ

Preamble

Whereas recognition of the inherent dig
equal and inalienable rights of all member
family is the foundation of freedom, justic
the world,

Whereas disregard and contempt for
have resulted in barbarous acts which hav

Article 6

Everyone has the right to recognition everywhere as a person before the law.

Article 7

All are equal before the law and are entitled without any discrimination to equal protection of the law. All are entitled to equal protection against any discrimination in violation of this Declaration and against any incitement to such discrimination.

Article 8

Everyone has the right to an effective remedy by the competent national tribunals for acts violating the fundamental rights granted him by the constitution or by law.

Article 9

No one shall be subjected to arbitrary arrest, detention or exile.

Article 10

Everyone is entitled in full equality to a fair and public hearing by an independent and impartial tribunal, in the determination of his rights and obligations and of any criminal charge against him.

Article 11

(1) Everyone charged with a penal offence has the right to be presumed innocent until proved guilty ac-

---

freedoms is of the greatest importance for
tion of this pledge,

Now, Therefore,

The General Assembl
proclaims
This Universal Declara
of Human Rights

as a common standard of achievement for
all nations, to the end that every individ
organ of society, keeping this Declaration
mind, shall strive by teaching and educat
respect for these rights and freedoms and
measures, national and international, t
universal and effective recognition and ob
among the peoples of Member States t
among the peoples of territories under the

cording to law in a public trial at which ne in
the guarantees necessary for his defence.

(2) No one shall be held guilty of any pen
on account of any act or omission which di
stitute a penal offence, under national or inte
law, at the time when it was committed. N
heavier penalty be imposed than the one tha
plicable at the time the penal offence was con

Article 12

No one shall be subjected to arbitrary int
with his privacy, family, home or correspond
to attacks upon his honour and reputation. E
has the right to the protection of the law aga
interference or attacks.

Article 13

(1) Everyone has the right to freedom of m
and residence within the borders of each Sta

(2) Everyone has the right to leave any cou
cluding his own, and to return to his country

Article 14

(1) Everyone has the right to seek and to
other countries asylum from persecution.

(2) This right may not be invoked in the
prosecutions genuinely arising from non-

Article 18

Everyone has the right to freedom of thought, conscience and religion; this right includes freedom to change his religion or belief, and freedom, either alone or in community with others and in public or private, to manifest his religion or belief in teaching, practice, worship and observance.

Article 19

Everyone has the right to freedom of opinion and expression; this right includes freedom to hold opinions without interference and to seek, receive and impart information and ideas through any media and regardless of frontiers.

Article 20

(1) Everyone has the right to freedom of peaceful assembly and association.

(2) No one may be compelled to belong to an association.

Article 21

(1) Everyone has the right to take part in the government of his country, directly or through freely chosen representatives.

(2) Everyone has the right of equal access to public service in his country.

Article 18

Everyone has the right to freedom of thought, co
science and religion; this right includes freedom t
change his religion or belief, and freedom, either alor
or in community with others and in public or private
to manifest his religion or belief in teaching, practic
worship and observance.

Article 19

Everyone has the right to freedom of opinion ar
expression; this right includes freedom to hold opi
ions without interference and to seek, receive and im
part information and ideas through any media and r
gardless of frontiers.

Article 20

(1) Everyone has the right to freedom of peacef
assembly and association.

(2) No one may be compelled to belong to an asso
ciation.

---

to manifest his religion or belie
worship and observance.

Article 1

Everyone has the right to fr
expression; this right includes
ions without interference and t
part information and ideas thro
gardless of frontiers.

Article 2

(1) Everyone has the right t
assembly and association.

Now, Therefore,
The General Assembly
proclaims
this Universal Declaration
of Human Rights

on standard of achievement for all p
, to the end that every individual
ociety, keeping this Declaration co
d strive by teaching and education t
these rights and freedoms and by p
national and international, to se
d effective recognition and observa
peoples of Member States thems

be imposed than the one th
me the penal offence was co

Article 12

ll be subjected to arbitrary in
, family, home or correspon
his honour and reputation.
the protection of the law ag
attacks.

Article 13

e has the right to freedom of n
within the borders of each St

e has the right to leave any co
n, and to return to his countr

States have pledged themselves to
n with the United Nations, the prospect for and observance of human
l freedoms,

understanding of these rights and
test importance for the full realiza-

ow, Therefore,

eneral Assembly
proclaims

versal Declaration
uman Rights

of achievement for all peoples and
d that every individual and every
eaching and education to promote
nd freedoms and by progressive
r recognition and observance, both
f Member States themselves and
territories under their jurisdiction.

science and should act towards one another in
of brotherhood.

Article 2

Everyone is entitled to all the rights and fr
set forth in this Declaration, without distinction
kind, such as race, colour, sex, language, r
political or other opinion, national or social
property, birth or other status.

Furthermore, no distinction shall be made
basis of the political, jurisdictional or intern
status of the country or territory to which a per
longs, whether it be independent, trust, non-s
erning or under any other limitation of sovere

Article 3

Everyone has the right to life, liberty and s
of person.

Article 4

No one shall be held in slavery or servitude;
and the slave trade shall be prohibited in a
forms.

Article 5

No one shall be subjected to torture or to cr
human or degrading treatment or punishment.

---

set forth in this Declaration, without distin
kind, such as race, colour, sex, languag
political or other opinion, national or so
property, birth or other status.

Furthermore, no distinction shall be n
basis of the political, jurisdictional or in
status of the country or territory to which a
longs, whether it be independent, trust, n
erning or under any other limitation of sov

Article 3

Everyone has the right to life, liberty a
of person.

Article 4

No one shall be held in slavery or servitu
and the slave trade shall be prohibited i
forms.

Article 5

No one shall be subjected to torture or t
human or degrading treatment or punishm

Article 16

(1) Men and women of full age, without
due to race, nationality or religion, hav
narry and to found a family. They are
al rights as to marriage, during marriag
olution.

(2) Marriage shall be entered into onl
e and full consent of the intending spou

(3) The family is the natural and fu
up unit of society and is entitled to pr
ety and the State.

Article 17

(1) Everyone has the right to own prope
ll as in association with others.

10

crimes or from acts contrary to the purposes a
ciples of the United Nations.

Article 15

(1) Everyone has the right to a nationality.

(2) No one shall be arbitrarily deprived of h
ality nor denied the right to change his nationa

Article 16

(1) Men and women of full age, without a
tion due to race, nationality or religion, have
to marry and to found a family. They are e
equal rights as to marriage, during marriage
dissolution.

(2) Marriage shall be entered into only
free and full consent of the intending spouse

(3) The family is the natural and fun
group unit of society and is entitled to
society and the State.

Article 17

(1) Everyone has the right to own propert
well as in association with others.

(2) No one shall be arbitrarily deprived of
erty.

---

(3) The will of the people shall be the basis of the
uthority of government; this will shall be expressed in
eriodic and genuine elections which shall be by
niversal and equal suffrage and shall be held by secret
ote or by equivalent free voting procedures.

Article 22

Everyone, as a member of society, has the right to
ocial security and is entitled to realization, through
ational effort and international co-operation and in
ccordance with the organization and resources of
ach State, of the economic, social and cultural rights
ndispensable for his dignity and the free development
f his personality.

Article 23

(1) Everyone has the right to work, to free choice of
mployment, to just and favourable conditions of work
nd to protection against unemployment.

(2) Everyone, without any discrimination, has the
right to equal pay for equal work.

(3) Everyone who works has the right to just and
favourable remuneration ensuring for himself and his
family an existence worthy of human dignity, and sup-
plemented, if necessary, by other means of social pro-

(?) No one shall be ar
e or by equivalent free voting procedu

Article 22

Everyone, as a member of society, ha
ial security and is entitled to realizat
tional effort and international co-oper
ccordance with the organization and
ch State, of the economic, social and c
ispensable for his dignity and the free
his personality.

Article 23

(1) Everyone has the right to work, to
mployment, to just and favourable cond
d to protection against unemploymen

---

shall be the basis of the
s will shall be expressed in
ions which shall be by
and shall be held by secret
oting procedures.

22
f society, has the right to
d to realization, through
ional co-operation and in
ization and resources of
social and cultural rights
and the free development

e 23
t to work, to free choice of
ourable conditions of work
nemployment.

ny discrimination, has the
work.

s has the right to just and
suring for himself and his
f human dignity, and sup-
other means of social pro-

Article 24

Everyone has the right to re
cluding reasonable limitation of w
periodic holidays with pay.

Article 25

(1) Everyone has the right to a
adequate for the health and well-be
of his family, including food, clot
medical care and necessary social
right to security in the event of un
ness, disability, widowhood, old ag
livelihood in circumstances beyond

(2) Motherhood and childhoo
special care and assistance. All chil
in or out of wedlock, shall enjoy the
tion.

Article 26

(1) Everyone has the right to ed
shall be free, at least in the element
tal stages. Elementary education sh
Technical and professional educat
generally available and higher e
equally accessible to all on the bas

(2) Education shall be

holidays with pay.

Article 25

Everyone has the right to a standard of living adequate for the health and well-being of himself and of his family, including food, clothing, housing and medical care and necessary social services, and the right to security in the event of unemployment, sickness, disability, widowhood, old age or other lack of livelihood in circumstances beyond his control.

Motherhood and childhood are entitled to special care and assistance. All children, whether born in or out of wedlock, shall enjoy the same social protec-

Article 26

Everyone has the right to education. Education shall be free, at least in the elementary and fundamental stages. Elementary education shall be compulsory. Technical and professional education shall be made generally available and higher education shall be equally accessible to all on the basis of merit.

It shall promote understanding, tolerance and friendship among all nations, racial or religious groups, and shall further the activities of the United Nations for the maintenance of peace.

Parents have a prior right to choose the kind of education that shall be given to their children.

Article 27

Everyone has the right freely to participate in the cultural life of the community, to enjoy the arts and to share in scientific advancement and its benefits.

Everyone has the right to the protection of the moral and material interests resulting from any scientific, literary or artistic production of which he is the author.

Article 28

Everyone is entitled to a social and international order in which the rights and freedoms set forth in this Declaration can be fully realized.

Article 29

Everyone has duties to the community in which alone the free and full development of his personality is possible.

In the exercise of his rights and freedoms, everyone shall be subject only to such limitations as are determined by law solely for the purpose of securing due recognition and respect for the rights and freedoms of others and of meeting the just requirements of morality, public order and the general welfare in a democratic society.

(3) These rights and freedoms may in no case be exercised contrary to the purposes and principles of the United Nations.

Article 30

Nothing in this Declaration may be interpreted as implying for any State, group or person any right to engage in any activity or to perform any act aimed at the destruction of any of the rights and freedoms set forth herein.

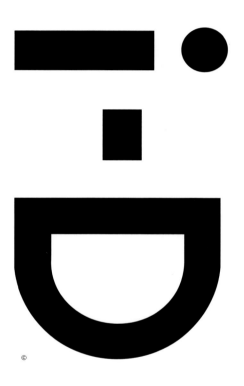

learn and pass it on

This picture is dedicated to the idea of leaving a beautiful place a little better than you found it - take someone else's rubbish home - why not?

A beach in Greece, 1978.

learn and pass it on

Two weeks ago today, Terry and I flew into New York to arrive at 11pm on Monday 10 September for a one week stay in downtown SoHo. In my bag I had a final print out of this book and my half-written introduction which I had promised to complete and send back to the office. I cannot pretend that the world is the same place as it was before September 11.

My overwhelming gratitude and relief at being safe with our family floats somewhere in space surrounded by the pain and sorrow of so many other families missing and mourning the people they love and my faith also has no answers yet.

How scary a place does this planet seem when religious fanaticism hitches a ride and the only way to make people listen and take notice is through carnage and tears.

What place for non-violent protest, for moderation, global responsibility instead of global destruction?

Terry always teased me and said that these books belong to the part of me that was a teacher in the years before i-D. He's probably right. I just know that it's been essential for me to be allowed to think about things other than fashion and frocks at regular intervals! So to all of you who have joined us on this particular journey, a huge thank you. It's been a privilege and an honour.

As always with i-D, you will find the famous and the private, the known and the anonymous voices. Some of us will explain everything, others leave you to find the key yourself.

The idea behind the book is simple. In all our lives there are talents and gifts that we are born with – if you like the things we "bring" with us – the result of genes and inheritance, but there are other things that we learn along the way. (Maybe from special friends, personal teachers or just life itself.) I wanted this book to be a present for all who pick it up: a combination of global experiences, inspirational heroes and simple observations.

We invited contributors and special friends to inspire, intrigue and fascinate us with the diversity of their contributions. This project continues the series of books begun by Family Future Positive and Beyond Price.

Tricia Jones 24.09.2001

This book, like just about everything I see and do, has been a learning experience for me; from the amazing people who've contributed to it, and the things they've shared, to the process of pulling it together. The events that occurred on September 11th happened after we'd finished this book, and have put a different slant on many of the contributions. To some, it's like a hidden dialogue's been added; to others, such as the Dalai Lama's, it's given a new relevance. Either way, the events underlined the media's growing presence in our lives, and its responsibility in what it chooses to pass on. If this book teaches just a few people to listen to others – no matter who they are – then it's done a bloody good job.

Liz Hancock

Ingenuity

Roberto's mother lived in London in the early 1970s (not many people know that Roberto, Britain's best known young Spanish designer, was actually born in London). These were hard times for the young Spanish mother and very cold too. Electricity was supplied by LEB and payment was commonly made by feeding the meters with coins. You were freezing – you stuck a coin in the slot to make the heater go on burning. Every time the LEB people came to empty his mum's meter, they found very little in it to reconcile with the cold winter. "We know you're fiddling!" they said. "But we have no idea how." Roberto's mum fought freezing with freezing.

In her freezer she manufactured ice coins in moulds she made, frozen clones of the real coins, to feed the meter with. A short time after doing its job, convincing the electricity to go on for a bit longer, the ice coin melted and eventually evaporated leaving no trace.

Roberto, an industrial designer, is also designing and manufacturing pretty cool things. Ingenuity, it seems, runs in the family.

Ron Arad

Most of the things that have had a deep impact on me have generally been related to books or music. I read *Chariots Of The Gods* when I was about 14 and I have never been able to quite shake the sneaking suspicion that there are aliens! And it was largely because of this that I spent nearly a year hitchhiking around South America. Ayn Rand's *Atlas Shrugged* changed forever the way I viewed the world. But above all, music means the most to me. Thankfully, my parents passed their love of opera and classical music onto me as a small child and there are pieces that I return to time and time again, such as Beethoven's *Pastoral* and *Eroica*, Bruch's violin concertos, Khachaturian's *Gayaneh* and *Spartacus*, and anything by Verdi. Most importantly, love comes and goes but music is always there!

Hilary Alexander

My mother was a very strong person who helped my father and never let us feel underprivileged just because there wasn't much money. She always made us feel comfortable with ourselves. She was a wonderful mother, without being too overbearing. Possibly by keeping quiet she taught us more than if she had said a lot.

Although my mother did not have a lot to spend on clothes, she nonetheless had her own style that was extremely personal.

She took what she found interesting from fashion and ignored other trends that she disliked. She never gave way to exaggeration. She had a very striking face. She never needed make-up; it didn't suit her. She had a very special beauty. She was a woman who had succeeded in matching her style to her temperament, rejecting artificiality, ostentation and caricatures. This rejection of so many things by my mother had a definite effect on me.

Giorgio Armani

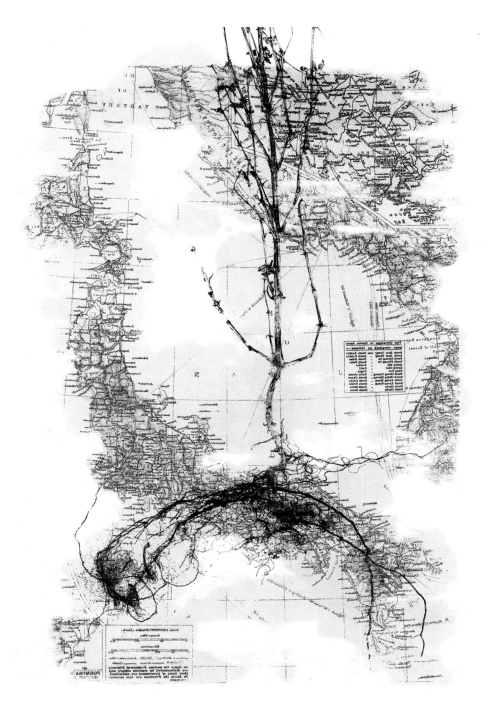

To be an individual. Difference is something to celebrate – it enlarges our world and adds to its wonders.

I was about to be born when my parents left France for Japan. Tokyo became my home until I left at the age of 17; my roots have spread over several countries since.

It takes courage, sometimes, to embrace what sets you apart. How wonderful to see – suddenly – the beauty that belongs to the unique.

Eloise Alemany

My name is Paul.

And how long have you been working in Regents Park?

24 years.

So you started as a young boy?

Yes, I started at 16. Right from school.

How did you learn about gardening?

Through all the gardeners that were here at the time. People who have been here 20 to 30 years. They showed me what to do and I learned from them really. It's just sort of passed on. They were taught by other people and they taught me. And I show other people now the same things they did.

And have roses become your speciality?

Yeah [laughs] at the moment, yeah. I sort of look after them all here in the rose garden. Do all the maintenance of them, the pruning, and the planting—everything.

The last couple of years have been incredible haven't they?

Yeah, it just hasn't stopped. It's just full time. I think it's nice to see something you plant grow and have people come up and say 'lovely job you do' and all of this. I mean not often do you get the satisfaction in a job of people coming up and telling you you've done a good job. Most places, no one wants to know really. Here people stop and ask you how to help them with their gardens… Do I know this disease? Do I know that? How do I get rid of it? What's the best time to prune? You tell them and they're pleased.

When is the best time to do everything, to look after roses?

Well, it's all year round really. You start in the winter. You do your pruning. Get all your weeds out, get all your old leaves off, so if there's any disease on them, they're out of the way… it's fresh. And then in the spring, you feed, to get your growth going. And in the summer you're dead heading, keeping your dead heads down so you get more blooms. And then it starts again in the winter. You start pruning again. It's a full circle. It never stops.

You obviously get incredible success. Is there a relationship with roses that you've got?

Yeah, I suppose so. I've never really thought of it like that. You just get into an automatic thing. You just go along… people come up and they think it's nice. It makes you feel good. It's just a nice feeling. You get a buzz. You see all of them come out in one go and you think: 'I've done that.'

And what have you learned in life through gardening?

Things take time. It's not just instant. You've got to give time for things to move on. You can't think it's going to happen in a split second. It takes time. You get there in the end, that's what I find. You don't need to rush flat out all the time. It's nice to take time to enjoy it. You'll miss it if you're in a hurry all the time. Life shoots by and you're missing things. It's the little things that makes it better.

What sort of little things?

Taking even just a nice, sunny day and just enjoy it. Not to think 'I've got to work, get this, get that.' Just enjoy the nice blue sky, nice bit of sun, heat on your face. It's nice, just enjoy it.

And when it's pouring with rain or freezing cold?

Rain makes things grow so enjoy it. It's a laugh. I mean it's nice sometimes just to go out in the rain. Have a walk. Freshens you up. I mean, the cold… I prefer the winter. Everything looks different. When you've got sun out, it's like a different world. Winter and summer are just so different. Everything has a different look.

Are there any particular gardeners that gave you a bit of knowledge or that you've learned from?

Yeah, my old friend who used to work here, Dave, he'd been here for donkeys' years. He showed me how to prune, how to be. And he still comes through every now and then, he still comes to visit. He taught me all that I know.

Is it in the pruning?

Yeah, if you prune it wrong, you don't get a good rose. You get a misshapen bed. You don't get the growth right. And if you don't get the growth right, you don't get your blooms. It's as simple as that, you have no roses at the end of it.

Is there still a lot to learn for you?

It's a never-ending job, learning. You never learn everything as a gardener. There's always someone coming up with new ideas, new ways of doing things. Every time you see a gardening friend you think, "Ooh, that's a good idea. I never thought of doing it like that." You're always learning. It's an ongoing process.

It's not a boring job?

Oh no, it's always changing. Your seasons change. The weather itself can make a difference to plants and things. You have a dry spell, a wet spell. This autumn we had so much rain. It made a big difference to how the roses grow. We're later with the bloom this year. We're about two to three weeks late. And some of them still haven't budded up properly yet.

And that's to do with the weather?

Yeah. The weather and the cold we had. Other winters people had very mild winters so they've been out really early.

Are there any gardens that inspired you?

Not really, no. I think ours is the best. I'm biased.

Paul Archer

Photography by Axel Hoedt.

My eyes were first opened to the world – of art, that is – by my family. The important thing was to make your talents bloom: material wealth didn't matter. Marie Crevoisier, my grandmother, a fervent disciple of Montessori, believed that the body is fashioned by the life around it and should function with it in symbiosis. Victorin Barbier, my grandfather, a self-taught man and a freemason, taught me to see the natural world. Thanks to him, wandering through the woods, I learned about butterflies and flowers, how to heal wounds by mixing the Turk's cap lily with alcohol. He was a pedlar by trade and also a healer. It was then I began to notice my surroundings, to call upon my senses.

My other grandfather, Charles Beaud, was a stonecutter. An artist in his way, he would draw pictures on cupboard doors, on the cellar door – but on the inside, because my grandmother wouldn't let him use surfaces that could be seen.

"It's allowed, but in secret" was an idea that made an impression on me as a child.

But the encounter that really made me what I am now, the turning point in my life, was with Maurice Besset. He was my tutor at the Faculty of Arts in Besançon. My parents had encouraged me to round off my Fine Arts studies with a "proper" course in History and Art History. As heir to Le Corbusier in 1965, Maurice Besset was already making daring comparisons between Leonardo da Vinci and Rauschenberg in the 1960s. He was one of those "turbo-profs", who at the time would travel back and forth by train from Paris to the provinces to give lectures all over the country. He taught me that art was a living thing, a thing that you could live with. "There is life beyond the studio." It was with him that ideas on movement between different forms of creation, especially between the Fine Arts and the Decorative Arts, became firmly rooted in my mind. In fact, he saw Architecture – the "conquest of space" - as the most accomplished art form. "In life," he would say, "anything can be a reflection on art and aesthetics, and therefore on ethics. Consequently, every act has a meaning".

He was from the mountains, like me, and from the same region. That may have helped to bring us closer. A native of Mouthe, the coldest town in France, "where the cherries ripen in October – if they can". He would come alive in natural surroundings, a trait he had in common with my grandparents. He transformed me, developed my curiosity. Art is everywhere, with no order of rank. It was at his home that I saw, for the first time, chairs designed by Alvar Aalto and Hans Coray, glasses by Virkkala, clothes by Marimeko. He lived with books too, in wonderful surroundings, though not necessarily those of a collector. Maurice Besset was an uncompromising person, upholding principles he would never betray. He infected me with the virus of contemporary art, the virus of living and living artists, of moderation too. It was he who brought me to the Grenoble museum as soon as I'd finished my studies, giving me three days to make up my mind to join him and leave the town where I was born. I worked hard after my first exhibitions with him. He taught me to be rigorous, demanding. Thanks to him, I had the privilege of meeting artists with a vision: artists like Naum Gabo or François Morellet, Cy Twombly or Christian Boltanski. He was already fascinated, at the time, by the media and the role of television. He loved the cinema: back in the 1950s, he invited Godard and the Nouvelle Vague to Innsbruck, where he was in charge of the French Cultural Centre. He also awakened my interest in graphic design, with Adrien Frutiger, who designed the "Univers" alphabet. He adored Frank Lloyd Wright, and although he'd never set foot in America, he knew the skyscrapers and streets of Chicago by heart. He sent me over there in his place when I was still just an assistant. So it was thanks to him I got to know America and the artists he loved. I met Trisha Brown, Philip Glass, Louise Bourgeois, Willem de Kooning. Another thing I loved about him was that after every lecture he gave, he would tear up his notes so as not to be tempted to say the same thing twice. As a teacher, he also gave me a taste for passing on knowledge to others. If I hadn't met him, I would probably have become a teacher in the provinces, I'd have started a family, a different one, not the one I have chosen for myself. He ended his career as Dean of the University of Geneva, because France – Paris, Grenoble – had let him leave. Maurice Besset was a demanding person, a tyrant and a genius who was instrumental in awakening a passion for contemporary art, and for life itself, in several generations of students in Besançon, Grenoble and Geneva.

Marie-Claude Beaud

To whoever it may concern:

We hold these truths to be self-evident
that all men are created equal
that they are endowed by their creator
with certain inalienable rights
that among these are LIFE
that to secure these governments
are instituted among men
deriving their powers from the consent of the government
that whenever any form of government
becomes destruct of those ends that it is the right
of the people to alter or abolish it
and to institute a new government.

Yes, we would like to think that certain truths are self-evident, but what I have come to learn in this life is that whether things are true or right seems to be of no real significance whatsoever, when the very people that we have given the power to enforce these rights have abused their power to the extent of juxtaposing the truth in whatever way they see fit, under the veil of protecting public interests. When one realises that politics have nothing to do with people at all, that it is merely a chess game played by a chosen few with many pawns, it seems ironic that in this age of Aquarius, this great time of unveiling /transparency, of going beyond the three-dimensional and uncovering all that has been occulted, that we still are not ready for the truth. It seems that the most terrifying thing that mankind will have to face is himself - he is able to embrace everything but, if the truth be told and the truth be said, I think we'd all rather be dead. And dead is exactly what we've become. Apathy reigns supreme – it's everywhere – apathy is death and this world has become a necropolis. People have resigned themselves to sleep; no one wants to know what's really going on. If it's not happening to them, then it's not happening, and if we don't know what's going on then we can't be held responsible in any way – even though the shit is on our shoes. We are all guilty. "Guilty of what?" you cry. "I never did nothing." And that's just it, no one ever does anything about anything because no one wants to acknowledge that anything is wrong. Well, it is. It's so wrong I struggle to see what's right, because all that is right is being destroyed at great speed; wo/man is an endangered species snared by itself and it doesn't even know it. The only civilised cultures left on earth whom the higher ground render uncivilised are quickly being wiped out, and with them their wisdom and their magic that helps keep this world alive. Through the higher consciousness of certain individuals a profound difference is being made. We have lost that magic and have embraced greed and ignorance. Instead, the super powers want to cultivate them, bring them round to their way of thinking which obviously is not the way, and our form of civilisation is quite frankly not working. The system that technocratic man has set up is just that – a set up. And it has failed. Man's vanity has led him to believe that he is destroying the world. We do not have that power – we may have convinced ourselves that we have created it, our greatest delusion, we have simply imposed our madness upon it. It is us who are being destroyed and who are destroying everything that nature has provided, thinking that we can put something better in its place, not really understanding how she works, constantly breaking the chain until there no longer is one. And nature is fighting back with a vengeance; she will simply press the eject button when she's good and ready because she has the power. It's so crazy that the people whom we employ to serve us are actually too busy serving themselves, and the sad thing is that people actually aspire to these powers by imitating their strategies on a microscopic scale in their pursuit for power and control in their own lives. Why man thinks that by unleashing psychological/physical warfare on any scale, that that somehow constitutes power, is beyond me. It's not powerful – it's pitiful. What I've learnt is power is in everyone and everything, people just don't know it. Society has bred a certain value system that has killed our autonomy; what we possess equates who we are, what we amass now speaks for us, possessions have become our power tools – that innate wisdom with which we came has diminished.

Power is about being able to stand with nothing, knowing that you have everything, and that ultimately no one can give you anything nor take anything away. It's about the interior, not the exterior.

We are all heroines and we are all heroes and we are all low-down motherfucking zeros – no one is higher or lower. We are all created equal but we don't live that way. The rich man feels he has more rights than the poor man, the poor man feels he has none: introduce a madman with a gun in his hand and he shoots both men, all you have are dead men – is it only then in death that we are equal? It seems that money is more valuable than life itself, and that these men that we employ to represent our values are prepared to sacrifice lives for it. All I know is there is no higher energy here on earth than love – this intangible thing we have such trouble trying to comprehend, define – I know changes everything. We have to diffuse the smokescreen and checkout the illusion within the illusion and get to grips with the realities. Even if you feel you can't change anything or do anything that would make a difference, you can by just being aware, being awake. Through this awareness there will be a major shift in our consciousness universally, so when shit happens you'll see how it permeates everything, and you'll start to feel it, and maybe when you start to feel it you might just feel you want to do something/say something about it – it's your right – godspeedyou.

Zoe Bedeaux

There are short instances
Such as an embrace
And hand claps
That savour time

There are silent moments
For which we stop
Ones that come to us when not looking
Waiting – watching
Or thinking about things for too long

There's time well spent
That's mostly one alone
One within us four
So close to the skies
Near by the water edge
Beside the trees
"For the trees have not been cut"
Is where we go

Yet hope has happened its way
That's way ahead for most of us
Like a secret
That once I've told you – it's bygone
Until tomorrow comes
All come again.

Mark Borthwick

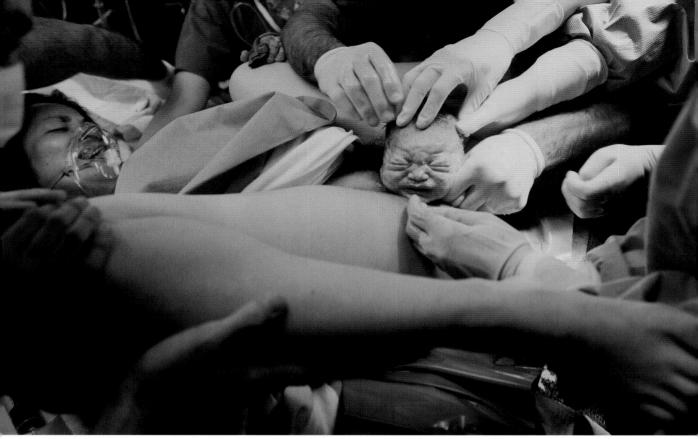

My friend giving birth.

Regardless of my absolute decision to have a natural birth nine years ago, I still had to fight off the nurses who automatically wanted to induce my labour with Pitocin (a synthetic form of a natural hormone, oxytocin, which causes uterine contractions). The nurse was about to call the anaesthetist who would perform the epidural. I said I didn't want to have an epidural. The nurse was surprised and proclaimed that 95 per cent of women in their hospital during labour would get the epidural. It seemed very inconvenient for them that I didn't want an epidural; it was 2am and they just didn't understand that I wanted to experience the birth of my child naturally. Their final meagre effort to convince me was to separate me from my partner. There was no free room in the maternity ward for my partner to be with me so they sent him home and put me in a dark room next to a sleeping woman who had given birth the day before. I didn't want to disturb the sleeping woman next to me so I endured my contractions silently until I felt that it was time, about three hours later. I pressed on the nurse call button; a nurse arrived, checked me and said that it was time to go down to the birthing room. I told them to call my partner, which they did immediately. Two hours later, with the support of a midwife who was motivating me to push by angling a mirror so that I could see the hair of my baby – the angle of the mirror was so wrong and I couldn't see anything – "push! push!" and my daughter was born. Twenty-two months later, I was pregnant again and was strolling around the flea market. It was 11am and my contractions commenced. This time I knew that I shouldn't go to the hospital too early so we continued to look around. We went home, had lunch, had a bath and I started to clean the house. Every time the contractions came, I ran to the sofa and tried to get into the most comfortable position until it went away, then continued my house cleaning. Around 4pm I knew that it was time to go to the hospital

which was ten minutes away. My partner and I walked to the hospital and within one and a half hours, with the guidance of a midwife, I pulled my son out of myself, slipped him onto my stomach, then he immediately took to my breast! The second time around, I made sure not to have the glucose IV and the bulky foetal heartbeat monitoring apparatus which I had the first time. I hated the IV because I couldn't move that arm and the electronic foetal monitor was just a bother. I wanted to have the freedom to walk around and do what I please.

Giving birth is the most magical experience I have ever had. My body did everything naturally and I just had to tune into what my body was signalling me to do. The contractions were like the ocean tides, coming and going. It was like the most challenging sport event in my life and so beautiful.

Last year my friend was having a baby and had agreed for me to be at the birth. Her water broke one month earlier than the due date and she rushed to the hospital at 6am. By the time I arrived it was 11am and she had the glucose IV, the foetal monitor and the Pitocin IV. A machine was beeping incessantly as doctors and nurses in blue scrubs came in and out of the room randomly. As the contractions got stronger, the doctor would come in to tell my friend that she had the option of an epidural anaesthesia. My friend declined several times but after a long wailing contraction at about 2:30pm, the doctor rushed in and proclaimed, "Oh you seem like you are in so much pain! You should have an epidural! Pitocin induction makes the contractions more painful," and so my friend nodded her head yes. Immediately, a nurse came in with some documents and was asking my friend to sign the contract in the midst of a contraction, although she was in no form to actually read all the technicalities. When birth time came, my friend was wheeled into the operating room, suddenly about ten new faces in blue scrubs arrived mostly just to observe. She pushed when she was told to and when the head came out there were so many pairs of hands to capture the newborn.

In ancient times the area of childbirth belonged to women. Older women, female relatives or friends and midwives surrounded and supported the woman giving birth. Obstetric management of childbirth within the dogma of medicine are seen to be successful and improving the safety of birth, however this medicalisation of childbearing has converted what is in most cases a healthy, natural process into a high tech event. Instead of supporting, encouraging, and nurturing a mother who is actively giving birth with patience and simple remedies, the accepted way now seems to be the obstetrician who comes and removes the baby from the mother with the automatic aid of drugs, procedure, technology, control, and predictability. I feel strongly that the injudicial medical invention of childbirth takes away women's sense of dignity, fulfilment, and autonomy – and it is only the beginning of motherhood. Ironically, until recently all obstetricians were male, and even if there are women obstetricians today, they have all been trained under curriculums mostly devised by men. There is an enormous increase in Caesarean births, Pitocin-induced contractions, epidural anaesthesia, episiotomy etc. The miracle of modern medicine and the advancement of technology seem to override the even greater original miracle, the most perfect machines, which are our natural bodies.

Anette Aurell

I inherited a saying from my grandfather which I have always remembered when making decisions.

'aim for the stars and you may fall in the clouds.
aim for the clouds and you may fall on the ground.'

It worked for me so far...
so maybe it may work for others.

Neil Barrett

Be faithful to
your dreams.

Véronique Branquinho

Climbing to the summit of Mt Kilamanjaro – Africa's highest mountain – has to be my most rewarding
achievement. I made the journey in September 1999, 20 years after my Dad completed the climb and six years
after my Mum's attempt in 1994. These portraits are of two of our guides from the Chagga tribe of Northern
Tanzania. Through countless generations, the Chagga have handed down the knowledge and skills necessary
to live on the mountain and surrounding area.

Gemma Booth

As a graphic designer, I have been experiencing a deep and growing unease for many years about what I do.

I started to look around for some possible clues in order to resolve an answer, to create a context in which I could begin to look at the role of design, and my role within it. At this critical juncture of the 21st Century, today's key question is one of identity and role. We increasingly define ourselves through input, and are under pressure to simultaneously publish, receive and edit a million messages a day. Digital is dead.

At the heart though, stands a question central to our industry – can design feed people?

Clearly, design itself cannot be used as physical sustenance, unless, of course, we find a way of pulping and recycling printed matter as edible fibre. Or redirecting all that energy towards other more humane uses. Still, that leaves an infinite space of digital matter that remains unaccountable.

I immersed myself in an online information jungle, and quickly drowned in an ocean of hard, devastating facts. Each fact led to another ten connections, and each in turn to another ten in a never-ending spiral of links. These facts were shocking to me and as each one was uncovered, the consequences of the statistics began to reveal my planet to be a planet I did not know. A culture shock.

And these facts, when laid out on the dining table, started to reveal links and parallels with each other, forming a matrix of echoes and reflections, a grid of interwoven cause and effect. Not the virtual web of computer cables, or the sprawling network of travel and tourism, but a flowing, fluid dynamic of extreme contrasts and seismic shifts, one set of facts overlaying another in a kind of disharmonic harmony.

The problem with human statistics is that they conceal the human. We hide behind a wall of figures and percentages, an infowall, hoping against hope that the world of real individual pain will remain a virtual one, one in which death and suffering is somebody else's problem, where any remote suggestion of real emotion can be buried beneath the white pages of statistical papers.

You see, from where we stand, it seems pretty perfect. Excitement about new technologies and software justifies all our inaction. We obsess about communication, and we dispense with content. We foolishly imagine that this will somehow save the planet, yet all it does is keep us so busy that we don't have to think about anything. We become obsessed with the how and the what, not the why.

Design cannot in itself feed people or replace governments. It cannot shelter homeless people, and it cannot in itself be a cure for Aids. But there are many things it can be. It can educate, instead of dictate. It can reveal and publicise, it can be a call to arms to help our neighbours. It can be a rallying cry to shake people out of their stupor, it can

undermine official disinformation, it can help create awareness; it can empower people to better communicate, to let others become aware of their problems, to reduce their reliance on outsiders, to become self-sufficient.

We still listen to the old instructions, repeating behaviours, and failed behaviours at that, instead of inventing new ones. The reason we as a race continue to exhibit old behaviours is that we have not given ourselves permission to stop listening to the old instructions. We need to encourage, stimulate or produce real behavioural change. The human revolution begins here, and you will need to be willing to be part of that risk.

The distribution channels are there, albeit reaching as yet small populations. We, as providers and content creators have the keys to unlock true communication, communication with real meaning and the power to alter our lives and the lives of others for the better through empowerment and respect.

We need to create a dialogue, not a monobrand, monothought monologue. One where the message itself may be altered, the grid rearranged.

If we are to not only survive as a species, but to prosper creatively and to evolve dynamically, we must recognise the whole human race as a brand, with all of its diversity and colour, its differences and sometimes its vetos. A brand based on respect, not power; possibility, not uniformity. Love, not fear.

Neville Brody

In 1997, 26,000 patent applications were filed to the African intellectual property organisation. Only 31 came from resident Africans between 1991 and 1997, the value of royalties to the US doubled to more than $33bn a year

less than 7% of the world is online or, 93% of the world's population has no access to the internet

patents are killing people

If the world was shrunk to 100 individuals (with all the existing human ratios the same) six people would own 59 per cent of the wealth and 50 would suffer from malnutrition

this year, 100million babies will be born. Today, the world will gain another 230,000 people

within 50 years europe will have 25% fewer people than today, and Japan 21 million fewer

In India, of 1billion people, 465m cannot read, 700m live in homes with no lavatories, 390m are too poor to summon the cash for basic food, and live on less than $50 a year. Less than 1 in 10 own tv's

and a new baby is born every 2 seconds

the rich get richer
and the poor get poorer

Pornography is a $12-$13 billion-a-year industry - more than the combined annual revenues of the Coca-Cola and McDonnell Douglas corporation

97% of those babies will be born into the developing world

only 10% of R&D goes on drugs that account for 90% of global disease, with the bulk spent on first-world afflictions such as obesity

UNICEF estimates that one million children are forced into prostitution or used to produce pornography each year

In 1900, Europe had three times the population of Africa;
by 2050, Africa will have three times the population of Europe

80% of the planet has never heard a dialling tone

all you need is love

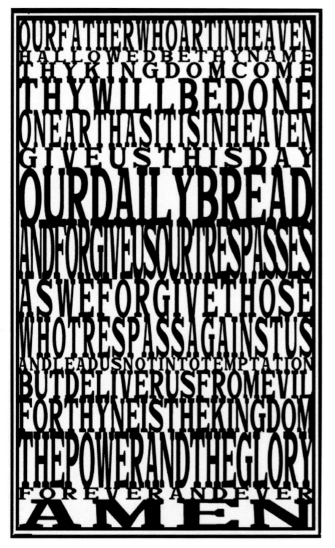

Here is my idea for learn and pass it on. Simple, really, it's the Lord's prayer, my personal mantra at bedtime, which I'm sure most people probably already know. It's very personal to me. Something I learned as a child, and something which forms part of my daily routine, which helps me to keep my feet on the ground.

Antonio Berardi

Here is my contribution to learn and pass it on, I'm afraid it's a little "dark".

There are times when I am convinced that I have never really learned anything in my life. When I began my career in fashion I was, however, lucky to have been given one piece of sage advice, which I took to heart and for most of my 20-something years in the business – except for some instances of blatant asshole-ism – I have tried to act accordingly. That is: the people you meet on the way up the ladder are the same ones you meet on the way down. Fashion people are notorious for their short attention spans and selective memory. They can also be extremely cruel. You can be up one moment, down the next, but never ever believe for a second that people like you for who you are.

Richard Buckley

I first met Chi Chi LaRue shooting stills for her directorial debut for the XXX feature *Billboard* in 1989. (She then told me I should be in the movies but that was a long time ago.) Chi Chi later art directed adult film box cover shoots that I would photograph, showing me the tricks of the trade on how to make the men look "THE HOTTEST!": secrets I've shared along the way with other models and photographers. But she shares a lot more than technique. Unfettered by what other people think, she says it like she sees it and when she does, it is funny as hell. Chi Chi, thanks for being unashamed, sharing your amazing sense of humour and ten or so years of watching your inspired direction that delivers the best of performances. For me, Chi Chi's talents aren't simply passed on in a literal sense. She makes people happy and comfortable, and this helps them express what talents they have to others. Thanks Larry for the education, great moments over the years and teaching me that things aren't always what they seem.

Chi Chi LaRue with adult film star Nina Hartley, Adult Video News Halloween Party 1995, at the Hollywood Palace dressing room.

Jeff Burton

These photos are of Pierre-Henri Beaubar. Here is a guy who has used narcissism in a very positive way. He has treated his life as a large body of work with narcissism being the concept from which to learn to love and accept himself, unlike today's generation who only use narcissism negatively, so there is nothing to gain. But from Pierre, you gain the love of oneself. Pierre never sought fame or fortune, because there was never a big void to fill. He is very content and so he has accomplished what he has set out to do, leaving a trail of loving oneself. Well, I am sure I have not done any justice to Pierre's life, but I am not a writer.

PS - I forgot to mention that he made and designed the costumes for himself, and he has an amazing collection of photos of himself he has had taken from different photographers for at least six decades.

Martha Camarillo

When I was a kid I had a Ladybird book about Jason and the Argonauts. I loved it and the stuff about the Golden Fleece and evil skeleton soldiers and all that. But one thing always bothered me. Jason didn't live happily ever after.

His adventures done, he settled down with the beautiful princess who nagged him a lot for reasons I can't remember. So Jason took to sitting under the prow of the Argo – now parked in his front room – reliving and ruminating and reflecting on his days of swash and buckle. The old boat creaked and strained above him and one day, riddled with woodworm and rot, it just came to pieces. Jason died under the debris.

Clearly there was a message in all this but I was too young to get it. Then I was watching that really good Clash documentary the other week. And Joe Strummer reminded me of Jason. There he was, on the edge of crying, saying how good the good ship Clash had been, how sturdy of purpose and fast. Not in a boastful way but a sad way, full of pride in what they had achieved and full of regret that their great adventure finished before it needed to (if certain crew members hadn't jumped ship, for instance).

The point is, I suppose, that if you're lucky, at some stage in your life you might find yourself amongst friends, united behind a common goal and set on achieving remarkable things. These special unions happen and for all sorts of reasons. And if that happens you will feel what Joe and Jason felt.

The thing is to cherish and marvel at it as it happens. And then move on. Don't sit under the boat.

Nick Compton

Maurizio Cattelan

Abruzzo 1979 – 2nd division drill camp.

We have much more strength than is imaginable or measurable. It might not flex its great big muscles on a whim, when we demand it. But rest assured that this Herculean power – to pursue and survive the passions and tragedies of Life – lies dormant within all of us. It can be awakened in an instant, when we need it.

Natascha Chadha

My little brother Robin, age eight.

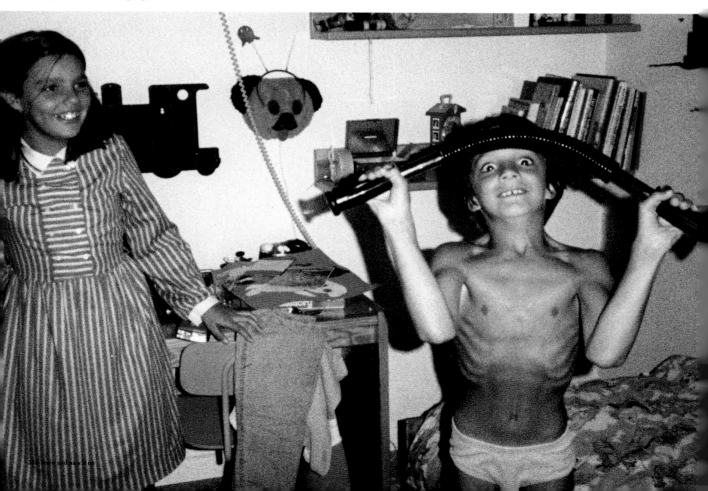

Zehra Ozel, age 80.

My maternal grandmother in Northern Cyprus has always been a
great inspiration to me – now and during my childhood. I especially
enjoyed Ottoman children's stories she recited. Her memory and
humour is the sharpest in my family. She has six children, my mother
being the sixth. As a child I always thought she was still pregnant
because her belly never went down. She particularly enjoys me
plucking a few hairs from her chin.

Hussein Chalayan

I did not know anything about my grandfather until my early teens when I found out he had recently died. He had left my dad's family in the late 1950s to work in South America and Africa – there are only a few photographs of him in existence.

Davey Graham is a self-proclaimed travel man and my guitar hero; these pictures were taken throughout his life. He travelled lots and so did my grandfather. There are also links between him and my dad. Davey was shut out by his father at a very young age; my grandfather left home when my dad was 14.

I've learnt that sometimes things that happen before we were born have a big effect on us. I think that my dad has tried hard to make a better relationship with me than he had with his own father. This is me trying to fill in the gaps.

Tim Chave

Things I've learned along the way.

1. Always keep cool if you want the edge – the psychological edge. That edge is the sharpest edge there is.

2. I never relinquish striving in a situation where things desperately need to be put right, until I can look myself in the mirror and know that I did everything I could to rectify matters. I may retire defeated, but I retire with a conscience I can live with.

3. During the worst times when I thought life was over, that was never the case. It was only on hold.

4. You can never love a dog too much or a man too little.

5. With a dog, what you see is what you get; they're genuine and, most importantly, a dog never lies about love.

6. Out of every situation, however bad or, funnily enough, good, I've learnt that I must be the best that I can be. That's the only way to grow.

7. Why me? Well, why not me. I never question the former when good things happen; why should I do so when the not so good visit for a while.

8. Some time ago during the floods and when the river Rodin was in full spate, Zara the golden labrador fell in – and she couldn't get out. There is always quite a current in that river when the Thames flood barriers are closed and the water backs up. I stripped off my heavy coat and what not and went in after her - and I have to say that there was a point when I didn't think we were going to make it. We got out considerably lower down the bank than where I'd got in. "Oooh, how brave," everyone said. That caused me to question the nature of bravery, because you see I didn't consciously commit an act of bravery. It was simply that I couldn't not try to rescue that dog, because I couldn't have faced her owners and told them that, as we spoke, their dog was banging up against the Thames barrier, had I not made that attempt. Therefore I think that 'bravery' is nothing special, it's just something you have to do. You can't not do it and live with yourself.

9. Nothing is forever. Not the good times, not the bad times, not the people or places. The old order always changes. It is this inevitability that I find comforting and that I feel prepares me for anything.

10. One wet morning I delivered a dog back to her owner and had a real bitch about life in general. The lady listened until I had wound down and, having remembered my manners, I asked how she was. "Actually," she said, "I'm a bit down myself. My cancer has spread into my brain and it means more chemo." It transpired that this lady had had a double mastectomy, and that there was nowhere that this disease had not been and ultimately did not get. We became friends and, during that friendship, I have never heard her moan, complain, ask for special treatment or behave in any way that is not perfectly dignified. She is dying. I am alive. I have nothing to grumble about. I try desperately hard not to.

11. The best and most reinforcing time of day is just before I go to sleep. My dog Baggins settles his head on my shoulder, makes a few settling sounds and then starts to breathe deeply. With my arms around him as he starts to snore, I am content.

12. Never trust a man who buys underwear. He isn't buying it for you, he's buying it for himself.

13. I've discovered that it is best to treat a second chance as your last chance. It very often is.

Suzy Crabtree

We all have something to give back; many organisations need our time and talent. The key to it all is to be selfless.

You aren't important. It's what you are giving to the organisation that counts.

These photographs were taken between 1996 and 1999 for St Johns Ophthalmic Hospital, Jerusalem. A hospital founded for the medical needs of the Palestinian people of the West Bank and Gaza. The photographs were used to expand the charity's picture library and in fundraising projects for them.

Donald Christie

Speech by His Holiness the Dalai Lama at the
Forum 2000 Conference, Prague, 1997

Today's world requires us to accept the oneness of humanity. In the past, isolated communities could afford to think of one another as fundamentally separate. Some could even exist in total isolation. But nowadays, whatever happens in one region eventually affects many other areas. Within the context of our new interdependence, self-interest clearly lies in considering the interest of others.

Many of the world's problems and conflicts arise because we have lost sight of the basic humanity that binds us all together as a human family. We tend to forget that despite the diversity of race, religion, ideology and so forth, people are equal in their basic wish for peace and happiness.

Nearly all of us receive our first lessons in peaceful living from our mothers, because the need for love lies at the very foundation of human existence. From the earliest stages of our growth, we are completely dependent upon our mother's care and it is very important for us that she express her love. If children do not receive proper affection, in later life they will often find it hard to love others. Peaceful living is about trusting those on whom we depend and caring for those who depend on us. Most of us receive our first experience of both these qualities as children.

I believe that the very purpose of life is to be happy. From the very core of our being, we desire contentment. In my own limited experience I have found that the more we care for the happiness of others, the greater is our own sense of well-being. Cultivating a close, warmhearted feeling for others automatically puts the mind at ease. It helps remove whatever fears or insecurities we may have and gives us the strength to cope with any obstacles we encounter. It is the principal source of success in life. Since we are not solely material creatures, it is a mistake to place all our hopes for happiness on external development alone. The key is to develop inner peace.

Actions and events depend heavily on motivation. From my Buddhist viewpoint all things originate in the mind. If we develop a good heart, then whether the field of our occupation is science, agriculture or politics, since the motivation is so very important, the result will be more beneficial. With proper motivation these activities can help humanity; without it they go the other way. This is why the compassionate thought is so very important for humankind. Although it is difficult to bring about the inner change that gives rise to it, it is absolutely worthwhile to try. When you recognise that all beings are equal and like yourself in both their desire for happiness and their right to obtain it, you automatically feel empathy and closeness for them. You develop a feeling of responsibility for others: the wish to help them actively overcome their problems. True compassion is not just an emotional response but a firm commitment founded on reason. Therefore, a truly compassionate attitude towards others does not change even if they behave negatively.

I believe that we must consciously develop a greater sense of universal responsibility. We must learn to work not just for our own individual self, family or nation, but for the benefit of all mankind. Universal responsibility is the best foundation both for our personal happiness and for world peace, the equitable use of our natural resources, and, through a concern for future generations, the proper care for the environment. My own ideas about this are still evolving but I would like to share some of them with you.

I believe it is important to reassess the rights and responsibilities of individuals, peoples and nations in relation to each other and the planet as a whole. This has a direct bearing on human rights. Because it is very often the most gifted, dedicated and creative members of our society who become victims of human rights abuses, the political, social, cultural and economic developments of a society are obstructed by the violations of human rights. Therefore, the acceptance of universally binding standards of human rights is essential in today's shrinking world. Respect for fundamental human rights should not remain an ideal to be achieved, but a requisite foundation for every human society. But, when we demand the rights and freedoms we so cherish we should also be aware of our responsibilities. If we accept that others have an equal right to peace and happiness as ourselves do we not have a responsibility to help those in need?

A precondition of any discussion of human rights is an atmosphere of peace in society at large. We have recently seen how new found freedoms, widely celebrated though they are, have given rise to fresh economic difficulties and unleashed long buried ethnic and religious tensions, that contain the seeds for a new cycle of conflicts. In the context of our newly emerging global community, all forms of violence, especially war, have become totally unacceptable as means of settling disputes. Therefore, it is appropriate to think and to discuss ways of averting further havoc and maintaining the momentum of peaceful and positive change.

Although war has always been part of human history, in ancient times there were winners and losers. If another global conflict were to occur now, there would be no winners at all. Realising this danger, steps are being taken to eliminate weapons of mass destruction. Nonetheless, in a volatile world, the risk remains as long as even a handful of these weapons continue to exist. Nuclear destruction is instant, total and irreversible. Like our neglect and abuse of the natural environment, it has the potential to affect the rights, not only of many defenceless people living now in various parts of the world, but also those of future generations.

Faced with the challenge of establishing genuine world peace and preserving the bountiful earth, what can we do? Beautiful words are not enough. Our ultimate goal should be the demilitarisation of the entire planet. If it were properly planned and people were educated to understand its advantages I believe it would be quite possible. But, if we are to have the confidence to eliminate physical weapons, to begin with some kind of inner disarmament is necessary. We need to embark on the difficult task of developing love and compassion within ourselves. Compassion is, by nature, peaceful and gentle, but it is also very powerful. Some may dismiss it as impractical and unrealistic, but I believe its practice is the true source of success. It is a sign of true inner strength. To achieve it we do not need to become religious, nor do we need any ideology. All that is necessary is for us to develop our basic human qualities.

Ultimately, humanity is one and this small planet is our only home. If we are truly to help one another and protect this home of ours, each of us needs to experience a vivid sense of compassion and responsibility. Only these feelings can remove the self-centred motives that cause people to deceive and misuse one another.

No system of government is perfect, but democracy is closest to our essential human nature; it is also the only stable foundation upon which a just and free global political structure can be built. So it is in all our interests that those of us who already enjoy democracy should actively support everybody's right to do so. We all want to live a good life, but that does not mean just having good food, clothes, and shelter. These are not sufficient. We need a good motivation: compassion, without dogmatism, without complicated philosophy, just understanding that others are our human brothers and sisters and respecting their rights and human dignity. That we humans can help each other is one of our unique human capacities.

We accept the need for pluralism in politics and democracy, yet we often seem more hesitant about the plurality of faiths and religions. It is important to remember that wherever they came from, all the world's major religious traditions are similar in having the potential to help human beings live at peace with themselves, with each other and with the environment. For centuries, millions of individual followers have derived personal peace of mind and solace in times of suffering from their own particular religious tradition. It is evident too that society in general has derived much benefit from religious traditions in terms of inspiration to ensure social justice and provide help to the needy.

Human beings naturally possess diverse mental dispositions and interests. Therefore, it is inevitable that different religious traditions emphasise different philosophies and modes of practice. Since the essence of our diverse religious traditions is to achieve our individual and collective benefit, it is crucial that we are active in maintaining harmony and mutual respect between them. Concerted efforts to this end will benefit not only the followers of our own faith, but will create an atmosphere of peace in society as a whole.

In the world at present, if we are serious in our commitment to the fundamental principles of equality which I believe lie at the heart of the concept of human rights and democracy, today's economic disparity between the North and South can no longer be ignored. It is not enough merely to state that all human beings must enjoy equal dignity. This must be translated into action. We have a responsibility to find ways to reduce this gap. Unless we are able to address this problem adequately, not only will it not go away, but it will fester and grow to give us further trouble in the future.

In this context, another important issue is overpopulation. From my Buddhist point of view, the life of every sentient being is precious, so it would be better if we did not have to practice birth control at all. But today, we are facing a situation where the growing number of people poses a threat to the very survival of humanity. Therefore, I personally feel we need to be pragmatic and adopt birth control measures in order to ensure the quality of life today in developing countries, and to protect the quality of life for future generations. Of course, as a Buddhist monk, I favour nonviolent forms of birth control.

Another issue which is dear to my vision of the future is disarmament. And that can only occur within the context of new political and economic relationships. Everyone wants peace. But we need a genuine peace that is founded on mutual trust and the realisation that as brothers and sisters we must all live together without trying to destroy each other. Even if one nation or community dislikes another, they have no alternative but to live together. And under the circumstances it is much better to live together happily.

To achieve global demilitarisation our first step should be the total dismantling of all nuclear, biological and chemical weapons. The second step should be the elimination of all offensive arms. And the third step should be the abolition of all national defensive forces. To protect and safeguard humanity from future aggression, we can create an international force to which all member states would contribute.

We also need to call a halt to the appalling international arms trade. Today, so much money is spent on armaments instead of feeding people and meeting basic human and environmental needs. It is a tragedy that in so many parts of the world there is no shortage of guns and bullets, but a severe lack of food. In such circumstances, thousands of innocent people, many of them children, are maimed or die. I believe there is a crying need for greater responsibility in the way we assess priorities in creating jobs, manufacturing goods and marketing them abroad.

The awesome proportion of scarce resources squandered on military development not only prevents the elimination of poverty, illiteracy and disease, but also requires the sacrifice of our scientists' precious human intelligence. Why should their talent be wasted in this way, when it could be used for positive global development? Our planet is blessed with vast natural treasures. If we use them wisely, beginning with the elimination of militarism and war, every human being will be able to live a healthy, prosperous existence.

Similarly, the problems of poverty, overpopulation and destruction of the environment that face the global community today are problems that we have to address together. No single community or nation can expect to solve them on its own. In ancient times, each village was more or less self-sufficient and independent. There was neither the need nor the expectation of cooperation with others outside the village. You survived by doing everything yourself. The situation now has completely changed. It has become very old-fashioned to think only in terms of my nation or my country, let alone my village. Therefore, I repeat that universal responsibility is the real key to overcoming our problems.

Today's problems of militarisation, development, ecology, population, and the constant search for new sources of energy and raw materials require more than piece-meal actions and short-term problem-solving. Modern scientific development has, to an extent, helped in solving mankind's problems. However, in tackling these global issues there is the need to cultivate not only the rational mind but also the other remarkable faculties of the human spirit: the power of love, compassion and solidarity.

A new way of thinking has become the necessary condition for responsible living and acting. If we maintain obsolete values and beliefs, a fragmented consciousness and a self-centred spirit, we will continue to hold to outdated goals and behaviours. Such an attitude by a large number of people would block the entire transition to an interdependent yet peaceful and cooperative global society.

If we look back at the development in the 20th century, the most devastating cause of human suffering, of deprivation of human dignity, freedom and peace has been the culture of violence in resolving differences and conflicts. In some ways the 20th century can be called the century of war and bloodshed. The challenge before us, therefore, is to make the next century, a century of dialogue and of peaceful co-existence. In human societies there will always be differences of views and interests. But the reality today is that we are all inter-dependent and have to co-exist on this small planet. Therefore, the only sensible and intelligent way of resolving differences and clashes of interests, whether between individuals or nations, is through dialogue. The promotion of a culture of dialogue and non-violence for the future of mankind is thus an important task of the international community. It is not enough for governments to endorse the principle of non-violence or hold it high without any appropriate action to promote it.

It is also natural that we should face obstacles in pursuit of our goals. But if we remain passive, making no effort to solve the problems we meet, conflicts will arise and hindrances will grow. Transforming these obstacles into opportunities for positive growth is a challenge to our human ingenuity. To achieve this requires patience, compassion and the use of our intelligence.

His Holiness the Dalai Lama

When our first baby arrived she had to teach us how to treat her.
We had no idea.
We do now.
Second baby came and they formed a gang. The older is the younger's horizon.
The older brings everything: toys, jewels, friends and chickenpox.
Our spotty girls.
The virus got the older first and was mild, but it learned by the time it reached the younger.
Our pebbledashed sumo.

Kevin Davies

Mother really does know best!

Fiona Dallanegra

'For a time, I held an unique position; among the hundreds of isolated creatures who haunted the streets of lower downtown Denver there was not one so young as myself. Of these dreary men who had committed themselves, each for his own good reason, to the task of finishing their days as penniless drunkards, I alone, as the sharer of their way of life, presented a replica of childhood to which their vision could daily turn, and in being thus grafted onto them, I became the unnatural son of a few score beaten men'.
Neal Cassady - *The First Third*

Jack Kerouac based the whole of *On The Road* on his personae and Allen Ginsberg dedicated some of his most howling poetry to him, yet history seems to have forgotten about Neal Cassady.

Not so strange, perhaps: apart from a shoddy book of letters and scribbled notes (*The First Third*, from which the above quote was lifted), Neal Cassady never produced anything tangible for future generations. Yet he remains a pivotal character in the story of the Beats and therefore in the never-ending saga of youth rebellion. In a funny way, Cassady's attitude, swagger and street wisdom inspired his typewriting and peyote-munching peers to produce important and life-affirming works of art, while he himself never even thought of securing his own legacy. Maybe he didn't feel like it. Maybe he was too busy being Neal Cassady. But he learned about life and passed it on, without him even noticing.

Peter de Potter

Photography by Johan Coppens.

When you asked me to participate in your new project; learn and pass it on,
I immediately thought about my grandmother Léone.

I had the chance to share with her my teenage years mostly in Biarritz.
She gave me the freedom and her car!
More than the foie gras, I learned life, happiness.
I learnt generosity, respect, humility.
I learnt how to welcome friends at home and to make their life easy.
I learnt how to pick mushrooms in the forest.
I learnt what love means and the sacrifice of a woman for love.
She's helping in my job, she's quite a guide, maybe she doesn't know.
She's in my heart and I want to pass it on.

Foie gras de canard from Mamy Léone
The duck has to be plucked and cleaned out.
Let soak half a day and renew the water.
Let drain off.
Add salt and pepper and cut one truffle from the French region of Lot.
Stuff the different part of the foie with the "truffe".
Put the foie in a preserve and sterilise it during 55 minutes.
Let cool down before taking out.
You have to wait one month before eating the foie gras.

It's delicious with a sweet white wine called Sauternes from Loupiac near Bordeaux.

Fred Dechnik

Mother Courage

My mother was born on the 6th of March 1934, 60 miles outside of Berlin. By then Hitler had already been in power for a year. When she was five, Germany declared war on the world and ultimately on itself. By the age of nine, the war had taken her father and laid the country in ruins. Despite wartime being hard and frightful for everyone, with bombings and shortage of every day supplies, the worst was yet to come. After 1945, production of goods had ceased in most parts of the country, and machines and tools were destroyed – that is, if they were not melted down for ammunition and weapons in the last months of the war. Germany was divided into sectors by the victors and while France, England and the USA couldn't quite make up their minds what to do next, the Russians were busy creating yet another dictatorship in their share of Germany. When I was growing up, stories from this time were all around me. Not one family meeting would go by without them. One of these stories I want to write about.

In her early twenties, my mother lived in the Russian sector and was working for the German railways or 'Reichsbahn'. Her workplace was located in West Berlin, even though the Reichsbahn itself was under control of the Russians. The Russians, always trying to be ahead of the class enemy, wanted to be the first to install a computer system for their railways, and to top it off, a woman was chosen to be its first operator - my mother. A brand new job title was invented: the English term 'dispatcher'. This word did not make much sense to the average German, but sounded very sophisticated and modern. In reality, the job was as badly paid as any other, and the money made hardly bought most foods, clothes or even books.

My mother's train ride to work every day was two hours long and would have been impossible to bear if it weren't for the few novelettes that her family had managed to hold onto from before the war. Unfortunately, one of the many Marxist/Leninist theories on how to make people good socialists was to have them read literature that was either political (socialist) or heavily intellectual (again in a socialist kind of way). Trivial literature and especially novelettes were strictly forbidden by law. In fact the new Government was so passionate about it that anyone found with one could immediately be jailed. My mother, on the other hand, didn't think she could survive these endless train journeys without anything to read, so she took the risk.

Everything went fine until one day two policemen unexpectedly came to inspect her compartment. These inspections happened quite regularly and there would have normally been enough time to hide everything. Maybe it was because she was distracted by taking out a sandwich from her lunch box.

"What have you got in your bag?" one of the men asked forcefully.

My mother was suddenly overcome with anger at the constant harassment of the so-called 'people's police' and replied: "What's it to you?"

"Open it," the officer went, not quite knowing what to make of my mother's behaviour.

"If you want to look in there you might as well check what's in my sandwich," she answered snidely. "It's cheese from the black market in the West sector."

At the time, importing anything from the West was even more of a reason to be jailed on the spot. Astounded and unsure how to react, the officer now shouted, "And what is it you are reading? You know that these are illegal – give it to me."

"This is mine," she replied "you're not going to get it!"

The officers had clearly had enough, even though they didn't quite know what to do. "You are under arrest. We'll have to take you to the station." They took her along the platform under the observing eyes of the other passengers. Most of them knew her because they all came from the same village. She was taken into the office of the police commissioner, which was located on the platform. The two policemen told him what had happened and he turned bright red from anger. "Hand me the bloody book now!" he screamed, "or you are going straight to jail!"

"This book is mine and if you take it you are a thief," she retorted. "On the other hand", she continued calmly, "should you want to borrow it I could leave it here and pick it up on my way back. But you must finish it by then because I'm not through with it yet."

The commissioner could not believe the insolence. "You don't seem to realise what you are gambling with!" came his reply. "I'll show you that I can take your book!" He walked to his desk opened the drawer and showed her defiantly and angrily all the books and novelettes that he had taken from other passengers.

But my mother was still not impressed: "You seem to have a lot of time to read."

The commissioner boiled over. "That's it – I'm booking you. You're going straight in and won't come out for a long time".

In the meantime almost all the passengers had left the train and were watching this spectacle through the open window. No one dared to breathe or say a word. In those days going into jail could have easily meant that you might not come out alive. This behaviour would have classified her as a political prisoner, and a sentence would have been extremely harsh.

"Fine," she replied, "then all you have to do is call the Reichsbahn central office in Berlin and tell them that the dispatcher won't be coming to work today because you have arrested her."

The commissioner, who just thought he had won back the upper hand, went silent. He was clearly confused about the term 'dispatcher'. It sounded like it was very important. Would his arrest cause major disruption or delays? Could this get him into trouble; was this woman so confident all along because she held an important position at the railways and would her arrest immediately cause a scandal? The crowd outside saw the commissioner hesitating and the silence slowly turned to cheering and hauling "You show him," some screamed. "Let him have it," screamed others.

The commissioner finally gave in: "Get out of my face and if I ever catch you again..."

A few months later during the big annual staff meeting while the general manager was busy praising the achievements of his division in particular, and socialism in the east sector in general, my mother stood up in front of 300 of her colleagues and superiors and said, "If we are so much better than the capitalists, why can't we even buy margarine? And if we get any then it's green and uneatable." She had always provoked police and authorities when she had a chance and got away with it. This time she seemed to have taken it too far.

A few days after the incident at the staff meeting, a woman from the mayor's office walked up to her mother (my grandmother) on the street. "Tell your daughter not to come home from work today. She can't ever come back. They want to take her tonight." And so she had to leave as a refugee with nothing but a handbag, leaving friends, family, land and memories behind. Soon after that her brother followed her into the West. A while later, her mother met the same woman from the mayor's office and was also told that she also had to flee immediately. The 'people's police' wanted to take her in revenge for the escape of her children. She took with her all she held in her hands.

A few months after that, Germany awoke to something no one had seen coming; a wall divided the country, and would keep those who happened to be on the wrong side imprisoned for the next 30 years. My mother and her family owe the fact that they were on the 'right' side of the wall largely to my mother's inability to keep her mouth shut whenever she saw injustice. She risked her life for what she believed in and was rewarded with freedom, leaving those behind who thought it would be cleverer to adapt, arrange and accept.

This has been a great inspiration for me in my life. It has taught me that people, influences, even governments come and go, and that all you have worth holding onto is what you feel in your heart.

Uwe Doll

Within the last decades mankind has accumulated more knowledge and information than in a few centuries before. Today it is impossible for one person to know everything like the "uòmo universale" of Leonardo da Vinci's time. We have computers and the world wide web seems to be able to answer all our questions, "information" is available 24 hours a day, 365 days a year, at reasonable costs for anybody in the first world, (we all know the third world, where – by the way – is the second one?) Where can we find "knowledge"?

We manage to reduce the variety of species on this planet every day, and at the same time we can see children knowing less about nature, having less understanding of nature and being less interested in nature: and us having less time for our children in a time when things run faster and faster.

What I try to pass on to my children is love and respect for nature, for the creation.

Growing up with nature teaches the basics, that fresh air and clean water is the real luxury.

Naturally kids come up with great and important questions, especially when they are interested in the matter, (why is grass green, why has an owl big eyes, who made all this…?). If they ask me something which I don't know, I try to look it up in a book or the internet, or ask grandma/pa (who still tend to know more about those things). Sometimes we try to find out more by patient observation of the animal, plant, stone or cloud.

A computer cannot eat a worm and the internet cannot help us to find out how a wet forest smells in summer.

PS: A few days ago I read in a newspaper that a third of the children being asked to paint a cow were painting a purple cow as seen in Milka chocolate commercials in Germany. A boy of eight years answered the question "which trees and flowers do you know?" with the remark that he would prefer to talk about cars.

PPS: an American told me that he grew up in one of the big US cities and thought of concrete as the natural surface of the planet and parks being "artificial" until he went to the countryside at the age of ten.

Thomas Degen

Photography by Anja Herdemerten.

I've been working on an alternative portrait of the nation, a project documenting the homeless and rough sleepers. What drew me to this project was that you can basically learn from all aspects of life. There's a fine line between the stars and the gutters. I've found people sleeping rough who came from all walks of life, from doctors to criminals and many in between. I wouldn't want to be in that position, but you've got to have compassion and understanding because actually, it could be you. It's just circumstances.

Larry Dunstan

Some things that we learn are not always pleasant lessons, and the things we take on board as a result are nasty reminders of these encounters or events. They are things that can't be taught as you only learn from experience.

Pete Drinkell

A-Z of unwanted pregnancy; How to deal with unwanted pregnancy for women.

a. Always use a condom, carry them with you 24 hours a day.

b. If things go a bit rumpy pumpy and the condom tears don't lie back and think of England, rush to the bathroom and standing up, spray your insides with a hard jet of ice cold water. A modern day old wives tale is to use coca cola. If you've been shagging alfresco, roll on to your back and have your young man assist with a bottle of Evian, then jump around on the spot for a good five minutes.

c. Go straight to the chemist and buy the morning after pill. The 'morning after' pill has a stupid name because it actually works up to 72 hours after, so don't freak out if you're nowhere near a chemist or it's a Saturday night. Also call Talking Pages, they can tell you the nearest 24-hour chemist.

d. If for some reason it was impossible to take the morning after pill in time, you could go to your local family planning clinic and ask to be fitted with a mini coil I.U.D. Keep it in for a month then have it removed, this will prevent a pregnancy going any further. It can be painful and bloody, I'm not even sure if it is legal, I actually did this a few years ago. True, it put me off sex for an extremely long time but at least I didn't have the fear of being pregnant.

e. If your period is one minute late waste no time, go to the chemist and buy two home pregnancy tests. Boots do a very good deal. Do one test straight away, preferably first thing in the morning and do the second in the evening, this way you can be sure of a true result. Home pregnancy tests can give the wrong result if you have some kind of hormonal imbalance.

f. If the test shows positive call a friend – someone you really trust, this could be your boyfriend – and discuss the pros and cons.

g. If you decide having a baby is impossible, call either the family planning clinic or Brook St advisory centre, or any place that can give you advice on unwanted pregnancy. If you have a good, understanding GP also call them.

h. Have a blood test and pregnancy test to be 100% sure you are pregnant.

i. Insist on having an abortion as soon as possible, if you have the money (300 pounds) you can be treated within 24 hours, if you go through the NHS you may have to wait up to six weeks depending on availability.

j. Do not keep your pregnancy a guarded secret like the crown jewels as you may need moral support; you will feel shit, weak, maybe sick and afraid to talk it through.

k. Go to the clinic with a friend, not just for the operation but for the preliminary visits: check that the place is clean and the staff are understanding.

l. Once a date is fixed for the termination do not go out on some awful god ridden drunken binge, try to stay calm.

m. Some women after termination feel fine, like almost nothing has happened, others may feel extremely weak. Make sure you have nothing to do the following 48 hours, make sure you have food at home and somewhere comfortable to be, you will need some care and attention.

n. You may also feel in a state of euphoria from the relief, be careful as depression will follow.

o. If for any reason after the termination you feel terribly ill, go back to the clinic immediately, 2% of terminations do not work, if it is not a clean evacuation there could be fatal consequences.

p. If you feel that you made the wrong decision or suffer from guilt, ask for counselling; this can be a natural feeling which passes with time. Also there is a possibility that you may take out some kind of guilt aggression on your partner (if you have one). There is also a possibility that the knock on affect of the termination can result in the end of your relationship, simply because you feel you have experienced something so utterly alone, this is why it is good to talk through all stages of the decision to terminate.

q. You will probably feel terribly broody and want to steal babies, but the reality is you stand an extremely high chance of falling pregnant immediately, so maybe for a short period like six months go on the pill, but make sure you are given the correct pill to suit you.

u. Drink lots of rosehip tea, take iron pills and eat beetroot and red meat, if you are a vegetarian the best thing is Floradix, available in tablet or liquid form from all natural health food stores.

v. Think positive and concentrate on all the things you couldn't do if you had a baby.

w. Exercise and try not to get too out of your head, as some weird deep-seated emotions could come flying to the surface when you least expect them.

x. Beware of phantom pregnancies.

y. Remember, no woman wants to have an abortion but it is far better than an unwanted child.

z. And most important, if you do decide you want to have the baby don't listen to anyone, just listen to your heart.

Tracey Emin

My mother suffered a stroke earlier this year. Six months later she is up and walking with the aid of a three pronged stick. Margot is a friend of my mother's.

Through these women I have learnt the healing power of friendship.

Edward Enninful

Initially I'd hoped to photograph my old history classroom, as my (cynical) Northern Irish teacher taught English history in a way which became very important to my understanding of politics. The classroom isn't there anymore. So instead I thought about what I'd learnt from photography: to appreciate and be thankful for beauty. These images reflect what I have learnt and, I hope, pass on some notion of the beauty I see.

Dedicated to Mr Keenan, who was a brilliant teacher.

Jason Evans

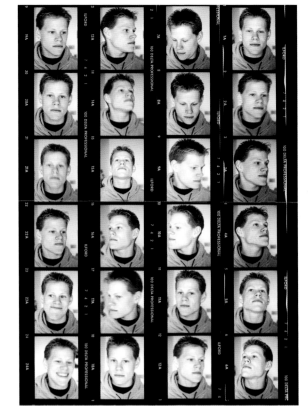

"And in the end
The love you take
Is equal to the love you make"

'The End', from *Abbey Road* by The Beatles.

Kevin Ellis

Values are possibly the greatest legacy to leave behind for the next generations. What we believe in, how to use these beliefs in the best way, and learning to remain true to a set of core values, will have a great impact on what our future world will be like to live in. This has certainly been my experience.

My father was an incredible wizard transmitting his values, never forcing his convictions on my siblings or me, but effectively leading the way with his example.

In dealing with shoes for more than a century, at Camper we constantly reflect on the meaning of walking. Walking means travelling, going from one place to another. Within a metaphoric sense it also means advancing, improving, developing, innovating. We aspire to a society that is open to all people who, while coming from diverse social, cultural, economic or geographic realities, dedicate their imagination and energy to bringing useful and positive ideas and solutions in order to have a better world. In a simple, anonymous and honest way. Rationality and intelligence are necessary conditions, but not enough, to achieve a society that is humanitarian, fair, balanced and practices solidarity. The time has come to think beyond reason and technology and to concern ourselves with sensitivity and will.

To create is to invent possibilities. People in the fields of design, fashion, architecture, art… have much to say in this regard and have much room for action. We believe that culturising product and humanising messages is a path worth walking to responsibly exercise the new role of business in civil society. We endeavour to achieve this. Discreetly. With humour. From the Mediterranean.

Lorenzo Fluxá

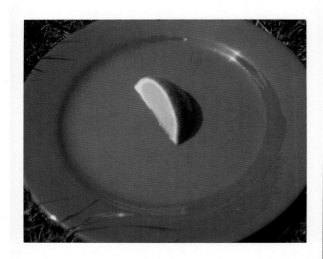

My tip: To cure hiccups, bite into a wedge of lime. It never fails.

Simon Foxton

Things I have learned along the way

That uncomfortable shoes stop you from travelling.

That everyday is a best underwear day.

That green grass is good for the soul.

That sorry is only hard if you don't practise enough.

That music is emotional first aid.

That you only grow old if you stop growing.

That love is to be given and received.

That history is only his story.

That health becomes very valuable once you become unhealthy.

That the tightest grip is an open hand.

That a man who allows the woman inside to flourish, understands equality.

That women are too hard on themselves and not hard enough on others.

That good, long, belly-churning laughter is better than most drugs.

That good friends don't need proof.

That survivors are those that refuse to be victims.

That my two small daughters are wonderful visitors to my life, who will leave long before I'm ready to wave them off.

That every woman is a witch cut off from her magic.

That vegetable oils are often cheap palm or coconut oils high in saturates, and no healthier than lard or dripping.

Caryn Franklin

Only hire people that you want to have dinner with.

Tom Ford

Sunset in Rejkavik, August, 2000 taken by Stephen Gan and Tobias Schweitzer.

SG: When I think of what I've learned and value along the way, I think of particular images…

TS: Images have different levels of how you perceive them. To describe it in an easy way you could say, "I fall in love with an image".

SG: When I see this picture again, the first things I notice are bits of glimmer and sparkle…

TS: First there are these strong colours, their strong contrasts and you can see the spots of lamps, the lines and light strings. But always deeper is what the image talks about. In this case there are two people who are sitting in front of a burning horizon in Iceland. They are above the city. They are behind this glass wall. These two people in front of the window are watching, astonished. Just watching because it's this tension of a miracle of nature which takes place.

SG: That summer I learned to experience the landscapes and nature, things I never noticed before because they were so far from my reality, and they were, I guess, things I had to be shown. What remains a couple years later are the memories of that incredible sunset, close to midnight, in that strange hotel room with the wraparound windows, one August, in Iceland. And that old saying, though it may sound corny: "Behind every dark cloud lies a silver lining".

Stephen Gan and Tobias Schweitzer

His name is Pablo Serrano, Yogi and photographer. What he has taught me is to listen to my body and give myself time to rest and recuperate from a hectic life. Without health, whatever wealth or success you manage to accumulate will become meaningless.

Kate Garner

After adolescence, when we are left alone and all shaped up, rare are those encounters that can alter our appreciation of ourselves and redefine our horizons. Our education, our prejudices, our timidity and our indisposition paralyse our attention and obliterate our judgement… and numerous opportunities are thus lost.

Sometimes though, if we are for a short period receptive and unoccupied, in some unexpected occasion, we meet people who can slightly modify our sensibility and have a certain impact on our destinies.

As 1970 had been a tumultuous year for me, one of my good friends suggested that I relax with him in Brittany for the Christmas week. It was one of those new centres of thalassotherapy, which are said to be revitalising. And there, a chain of introductions brought together since that first day, and from breakfast till dinner thereafter, eight people whose occupations, mentalities, ages, origins and centres of interest did not predestine to talk for more than two minutes.

Among them was Andrée Putman, a stylist who later became a famous international designer and has been, since that first week, one of my constant sources of inspiration; Claude Serreules, who had been Charles de Gaulle's pilot during the war, was Grand Chancelier de l'Ordre de la Liberation and later became for me a decisive intercessor; his wife, Marie-Hélène de Ganay, who had initiated the boutique Dior with Christian Dior, and taught me a lot of things on what should become fashion history; and Ida Chagall, who knew how to make the artists seem familiar. There was also Michel Warren who, having started his career as a fashion designer under Madame de Polignac at Lanvin, later became a successful New York gallery owner, with painters like Dubuffet, Bram van Velde, Fernand Léger etc, and finally chose to be a Parisian artist.

Michel was gifted with clairvoyance and had intuition about people and events. This appeared in our group when – having been fascinated by a very ordinary couple having lunch close to us – he invited them to our table for coffee. Flattered to be singled out by the most glamorous and joyous assembly, they happily joined us... and then, without exchanging a word, they engaged in a mute dialogue with Michel Warren, which ended in screams and insults. The scene was frightening and embarrassing. Michel Warren was livid... the hand he held out to me after the couple had fled was as cold as ice. None of us dared to ask him what he had seen.

Every day of his life a different incident occurred. This created a permanent tension around him... he could read and assert our futures. Some viewed him as a sorcerer and the legends around him flourished.

Some accepted his power philosophically; others ran.

Though his education had been minimal, his erudition was encyclopaedic. He knew about cancer research as much as any specialist; had dinner with Lacan and had published the *Antisteak,* an excellent cookbook. His conversation, his extraordinary sense of narration and his table were fabulous.

But his main interest was in art, as a collector and as an artist. As a collector, he entertained with the business people, among whom Claude Bernard was the one he most referred to – a relationship which could be compared to duellists. Each negotiation was a new drama. Bacon, López García, Dado, Raynaud were among the very eclectic artists he revered. As an artist, his relationship with the collectors was, all the same, a romance and his apartment, the former Antoine's Studio in the 16th arrondissement, was the place where the scenario was played. As a collector of his works, I have often been part of the intrigue and today, 25 years after his death, I love his paintings as much as any other I own. His work, which was figurative when abstraction was the only thing considered valuable, could be qualified as postmatissian.

The young gallery owner Yvon Lambert had already converted me to Malaval or Twombly but, up to my late friend, writer and critic Bernard Lamarche-Vadel, who constantly preached about the artists he loved – nobody before Michel Warren had ever shown me that art could be so essential to life.

Fabrice Emaer, one of his devotees, and the roi de la fête in the '70s, had asked him, before he commissioned Gerard Garouste to do a décor for the Palace, to create a fresco for a wall of the Club 7's basement – a big smoky room where mostly men danced till dawn. Michel Warren chose La Cene as his theme and started looking for models. When Leonardo da Vinci was commissioned by Ludovico Sforza, he had wanted a papal authorisation before accepting, as depicting Christ and the saints was then a sacrilege. Michel Warren had read Leonardo's notebooks and knew numerous pleasant anecdotes about the subject. His own enterprise would result in many melodramatic scenes. The work was never quite finalised...

A few months later, Michel Warren had three personal exhibitions in town. One of them was at the Espace Cardin. His paintings were huge and all depicted the same man – nude and bloody with bandages and broad empty eyes. Surprisingly this is the very way Michel Warren was found in the street a few days later. Nobody has ever been quite sure how it happened.

Since then, I know that life can be art and believe that we are born with our written story and built for facing it, that we can get rid of our roots, if we are given time, look at our relatives as admirable friends, ignore religion, sex inclination, and social blahblah, and peacefully enjoy the end of the play.

Didier Grumbach

Last March I visited Tane Mahuta. Standing in front of this beautiful tree made me feel so much... Everything. My mind began to interconnect history, experience, inspiration, and dreams. The past, the present, the future. The earth. Civilisation. The joy of our immortal souls. Mortality. The infinite amount of experiences that have happened, are happening, could begin to happen, and would happen. The infinite amount of possibilities that have been offered to us. How every experience and every encounter with everything has effected, and is creating some influence that will transform as we recognise and accept our relationship to it. What we have will pass onto us, from every moment. When we are open. Intuition and natural response... we pass it on. Every second we experience something in-between things, places, people, animals, technology,...
Every second something changes. In one moment, something makes sense; in another it doesn't. It all keeps changing.

Tane Mahuta, God of the Forest. It is estimated that Tane Mahuta is around 2000 years old. Tane is the largest kauri tree in New Zealand. Dimensions: trunk height: 17.7 meters, trunk girth 13.8 meters, total height 51.5 meters Photography by Laura Genninger. Digitally mastered with love by David Ortega.

Laura Genninger

Creativity and thinking should only be guided – not restricted or limited. My mum's a teacher and my dad's an all-round creative, and both of them taught me the basics, with the sense of freedom not to over-correct.

Like when I used to get frustrated at not being able to draw like a proper artist, they told me that Picasso spent years learning how to paint like a child;

and when I wrote fun stuff, that the spelling wasn't as important as what I was saying. They never told me "you can't", they just let me go for it and figure out for myself what worked and what didn't. I know lots of people, kids and adults, who are too scared to try. They don't realise it's the only way you'll find out what you can and can't do, because they're always being told "it's not possible". Like a really close friend once told me: "Just tell yourself it's easy and do it". I wish there were more parents out there who told their kids a flavour could be anything they wanted it to be.

Liz Hancock

My sherbet recipe, age seven-ish.

Genes and jeans form part of who we are, the rest is up to you.

Matthew E. Hawker

'Rotation' thanks to Finley Walsh.

If you try your hardest and give your best in each passing moment of the present, with respect to the past and an eye on the future, then you will find your peace.
I have learnt this from the smiles of two farmers who have always helped me even when their own stories have looked black. One, Neil Griffin, has lost his entire dairy herd and hill flock through a terrible contiguous cull; the other, Pete Jones, has had his young family's home and farm under silty flood water three times in the last six months and, because of the foot and mouth restrictions and constant threat, cannot farm.

Amanda Harlech

I've learnt to accept people for who they are and not for the job they do. "What's your background?" has been replaced by "what do you do?", in a world of upwardly mobile chic snobbery. This perpetuates the notion that unless you fall into a particular job-type, your social standing is limited. We are learning to address racism, sexism and ageism. Maybe "jobism" is the next challenge?

Steve Harris

Juergen.

Mark.

Alistair.

Carol.

Sorcerer and apprentice. Photographer and assistant. What makes a good photographer? Who knows? Can whatever makes a good photographer be passed on? I don't know – but I'm keeping my fingers crossed.

My mum and dad – who are celebrating their 40th anniversary this November – have given me a life from which I truly derive enormous joy and pleasure. At the risk of descending (further) into schmaltz, I hope that, just in doing what I love doing most – taking photographs – and by being glad that I'm me, I'm able to pass on some of that happiness to them. Even if ma can't stand the portrait I took of her…

Jake Gavin

Perseverance: a continued steady belief of efforts, withstanding discouragement or difficulty, persistence.

My parents brought me up to believe I could do anything or be anything I set my mind to as long as I persevered. My father, who was a great man, taught me this word. I was young and I can't remember exactly when but I remember him saying it to me in his loud voice, enunciating every syllable slowly and occasionally making me spell it. It was our word for when things weren't going well at school – I was an academic underachiever; he was one of England's top academics, (professor and lecturer of Art History, Principal of the Slade School and Chelsea Art School, writer of art history books and Doctor of Literature) – when things weren't going well with my endless music lessons, or at home or with my friends. He knew if I persevered things would eventually turn themselves around, sort themselves out. Because he always believed in me, often when everyone else, even me, had given up hope.

It was only after he died, in 1991, that I really started to live by this word. There have been so many times when I have taken on tasks that are too big, too daunting, but I've persevered. I've done things that scare me, stayed at places where I know they don't want me to be, because I know it's the right thing for me to do. I had an unusual upbringing – I was adopted at the age of three with my black half-sister by white middle class parents. I have two sisters (one white, one black) and three fathers (two black, one white) and two mothers (one white, one black).

Outside my family I was constantly being told there were things I couldn't do or achieve because I was black. At infant school they wouldn't teach me to dive because black people don't swim well enough. At secondary school I was told that I wouldn't pass any O or A levels or get into any polytechnic because I wasn't bright enough, and this was often the way with black children, they didn't have the right genes or attitude to excel. (Just for the record, I graduated from a university and am now a fashion journalist.)

Two years ago I moved to South Africa and came across an ingrained racism and my everyday life became a battle with other people's racist beliefs. So perseverance became my daily mantra.

Often taking a deep breath, counting to ten and slowly saying the word. Perseverance is the seminal word in my life and the word I would pass on to my children, to anyone. I know I wouldn't be the person I am today if I hadn't lived by this word. It has made a stronger more determined person, but it also makes me smile, because it reminds me of my father. Whatever the situation. It can be done. It just takes perseverance.

Amanda Gowing

My dad taught me how to keep my head above water.
My friends have always been there to watch my back.
Between them, they've taught me that you can't achieve
anything without having someone you can put your
complete trust in.

Mark Hooper

The most important thing that I
learned in the last five years, very
slowly but still, is to relax, thanks
to Ines, Giovanni, Jane and
Jacques. In the past, learning by
itself was a kind of obsessive,
restless hobby for me. Now, the
things that I want to learn have
changed and this changes
everything.

Desiree Heiss

What I have learned, and, would like to pass on is as simply put as the title of the Verve song… 'The Drugs Don't Work'. I have learned this lesson over and over again, and have gratefully, FINALLY, come to accept it as the truth.

Marc Jacobs

When I go to travel, I meet a lot of people and find a lot of things. But when I am in a hotel room, I'm alone. I can feel I'm standing on the earth by myself. A hotel room in travel lets me strengthen my weakened heart.

Gramercy Park Hotel NYC, 2001.

Takashi Homma

Inhale and exhale deeply every day.

Jicky, Joshua Tree 2001.

Matt Jones

Five minutes after leaving a Comme des Garçons outdoor fashion show at Place Vendome, the skies opened. July 2000.

Taking a sunshine shower – Mexico, 2000.

This thought is dedicated to my mum who initiated and encouraged my application to art college, but who had also pleaded with me to jump with her out of a second floor window when I was ten years old.

She spent the rest of her life suffering from manic depression and died 15 years later in a psychiatric hospital outside Warrington. I learned to survive – whatever the weather, to believe that there is a sunny side to life, and that positive thoughts make positive energy.

Terry Jones

About Repeated Situations in Life…These come much and often to you, until you have learnt your lesson and finally make the right decision.

About Love…
Needs attention 24 hours a day. If you don't take care, it will fly away as fast as it came.

About your Inner Voice…
After I learned to listen to my inner voice, mistakes and wrong decisions don't happen that much.

About Relationships…
The longer you keep the rope, the closer people want to be with you.

About Money…
Needs to come and go. If you hold it tight, it will leave you; if you let it go, it will come back to you.

About Moments…
Enjoy a wonderful moment, take a deep breath and give your heart and mind a big smile – cause every moment is unique and will never come back.

About Lies…
No lie is knitted so thin that the early morning light won't show through.

About Health…
Is the most important thing in life and needs to get treated well and consciously.

About Age…
Exists only in your head – the moment you think you're old, you become an old person.

About Fear…
Is one of the biggest handicaps in your life and destroys dreams. If you can work against it, you get freedom and happiness.

About Thoughts…
Are magic and will be material one day.

About Wishes…
Come true one day, as long as you believe and want it really deep from your heart.

About Possessions…
Is very nice to have, but you came without and you will go without – so don't pay too much attention to them.

About Death…
Belongs to life and is a natural thing. Face it and enjoy each single day on earth.

About Work and Business…
Should only occupy maximum three-quarters of your day. Life is too short and too extraordinary to spend eight hours almost every day for one thing like this.

About Happiness…
Does only exist in you. If you are not able to make yourself happy, nobody else will.

About Nature…
Is one of my biggest loves and the most beautiful thing on earth.

About Beauty…
Is ageless and comes only from your heart.

About God…
He's always with me – I believe in Him, trust Him and talk to Him sometimes.

About Children…
Looking into their wonderful eyes makes me silent and respectful.

About Priorities…
Are individual and have to be made in each life. Try not to lose focus of your personal priorities and don't listen too much to people who maybe try to take you away from your goal.

About Humour…
Is one of the best and healthiest things in life. To be with people who make you laugh from the bottom of your heart is Heaven.

After all I have seen, felt, given, become and had to let go, I try to live in the moment, enjoy each second and live like it would be my last breath – because nobody knows how much time is left to enjoy life.

Gabriela Just

Twenty-five years ago my one time vegan-eating, acid-taking younger brother became a born again Christian, with all the scary over zealousness that the newly converted bring to the party. For years he tried to convert us – there were big arguments over family teas and Xmases – we were having none of it. But over the years I began to notice a change in him and his life, I remember during one of our, by then infrequent discussions, he reminded me that it says in the Bible, "ask and it shall be given to you", ask for help and you will be given it. It was a bit of a seminal moment. Quietly, telling no one, I began to try it out for myself. That was 15 years ago. Privately and secretly God and my nondenominational faith have become an integral part of my life. As an adolescent, whose common sense had told me quite categorically that religion (school, family or otherwise) and life after death were obviously just in place to make us all feel better while we're here, it came as a huge shock. But I have learnt with amazement and disbelief, as my brother told me so many years ago, that prayers are answered, that somehow if you ask for help it is given to you. My rational self still does not understand at all. My brain can still argue and question what my spirit and soul have found to be true. I can only, with the utmost humility, acknowledge and pass on this truth that I have found. Up until now I have only ever mentioned this to certain close friends who might have been in the middle of difficult times and the analogy I have always thought of is this. There is a coat in a corner of the room – it does not have your name on it, it belongs to anyone or no-one. Call it God, call it faith; one day if you're cold or if you need help you might try it on. There is no price tag, no obligation to buy; but if, as happened to me, it seems by some miracle to fit you, in spite of all your preconceptions and prejudices, feel lucky and one day as my brother did for me, tell a friend about the possibility.

As a child I was frightened of everything. The lift I was in would stop, so I walked up countless flights of stairs. The house I slept in would be struck by lightning, so thunderstorms had me wide-awake and terrified in the middle of the night. A natural born worrier. But over the years I've found the confidence to let go. What I've learnt is that worrying doesn't help anything at all. It's a totally negative place, which undermines our energy and limits our possibilities. If something is bad you're going to find out soon enough and will have to deal with it, as well as you can at that moment. If it doesn't happen, as often things don't, then you have saved yourself the bother. Now I believe that many things happen for a reason and with a wing, a prayer and a lot of positive thinking, I'm learning to go with the flow.

Tricia Jones

Photography by Tricia Jones.

© Richard Davies at David Chipperfield Architects.

Build a modern house

1. If you ever can, build a modern house! This is so important. Otherwise what legacy are we leaving for our children? What will people conclude when they look at the architecture of our generation? That we had such contempt for our own time, for our own lives, that we wanted nothing to be remembered of it. We believed that, unlike fashion, art, music, that when it came to architecture we had nothing to offer? Nothing to say?

2. I would strongly advise, however expensive, to choose the best architect. Don't go for second best and don't try and half do it yourself. The best architects will be able to think of things you could never possibly imagine once you've employed him/her – don't try and clip his/her wings – enjoy the ride – it won't happen too many times in your life (that you have a whole office of people worrying about what shape bath you will like most or what shadows the sun will cast as it rises on your birthday). Think how you would approach it if you were commissioning art – which is, in effect, what you are doing…

3. No couture dress, no piece of music, no painting will so profoundly change your life, consistently alter your preconception of the world around you and so frequently immerse you in moments of beauty as a fantastic modern home.
In summer evenings great shafts of orange light enter deep in my house and turn each room into fantastic glowing colour spaces – Rothko in 3D. The house literally bursts into colour. On rainy nights the white walls become ever-changing Op Art paintings as the outside lights project the concentric circles of raindrops falling onto the glass roof.

4. Opposition – you will encounter opposition. We fought very long and very hard. Four new planning permissions – means four heavy and terribly emotion-filled planning meetings. I still feel physically sick whenever I get a letter with my local council's logo on it. It was deeply, deeply unpleasant. I cried. I was fighting for my dreams. However we got through and there are a few things to remember.
    i. Never let it become personal.
    ii. Everybody is entitled to their opinion – people are very wary of change, it is natural, but I find it sad.

Intellectually I can't hold with the 'it doesn't fit in' argument – surely diversity of form is infinitely more exciting than repetition?
People opposed to you feel just as strongly as you do. They will be very vocal – sadly the people who like what you do or just don't mind will not. You will feel in a minority. Time will reveal however that you are not. Over the years people have written to me, come up to me in the street and praised my house. One man shook me by the hand.
Every weekend we get students sitting outside the house sketching. We've had coach loads of foreign students on architectural tours – it's a very strange feeling to look out of your window and see 30 students smiling hopefully at you. It's a bit like your house is a pop star. And, of course, every magazine and newspaper wants to run a feature. Photographers want to use it as a location and we get asked to hire it out for films. We even had requests from a contemporary artist to do a painting of it.

5. Once you've finished building it (no comment) it may sound odd to say but for God's sake live in it – it's not a museum. A good house looks better really lived in. Put your children's paintings on the walls – have parties – let it get trashed.
The first scratch on the black American walnut table is the hardest; after that it just looks more and more like it actually belongs to somebody. I'm sure Charles and Ray Eames, Marcel Brauer, Alvaar Alto et al would want to see children's sticky ice cream hand prints on their chairs – they look better that way. Any awful pink plastic toy, however crap, suddenly looks like art in a modern house!

6. Finally, the only real problem. Anything this fab - this all encompassing, that can so easily transport you to a higher mental and physical state – is addictive. And this is the most expensive addiction ever!

Nick Knight

If I don't become myself, who will be myself?

Poem by Mitsuo Aida.

Hiroshi Kutomi

Photography by Yoko Miyake.

Take risks and challenge yourself.

Calvin Klein

As the saying goes, 'you always learn by your mistakes'! Life itself is hard in many ways, but the experience that comes with age is the greatest of all. In these uncertain times where disease, war and fatal accidents sadly become part of our everyday lives, it is humanity that conquers all. But remember, try to always be nice to everyone because one day even your greatest enemy could become your saviour.

Julien Macdonald

The 10,000-year Clock.

What can we see on the image?

This image is a detail of the drive system for the prototype of the 'The Clock Of The Long Now', which is nine feet high and ticking in public glory at the Science Museum in London. It has the position of honour at the conclusion of a wonderful new permanent exhibit called 'The Making Of the Modern World'. The Clock is being designed by Danny Hillis, designer of some of the world's fastest computers. Entirely mechanical rather than electronic, the Hillis clock design utilises a new form of digital calculation and synchronises with the noon sun to achieve reliable accuracy over very long periods of time and will keep time for the next 10,000 years. As Hillis first described the Clock in 1993, "It ticks once a year, bongs once a century and the cuckoo comes out every millennium." The Long Now Foundation is aiming to put a monumental version (60 feet high) of the prototype clock inside the 2,000-feet high white limestone cliffs of eastern Nevada's Mount Washington.

The project summary of the Long Now Clock in 1998 read,

"Civilisation is revving itself into a pathologically short attention span. The trend might be coming from the acceleration of technology, the short-horizon perspective of market-driven economics, the next-election perspective of democracies or the distractions of personal multi-tasking. All are on the increase." What perspective does 'The Clock of the Long Now' offer the future? What can we learn from the clock?

All the Clock can do is give permission to think long term and lengthen cultural attention span. Amid all the demands on us to think short term and fast, that may be kind of refreshing. Mostly we discount the future. The Clock treats the next minute, a minute ten years from now, and a minute 10,000 years from now exactly the same. It's like a currency that doesn't inflate. Hopefully, the Clock does for thinking about time what the photographs of the Earth from space have done for thinking about the environment.

Stewart Brand, 63, creator of the Whole Earth Catalogue and author of *The Clock Of The Long Now*, is president of a foundation building a 10,000-year clock and library.

Joerg Koch

Photography by Rolfe Horn.

There's no answer to every question. And the strength you get from living with this fact lies simply in having to cope with these uncertainties and non-answers. In truth, this is much harder to practise than it seems. You could easily become a victim of this reality, helpless over destiny and let the lines that run on the palm of your hand rule your fate. So the one thing I've learnt is adaptability, and to make the most of what I have and in situations. Or, as in the words of Jean-Paul Sartre, "Man is nothing else but what he makes of himself".

Karen Leong

The essence of Aikido.
To my sensei Patricia Guerri, for the trusted love; to the open hand showing the path to fulfil my goal.

Duc Liao

L'Expérience est un Merveilleux héritage qui est difficile a trouver et difficile a laisser derrière soi.
(Experience is a wonderful legacy that is difficult to come by and difficult to leave behind.)

Jenny
President and co-founder.

Martin
Designer and co-founder.

Photography by Axel Hoedt.
Photographic assistance by Kim Curtin.

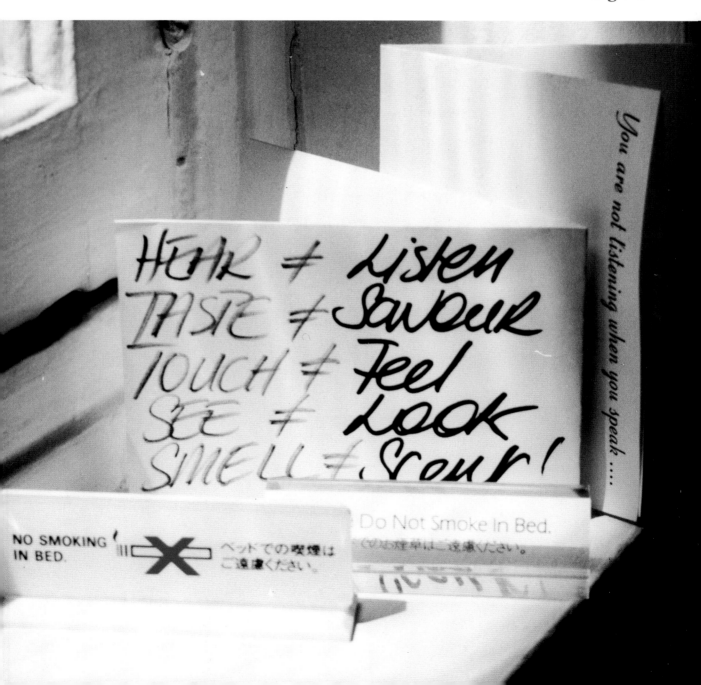

Learning and discovering
from those you have
passed it to.

Wyatt in a Welsh forest.

Mark Mattock

I've learnt so much from my father about cars and motorbikes. Every Sunday I used to spend at the racetrack with him, and this picture reminded me a lot about my childhood and my father. This boy is not me, but could have been me. Dirty Sundays racing in motocross around the track.

Craig McDean

Leigh Bowery 1986, Jasmine McKell with drawing, felt pen on wiper board, 2001.

The picture of Leigh Bowery was taken in 1986 and I
have a print of it on my wall at home. One day last
month Jasmine (my five-year-old daughter)
spontaneously drew this picture.

Iain McKell

Photography by Iain McKell.

DAD

HOME

This is dad, this is home. I grew up in this house built by my father in the '70s. Dad's an artist, architect and a dreamer. I can always remember him saying: Let's try things out!

Ernesto Mallard at his house, Mexico City (hometown), May 2001.

Michel Mallard

one year anniversary of Zapatista rebellion at Aguas Caliente

JUSTICE AND DIGNITY

Zapatista women Chiapas, Mexico 1994 Celebrate their struggle for Justice and
~Shawn Mortensen 2001 Dignity

My heroes and their lesson…
Zapatista women and their lesson of dignity.
In 1994 my personal and creative life were at a crossroads. I was doing a
lot of work and travelling, and began to feel sad at the shape the 'New
World' seemed to be taking. I felt a good portion of humanity was
being left behind in our modern-techno worldwind. After a recent
return from a trip to Mexico, I began to read about these poetic peasant
Indian farmers and their democratic movement against 500 years of
abuse. I decided to see for myself if what I had read was true.
Unfortunately, conditions in Chiapas were as bad as they had said.
I was utterly shocked at their resolve – to struggle for justice, even in
the face of death – for as long as necessary to make the world a better
place for their children. They had such great dignity – more than I'd
ever seen anywhere.

Shawn Mortensen

From a rural local struggle to one that has captured the imagination of the World

JUSTICE AND DIGNITY

Indigenous Mayan women New Year's Day January 1995 Aguas Caliente-Chiapas, Mexico
—Shawn Mortensen 2001

Daniel Stephenson sat in a field on the outskirts of Doncaster, 1987.

I was given a camera on my 13th birthday by my mum and dad; the camera was the Halina 180. This was one of the first photographs I took with it. The photo of Daniel was taken in the summer of 1987 – we were on our way to my girlfriend-at-the-time's house. She lived on a farm surrounded by fields; this is where the picture was taken. It was a rubbish camera, but it didn't seem to matter.

Alasdair McLellan

1. In my life, I've spent long periods living in both town and country. I believe that the two are the yin and yang of a fulfilled life: if we forget the mountains and waters of the wild, we diminish our spirit. If we turn our backs on city life and metropolitan cultures, we starve our intellects. The trick lies in the balance.

2. The Gods are prodigal; they give all of us many gifts. For example, we all 'know' we could be a novelist; we're sure that we might easily be a painter. Who is to say we're wrong? This is not necessarily self-deception but I believe that the real gift of the Gods, given only to the few, is focus – the ability to decide which gift (or gifts) to develop, rather than frittering energy on them all, or doing nothing with any of them. Those who are a success at any level in life know this.

3. Diana Vreeland once told me when I thought she was being embarrassingly demanding at an airport terminal that she felt that the British 'sickness' was our determination not to offend others. "What you must understand, Colin," she said to me, prodding the air with a dramatically raised hand, "is that they must get it RIGHT. And that means right for me, not for them." It was a seminal moment.

Colin McDowell

I am, somewhat perversely, thankful for growing up in the tumult which was South Africa in the '80s... An unholy system of social engineering that stripped a people of their dignity and birthright. It's given us a unique endowment – a social conscience. A moral compass, to orienteer ourselves into the bold unknown. As we countenance the grim realities of growing a country out of the ashes of apartheid, we are very aware that progress and growth means taking everyone along. It means raising the standards of living for all our people, irrespective of colour, class or creed.

It is this reckoning that will serve our generation well. We are a pilot project for Planet Earth. After spending our time breaking a system down, we must accept a new challenge – building a new order. From our pragmatic leaders that negotiated a revolution, but a decade ago, we are imbued with the power of the possible.

We are only too aware that the complexity in this modern world is not merely in the technological domain... It remains, as we enter this new century, our ability to understand people, and co-exist in harmony. The hard fought gains of our fledgling democracy inspire all civic-minded and patriotic South Africans.

As our fractured, dismembered society repairs, and we start to celebrate the harlequin patchwork of cultures in South Africa, we shall show a world riven by ethnic and religious conflict that there is hope.

Hope that we may, as a wise man once said, elevate humanity beyond all nations – because the message that history has borne, is that nations, and indeed civilisations are transient. All that prevails is humanity.

One of the early discoveries our country has made, after we ascended to the world stage, is that the relationship between countries is as inequitable as the apartheid we destroyed. Vested interests of centuries old make it difficult for a newcomer to compete on an equal basis. When we try to negotiate trade deals, for example, we face similar prejudices to those of old. How can the farmers of Africa compete with European Union farmers, when the latter receive more in subsidies than the combined economies of all Africa!

Despite this, our future in South Africa is pregnant with potential. We look at the world through a unique prism. We live in the Second World. We move seamlessly from the high-tech to the dusty townships of Africa – and in so doing, find that we have a gift in being able to develop products and services that could serve the two-thirds of humanity that exists beyond the Greedy 8 or the EU and their narrow interests.

We could be the engines for the world's development over the next century. The developing world must become a more united force in addressing its own problems. The age-old North vs. South divide must be bridged. Europe, with its ageing populations and low birth rates, may yet realise that they need us...

Ravi Naidoo

Photography by Roy George.

I have been working in fashion for years and yet I still cannot find a satisfactory definition for 'fashion': industry, economics, art, communications, entertainment, costume, sociology, philosophy, technology? Is it something that concerns the body, the mind or the soul? The individual, the group or the tribe? Is it an expression of conformity or nonconformity? Of power or creativity? And do this power and creativity impose themselves from the top down or do they grow up from the roots?

Perhaps this is why I still enjoy working in the field so much. I have had the opportunity to meet many very different people and I have tried to learn as much as possible. 'Professionalism' is often just a token word. I would take away the mystique, the presumption, the lack of wit and the 'double-breasted' attitude that surround it and I would leave the intensity, the preparation, the quality of what we do, along with the curiosity and the willingness to keep on learning.

They say that the eye of the storm is perfectly calm. This does apply to fashion: it is the contemporary business that best corresponds to the concept of continuous change; it is a perfect metaphor for the world we live in. It is like a pill for airsickness: if you take it, you move quickly through space and time without any severe consequences – maybe a little headache. You can stay still – sometimes it is useful to stop – only if you keep moving. Above all, working in fashion has taught me to appreciate change and not to fear the transformations that take place inside and outside of ourselves, or of the uncertainties that we inevitably face that are often worth more than solutions we find to allay our doubts.

I come from an upper middle class family that was respectful of form, concreteness and understatement. In my family's wardrobe these qualities become sober clothes, with classic and classic-sporty lines, in good material and never in loud colours.

Through my work in fashion I have come to understand the value of difference, the pleasure of contradictions.

'Multiple', 'complicated' and 'explain' are words that come from the same Latin root that means to 'fold': and we all know how important folds are in making any garment. My father was a notary. He taught me the importance of logic and precision in our choice of words. In fashion, I learned the importance of images: images can never contradict each other, they work through accumulations and density, they can appear confused (like the pictures in fashion magazines today where the product is barely visible) yet still be significant, explicit and obvious. Fashion succeeds in making images think (even our own image) and in making us think through the images.

I believe that fashion is concerned essentially with the issue of identity, the search for identity. It is a difficult and very current problem. Fashion can contribute in helping us with identities that are more complex, fragmentary and intermittent than those to which traditional society had accustomed us. It has served to help me discover the profound and stable value of the superficial and ephemeral. As a personal design of the body it has certainly contributed to supporting reason: and the body is the last frontier that we have.

Now, I think I have dispensed enough 'wisdom'. I do not feel like a teacher, I would like to keep on learning. And as someone once said – and I don't remember who – "the things I have done interest me less than those that are still to be done".

Raffaello Napoleone

I found this poem called *Children* – the writer didn't publish their name.

If children live with criticism, they learn to condemn.
If children live with hostility, they learn to fight.
If children live with ridicule. they learn to be shy
If children live with shame, they learn to feel guilty
If children live with tolerance, they learn to be patient
If children live with encouragement, they learn confidence
If children live with praise, they learn to appreciate
If children live with fairness, they learn justice
If children live with security, they learn to have faith
If children live with approval, they learn to like themselves
If children live with acceptance and friendship, they learn to
find love in the world.

I pass this on to all those who have children and dream of having children one day... they are the future. May we teach them that their world is in a grain of sand and their heaven in a wild flower.

My dad aged 29 and me; me aged 29 with my goddaughter.

For D and everyone else that has a dream.

Since the publication of my submission to Learn and Pass It On my father died. I think i finally got all that he was trying to pass on now that he has gone! Thanks Dad!

Nadia Narain

Sorry, handwritten ~ secretary on hols./

When the Australian Army discharged me after the war I went to Sydney to apply for a job at the Sydney Morning Herald. They published a weekly magazine and I thought they might need a young & ambitious photographer. The man who interviewed me, looked at my photos and said: "I'll give you a job and pay you 10 quid a week which means you must be worth 20 to me I advise you to be your own boss and make the 20 for yourself". This was the one and only lesson in economics I ever got. I went back to Melbourne, opened a little studio and never ever worked for a boss.

H. N.

Helmut Newton

316 learn and pass it on

Two years ago I started taking portraits of Lucenda –
since then she has been a big inspiration for me. The first
time I photographed her was when she was about 15 and
since then I've been taking photos of her for lots of
things because she's got a special face, a strong look. It's
nice because I've watched her change. When I first met
her she was really a girl; now, at 17, she's becoming a
woman. It gives me a strength when I look at her, and it
makes me happy to take photographs of her and the
special way she is, that's really good to look at and to see.
And the animals give me the unexpected – that's why
they are so much fun. I've always taken photographs of
animals, so for me it all fits, to make another world that
all goes together.

Bianca Pilet

She taught me how to sew.

Jessica Ogden

Photograph of Annabella and Jessica by Maria LaYacona, 1973.

My mime teacher at the Piccolo Teatro in Milan, who was a student of Etienne Decroux, one of Marcel Marceau's teachers, used to tell us how Decroux spent an entire month teaching them how to move each single part of a finger independently. Then they passed on to completely spontaneous improvisations.

And that's what our teacher taught me and my companions: great involvement, strong effort, serious patience in order to completely dominate our bodies. Through this our bodies turned totally flexible and free, and we were able to express whatever we wished.

This lesson has always meant a lot to me. The more you learn, the more you are free to express yourself without limitation.

Miuccia Prada

I always know when I have to visit – the giant 40 foot waves come into my dreams, reminding me that I need to hear the voice that whispers as the sea rolls in. Breathing with it, following the tide go out and come back in, reminds me what a small and precious thing life is.

Jane Peverley

Technology constantly bombards us with information these days, which not only teaches us things, it's also the way most of us pass on information to each other today.

Tesh Patel

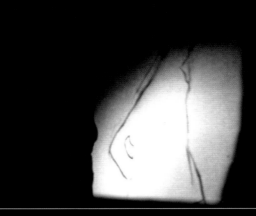

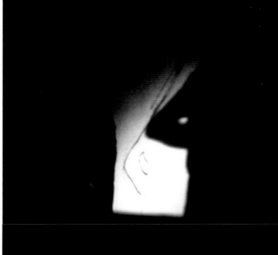

La Fine di Dio by Lucio Fontana.

Enthusiasm and Respect, for oneself and for others.

The holes represent enthusiasm but they are limited by a 2cm wide surface that runs around the painting and this for me is respect.

Clarice Pecori-Giraldi

A Shadow Fitting

These movies I was working on; I was working with shadows. The hardest thing for anybody to pass on to you is self-knowledge. The shadow is a portrait of who you really are, but you have to give life to that portrait and also to fit into that shadow. It's like self-discovery, you have to fill in the body and soul – the essence of who you are.

Shannon Plumb

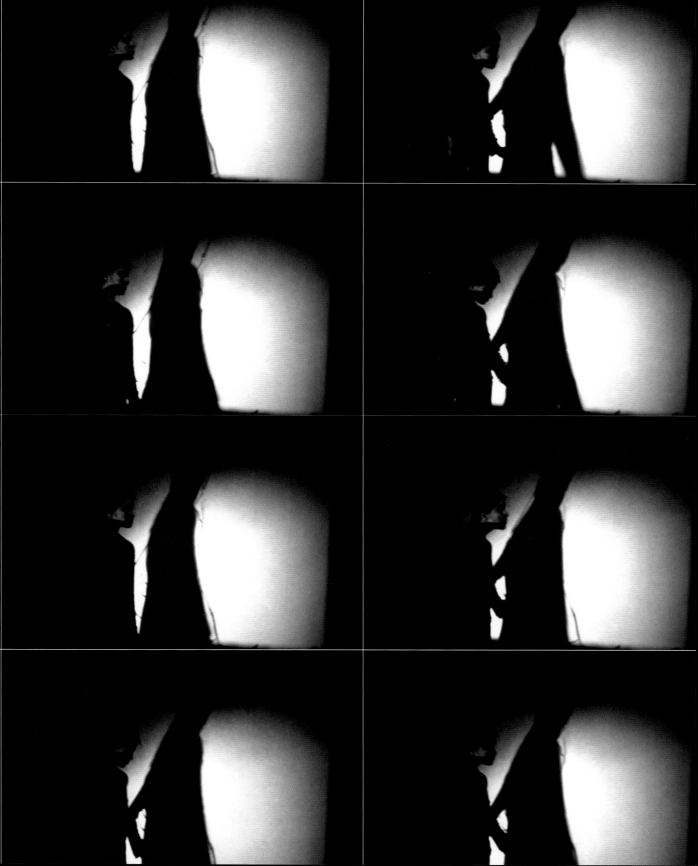

Back when I was a kid in Rio, I used to cut school every time that the waves were good. In its own metaphoric way, surfing taught me things that I knew I could not learn in a classroom. Fear, grace, balance… How to ride the flow of raw energy that can only be found in nature… How to be connected, mind and body. But, most of all, surfing taught me that some of the greatest things in life require great effort and still, at the end, produce nothing that can be shown to prove it (no tracks, no score, no commodity). Like love. Surfing is unpredictable, unmeasurable. It hurts sometimes, but we still can't live without it.

Vava Ribeiro

Naked surfing photographed by Vava. Ubatuba, SP Brasil, February 2001.

THIS IS ME CUTING SCHOOL

Just say no!

Terry Richardson

Mischa Richter was a cartoonist and a painter. He was also my grandfather and he taught me about composition, colour, timing, respect, pride and laughter. I will miss spending time with him but I will never forget what he taught me. That is with me everywhere I go.

Him on his porch, Summer 2000.

Mischa Richter

The learning process is one of the most critical phases in human life.

But I have discovered that it is even more difficult to pass on one's knowledge. Especially in the world of work. Diffidence, fears and absurd defensive positions make it difficult to pass knowledge and experience from the old to the new generations. I represent the eighth generation of the Rivetti family to work in the field of textiles and clothing. I had the misfortune not to get to know directly the person from whom I've learnt most, or at least I don't remember him. He was my father. He died when I was only three years old.

He was a great inventor. After the Second World War, he was the first to introduce clothing made to theoretical measurements or sizes in Italy. Then he revolutionised the production process.

The great testament that he left me was to give extraordinary importance to human relationships and values.

This was passed on to me, in a modern world, using the oldest form of memory: the oral tradition, the story. Countless persons, a new kind of story-tellers, have described this man, who both they and I regard as a mythical figure. He was a good man. He got what he wanted with the sweetness of his smile and he also managed to help those in need. As proof of his being above factions, I jealously conserve his pass in the CLN, The National Liberation Committee, or the Italian partisans during the Second World War. He was unique in having stamps of approval from all the Partisan brigades. From the Catholics to the communists, from the monarchists to the socialists. It goes without saying that he was a liberal. Now, it's my turn to communicate to the ninth generation, to my three children. I try not to talk too much, as the Latin saying warns "verba volant", but instead I try to leave them something through everyday example. I would like my sons to understand in full and support the values of ethics, which unfortunately now are all too often forgotten, trodden underfoot and derided.

Carlo Rivetti

Las Paredes Hablan: The Walls Speak

History and love all reach the surface at some point.
There are very special surfaces in the world which catch the residue of small big everyday moments. This always amazes me because our surroundings teach and inform.

They could be the doorway where we catch two lovers kissing; the rift in the pavement where some green grows; the orange rind sitting in a garbage bin; careless and careful graffiti – or the muted music in the street from open windows that can sink into concrete or suspend itself in the air.

Listen to the things close to you. Try to make sense of all the existing layers, the voices in the void – all the quiet noise.

Oriana Reich

The Man Who Painted a Mountain

I learn from outsiders. Leonard Knight lives just outside the small community of Niland in the Southern Californian desert, in an old military installation called Slab City. He's a 70-year-old Korean war vet who has devoted his life to spreading the word that 'God is Love'. He originally spent nearly five years painting his message on a 50-foot sandbar. Then it collapsed. So he started from scratch in 1990, building a structure out of hand-mixed adobe made with dirt and water from a nearby stream. Salvation Mountain has been growing ever since. Baked by the sun, sealed by many coats of paint, it is now invulnerable. A primary-coloured riot of waterfalls, flowers and Biblical lore, it has inevitably become a cause celebre. The local authorities declared it a toxic dump and wanted to bulldoze it. They backed off when Leonard's independently analysed gravel samples came back clean. Now people drop by from all over to give him more paint. Even the State of California, which owns the land, donated gallons of the yellow normally used for painting lines on roads. Museums, art critics, sociologists and film-makers have also come to see one of America's most extraordinary expressions of visionary art. But, however obsessive the project may seem, Leonard himself is no wide-eyed cultist. He calls himself "a desert hobo bum". Sweet, sharp and funny, he lets his mountain speak for his faith.

Anita Roddick

Photograph courtesy of The Center For Land Use Interpretation.

The spirit of growth.
Michel and Lucien Momy building together, the little
one also giving advice to the grown up one.

Myriam Roehri

Many things I have learned along the way, in my personal as well as in my professional life.

I have learned to make people feel responsible, at all levels, for the success of any enterprise: this motivates them and makes them give their best. I have learned to act promptly when I see someone having a hard time: this person will not only suffer but also create unhappiness around him or her. I have learned to listen to people who need to speak out what is on their mind to be able to look ahead. I have learned the power of values – human, familiar, traditional values: respect, honesty, help.

These things were passed on to me by my family, simple farmers who lived every day as a gift. These are the values I want to pass on to my children.

For successful living.

Renzo Rosso

It is a luxurious thing to have a passion becoming your own job. You feel like you wake up every day to accomplish something you love. But by the time you will succeed, you have to be ready to "eat potatoes" for maybe quite a long time – that is sometimes the price to pay. But, at the end, you will laugh about it...

Gilles Rosier

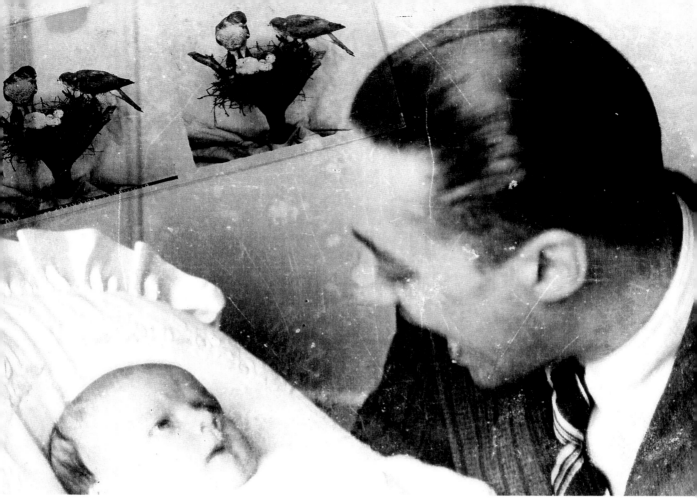

A little song.

Paolo Roversi

My granny's dressing table has always been a fascinating place for me. As a child it was the first place for me to go when visiting her. I would use her make-up, try on her jewellery, then raid her wardrobe. It was one of the first places that I experimented with my femininity and learned about being a woman.

Amber Rowlands

Kris Ruhs

There was always lots of interesting people around and we got to paint & play on large canvases

Taking the walls down caused the ceiling to sag, the neighbours were waiting for the house to fall but our house was different it was held up by our energy

From the time we are born and right through our youth, some of the most fundamental things that shape our character and subsequent adult lives are learned or acquired, and the people with the greatest impression on us at the time are our parents, older brothers and sisters. There are certain qualities we have to deal with, and eventually let go of, while others we nurture in becoming a part of our own lives, and then in turn hopefully pass on to others.

My dad was Italian, but emigrated to Switzerland as a baby with his parents, looking for something new. Years later, he left his family and came to London, also looking for something. Before I knew him, my older brother Bruno left Scarborough to study design in London, but I kept hearing all these things about him and his work, and he became the greatest inspiration in my life. Him getting out of Scarborough and pursuing what he wanted to do, made me realise there was so much more to life than meets the eye, and to go and find it, as he had done years before me, and dad had done years before him: leaving, moving on, looking for something else and pursuing your dreams. So from childhood through to adolescence, I learnt about Bruno's very different world, and consequently through him and his art, I found myself and my art – and eventually, when I came to London, we found each other.

Love, Bro.

Derrick Santini

For me, what I've learnt and would like to pass on is to never speak badly to the persons you love. They can disappear anytime and after you have the bad words in your head forever. Sometimes it's difficult when the person you love does something you're not happy with and you're particularly vexed, but it's important to always try to understand.

Sarah

Cat's cradle fascinated me ever since I saw my sister playing it monotonously for hours. I want to pass on proverbs and tradition. The real thing everybody should experience by themselves.

Stephan Schneider

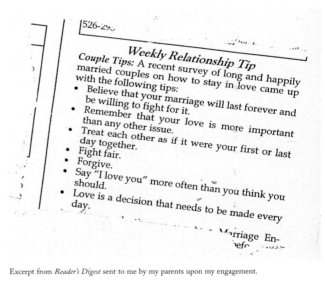

Weekly Relationship Tip

Couple Tips: A recent survey of long and happily married couples on how to stay in love came up with the following tips:

- Believe that your marriage will last forever and be willing to fight for it.
- Remember that your love is more important than any other issue.
- Treat each other as if it were your first or last day together.
- Fight fair.
- Forgive.
- Say "I love you" more often than you think you should.
- Love is a decision that needs to be made every day.

...Marriage En-
...efo...

Excerpt from *Reader's Digest* sent to me by my parents upon my engagement.

Jicky Schnee

1. Take pleasure seriously.
2. Life is about every hour.
3. Look at the world through the eyes of someone you respect; admire and love.
4. You can't do it, without doing it!
5. Stop making sense… logic is predictable.

Paul Smith

Ugandan Benedict was barely 20 when she lost her sight after drinking what she believes was badly-brewed alcohol. Today, despite her blindness, she insists on teaching her five-year-old daughter how to read. For that she uses boards which are both in Braille and alphabet.

Shambhala

Love

And now I will show you the most excellent way.

13 If I speak in the tongues[a] of men and of angels, but have not love, I am only a resounding gong or a clanging cymbal. [2]If I have the gift of prophecy and can fathom all mysteries and all knowledge, and if I have a faith that can move mountains, but have not love I am nothing. [3]If I give all I possess to the poor and surrender my body to the flames,[b] but have not love, I gain nothing.

[4]Love is patient, love is kind. It does not envy, it does not boast, it is not proud. [5]It is not rude, it is not self-seeking, it is not easily angered, it keeps no record of wrongs. [6]Love does not delight in evil but rejoices with the truth. [7]It always protects, always trusts, always hopes, always perseveres.

Venetia Scott

Survive

When the request of learn and pass it on came from Tricia and Terry Jones, I felt very honoured and faced this homework very relaxed. Days were going by and I realised it was much more difficult for me than I thought… and struggled until the deadline, here we are now! It became so clear that my inheritance came from the spirit of my mother and her eight brothers and sisters.

My father disappeared in the Holocaust and a sort of miracle happened – my uncles and aunts and my mother all survived. I know that the main thing I learned from life is itself; live now, not yesterday or tomorrow, just now and respect life.

My daughter went through some difficult moments this year and most naturally I told her: "If our family survived there must be a reason, so we have to do the same, not give up." My mother taught me to live just by living, so that was my inheritance and I passed it on and so my children would do the same…

Irene Silvagni

LIGHT

WORSHIP

<u>DETERMINATION</u>

VIGILANCE

WANDERLUST

<u>NATURE</u>

VISIBILITY

ORGANISATION

FAITH

HUMILITY

RESISTANCE

HOPE

<u>COMPANIONSHIP</u>

INDEPENDENCE

Raf Simons

Text by Peter de Potter and Raf Simons.

The two year journey we travelled before finally completing the adoption of Matteo was a rollercoaster ride. We experienced every emotion from anguish to exultation and from deep depression to intense joy. Above all, we found unconditional love in a little boy who is now part of the fabric of our lives and who makes every waking day and sleeping night a cause for celebration. We hope that others who have dreamed of adoption will be encouraged. There are so many beautiful children out there in need of loving parents. (Hopefully one day they will also come up with the single sex birth certificate!)

Robert Triefus and Caleb Negron

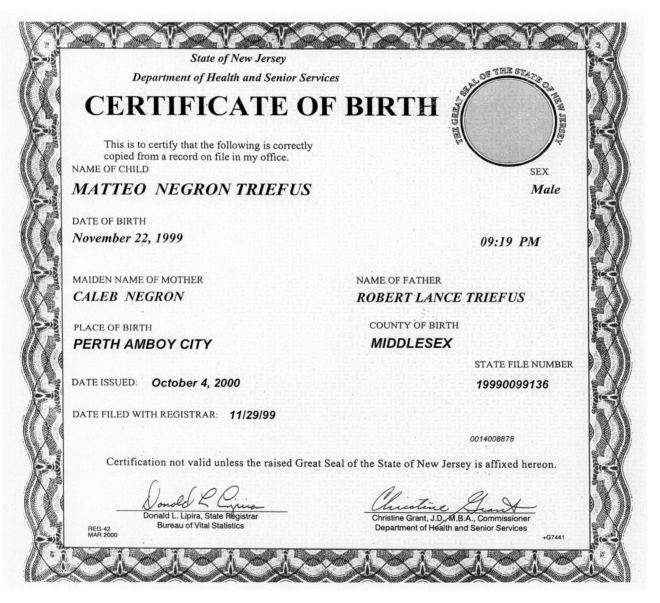

State of New Jersey

Department of Health and Senior Services

CERTIFICATE OF BIRTH

THE GREAT SEAL OF THE STATE OF NEW JERSEY

This is to certify that the following is correctly copied from a record on file in my office.

NAME OF CHILD

MATTEO NEGRON TRIEFUS

SEX

Male

DATE OF BIRTH

November 22, 1999

09:19 PM

MAIDEN NAME OF MOTHER

CALEB NEGRON

NAME OF FATHER

ROBERT LANCE TRIEFUS

PLACE OF BIRTH

PERTH AMBOY CITY

COUNTY OF BIRTH

MIDDLESEX

STATE FILE NUMBER

DATE ISSUED: *October 4, 2000*

19990099136

DATE FILED WITH REGISTRAR: **11/29/99**

0014008878

Certification not valid unless the raised Great Seal of the State of New Jersey is affixed hereon.

Donald L. Lipira, State Registrar
Bureau of Vital Statistics

Christine Grant, J.D., M.B.A., Commissioner
Department of Health and Senior Services

REG-42
MAR 2000

+G7441

Precious Consequence

AGE 3
"I want mommy"
AGE 10
Barbie
Fairies
Coney Island
Mistakes
AGE 14
Marry a Beatle
Be famous
Be beautiful
Have tits
Mistakes
AGE 18
Have fun
Have sex
Handsome husband
White picket fence
Career
Mistakes
AGE 21
Have fun
Have sex
Handsome husband
White picket fence
Career
Babies
Mistakes
AGE 28
Have fun
Have sex
No husband
No white picket fence
Career
Babies
Mistakes

AGE 35
True love
Great sex
Kids
Career
Mistakes
AGE 40
Womanhood
True love
Great sex
Teenagers
Career
Mistakes
AGE 47
Confusion
Sorrow
Tragedy
Questions
Mistakes
AGE 50
Compassion
Understanding
Nature
Sadness
Smiling
Remembering
Changing
Grandchildren
Maintaining
More questions
No answers
Sex
Fewer mistakes

Francesca Sorrenti

Co-existing is a balance – a fine line between the birth and death of something and nothing. To walk side by side with pain, shake hands with sorrow and befriend grief. To allow creativity to take its course and try to see beyond what seems… By the time I finish asking, the answer has wrapped itself around me. Amour. Esperance. Foix. Mom, you're the bomb.

(Baby) Arsun and Mary 1999 (Door) East 12th Street, New York City, 1997.

Vanina Sorrenti

What I learned that's helped me the most that I'd want
to pass on is what my dad and Andy Warhol said to me:
"Don't give up".

Stephen Sprouse

Dear Tricia

Shame on me. I wanted to call or fax you since such a long time. It is
especially embarrassing for me that I did not come back to you, because
I wanted to write only a few lines about what to learn and to pass on
which was including good manners, behaviour, being on time, being
professional etc, and I do the opposite. I am ashamed.

If you still need my text and it is not yet too late, please take the
following (or the complete letter because it includes a human aspect to
the Prussian discipline I am voting for):

1. family values
2. good manners and behaviour
3. compassion and tolerance for everybody and every aspect of life
4. respect for every human being and nature
5. being on time in respect to the waiting person
6. being professional
7. love for nature which means happiness without material possessions
8. being patient (I still am working on it)

Angelika Taschen

My mother is a mother to all children. I can remember her saying to a family friend who was nursing a broken heart: 'Never run after bus, train or man, because as one leaves another one arrives'.

Marcia Taylor

A survivor of the Holocaust talks to citizens of Dresden at a Jewish cemetery.

Wolfgang Tillmans

My mother, my father and me. Bubenreuth Germany, 1999.

Juergen Teller

Nicoletta, my wife, completes.
She has all the qualities that I don't have; she
completes who I am. Nicoletta has been a
great teacher to me in all respects, and I'm
always surprised by what she teaches me.

Max Vadukul

Photograph of Nicoletta Sontoro by Max Vadukul.

Lovers can sleep, love never sleeps.

Willy Vanderperre and Olivier Rizzo

never regret,
never hesitate,
to give,
to open,
your heart.
never sell,
never forget,
your soul.

Milan Vukmirovic

Photography by Mark Borthwick.

My daughter Rebecca, ten years old, in Normandy.

Jamaica, 2001.

How to wear a snake:
as a hat, as a belt, as a neck tie, packs away easily

Enjoy nature and freedom in a
preserved environment.

Ellen Von Unwerth

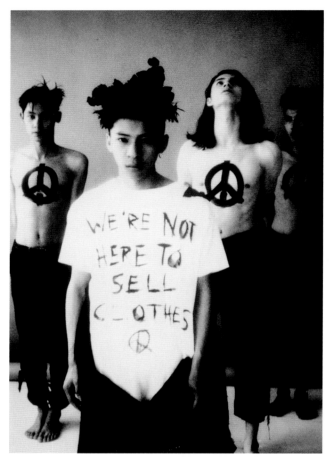

Never give up on a dream.
Subvert from within.
Dream Big.

Iain R. Webb

If I risk and fail, will I die? If no, then risk.

Jules Wright

A lady asked me the other day, "Did you learn something with age which as a young person you could have never expected to discover? Something by way of advice that you could pass on to young people?" There have been small flashes of insight – one tends to remember most particularly the ones when one was very young.

And the nearest thing to a revelation was when, at the age of 22, I gave birth to my first child. He was nothing to do with me, an independent stranger who I loved and cared for of course and tried to guide, but this was only possible according to his own lights. His character was there from the minute I first saw him and he hasn't changed.

This applies to my second son but then I was prepared. The only way in which I have influenced my sons is in that they have sound morals, because I respected them and tried to see their point of view, even at a young age. Therefore they respected and listened to me. Character is there from birth and each individual will react to circumstances according to their character.

Discipline can be imposed on children; it builds character. It's important that children are encouraged and, if necessary, made to accomplish what they set out to do. Achievement gives the confidence to attempt again something new and difficult. In the end the only discipline that counts is self-discipline. A few golden children will do this independently but this is now harder for them because of the accelerating bombardment of non-stop distraction.

Today we suffer from a lack of solitude. It's only by being alone that one can think. I include reading as a crucial part of being alone; reading is the most concentrated form of experience it is possible to have.

There we have it – I can't read the book for you and all the advice in the world won't read the book for you. My younger son (now grown up) is not a reader – yet. (I still have hopes.)

So, although the above may offer some advice to parents, I have no advice to pass on to younger people. Parents, take away that mobile phone, don't let them fiddle around with computer games. Don't just believe in your children because you love them. Don't just believe in the future, do something!

My experience has been gradual. I have strong opinions which have been forced upon me by the unpleasant fact that people have become more and more ugly. This is the result of consumerism and in developed countries ugliness is now almost universal. On the other hand I have learnt something of the awesome potential realised in past ages by a small number of human beings who cultivated beauty. Culture is defined by perfection.

I have been shocked by beauty; it is the only mystery, though it cannot grow where it is not cultivated.

There must be a hierarchy of values. When there are no judges there is no art and when there are no ideas there is only popular opinion.

Vivienne Westwood

Play with it.
Have fun with it.
But don't buy into the fashion bullshit!

Patti Wilson

I'm learning
something marvellous
and new every day
being a father.

Paul Wetherell

"SOME THOUGHTS"

(1) Start Something New

② Work is not about shorter hours or longer hours, it's about <u>every hour</u>

(3) You cant do it, without doing it.

(4) Make Room to break the RULES

Paul Smith

again....

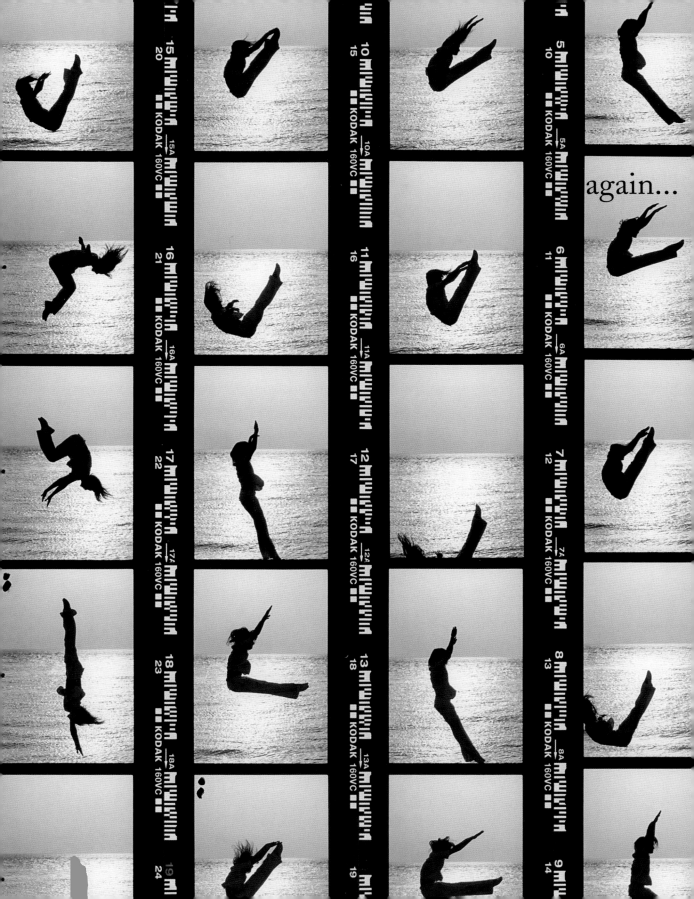

again...

again...

synchronicity... Y-3

tilda swinton *photographed by* **craig mcdean** june 2003

06>

9 770262 357068

£3.50 US$9.99 YEN1850

©

Rebel!

Beyond our
control,
part of a game
whose rules we
haven't set,
we go about
our ordinary
lives as though
everything is
normal, nothing
has changed.

But in the
background the
news and media
hype war.
The munitions
factories are one of the few
beneficiaries of
control by fear...

and down the
catwalk models
glide,
cushioned and
cocooned within the
fantasy bubble
of fashion.

Yesterday for the
first time
I felt myself
not alone within
the group. We
were, by any
standards, a
gloriously mixed bunch –
shouting for
peace, reclaiming the
streets, freezing for freedom.

But the fact
that all around
the world other
like minded youngs,
olds, mums, dads,
cowards and heroes
were on their local
patch to be
counted too, made
it in the end
the coolest
catwalk, and by far
the very most
relevant show that
I had seen
all week.   TJ 16.02.2003

not in our name

The following section is dedicated to peace and a future that does not rely on bombs, tanks and guns to solve the problems of the world.

The idea for this project started during Fashion Week in New York, with tanks at Heathrow, helicopters over Manhattan and peace marches planned across the world for the following Saturday. It seemed that we had to do something; that however small our contribution, we had to stand up and be counted, to lend our voices to the growing consensus of dissent – because the truth is that if we stay silent, it can only be presumed that we acquiesce.

We wanted to be a conduit for creative people internationally who disagree with war. So we sent out the following brief: 'Let us know your views, your message, your image and your ideas in whatever way you want to. We suggest using a white shirt or T-shirt as a canvas, and would ask you to be photographed with it if you don't mind, but you do not have to.'

The next 44 pages are the voices and images we were given as a result. As always, we feel honoured and privileged by the response that we have received.

Tricia Jones 2003

With social consciousness comes responsibility. The responsibility to take advantage of the opportunity our position affords us, and convey our feelings through imagery to promote awareness.

Photography by Jérôme Albertini.
Styling by Miguel Adrover.

Miguel Adrover

NOTHING IN THE WORLD IS
MORE DANGEROUS THAN
SINCERE IGNORANCE AND
CONSCIENTIOUS STUPIDITY

MARTIN LUTHER KING

This image is based on dispute over territory.

Photography by Andy Atkinson.

Hussein Chalayan

What we know about
the American psyche
so far.

Photography by Johan Coppens.

Peter de Potter

Docket sez Stoppit.

Peace in my Garden.

Tracey Emin

War is the real enemy.

Sophia Kokosalaki

Photography by Bill Georgoussis.

Terry Jones

Point the finger... there are three pointing back at you

Human Nature

Human Beings

Nothing can be done

Many thanks to Charty for proving to me that something as well as nothing can be done, and to Noam Chomsky for his honesty, integrity and inspiration.

Photographic assistance by Kristian and Tyrone.

Mark Lebon

Left to right: Arielle Dombasle, Loulou de la Falaise, Betty Catroux, Mouna Ayoub.

I remember as a kid in Iran, waiting in the cellar for the bombings to stop, when my most exciting thought was the idea of running away from that country and coming to Paris in quest of a glamorous life. I would even request that my family call me Saint Laurent, I would sign my drawings Hermès, not to mention my imaginary aunt Cathy, in homage to Catherine Deneuve.

Ali Mahdavi

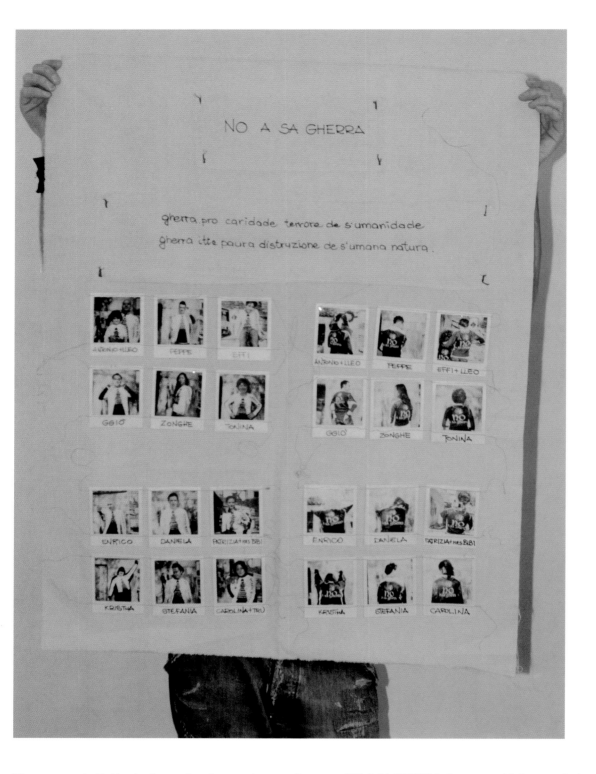

The poetry on the T-shirts has been written by an ancient poet from Ittiri (a small village near Alghero, the place where we live and work). He cannot write but he composes oral poetry in the Sardinian language at the same time you ask him to do it. We asked him: tell us something against war and he told us in Sardinian language the sentences we wrote on the T-shirt. We have made the translation: Sardo -> Italiano -> Inglese.

NO A SA GHERRA gherra pro caridade terrore de s'umanidade gherra ittepaura distruzione de s'umana natura. NO ALLA GUERRA guerra per carità terrore dell umanita guerra che paura distruzione dell umana natura. NO WAR war for God's sake terror of human beings war what a scare destruction of human nature.

Antonio Marras

II faced.

Alexander McQueen

Pauline Takahashi with her mother's melted breakfast bowl from Hiroshima.

Shawn Mortensen

Waris.

It's a shame that it takes war to inspire people (myself included) to be politically creative - I mean, some of these images are fucking great. Maybe if we all got off our arses between wars and said something, we could give the next one a miss.

Keiron O'Connor

Nathalie Ours 'Extracts from a letter from Michael Moore to George W Bush on the eve of war, March 17 2003

George W Bush, 1600 Pennsylvania Ave, Washington, DC

We love France. Yes, they have pulled some royal screw-ups. Yes, some of them can be pretty damn annoying. But have you forgotten we wouldn't even have this country known as America if it wasn't for the French? That it was their help in the Revolutionary War that won it for us? That our greatest thinkers and founding Fathers – Thomas Jefferson, Ben Franklin, etc – spent years in Paris, where they refined the concepts that lead to our Declaration of Independence and our Constitution? That it was France who gave us our Statue of Liberty, a Frenchman who built the Chevrolet and a pair of French brothers who invented the movies? And now they are doing what only a good friend can do – tell you the truth. Michael Moore

Nathalie Ours

So sad, Mr Blair, that your pro-war stance not only helped solidify support for Mr Bush's war in Iraq, you also helped convince us that it was moral. Not a small achievement. You are a hero in America and many people in Europe see you as the new American prime minister… So sad for Iraq, so sad for Europe.

Maryvonne Numata

Pacifists on show

Nothing has really changed. Man is still the same, as fragile and powerless as he always has been. This is the thought that comes to mind when looking at the portraits of people posing naked before the camera for photographer Gianni Berengo Gardin. Twenty-seven statement-making portraits taken in 1968 at the time of the great peace protests against the Vietnam War make up the feature simply entitled *The last pacifists in Milan. Leave us alone, we are vulnerable* and published in the 2nd-3rd 1968 winter equinox edition of avant-garde magazine *Pianeta Fresco*, founded by Fernanda Pivano and Ettore Sottsass, a leading tool of the great cultural, social and ideological turmoil of the time, particularly linked to the beat generation. Men and women showing their vulnerability and their desire for peace by posing naked, covered with just one belonging or their most prized possession, such as the self-portrait of Berengo Gardin with his son Alberto. Black and white photos with hairstyles, make-up and details that clearly show the time they belong to and which today are more relevant than ever. Archive photographs from the Contrasto journalist photography agency, with thanks to the co-operation of Renata Molho who featured them in an exhibition on the 1960s for the Fondazione Mazzotta, have been used by CP Company to make a 16-metre banner to show as a tribute to those who have not forgotten human fragility and want to defend human rights. All of this was exhibited at the Milan showroom, at the same time as CPictures, a photographic behind-the-scenes of the reality and activity of CP Company by four great contemporary photographers including Berengo Gardin.

Carlo and Sabina Rivetti

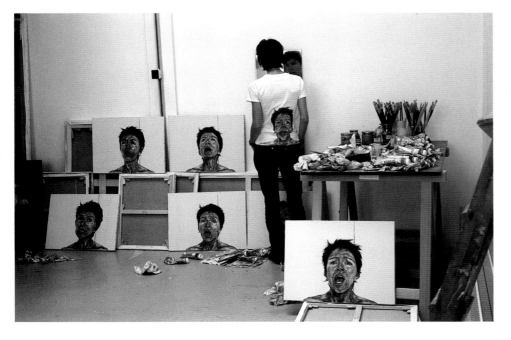

Silence kills. My voice against war. Cette peinture est ma voix, mon cri, ma résistance, contre la guerre, les massacres, les mutilations, de ce nouveaux siécle Américain.

Dominique Renson

HELP

HEALTH EARTH LOVE PEACE

PHOTO ALFREDO CELLA
SPECIAL THANKS CATERINA AMATO

MILANO 31·3·03

These 3 signoras, Virginia Poggi, Giuseppina
De Masi e' Luigia Medaglia spend a great deal
of their time + energy helping stray animals
and bringing joy + confort to those in need.
They carry the Flag of Peace everyday.

Kris Ruhs

Kris Ruhs

My daughter Elsie Pearl.

Mischa Richter

Bob and Roberta Smith

389

i-D Magazine
124 Tabernacle Street
London EC2A 4SA
Tel.029 7490 9710
Fax.020 7251 2225

RAF SIMONS

DETLEF BVBA - ROSIER 32-34 - B 2000 ANTWERP, BELGIUM
PHONE: ++32 3 233 11 23 - FAX: ++32 3 233 98 16 - E-MAIL: RAF.SIMONS@PANDORA.BE
VAT: BE 473 320 606 - BANK: BBL 320-0137597-24

Not in our name...

[handwritten: RAF SIMONS, ROBBIE SNELDERS, PIETER MULIER, ...]

would like to be a conduit for creative people internationally who disagree with the war.

It would be good to be part of, to lend a voice to the growing consensus of dissent — because the truth is that if we stay silent it can be presumed that we acquiesce!

If you would like to join us in this, we will be devoting as much space as is needed in our June issue, on the bookstands in mid-May. This is not one of i-D's special issues, unfortunately, as these take many months to put together — we need to do this immediately and publish as soon as we can.

The brief is absolutely free: let us know your views, your message, your image and your ideas in whatever way you want to. We suggest using a white shirt or T-shirt as a canvas and would ask you to be photographed with it if you don't mind, but you do not have to.

The dea...   to
i-D for ...

If you h...   ctly
on Tel.   90
9720 o...

With ve...

Tricia J...
10.3.20...

Raf Simons

No War.

Paul Smith

Name: Yusuke 802
Occupation: Invisibleman
Age: 28+alpha

Jun Takahashi

encroachment

USD vs JUR

WAR IS PEACE.
FREEDOM IS SLAVERY.
IGNORANCE IS STRENGTH.
UNDERCOVERISM 2003.

A BRUTE OF A MAN

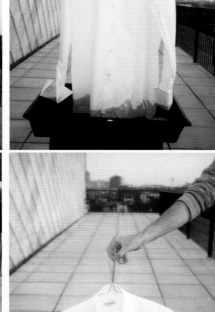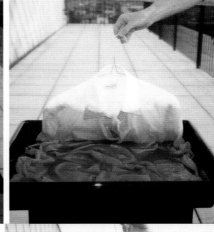

Dries Van Noten

Above: Richard Buckley.
Right: Francesco Vezzoli.

Matthias Vriens

Photography by Matthias Vriens.

Charlotte Gainsbourg for peace.

Styling by Martine de Menthon.
Make-up by Kathy le Sant.
Hair by David Mallett.

Ellen Von Unwerth

i-D

9 770262 357075

06 >

£3.80 US$9.99 YEN1800

PLUS SPECIAL PORTFOLIO:
i-D SUPPORTS
MAKE POVERTY HISTORY

...TION ISSUE NO. 255

M.I.A.

LOUDER THAN BOMBS

The global campaign for Action Against Poverty can take its place as a public movement alongside the movement to abolish slavery and the international solidarity against apartheid… Like slavery and apartheid, poverty is not natural. It is man-made and it can be overcome and eradicated by the action of human beings… And overcoming poverty is not a gesture of charity. It is an act of justice. It is the protection of a fundamental human right, the right to dignity and a decent life.

Nelson Mandela, February 2005, London

If everyone who wants to see an end to poverty, hunger and suffering speaks out, then the noise will be deafening. Politicians will have to listen.

Desmond Tutu

i-D unconditionally supports
make poverty history

Two months ago we sent a letter to our contributors explaining that we wanted to support, in our own personal way, the global initiative Make Poverty History. We asked contributors to respond as they felt appropriate whether with photographs, sentences or a written piece. As always the i-D team have learnt so much from the responses that have come in. It's been a privilege and an honour to work on this project but more than anything it's felt essential! Among the many things that have stuck in my mind… Koto Bolofo who, when he explained his chicken head photo said simply, "all poor kids will relate to this because it's the only bit of the chicken that our mothers could afford". The message from Edun, "we carry the story of the people who make our clothes around with us" which immediately makes it unallowed to detach yourself from the 12 year-old who might have made your cheap trainers. The aim of this portfolio was to try and look at the issue from all angles. This is not just an African problem because that sees Africa always as only the victim. (Hence our inspirational pictures and stories from Kenya, Ghana and South Africa.) As we all know, poverty and our abuse of global responsibility with regard to the developing nations is a worldwide challenge. With this section we hope to inspire and provoke all of us into some sort of response. None of us can do enough, we can all do more and there will always be extra to do. But at least if we really think about our actions, question our beliefs and preconceptions, then finally the situation must improve. It is no longer an excuse to say "things will never change", "the problem is so enormous there is nothing we can do"… then put our hands in our pockets for the note that quietens our consciences. It is up to all of us to stand and be counted, to force governments into action and look at any individual efforts that we can all make to affect the future of the world's children. It's very simple: at the end of the day where there's a political will there <u>is</u> a way. We just have to collectively believe that and make it happen.

Tricia Jones 2005

My huge thanks to all of you who have made time in your busy schedules to contribute to this issue and to Ashley Heath who, when he heard in early December about the campaign, so correctly knew we would want to support it.

The Need for Knowledge.

Dennis Morris

Masai Mara, Kenya, 2004.

No one – especially not a child – should face a life of poverty in this age where technologies change before one's eyes. It is simple to say 'Make Poverty History', but much harder to achieve. For all of us who are fortunate to 'have', we can make a difference for those who 'have not'. Random acts of kindness count.

Giorgio Armani

The rich nations need to lift the bars that are holding back the poor in the developing world.

Cuba, 2005.

David Bailey

Journalists keep asking me why I'm supporting Make Poverty History – whereas I think they should be asking the people who aren't, why they are not. If you need to ask me why I'm supporting Make Poverty History......?!

Johnny Borrell

This image is about how some of the world can afford luxury and weapons and the others can't. The pain and suffering which results from rich nations bombing poor ones is so unfair. Put the budget towards aid not arms.

Judy Blame

Left: Business district in Tokyo 2004. Right: Dublin.

"Poverty is the worst form of violence." Ghandi
"The mother of revolutions and crime is poverty." Aristotle
"Wealth consists not in having great possesions, but in having few wants." Epictetus
"A fool dreams of wealth: a wise man, of happiness." Turkish proverb
"Reality leaves a lot to the imagination." John Lennon
"Riches are rarely found in wallets." Orion Best
"The world is full of suffering. It is also full of overcoming it." Helen Keller
"The mind is its own place, itself can make heaven of hell and hell of heaven." John Milton

Orion Best

Rose Bakery 46 rue des Martyrs 75009 Paris

supporting 'makepovertyhistory'
way beyond charity
more than a priority
the bowl on top of RB
should be full for everyone

Rose Bakery

Chicken heads and chicken feet is what
my mother boiled to make me strong.

Koto Bolofo

Joe Casely-Hayford

Poverty is my identity
my situation is visible
but can you see me?

413

Shot in Gaya, India, during the Kalachakra teachings, in which the Dalai Lama prays for world peace.

Larry Dunstan

It's easy to forget that there is a flipside
as we are travelling to see the world's
most beautiful sites.

That this beauty may have little or no use to those who
are closest to it as they are struggling from day to day. We
may turn them into onlookers as we thoughtlessly display
our wealth, as we revel in an exchange rate beneficial
beyond our wildest expectations. We might degrade them
to the role of extras in our holiday movies and snapshots
or inflict on them the ultimate defeat of the human spirit,
which is prostitution.

Uwe Doll

Rio De Janeiro, 2005. Artwork by Wilhelm Finger.

Olafur Eliasson

The weather project, 2003 Turbine Hall, Tate Modern London (The Unilever series)
Photography by Nicoline L. Refsing.

Fran, Vanessa, Andrea and Warren.

Growing food on an allotment and saving seeds isn't exactly a revolutionary act is it? Well, across the world agriculture is in crisis as multinational corporations gain increasing control of the food chain. The UK has lost 90 per cent of its vegetable varieties in the past one hundred years, a loss of diversity every bit as damaging as the loss of rainforests. Meanwhile supermarkets have a stranglehold on the high street and have become so powerful they can make or break farmers. Currently, they pay farmers less for a pint of milk than it costs the farmers to produce. In Canada, farmer Percy Schmeiser was successfully sued by Monsanto for stealing their 'intellectual property rights'. His crime? Percy's land was contaminated by Monsanto's genetically modified rape seed. But the court ruled that he was stealing off Monsanto by infringing on the corporations patent rights!

Bio tech corporations that are trying to force feed us their genetically modified greens are also producing terminator seeds, which prevent poor farmers saving their own.

In Iraq, America just passed a law making it illegal for farmers to save seed! In India thousands of farmers have become enslaved by debt and committed suicide. So Seedy Sunday is a green two fingers up to those who control the food chain. And like all good ideas it's a simple one, swapping seeds with fellow gardeners to keep outlawed and old fashioned varieties alive. But across the world, saving seeds is becoming a matter of life and death.

Text by Warren (info@forestgarden.fsnet.co.uk). For further information go to www.seedysunday.org, www.percyschmeiser.com, www.grain.org

Jason Evans

Theres no Reason
why WORLD DEBT can't
be paid off
Tomorrow

Tracey Emin
2005.

Tracey Emin

418 make poverty history

Poverty is many things.

Emotional poverty is an inability to give.

Spiritual bankruptcy is an inability to love.

Educational destitution,

Leads to polluted institutions,

A soulless death,

An empty life.

And a waste of all we can be.

If knowing this, I still choose not to see,

Then poverty grows, nourished by me.

Caryn Franklin

It was our last day in Ghana. I'd been travelling around the poor rural north of the country with Chris Martin from Coldplay, i-D photographer Matt Jones and a team from Oxfam. It had been hard work, but after a grueling 14 hour drive back to the coast, we'd returned to the bustling modern capital Accra feeling that the job was done. That night we'd gone out for a meal to celebrate, sitting outside in the warm night air while a live band played requests for money. Sam, the likeable programme director of Oxfam Ghana, requested *Welcome Home* by Osibisa, the group that put Ghana on the map with their disco hits in the '70s. Chris requested a Bob Marley tune, an idea the band liked so much that they played several in a row, with us all singing along to every word. The following day the schedule promised 'informal interaction with Ghanaian musicians'. Sam was vague about the details, but we piled into the truck expecting to meet perhaps some of the band we'd seen the night before – a pleasant way of passing the last few hours before going to the airport. Chris had brought along a guitar in case it was needed, and on the way entertained us with Johnny Cash songs (his dad is a big fan of country music). But when we got to the hotel venue, he wisely slipped it out of sight, because it quickly became clear that this was no informal meeting after all. It was a conference gathering together some of the country's biggest cultural figures: not just musicians like veteran high-life star George Darko and Mac Tonto from Osibisa (now Ghana's Director of Culture), but also actors, producers, arrangers, writers. As Chris later commented, it was like sitting in a room with Ghana's equivalent of Bono, Thom Yorke, Mike Skinner, Jamelia, Nellee Hooper, Kate Winslet, Sam Mendes, Robbie Williams, Simon Pegg and Ant and Dec. They had gathered to talk about Fair Trade. Oxfam explained how Coldplay and other artists have helped raise awareness of the issue in the West; now they were hoping African artists might start to pressure their governments to defy the punitive rules laid down by the World Bank. Chris was embarrassed to be held up as an example, and quickly made it clear that he was here to listen and to learn. And learn is what we did, because although we both knew a fair bit about the music and film industries, once these artists began to speak – passionately, movingly, and with a fair bit of debate and disagreement amongst themselves – it was clear we knew nothing at all about their world. At first, the view seemed to be that there was no way struggling musicians and actors should fight for poor farmers. "We ourselves are endangered species. How do we champion any global cause?" asked one man. The actors talked of the lack of any local industry, with most films coming in from Nigeria. Mary Urenkyi, an older woman who had also once been well known on stage and TV, said she hadn't acted since the '80s because

as a single mother she simply couldn't make ends meet. Instead she now worked for the Forum for African Women, promoting education. She'd recently made a documentary about the huge numbers of girls dropping out of school because their parents can't pay the fees imposed by the World Bank. When she presented it to one of the main TV stations, they charged her money to show it. This was no news to the musicians. Western artists get paid when their music is played on the radio or TV; in Ghana, they have to pay the stations for the exposure. (This explains why nearly all the music I saw on TV there was gospel, funded by evangelist groups.) Musicians cannot afford to buy instruments, or to rehearse regularly. With no major record companies, artists have to set up labels of their own to release their music, often travelling to Europe and working menial jobs to raise the money for the next recording: "No matter how unprofessional the recording is, you have to release because otherwise you go hungry and your children will not eat," explained one musician bleakly. Panji Anoff, an articulate young producer with the most inventive facial hair I've seen for some time, also said there was little point pressuring Ghanaian politicians because their hands were tied by the stringent conditions the World Bank had imposed since Ghana accepted their loan in 1983. But slowly, the mood changed. "We have a wealth of talent and potential in this country," declared Rex Omar, pointing out that musicians have been central in spreading the word about HIV and AIDS. "Why are we acting as if we are nobodies? We have influence!" Singer Kojo Antwi pointed out that trade affects everyone. If farmers had more money, they'd be able to spend some of it on entertainment. People would hire live bands for weddings again. They would buy records, go to concerts, movies and plays. Amandzeba Nat Brew is the leader of a popular 24-piece band, but he said he wasn't just speaking as a musician when he supported Fair Trade. "In Africa, everyone is a farmer or a hunter. I come from the coast, so I am a fisherman, and I see big foreign trawlers coming in, dumping fish on our markets, so the local fisherman in their small boats cannot compete. The chicken we eat is imported, the rice is imported. This is why we are dying." Fired up by such talk, the artists agreed to keep on meeting, to keep discussing what they could do. And as we all chatted over drinks round the hotel pool afterwards, the differences fell away. Chris Martin and Panji Anoff quickly found a shared love of the Neptunes and Timbaland. I met one of the country's biggest rap duos, who had heard Shystie and Dizzee Rascal via cousins in the UK and were keen to incorporate more garage/grime sounds into their own mix of hip hop and Ghanaian high-life.

We saw many things in Africa that stayed with us long after we'd gone home. Early one morning in the fields, we met Nyaba Atampugre, a skinny 18 year-old in a ragged Adidas tracksuit that barely fitted him anymore but was still clearly his pride and joy. His sole income came from a patch of land which he tended with a primitive hoe made of stick and stone to somehow produce tomatoes. But he couldn't sell them because the markets had been flooded with tins of cheap tomato paste from Italy. Once there'd been a canning plant in his area, run by the government. But after Ghana took its loan in 1983 all state-run enterprises had to be sold off, and there was no buyer for this remote tomato business in the north. So it closed, and now middle-men come along when the tomatoes are so ripe they are falling off the vine, and he has no choice but to sell his crop at a knockdown price.

We went to a club one memorable evening in Bolgatanga just by the border with Burkina Faso, where Aaliyah and Missy Elliott mingled on the decks with local hip hop, where the girls teased on the dancefloor, the boys tried to stay cool and the atmosphere was heavy with sex and cigarettes and longing just like any other club anywhere in the world. That night in the guesthouse where we were staying, most of us lay awake all night listening to the sound of drums: apparently an old lady had died in a neighbouring village. When we passed back through the same area the following afternoon, the urgent rhythms were still going. "They must have loved that lady," says Chris, and Sam simply shrugs. "Of course!" In closeknit communities like these, the old don't die unnoticed. "We may be poor economically," Sam points out over dinner that night, "but socially we are rich." In Accra especially we met many people like Sam: lawyers, journalists, activists, educated people who had often been offered big jobs in the West but decided to go home because they genuinely believe life is better there. All of this stayed with us, but a few weeks later I was chatting to Chris on the phone and what had moved us both most was that last, unexpected day. "That really got to me," he said, "because the artists we met were just as talented as me – if not more so – and just as intelligent, but with different opportunities. It was fucked up, wasn't it?" When Coldplay started, they rehearsed every day not because they wanted to be rich but because they wanted to be good, because they felt they had something to say. I'm pretty sure that had they been born elsewhere, Chris, Jonny, Guy and Will would still be making music. As one of the actresses at the conference remarked, "This is a calling. It is something we feel we have to do." But I'm just as sure that if the stylish producer Panji Anoff or some of the rappers I'd talked to afterwards had been born in the UK, they'd be regular fixtures in magazines like this, their obvious talents recognised and supported.

It's weird to think how different life would be for any of us if we'd been born elsewhere. Ghana, like many developing countries, is prevented from moving forward by the West. Farmers are starving, artists are struggling – and all of this could be prevented by a few small changes to our trade rules. Most us don't know about the trade barriers imposed by the World Bank, we don't know that governments in peaceful, democratic countries like Ghana aren't allowed to control foreign imports or help their own people. And if we do know, we feel helpless to do anything about it. But we too have more influence than we think. Politicians want our votes and if enough of us speak, they tend to listen. You can find out more at www.maketradefair.com.

Sheryl Garratt

The Commission for Africa finds the "condition" of the majority

of Africans to be intolerable + an affront to the dignity

of all mankind. We insist upon an alternative

of these conditions through a re-alignment of policy

instruments — in favour of the weak. Here conclude with analyse + costs

an analysis of how this may be achieved + call finally

for these conditions to be implemented now in the name of

our shared humanity.

right, justice and in the name of

On the edge of this new century, in an age of unprecedented wealth

+ financial progress on nearly all continents Africa drifts

further from us all, unseen in its misery + ignored in its weakness.

As remote as it has for 2000 years the Dark Africa, is kept obscure by our

indifference + our fear that were we to cast our

unwelcome light onto it, economic likelihood

we would only reveal the empty mirror image of our success

our dark secret, our moral void which is our indifference.

which is not a failure, it is worse, it is indifference.

The darkness is in the ed ours, but ours is our moral failure.

The Commission

We have assembled the analysis of yours + all extant contemporary reports into our

conditions + while some are now redundant all of them show show clearly how

things may have been Africa.

However we exist in contemporary realities. The world is vastly different now

to 20 years ago when the world forcefully acknowledged the pity of the great famine

of 1984:85.

Our world locked into its political stasis of the cold war and its equivalence of

terror remained rigid in its competitive ideologies. Trade consequently

First draft written on the plane coming back from the Ethiopian capital, Addis Ababa, November 2004

Commission for Africa

DECLARATION

The Commission for Africa finds the condition of the lives of the majority of Africans to be intolerable and an affront to the dignity of all mankind. We insist upon an alteration of these conditions through a change of policy in favour of the weak.

Having analysed and costed how this may be achieved, we call for our conclusions to be implemented forthwith in the cause of right and justice and in the name of our shared humanity.

On the edge of this new century, in an age of unprecedented wealth and economic progress by all continents, it is unacceptable that Africa drifts further from the rest of the world, unseen in its misery and ignored in its pain.

The Commission, its members acting in their capacity as individuals, has assimilated the analysis of years and all extant reports into our findings. These clearly show how things may have been otherwise.

However we exist in contemporary realities. The world is vastly different to that of 20 years ago when we forcefully acknowledged the pity of the Great African Famine of 1984-85. The world, then locked into its Cold War political stasis, remained rigid in its competitive ideologies. The breaking of this deadlock, and the increase in global trade that followed, allied to new technologies and cultural shifts, have created a more fluid, less predictive yet more interdependent world.

This world in flux has brought great opportunities along with confusion, change and anxiety. But such change poses great possibilities for us all and especially for Africa, that great giant finally beginning to stir itself from its enforced slumber. We need, then, to seek to understand these newer forces in play about us, attempt to define them and in so doing set the framework for policies that favour the poor.

The great nations of the world, in alliance with their African neighbours, must now move together, in our common interest. How they may proceed will be determined by each nation's needs and desires. But all must immediately begin the journey that leads us to the ultimate common destination of a more equitable world.

Our task was the first step. It is done.

11 March 2005

Bob Geldof

Prime Minister Tony Blair	Dr William S Kalema
Fola Adeola	Trevor Manuel
K. Y. Amoako	President Benjamin Mkapa
Senator Nancy Kassebaum-Baker	Linah Mohohlo
Rt Hon Hilary Benn MP	Ji Peiding
Rt Hon Gordon Brown MP	Tidjane Thiam
Michel Camdessus	Dr Anna Kajumulo Tibaijuka
Bob Geldof	Prime Minister Meles Zenawi
Hon Ralph Goodale PC MP	

Four hundred million cotton farmers in the developing world are living in conditions of abject poverty due the collapsed world price of cotton due to US and EU and Chinese cotton subsidies and due to high costs and negative health impacts of pesticides used on cotton (25 per cent of world pesticides).

Between 20,000 people per annum (WHO figures) and 100,000 people plus per annum (Pesticide Action Network) are dying of accidental pesticide poisoning. Up to one million per annum are suffering from acute long-term poisonings. Two hundred thousand farmers commit suicide per year. Conventional cotton farming also causes long-term contamination of aquifers, rivers, and desertification. However growing cotton organically can reverse this situation, it delivers a 50 per cent increase in income by cutting cost of inputs by 40 per cent and allowing farmers to access the 20 per cent premium for certified organic. It allows them to feed and educate their children, dig wells and afford healthcare. It makes agriculture viable, it stems migration to the cities and helps stop the accompanying spread of HIV. Farmers do get a drop in yield initially but this is more than compensated for by the drop in cost of inputs. Organic cotton is neither brown or lumpy, it's an identical fibre to non-organic cotton – if you're in any doubt about this visit the V&A textile dept or the Bath Museum and look closely at pre-1840 clothing and you will see that the cotton, all organic, is a finer quality than virtually anything on the market today. It's marginally more expensive. Typically the value to the farmer of the cotton in a T-shirt is four to five per cent, organic cotton fibre is 20 per cent more expensive than conventional cottons. Conventional cotton agriculture in Africa is bordering on collapse. An African farmer said to me, "When we have sold our crop we have nothing left." Growing cotton organically tips the balance for them from extinction to beyond survival. It makes farmers' communities sustainable. All of this without outside international aid, all of this for one per cent more on the price of a T-shirt. Another farmer in Africa said to me, "When we grow cotton organically all the money is ours and we have our health." It's unarguable. People say what can we do? Use your power as a consumer. Industry listens to consumers even if governments don't. Buy one organic cotton garment this year. Write to your favourite brands and tell them you love their stuff, have bought loads in the past but in three years time you want all the cotton that you buy from them to be organic and if they don't have it you won't buy from them anymore until it is.

Katharine Hamnett

Cut the imperial red tape!
Press shift!
Make History!

Terry Jones

As a stone ripples the water so we all have the ability and responsibility to spread ideas and actions. Accept the challenge: believe in the power each one of us has to create change and act accordingly.

A challenge to all politicians: Prove to us that you are not in the hands of big business. Make your money from taxing junk food and benefit the health of the nation and the world by subsidising organic and fairtrade food.

...To remember when you drink your next cup of coffee!

On top of the Fair Trade price a 'Social Premium' is paid to the producer's cooperative for education and health care. Producers are paid up to three times more than conventional world market prices. Environmental benefits: Fair Trade cuts down on pesticide use improving the soil, worker's health and protecting wildlife.

Coffee has been produced for more than 100 years in Honduras and is one of the country's main exports. More than 112,000 families grow coffee and ten per cent of the population is dependent on coffee for its livelihood.

The fall in coffee prices has created a major crisis in the Honduran economy, and is having a devastating effect on the lives of everyone who depends on it. Coffee farmers are being forced to sell their coffee at prices which do not allow them to cover their basic needs. Many are no longer able to afford basic medicines, are cutting back on food, and are pulling their children out of school. Seasonal workers are being laid off as the land-owners can no longer afford to pay them.

One of those farmers is Marta Alicia Zepeda: "I am 36 years old. I work in the national Post Office here in San Juancito, and I also have my own shop in the Post Office where I sell school books and materials. Coffee is our family's main source of income. I own a coffee plantation of 15 manzanas (25.5 hectares). As a farmer I am privileged because I work in Fair Trade. This means that at the moment, I get $125 per 100 lbs. If the price of coffee increases then I will be paid the difference but if it falls I will receive the same amount.

My message to big companies would be this: stop playing with the lives of coffee producers. It is the big producers who have all the influence – we, the small producers, don't have a voice or vote. Please continue your efforts to make trade fair. Remember that we are behind you, and there are millions of us."

Extract from the PEDEC FairTrade guide with thanks. For more information go to www.maketradefair.com.

Tricia Jones

MAKE POVERTY HISTORY – TAX:

APATHY BIGOTRY COMPLEXITY DEVIOUSNESS EXPLOITATION FASCISM GREED

NATIONALISM OPPRESSION PHILISTINISM QUITTERS RACISM SELFISHNESS TORTURE

HATE ISOLATIONISM JINGOISM KNAVERY LETHARGY MENDACIOUSNESS

UNFAIRNESS VICTIMIZATION WASTE XENOPHOBIA YOBBERY ZEALOTS

Nick Knight

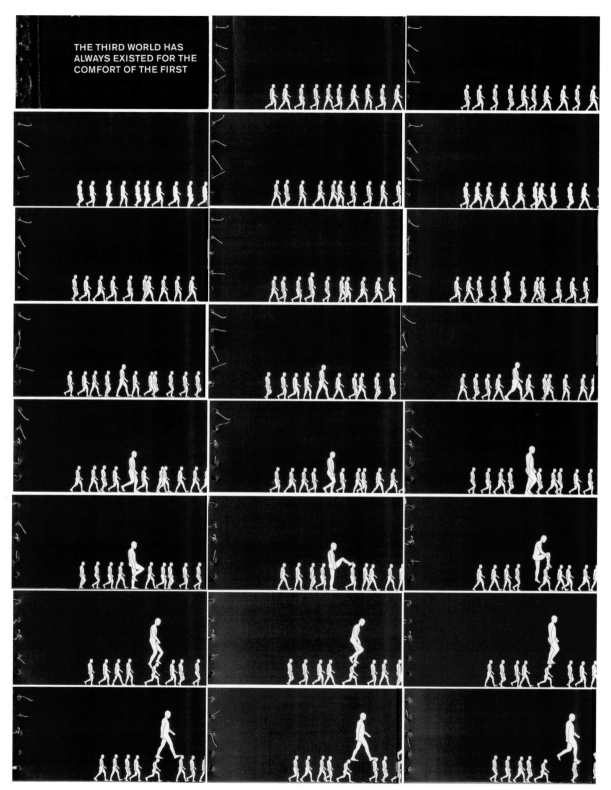

THE THIRD WORLD HAS ALWAYS EXISTED FOR THE COMFORT OF THE FIRST

Pages from a flick book, 2003.

The third world has always existed for the comfort of the first. Naomi Klein.

Jessica Landon

Sometimes we are all hungry... for love, but we live in fear anger and resentment...

STOP HUNGER
sooner better
Later greater

NOW's the best.

Live in Faith, Love and Acceptance.
4 ^ ever Be Live

Shirt and T-shirt by Dave Baby. Many thanks to A.Grey for her inspiration, and to LCF and The University of the Arts London, for their continued support.

Mark Lebon

Photography by Frank Lebon, age 11.

She explodes into the room. There are hugs, kisses and – above all – there is laughter. Wangari Maathai, Nobel Peace Prize winner and tree planter extraordinaire, settles herself down. "These days everyone seems to want to chat to me," she says. "I never dreamt I would be so popular." There is a further bout of deep, infectious laughter. Maathai, a young looking 65 year old, has suddenly become one of Africa's most well known people. For the last 30 years Maathai has fought to preserve the environment in her native Kenya and elsewhere in Africa. Then, in November last year, she was awarded the Nobel Peace Prize – the first woman in Africa to win the coveted award. "We have to manage resources like water, forests, land and oil: if not we will lose the fight against poverty and then there will be no peace," says Maathai. "This is a matter of life and death." Wangari Maathai's main claim to fame is connected with her statistically mind-boggling tree planting activities. Back in the mid-'70s Maathai, a professor of biological sciences, was becoming increasingly concerned about deforestation around her home in Nyeri, in Kenya's uplands north of Nairobi, the capital. Together with a group of local women – mostly peasant farmers – she founded the Green Belt Movement, which over the last 30 years has been responsible for planting between 20 and 30 million trees throughout Africa. "I love trees, I love the colour," says Maathai, known as Africa's 'Forest Goddess'. "To me they represent hope. I think it's the green colour." There's a further bout of laughter. "I tell people I think heaven is green." Maathai has had to endure some very tough times. She became involved in fighting for women's rights. "In Africa it's the women who bear the burden, not the men," says Maathai. "We've been waiting for men to change. We women have an important role in challenging them to be responsible to us and to our children – to stop sending them off to die on the front lines. We see our children dying in the fields, we see the future slipping away. I've been calling on Africa's leaders, who are mostly men, to make sure resources are exploited for people's benefit, to help them out of poverty, ignorance and disease." In the 1980s Maathai's marriage ended in divorce: her husband described her as "too educated, too strong, too successful, too stubborn and too hard to control". Shortly afterwards the Nobel Peace Prize winner fell foul of Kenya's then ruler, the dictator Daniel Arap Moi. After questioning various shady business deals involving Moi and his supporters, Maathai received a series of death threats. She and her two children fled the country. "They (Moi's politicians) are so incompetent that every time they feel the heat because women are challenging them, they have to check their genitalia, if only to reassure themselves. I'm not interested in that part of the anatomy. The issues I'm dealing with require the utilisation of what is above the neck," said Maathai at that time. Returning to Kenya Maathai was imprisoned and beaten unconscious by police for protesting about human rights abuses. When she was released she led a protest in which she and a group of women supporters took their clothes off in central Nairobi. Since 2002 Maathai has been a minister in the government of Mwai Kibaki, Moi's successor. Now she is part of the political establishment. "That makes me sound too respectable," says Maathai. "I hope I can still cause a stir," she says, slapping her thigh and laughing. "You've always got to create waves – it's the only way to get things done."

For more information check out www.wangari-maathai.org
Text by Kieran Cooke.

"My inspiration partly comes from my childhood experiences and observations of nature in rural Kenya. It has been influenced and nurtured by the formal education I was privileged to receive in Kenya, the United States and Germany. As I was growing up, I witnessed forests being cleared and replaced by commercial plantations, which destroyed local biodiversity and the capacity of the forests to conserve water.

In 1977, when we started the Green Belt Movement, I was partly responding to needs identified by rural women, namely lack of firewood, clean drinking water, balanced diets, shelter and income. Throughout Africa, women are the primary caretakers, holding significant responsibility for tilling the land and feeding their families. As a result, they are often the first to become aware of environmental damage as resources become scarce and incapable of sustaining their families. The women we worked with recounted that unlike in the past, they were unable to meet their basic needs. This was due to the degradation of their immediate environment as well as the introduction of commercial farming, which replaced the growing of household food crops. But international trade controlled the price of the exports from these small scale farmers and a reasonable and just income could not be guaranteed. I came to understand that when the environment is destroyed, plundered or mismanaged, we undermine our quality of life and that of future generations.

Initially, the work was difficult because historically our people have been persuaded to believe that because they are poor, they lack not only capital, but also knowledge and skills to address their challenges. Instead they are conditioned to believe that solutions to their problems must come from 'outside'. Further, women did not realise that meeting their needs depended on their environment being healthy and well managed. They were also unaware that a degraded environment leads to a scramble for scarce resources and may culminate in poverty and even conflict. They were also unaware of the injustices of international economic arrangements.

In the process, the participants discover that they must be part of the solutions. They realise their hidden potential and are empowered to overcome inertia and take action. They come to recognise that they are the primary custodians and beneficiaries of the environment that sustains them.

In time, the tree also became a symbol for peace and conflict resolution, especially during ethnic conflicts in Kenya when the Green Belt Movement used peace trees to reconcile disputing communities. During the ongoing rewriting of the Kenyan constitution, similar trees of peace were planted in many parts of the country to promote a culture of peace. Using trees as a symbol of peace is in keeping with a widespread African tradition. For example, the elders of the Kikuyu carried a staff from the thigi tree that, when placed between two disputing sides, caused them to stop fighting and seek reconciliation. Many communities in Africa have these traditions.

Such practises are part of an extensive cultural heritage, which contributes both to the conservation of habitats and to cultures of peace. With the destruction of these cultures and the introduction of new values, local biodiversity is no longer valued or protected and as a result, it is quickly degraded and disappears. For this reason, the Green Belt Movement explores the concept of cultural biodiversity, especially with respect to indigenous seeds and medicinal plants.

It is 30 years since we started this work. Activities that devastate the environment and societies continue unabated. Today we are faced with a challenge that calls for a shift in our thinking, so that humanity stops threatening its life-support system. We are called to assist the Earth to heal her wounds and in the process heal our own – indeed, to embrace the whole creation in all its diversity, beauty and wonder. This will happen if we see the need to revive our sense of belonging to a larger family of life, with which we have shared our evolutionary process.

In the course of history, there comes a time when humanity is called to shift to a new level of consciousness, to reach a higher moral ground. A time when we have to shed our fear and give hope to each other. Those of us who have been privileged to receive education, skills, and experiences and even power must be role models for the next generation of leadership. In this regard, I would also like to appeal for the freedom of my fellow laureate Aung San Suu Kyi so that she can continue her work for peace and democracy for the people of Burma and the world at large. There is also need to galvanise civil society and grassroots movements to catalyse change. I call upon governments to recognise the role of these social movements in building a critical mass of responsible citizens, who help maintain checks and balances in society. On their part, civil society should embrace not only their rights but also their responsibilities. Further, industry and global institutions must appreciate that ensuring economic justice, equity and ecological integrity are of greater value than profits at any cost.

As I conclude I reflect on my childhood experience when I would visit a stream next to our home to fetch water for my mother. I would drink water straight from the stream. Playing among the arrowroot leaves I tried in vain to pick up the strands of frogs' eggs, believing they were beads. But every time I put my little fingers under them they would break. Later, I saw thousands of tadpoles: black, energetic and wriggling through the clear water against the background of the brown earth. This is the world I inherited from my parents.

Today, over 50 years later, the stream has dried up, women walk long distances for water, which is not always clean, and children will never know what they have lost. The challenge is to restore the home of the tadpoles and give back to our children a world of beauty and wonder."

Text taken from Wangari Maathai's Nobel Peace Prize acceptance speech, 2004.

Prof. Wangari Maathai

We have got to stop feeling so insignificant and know that we all can make a difference. Sponsoring a child costs £15 a month.

Go to www.actionaid.org.uk

Matt Jones

Photography by Matt Jones.

I went to Ghana recently, travelling to the north of the country with Oxfam to see how the trade rules work against poor farmers. At the time, I wasn't sure what the kind of low-level subsistence farming we were seeing had to do with world trade. But when Ghana asked for a loan from the World Bank in 1983, they were subsidising farmers like these – who make up 60 per cent of the population by giving them cheap fertiliser and seeds. When the loan came in, they had to prioritise paying it back with interest, so anything that wasn't high profit-making was put on a back burner. In Ghana they prioritised gold and timber, which only two per cent of the population are involved in but which obviously make a lot of profit. The farmers got dropped, and that's why it's a real struggle for them now.

Which is how it links in with Fair Trade – a lot of developing countries were prevented from looking after their own people by trade rules imposed on them from outside. The World Bank needs to take interest in the lives of real people, not just look at the profit balances.

The good thing is that everybody in the world seems to be learning more about these issues. A few years ago, no one really talked about it, no one knew there was a problem. Now we do. That's the first step towards change. And in Ghana, we saw peasant farmers banding together to make their voices heard too. It's not all negative. If we all make our feelings clear to politicians who want our votes, we can force these institutions to change.

Chris Martin

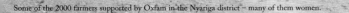

Some of the 2000 farmers supported by Oxfam in the Nyariga district – many of them women.

A farmer in one of the three Weiga rice valleys, vast natural basins with fertile soils that can only be used after the raining season due to lack of irrigation. With £600,000 spent on irrigation, a combine harvester and a few tractors, these valleys could produce enough rice all year round to feed the whole of Ghana.

In Zugu, a traditional village where the rice and maize farmers were no longer able to make a living due to the cheap US rice flooding the local markets.

Alexander McQueen

ROMA
26.3.2005

This image of an installation made by a homeless street artist is part of a series of his personal reflections on what life means living in poverty. In this case what does fashion mean when you have no money to buy food, let alone clothes? The task of ending poverty is everybody's responsibility for the future – governments, companies, individuals. For a FAIR successful living.

Renzo Rosso

A dream you dream alone is only a dream, but a dream we dream together is reality.

Yoko Ono

Chumbe Island is a tiny educational and eco-tourism project 40 minutes' boat ride from Zanzibar, where the community leaders are educating local fishermen to protect the coral and marine life of the area. Frequent trips are organised with schools from the mainland and a resource area is available. Khamis Ali Pandu, 23, was a ranger and student at Chumbe Island. Nine eco-huts are available for intrepid and eco-minded travellers to stay in.

Khamis Ali Pandu, 23, Tanzanian
What makes you angry? Low education of most Africans, selfishness of many leaders, the undermining of women in African societies, prestige leaders that have led civil war in Africa; nepotism in terms of employment. **What are your hopes for the future?** I look forward to being a good mirror in my society. The only thing that helps me is education so I shall try to achieve my best level in education.

What would make the world a better place?
To stop pollution, emission of poisons from industries, freedom of press in African societies, to invest in education because it is there for all. I should like to avoid all ways that allow erosion of the land to take place, strengthen democracy.
Favourite books? Geography books, novel books which show African society, for example. *Things Fall Apart, The Beautiful Are Never Yet Born* and other books concerned with different societies and things all over the world. **How would you like to influence the future?** I would like to get some assistance in order to improve my view for myself and my society. Really without some aid it is difficult to achieve, especially in terms of education. My family is so poor so I want to change my society which is falling into trouble. **Who and what has inspired you?** (Some trouble that occurs in our societies like early pregnancies, the increase in uneducated persons in my society and trouble with our leaders). Also inspirational leaders such as Jomo Kenyatta from Kenya as well as the late Julius K Nyerere from Tanzania, due to their policies during the struggle for independence and economic strength.

Khamis Ali Pandu

I believe that if western governments are to help, they have to put the poor first as active participants, advisors and leaders because the only true experts on poverty are the poor.

Anita Roddick

Kris Ruhs

Why don't we pay for air?

Rainforests provide most of our planet's oxygen. The forested nations hold the most valuable resource on earth. What if we were to prioritise between oil and air?

Surely we should pay these nations for the air we use?

F<u>air</u> trade would change the economic map.

Peter Saville

Photography Parris Wakefield, Saville Associates

The cover story of *Time* magazine of March 14, 2005 was dedicated to the theme "How to End Poverty". The photos accompanying the essay are homeless children, scavengers in garbage dumps, heroin addicts. These are images of disposable people, people whose lives, resources, livelihoods have been snatched from them by a brutal, unjust, excluding process which generates poverty for the majority and prosperity for a few.

Garbage is the waste of a throwaway society – ecological societies have never had garbage. Homeless children are the consequences of impoverishment of communities and families who have lost their resources and livelihoods. These are images of the perversion and externalities of a non-sustainable, unjust, inequitable economic growth model.

It is useful to separate a cultural conception of simple, sustainable living as poverty from the material experience of poverty that is a result of dispossession and deprivation. Culturally perceived poverty need not be real material poverty: sustenance economies, which satisfy basic needs through self-provisioning, are not poor in the sense of being deprived. Yet the ideology of development declares them so because they do not participate overwhelmingly in the market economy, and do not consume commodities produced for and distributed through the market even though they might be satisfying those needs through self-provisioning mechanisms. People are perceived as poor if they eat millets (grown by women) rather than commercially produced and distributed processed junk foods sold by global agri-business. They are seen as poor if they live in self-built housing made from ecologically-adapted natural material like bamboo and mud rather than in cement houses. They are seen as poor if they wear handmade garments of natural fibre rather than synthetics. Sustenance, as culturally perceived poverty, does not necessarily imply a low physical quality of life. On the contrary, because sustenance economies contribute to the growth of nature's economy and the social economy, they ensure a high quality of life measure in terms of right to food and water, sustainability of livelihoods, and robust social and cultural identity and meaning.

On the other hand, the poverty of the one billion hungry and the one billion malnutritioned people who are victims of obesity suffer from both cultural and material poverty. A system that creates denial and disease, while accumulating trillions of dollars of super profits for agri-business, is a system for creating poverty for people. Poverty is a final state, not an initial state of an economic paradigm, which destroys ecological and social systems for maintaining life, health and sustenance of the planet and people. And economic poverty is only one form of poverty. Cultural poverty, social poverty, ethical poverty, ecological poverty and spiritual poverty are other forms of poverty more prevalent in the so called rich North than in the so called poor South. And those other poverties cannot be overcome by dollars. They need compassion and justice, caring and sharing. Ending poverty requires knowing how poverty is created. The poor are not those who were left behind, they are the ones who were pushed out and excluded from access to their own wealth and resources.

The poor are not poor because they are lazy or their governments are corrupt. They are poor because their wealth has been appropriated and wealth-creating capacity destroyed. The riches accumulated by Europe were based on riches appropriated from Asia, Africa and Latin America. Without the destruction of India's rich textile industry, without the take-over of the spice trade, without the genocide of the native American tribes, without the Africa's slavery, the industrial revolution would not have led to new riches for Europe or the U.S. It was the violent take-over of Third World resources and Third World markets that created wealth in the North – but it simultaneously created poverty in the South.

One of the myths that separates affluence from poverty is the assumption that if you produce what you consume, you do not produce. This is the basis on which the production boundary is drawn for national accounting that measures economic growth. This myth contributes to the mystification of growth and consumerism, but it also hides the real processes that create poverty. First, the market economy dominated by capital is not the only economy, development has, however, been based on the growth of the market economy. The invisible costs of development have been the destruction of two other economies: nature's processes and people's survival. The ignorance or neglect of these two vital economies is the reason why development has posed a threat of ecological destruction and a threat to human survival, both of which, however, have remained 'hidden negative externalities' of the development process. Instead of being seen as results of exclusion, they are presented as "those left behind". Instead of being viewed as those who suffer the worst burden of unjust growth in the form of poverty, they are falsely presented as those not touched by growth. Without clean water, fertile soils and crop and plant genetic diversity, human survival is not possible.

People do not die for lack of incomes. They die for lack of access to resources. The indigenous people in the Amazon, the mountain communities in the Himalayas, peasants whose land has not been appropriated and whose water and biodiversity has not been destroyed by debt-creating industrial agriculture are ecologically rich, even though they do not earn a dollar a day. On the other hand, even at five dollars a day, people are poor if they have to buy their basic needs at high prices. Indian peasants who have been made poor and pushed into debt over the past decade to create markets for costly seeds and agri-chemicals through economic globalisation are ending their lives in thousands. When seeds are patented and peasants will pay $1 trillion in royalties, they will be $1 trillion poorer. Patents on medicines increase costs of AIDS drugs from $200 to $20,000, and cancer drugs from $2,400 to $36,000 for a year's treatment. When water is privatised, and global corporations make $1 trillion from commodification of water, the poor are poorer by $1 trillion.

The $50 billion of "aid" North to South is a tenth of $500 billion flow South to North as interest payments and other unjust mechanisms in the global economy imposed by the World Bank, the IMF. With privatisation of essential services and an unfair globalisation imposed through W.T.O., the poor are being made poorer. Indian peasants are losing $26 billion annually just in falling farm prices because of dumping and trade liberalisation. As a result of unfair, unjust globalisation, this is leading to corporate takeover of food and water. More than $5 trillion will be transferred from poor people to rich countries just for food and water. The poor are financing the rich. If we are serious about ending poverty, we have to be serious about ending the unjust and violent systems for wealth creation which create poverty by robbing the poor of their resources, livelihoods and incomes.

Ending poverty is more a matter of taking less than giving an insignificant amount more.

Dr. Vandana Shiva

Politicians must learn to give enough time and energy to stamping out corruption and feeding the hungry (and not just at election time)!

Paul Smith

In developing countries, there is a culture of reuse and recycling. Waste collectors roam residential areas in large towns and cities in search of reusable articles. Some of the products that result from the processing of waste are particularly impressive and the levels of skill and ingenuity are high.

Recycling artisans have integrated themselves into the traditional market place and have created a viable livelihood for themselves in this sector.

In Karachi, Pakistan, for example, tyres are collected and cut into parts to obtain secondary materials which can be put to good use. The beads of the tyres are removed and the rubber removed by burning to expose the steel. The tread and sidewalls are separated, the tread is cut into thin strips and used to cover the wheels of donkey carts, while the side walls are used for production of items such as shoe soles, slippers and washers.

Extract taken from Waren Report, Intermediate Technology Development Group. Go to www.itdg.org and www.wrf.org.uk

Marcia Taylor

Tennekoon was the inspiration and life force behind a unique Sri Lankan experience. Born in 1933, he died on February 5 2005, but through the village of Ulpotha his vision and work will live on.

Tennekoon's idea was simple: to bring back to the people of Sri Lanka a system of agriculture and irrigation which existed before the British colonised the island.

As a result, Ulpotha has an amazing fresh water 'tank' (lake) which feeds the fields where the villagers have been cultivating different varieties of indigenous and organic rice. This is a very special experiment because not only has it become a relatively self-sufficient community, but it also invites visitors to stay during certain months of the year. In keeping with his wishes, he was buried as he wanted and a Dhung tree was planted at his feet and a Kon tree at his head. He said birds loved these trees and he liked the idea of his remains giving sustenance to the tree and the tree in turn being enjoyed by the birds.

For more information, go to www.ulpotha.com
Tennekoon photographed in 2002 on the village ox-cart – his favourite mode of transport!

Tennekoon

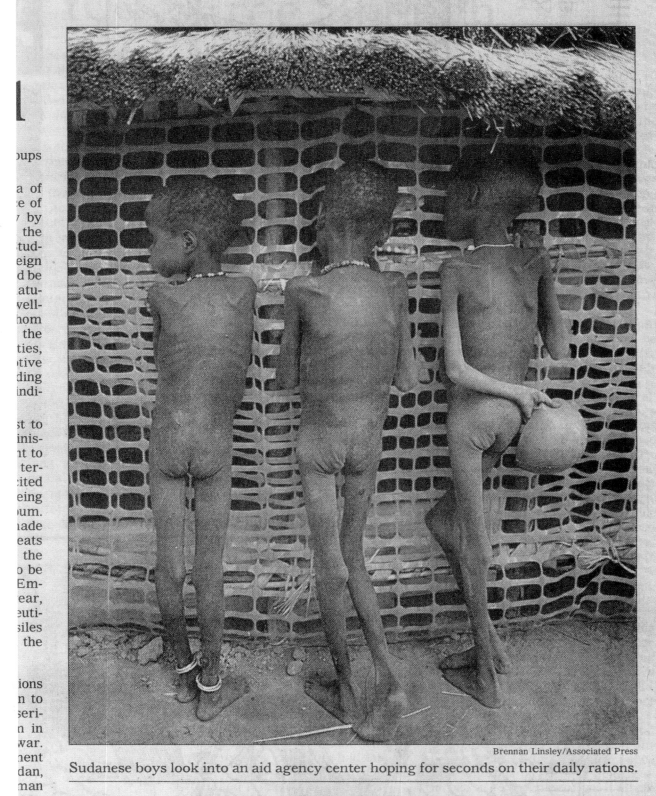

Brennan Linsley/Associated Press

Sudanese boys look into an aid agency center hoping for seconds on their daily rations.

Washington has restated its determination to isolate Khartoum. But this may prove

of China's largest state enterprises, has invested in Sudan's oil fields and is planning

Wolfgang Tillmans
The Colour of Money, 2004 (City of London,

445

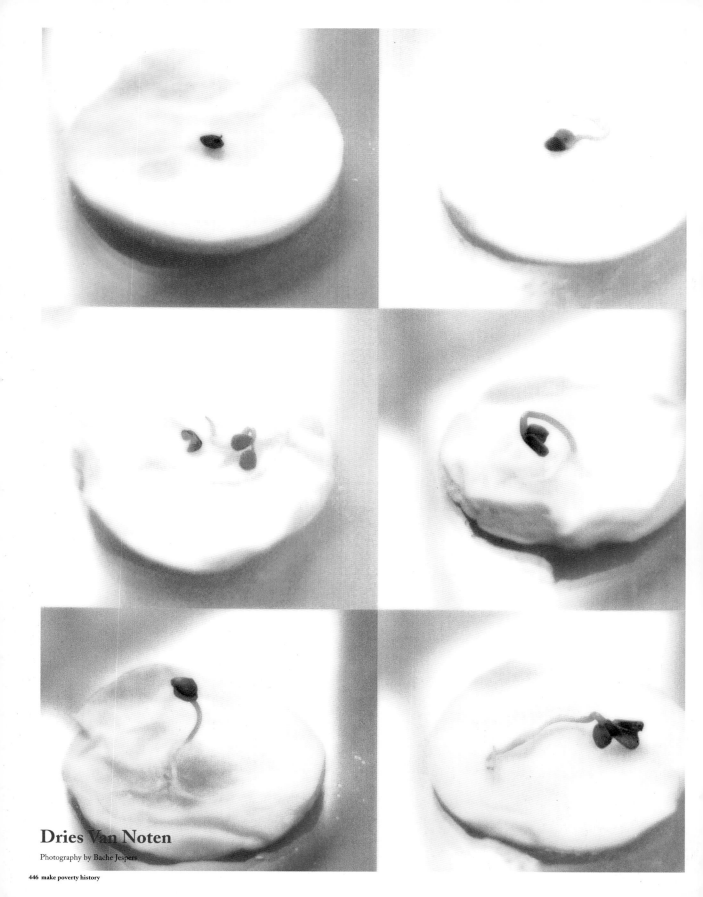

Dries Van Noten

Photography by Bache Jespers

THE DESIRE TO USE FOOTBALL AS
AN ENGINE FOR EDUCATION TO
TRANSMIT THE KNOWLEDGE TO OUR
KIDS AND TO THE NEW GENERATION.
THE BEST CONDITION IS THE WAY
WE DO IT ON THE PITCH.

KEEP THE BALL MOVING.

Patrick Vieira

Patrick Vieira

(RED)

GIORGIO ARMANI ON WHY WE HAVE A

ALERT

RESPONSIBILITY TO SAVE OUR SOULS

I make no claim to be an expert on world affairs, and I am entirely aware that as a fashion designer I am involved in an industry which many consider – quite rightly – to be essentially ephemeral in the impact it has on most people's lives. I write this therefore as an ordinary man. And like ordinary men everywhere I observe the world around me, and some of what I see saddens me. In particular, I see a place where the innocence of childhood is being eroded by hardship and sickness, by fear and danger and poverty. What I take from this is that we are witnessing the end of The Age of Innocence. >>

The English poet William Blake said that innocence and experience were "the two contrary states of the human soul". If that is so, then what a dear loss the loss of innocence is.

I had my childhood taken from me by the Second World War, and so I can empathise with the kids I see in the papers or on TV who are also losing that special piece of their lives. And it seems to me that today too many children are growing up in situations where the innocence and naivety of childhood that is rightly theirs is snatched away too early through war, famine, poverty or disease.

Every day we see images of children who have suffered this fate in Iraq, in Lebanon, in Sudan – the list goes on. There are so many conflicts in the world, so many countries defined as being in poverty, so many children

"SINCE LAUNCH (RED) HAS RAISED $57 MILLION, BUT THERE IS STILL SO MUCH TO BE DONE WHEN YOU CONSIDER THAT 1,000 CHILDREN ARE INFECTED WITH HIV EACH DAY IN AFRICA"

living with AIDS, inherited at birth, so many others living with unclean water or without enough to eat, so many orphans, abandoned to a cruel fate. For all of these children there has been no age of innocence nor will there be.

So when Bono and Bobby Shriver told me about their business idea for (RED), I signed up straight away. What a brilliant concept – sell consumers products they want and give a percentage of profits directly to the Global Fund, to help fight AIDS in Africa. In the case of Armani, we contribute 40 per cent. In this way, maybe we can make a real difference.

I am proud of Armani's involvement with RED). In just under two years since its UK launch on March 1, 2006, (RED) has contributed more than $57m to fight AIDS in Africa, with a focus on women and children, specifically in Swaziland, Rwanda and Ghana. It sounds a lot

but there's a lot more to do when you consider that 1,000 children are infected with HIV each day in Sub-Saharan Africa.

But it's a start, and a good one at that. Over 11.5m (RED) products were sold as of the end of 2006, and now (RED) contributes more to the Global Fund than 25 actual countries! That tells me that people can make a difference. And surely if there is one thing that we should all be able to agree upon, whatever our faith or race, it should be that we have an obligation to protect the age of innocence for the world's children, today, and for all our tomorrows? And who knows? By helping protect the character of their childish souls, we may perhaps find we recover some of that quality of innocence for ourselves?
For information go to www.armani.it (click on Emporio Armani), or www.joinred.com

ABOVE:
[Top left] Rose Uwabasinga, a 45-year-old grandmother (with Eliora Joyce, her granddaughter), has been HIV-positive for 12 years. She is vice-president of Rwanda's main national association for people living with HIV, whose activities are partly supported by (RED) funds.
[Top centre] A beneficiary of daycare at the Fonteyn neighbourhood care point.
[Top right] Inkhosikati LaMtsetfwa, head of Esitjeni KaGogo, one of almost 300 "kagogo"

("granny") centres in Swaziland that provide food and daycare for AIDS orphans and vulnerable children. *[Below left]* Denyse Mushimiyimana, a 9-year-old HIV-positive girl who is living a norma life with the help of antiretrovirals provided by Rwanda's national AIDS program, which is supported by (RED) funds.
[Below right] An Esitjeni Kagogo beneficiary, with a volunteer caregiver

Every Minute a Child Goes Blind

An estimated 1.4 million children are blind, up to a million of them merely because they lack access to adequate eye care. Imagine them all holding hands in a line that would stretch for an incredible 500 miles! Such a line would be front page news and cause a public outcry. But, instead, these children go unnoticed – out of sight and out of mind.

ORBIS, a nonprofit global development organization dedicated to saving sight worldwide, is working to change that.

Since 1982, ORBIS volunteers and staff have restored the vision and transformed the lives of more than 4.4 million people in 85 countries. At the same time, ORBIS has been building local capacity to provide eye care in those countries by training more than 154,000 eye care professionals aboard the ORBIS Flying Eye Hospital – the world's only airborne ophthalmic training facility – and in local hospitals in developing countries. Long-term national blindness prevention programs also take place in Bangladesh, China, Ethiopia, India and Vietnam.

The impact of ORBIS is far-reaching. But, the need remains great. We can and must do more to help the 37 million people in the world who are blind. To learn how, visit www.orbis.org.

Left Photography by Geoff Oliver Bugbee
Top Photography by Raul Vasquez

ORBIS
saving sight worldwide

Click Campaign, 2005.

Marcus Tomlinson

safe + sound

"To laugh often and much, to win the respect of intelligent people and the affection of children, to earn the appreciation of honest critics and endure the betrayal of false friends, to appreciate beauty, to find the best in others, to leave the world a bit better, whether by a healthy child, a garden patch… to know even one life has breathed easier because you have lived. This is to have succeeded!"

Ralph Waldo Emerson

safe+sound

The idea for this book was initiated by Mark Lebon, who approached Terry and I at the end of 2005 to say that one of his best photographic students at the London College of Fashion, Charlie Green, had been killed as a passenger in a drink related car accident. Mark had the idea to make something in memory of Charlie, but also to support young people at risk internationally. The title "Safe+Sound" was his, the request to make one of our special projects like Family Future Positive, Beyond Price and Learn and Pass it On. The brief was then mine, thinking how we could involve our contributors and what questions to ask. Initially my letter, too abstract this time I fear, was asking for positive stories of people who had inspired us by coming through difficult times including drugs, drink, anorexia, loneliness, depression or serious illness. However, as with the best projects this has grown organically and led by our contributors the contents have broadened and become more layered. We have difficult moments many times in our own lives. So the aim of this book has become to inspire, even in a small way, with personal stories and creative images and help all of us realise we are not alone.

Different people have earned and wear different life experience t-shirts and hopefully this book will show you some of those.

Once again a huge thank you to all of you who have found time in increasingly busy schedules to participate in this project. As always it's been a great pleasure and honour to be a part of it.

Tricia Jones 2007

Hootdrum is a youth project, run by professional musicians, that teaches kids from deprived inner city backgrounds to drum, dance and play percussion. It has organised workshops in over 100 schools involving 6,000 kids in the last five years, as well as in hospitals and mental health centres among children with extremely serious illnesses.

Drumming gives the kids a healthy, creative outlet for their energy and teaches them how to work together and socialise as a team. Many of the kids have attended weekly workshops for several years and some show massive musical potential.

Learning these new skills has a tremendous positive impact on their self-esteem and overall well-being. The three kids in the photographs (Christopher, Yassen and Isaac) all live on the Lisson Green and Church Street Estates – two of the most notoriously drug-ridden and dangerous estates in central London,

sandwiched between the extremely affluent areas of Marylebone and St John's Wood. They all come from single parent families (often with many siblings) except for one whose parents are together but sadly both HIV-positive.

Before they started drumming, the boys were considered the most unruly and disruptive in their primary school and probably headed for serious trouble.

Their behaviour in school, academic performance and social skills have all improved since drumming. These kids are truly amazing, with phenomenal energy and infectious enthusiasm. They are warm, witty and inspirational. The guys running Hootdrum invest tremendous amounts of love, time and energy to help improve the quality of life for some of London's most vulnerable kids – it's uplifting to watch! These pictures were coincidentally taken on July 7, 2006, exactly one year after the London bombings and show a side of London where people are coming together to create a more positive future.

Chidi Achara

"In sport we witness the struggle to excel, whether mentally or physically, and it is this inner drive that I admire above all. People are always fascinated by the bodies of athletes, but the secret of their motivation, ambition and passion can only be read in their faces and interpreted in their expressions. The faces of athletes at the Special Olympics invite the world to see their potential to achieve in a different light."

Giorgio Armani

friend |frend|

noun

a person whom one knows and with whom one has a bond of mutual affection, typically exclusive of sexual or family relations.
• a person who acts as a supporter of a cause, organisation, or country by giving financial or other help : *join the friends of Guilford Free Library.*
• a person who is not an enemy or who is on the same side : she was unsure whether he was **friend or foe**.
• a familiar or helpful thing : *he settled for that old friend the compensation grant.*
• (often as a polite form of address or ironic reference) an acquaintance or a stranger one comes across: *my friends, let me introduce myself.*
• (**Friend**) a member of the Religious Society of Friends; a Quaker.

verb [trans.] archaic or poetic/leterary
befriend (someone).

DERIVATIVES
friend.less adjective

ORIGIN Old English *fréond*, of Germanic origin related to Dutch **vriend** and German **Freund**, from an Indo-European root meaning 'to love', shared by **FREE**.

Extracted from OUP Oxford English Dictionary

Christopher Bailey

I am now more than halfway through my second year at university and more importantly, living away from home. The last 18 months have been an extremely hard and steep learning curve for me as a human being.

The biggest hurdle I have to overcome is 'loneliness'.

I feel after a year of extreme struggle I am coming out the other side allowing me to look at the emotions a lot more easily than if I was still in that particular state of mind.

Ben Benoliel

I have suffered with my black dog now for as long as I can remember and I still am. Sometimes I can feel really alone with my thoughts in the company of my black dog. Now as I am getting older I am beginning to realise that it is okay to feel; without these feelings I may not have begun to understand myself and life's ups and downs. I am starting to open my eyes to the important things like laughing, being around my boyfriend and mates, having a loving family and a beer on a nice sunny day.

I know my black dog will always be with me, but sometimes it's more fun not to have all the answers.

Clare Bennett

Happy and interesting and clever and fun
The change took place after a couple of months

Small white lies and ever more frequent mood swings
Which, at first, were ignored in the hope that they would end
But they continued, and it turned darker and more complicated
When one of the most unenviable of memoirs was bluntly uncovered

How to bandage the emotional wounds that had been inflicted
How to erase the non-memories causing so much pain
How to put a stop to the self-hatred and deliberate deterioration that ensued
And how to prevent the ever-threatened end to it all

The advice was made up on the spot and the amateur therapy a guessing game
Neither made easier with the empty suicide threats and tests on loyalty

The biting of the lip became harder and more frequent
And the desire to help began to pour, not ebb, away

All culminating in the time that the threats became real
The end of it all suddenly a promise only an arm's length
And the fear that set in with this realisation

Somehow it passed, resulting in a relief that was so strong and overwhelming
The ridiculous pretence of being able to handle the situation could finally end

All, surprisingly, in a whimper and not a bang

The dependency either went, or moved onto someone else
The latter probably holds more truth, but when we meet you tell me it's the former

Either way, it means that the self-deprecation has diminished, if only slightly
As pride and a career and a life have overtaken desperation

The memories of the hardships now just that, memories
Making way for a new strength of character
One that knows it can cope in situations it never imagined would happen.

Claire Badhams

The future's here, the future's QQQQ

Twelve year-old Jamaican child prodigy, reggae singer QQ, is what his countrymen would call, 'a blessed child'. His hits 'Poverty', 'Better Must Come', 'Mrs Babylon' and 'Never Know The Use Of Her' are potent conscious anthems with the power to touch kiddies and adults alike. At downtown Kingston street parties he captivates revellers who happily halt their X-Rated grooves to sway and sing along to his set. Around Kingston, youths from tots to teens can he heard singing his wholesome songs with the passion they'd previously hollered Vybz Kartel's hardcore 'Picture Me And You' ("...under the tree, F.U.C.K.I.N.G"). His sportswear, chains, cane-rowed hair and heavy patois mean he fits into Jamaica's bashy dancehall scene; yet his innocent, ethereal voice and positive words are a slap of genteel reality in an otherwise hardcore spectacle where supposedly devout Rastafarian artists curse and chant about sex and guns. "The big artists need to realise music has powers," QQ says from his family home. "Music can make you do things, and make you not do things. It sounds like a big claim, but I think music can change life." The idea of music as a positive force on people, particularly Jamaica's ghetto communities, was part of reggae's original mantra. But amongst the devout and debauched reality extremes of Kingston and the increasingly money and image focused contemporary dancehall scene, the concept's been lost, until now. With the conviction of a young Dennis Brown, a roots reggae legend who began his career as a child, QQ states he wants to make music purely to "help people unite and love each other".
And with an ethos like that, Jamaica's up and coming generation needs QQ like air needs oxygen.

Debbie Bragg and Sarah Bentley

Show some support and log on to www.qqworl.com Photography by Debbie Bragg.

I was taking some pictures of an old friend in the park, enjoying the sun and being amazed by his skill at the Brazilian art of capoeira. After an hour of watching one handed high kicks and contorted gymnastics, I found myself considering what an evolution he had experienced with his life.

We were all from Ladbroke Grove in London. All of us had sacrificed our innocence to the god of 'cool' way before we ever needed to and in the end many of us had ended up in jail, rehab, and saddest of all dead... but not all of us. Those who managed to find their way out of the nocturnal life of parties and drugs had done so through very personal awakenings. Maybe the catalyst to an awakened existence was their work, having a child or falling in love, but for this friend of mine it was capoeira. Capoeira has a long history with its roots in Brazilian African slavery. Forbidden to practice any martial arts, by their European 'masters', the slaves of Brazil hid their secret fighting techniques in music and dance. Capoeira was the rhythm and spirit that struck a cord with my friend. A strong enough note to turn his life around completely and irreversibly. He is a teacher of capoeira now, with a new school opened in London. He once said to me that he knows more about Brazilian history than English. Could it be that our lives don't really start until we try to find

out who and what we really are? Maybe my friend from London is more Brazilian than he is English now, or maybe he is more himself than he ever could have been living life without purpose and focus. In my opinion, he is a rich man to know what he is.. and to do something with it. He showed me that a willingness to change, learn and master 'anything' in life, can save us from the hole that is to be ignorant and self-destructive. There is clarity in effort. For me it was art that turned me around, for him capoeira...

Someone once said: "Life is something that everyone should try at least once. For me, nothing worth having comes easily."
It took determination, will power and help from Capoeira Mestres to turn his life around. Capoeira is not just fun but a Philosophy and a way of life."

Monitor Risadinha (Jacob Rety) Capoeira Teacher
www.capoeiracanal.co.uk Jacob@capoeiracanal.co.uk 07910 288 091

Orion Best

The water curtain falls to a god's applause.

Like a cool sheet flung across a bed of nails, the wave feathers and breaks over the shallow coral reef. A hot zephyr blows into the faces, opening eyes to see behind the falling curtain of indigo water. The tube is the ultimate destination for every surfer. Time seems to expand and happen in slow motion – strangely silent. Surfing awakens the senses and touches the ineffable. But my wings are clipped into the midst of reverie. Flipped by the deadly wipeout, I'm dragged across the live razorheads. Water's motion is the flux of the Tao – the forgiving yin against the fearless yang. "Under heaven nothing is more soft and yielding than water. Yet for attacking the solid and strong, nothing is better; it has no equal," wrote the Chinese philosopher Lao Tzu. "Highest good is like water…it comes close to the Way," he concluded. Surfing and life can be defined as how well you can get on the back of this shifting beast.

The sport has given me an image of the clear minds that Taoism recommends. But you've got to accept that when the curtain falls, and you are deep in the tube ride, you may or may not make the exit. Riding waves is all about timing. The best moves are syncopated, just behind the beat: invention, not imitation. If the pulse of jazz is the ocean swell, the musician is the surfer improvising against that backdrop, not by stating the obvious, but by creating space through style. I've surfed all over the world, but the heart of my style is in Cornwall. West Penwith's rugged beauty and crystal water has been a continual source of inspiration in my life, and surfing has kept me focused. When the coke got lined up on the counter, I went home early to surf in the morning. When school got hard I cleared my mind in the sea. It was not until I moved away from the ocean to study Geography at Pembroke College, Cambridge that I realised how my strength of character and fulfilment in life depended so much upon sliding waves. Family support (a dad who surfs) and a firm passion for my local beach helped me to become a multiple national and European longboard surfing champion. Still studying, I signed a professional surfing contract with Oxbow and Vans. Since graduating, they continue to support me to compete globally and specialise in surf exploration to remote corners of the world. The safe waves of home mix with the thrill of foreign shores and new surfing frontiers.

I share Joseph Conrad's passion for maps. Like Marlow, "I would look for hours at South America, or Africa, or Australia and lose myself in the glories of exploration," wrote Conrad, in Heart of Darkness. "At the time there were many blank spaces on the earth and when I saw one that looked particularly inviting on a map (but they all look that), I would put my finger on it and say: When I grow up I will go there." A local, global lifestyle developed. Cornwall kept me grounded, earthy and sane. But the far-flung kept pulling – Liberia, Korea, the Philippines, Ecuador, Ghana. It sounds like a sweet life filtered through a turquoise curtain – a sea-through. My eyes were wide open, but blinded by the brilliant light, until writing helped me to get to grips with what I was really seeing – paradise is so often a political hell. Utopia literally means 'No Place'.

The 'good life' conceals a crude survival of the fittest. Like the time the Hawaiian surf pirates arrived on Tortola in the Caribbean. The beach turned into a cross between a Scorsese gangster movie and an 18th Century pirate sloop. The mob meets the surf culture, where the Hawaiians play the pirate mafia, Lance and Ho'okano standing proud at the crest of the hierarchy. A local snatched a wave from Lance. "He thinks he can snake me," exclaimed Lance. "I normally give 'em three chances," I said. "This ain't baseball," replied Ho'okano. "If you see him with two black eyes tomorrow, don't worry; there'll be one from my right fist and one from my left." A school of tarpin burst from the sea, chased by a frenzy of splashing – maybe a shark? "When you paddle out, you enter the food chain," remarked Ho'okano, casually.

In Kenya, I finally did get my encounter: the tiger shark spoke no words, but I felt his presence. Poised with indecision, I lay on my board, looking, until I met the black mirror of his pupil. His burnt stare scorched my nerves and I conceded to his position at the apex of the food triangle. In the God's country, always honour the God. Twelve feet of carnivore glided with the current. My heart pounded, but I felt strangely calm. In Africa, you've always got to be in your senses. Don't challenge nature, adapt. Stick with your animal instincts and stay tuned. I live to tell the tale.

A felt presence turned positive in a rural backwater of China. Scouting the horizon for waves our senses magnetised towards some greater force. Turning away from the azure sea, a huge golden Buddha sat, elevated by a temple of steps, watching the ocean, contemplating existence, juniper smoke feathering from a shrine scattered with incense. Communist Chairman Mao erased history to enforce the present. But here in the periphery, on Hainan Island, remained a striking vestige from the Buddhist past that ironically taught the value of staying in the present. We had come as tourists, perhaps shaping the future of this island, with our cult of individualism and free expression. 'Right now' was a reminder of an eternal present, the calm screen upon which our short and frantic lives are projected.

The strange and rather beautiful collision of cultures that occurs at the expense of jet pollution is fascinating. But the globe is steaming, people are starving and there is an ugliness to global capitalism that marches to a fixed beat, the antithesis of style. As a transient, serving at the altar of travel, I try to give something back. Being a "carbon neutral surfer" helps, travel writing inspires, I hope, but home and family eclipse it all. I love to return to the West Country – the vaulting granite, a skirt of quartz sand, the anticipation of the changing season. The rock spine that forms the Cornish peninsula has created many lives in its own image. People see the stone as dead, but the minerals, crystallised from cooling magma, are spiked with static, broadcasting to those who can hear. I try and tune in during heated moments of competition. But for the European Championships final in France I tuned into something more immediately pressing – my mother and her recovery from breast cancer,

enduring months of surgery, chemotherapy and radiation treatment. Instinct prevailed and I successfully defended my European title, thanks to the folks back home, as the Buddha backdrop.

Suffering and success go hand in hand in our family. But happiness endures.

Bizarrely I never met my first cousin Charles Green. Charles's charm and beauty for me is then the unknown, the ineffable. But we share blood. "Charles was always looking for an alternative," said Mark Lebon, who has seen me surfing in Cornwall for the past ten years. "And you symbolise that." Charles and I had plans to meet in Cornwall before the tragedy struck. In his absence Charles has brought me into his circles. The social butterfly endures. I could see the sparkle for adventure in his eyes, caught by graffiti art on Lebon's studio wall. Charles would have

loved surfing. It suits the open minded, the restless and the complex. Charles found the gaps you can pass through to engage with beating hearts. He touched the animal pulse. He sensed the absence of everything deep in the tube, as the water curtain falls to a God's applause. He would have danced with the locals in a cramped bar in South America, their measured merengue steps doing more to announce nightfall than the setting of the sun. We would have raised a glass to the untiring spirit of life. Sometimes living must be about intensity and quality, not longevity – a hot coal in a rainstorm. Some pack more into one moment than many do in a million moments. Charles had timing and style. It let him inhabit new places. He found the space between gravity and levity – an eternal presence.

Sam Bleakley

Spirals

Spiral One

The London College of Printing was by far the most disciplined, strict and conservative school for design in Europe when I applied, while still on the Foundation course at Hornsey College of Art. Hornsey, you see, was the hotbed of student rebellion, or rather, it had been in former times. It had been the seat of the student uprising in this country during the anti-war demonstrations of 1967. By the time I studied there it had been considerably quietened, this process continued for a few years under Thatcher until the fateful day, not long after I left, when it was finally closed, amalgamated into Middlesex Polytechnic, and, ironically, eventually turned into a TUC centre.

So, having realised that in order to understand the process of design from the inside you had to study the rulebook, I arrived as a wide-eyed student at the LCP, now renamed the London College of Communication, whatever that means. I had chosen a strict school, because part of my drive had been that if you were to understand how Media and Advertising subverts society through manipulation, you had to understand how that worked, and a soft school would have been of no help whatsoever. I had originally intended to be a painter, but felt that the self-elected elite world of Art was a far more hypocritical place to be in than Graphic Design; and that if you made a choice to communicate something, then you should choose the broadest canvas possible. My aim was to understand the rules so that I could undermine them, to learn the tricks so that they could be revealed.

I worked hard, 24/7, to reach that goal. I had reached the understanding that being at college represented a golden opportunity, one that would likely never repeat itself, and that the career and business stuff was something that I would be able to learn later on, on leaving and going out into the world. No, this was an amazing opportunity, a gateway to exploration, to experiment, to develop my own creativity, to develop myself. I understood then that I was not there for the school, that, when I left, the school would continue regardless. I was there for me, not for the tutors. They were there for me, supposed guides, supports and gurus to my learning process. This was ultimately wide of the mark. The school at that time, it turned out, was obsessed with "the right way" to do things, that there were laws regarding design, that society and culture has a fixed position therefore its language must also be fixed.

The understanding occurred to me that there are two types of convention. One, the convention of pragmatism, meant that certain rules exist through a functional imperative, one that could be based on the need to find a page in a magazine, for example, or the need to understand a left turn. The other imperative is to do with culture, ie. one to do with taste or tradition. This one I felt was always challengeable, and led to a place of inevitable confrontation. My tutors did not understand this, and ridiculously tried to throw me out of school for turning the Queen's head sideways on a stamp project. They had called my work Punk Graphics as an attempt to box it up.

The ultimate outcome was that I was failed by the school at my degree assessment. The internal assessors, my tutors, stated that I had no commercial potential, and that I hadn't answered the course. By contrast, the external assessors gave me a first. When I revisited the school some years on, the head of graphics said to me that " we knew if we gave you a hard time you would do well." Well.

The work I did from there on in was largely led by my desire to show students that it was their duty to follow a course of self-development; that they were studying for their own deep benefit and not for the benefit of the school. That my success was a clear pointer to say trust in yourself, follow your instinct, question everything, and never compromise if your belief is strong in something. Formulaic design never works, as you are removing the human from the equation, but a process of internalisation and inner change is a more honest place. I always stated that if you approach design purely as problem solving, all you can ever hope to communicate is the problem itself.

As a result of my obstinacy, I was close to a place of poverty for a good four years after leaving school, but vowed never to weaken my resolve or beliefs. Now, some years hence, I have been asked to return to the LCP, sorry LCC, as a visiting professor, a role I have gladly taken on. And my message is the same now as it was then, look inside, trust yourself, stay true.

Spiral Two

In 2004 I was invited to Moscow for the first time, to show my work and give a series of lectures. Alexander Rodchenko had been my hero at school, and continues to be so to this day. He was the most influential of Russian Constructivists, unbending in his desire to explore, experiment, discover, and try new things. His restless creativity produced an astounding amount of inspirational material, much of which we haven't bettered since.

I was strongly influenced by his approach to visual communication, melding art with design, experiment with structure, and my muse was always the thought "if Rodchenko was alive today, what would he be doing with all this new stuff?". He was the invisible tutor and judge in my head.

With much trepidation I agreed to go to Moscow. It felt like taking coals to Newcastle, that the birthplace of constructivism and modern design would politely listen, pat me on the head with the comment "nice try, son", and send me on my way, red-faced.

Imagine, then, my surprise and sense of awe at being introduced to the grandson of Rodchenko, Alexandr Lavrantiev. A wonderful man, still living in the same apartment as then, he turned out to be a little older than me, and is now head of Photography at the University in Moscow where I was speaking. Imagine then my shock at discovering that he teaches my work to his students.

I felt both humbled and filled with joy. Now, I thought, I can stop doing this graphic stuff, I have reached the highest point. It also felt like a complete validation of everything that I had ventured, that all my belief systems were somehow right, that to trust in yourself is the only way to change the rules.

Neville Brody

Last month I completed a project with King's College London, photographing students from its 'Access to Medicine' extended degree programme.

The project was launched in June 2001, and since then has helped 136 young people from disadvantaged backgrounds to train as doctors.

It has also involved over 5000 local teenagers in community activities promoting medical education.

This programme, which is funded by the Pool of London Partnership, helps talented people from non-traditional backgrounds become doctors. 136 students from ten inner London boroughs are currently enrolled on the course.

During the last year, the project has been working with young people of Caribbean heritage to explore why their peers remain underrepresented amongst the medical student population.

In October 2005, Damilola Taylor's father, Richard, formally opened the Damilola Taylor Room at King's. Damilola was killed on a Peckham estate in November 2000 but had always wanted to become a doctor. The room is provided for the exclusive use of the Extended Degree students, who use it for study, relaxation and socialising. It is a particularly useful resource for students who don't have a suitable study space at home.

Gemma Booth

Here you can find some drawings of my graduate collection (1995).

The night after my graduation show, my whole collection got stolen out of my car. Never a trace was found… My sketchbook is the only thing left of this collection. To me, it was a great loss. Finally graduating, and a whole year of hard work was gone. But, at the same time, this also liberated me from my past, and it gave me the power to move forward. Having nothing to lose has always been a good drive!

Véronique Branquinho

On September 9 2004, I spoke to my friend Amiel Grumberg for two reasons: It was my birthday and I had just won a Biennial Award from Gwangju, South Korea.

I dedicated the award to him and then I asked him to prepare himself for a trip to Italy to see the exhibition by Anish Kapoor at the Minini Gallery. The plan was to talk about our future artistic projects, sitting on a balcony, drinking and looking at women!

He laughed and explained to me the proposition he would make to Massimo Minini for an exhibition, he told me he was trying to forget about Maud, a beautiful opera singer, that by pure coincidence was going to be singing that day in London for the first time. I don't remember when, but he had told me that he intended to live in Amsterdam and he spoke about finishing the final projects for the famous Rumanian artist Mircea Cantor. Everything appeared to be perfect. Today I remember his voice, completely solid for a 24-year-old young man, he wished me "happy birthday", we exchanged some sweet words about our future together and our future ambitions, I said "goodbye gypsy" (it was the nickname we used between close friends) and the conversation ended there. I went to celebrate my victory. He left forever.

That same day he jumped out of the window of his room at the Maison Descartes in Amsterdam, at the same time the organisers of a biennial in Romania were arriving. They found his body lying in the Dutch street, a long time ago now, but I don't think anyone has ever unknowingly hurt me so much.

I went almost a year thinking about him constantly. My wife who also liked him very much, said that Amiel had to have seen the stupidity of what he was doing as he was falling to his end. (This idea helps me feel better, Amiel was impulsive and proud, often his first ideas or affirmations were forcefully in favour of something or against something – but in the end his ideas were always very clear.)

When somebody so young decides to go away, I cannot avoid but think about the melancholic state they are in, that they think that nothing has a solution and that the best thing is to leave this world. Lamentably in the case of Amiel, to these extreme reasons, you must add the antidepressants that he took (I didn't know) and the amount of alcohol and drugs Amiel consumed, this I did know.

So many times we were under the same roof and I never saw in his bags any of these medicines, that in addition were not compatible. His doctor from his hometown in France had prescribed them, peculiarly his parents had requested medical aid from fear that Amiel consumed drugs (easy to buy in Amsterdam). I believe they never knew that Amiel smoked daily way before leaving Paris where he worked in the Palais de Tokyo. He said that to study in the curatorial programme "De Appel" with Saskia Bos – who would come to be his adoptive mother in terms of art – would be a wonderful experience, according to him. He also added that to live near a coffee shop would be a pleasant experience...

Sometimes we spoke of suicide. Like in my version, I said I would do it if my body or in particular my brain became too heavy for my loved ones to handle. He said: "No, Jota, suicide is not the solution, it is cowardly."

Why do so many young people succumb to their ego? Why? How can so much pain hide the sun? Why is the love and the respect of your loved ones not sufficient?

My gypsy was brilliant and stupid at the same time.

He was as generous as a perfect mother but as destructive as a missile at the same time. He was religiously proud, but agonisingly shy.

When he was 24 years old, three big problems occurred:

A: A woman left him.

B: He didn't get the position he was promised at the Palais de Tokyo.

C: He didn't manage to find 20% of the money he needed to start his first mega tourism show.

What I can say of this young man is, he was someone that would have been able to revolutionise the way to show or to see art at the beginning of the century, somebody who loved artists in such an intense way? Without wanting to, I realise that flattering his memory is the best way to forget his final act...

I lost a friend. Art lost a lover. Life seemed so hard, but life is very hard... He could support his doubts and rejections, not the lack of economic support.

Today, I have a two-year-old daughter. I have shown her a few times photos of Amiel; the last photo I have of him alive, the photo is fading due to the sun that hits that part of the house. My daughter listens to what I say about the photos, she smiles just like Amiel in the photo, as the photo continues to fade. The photos that are with this article show "Amiel, the bridge" a work that I finished just one month after his death. The wooden bridge represents the road you should never be far from when you try to be creative, the ground is covered with glass and at the end of the bridge the glass is broken, just like Amiel's life.

I ask myself so many times, what can I do so that his suicide is not left meaningless. How can I help young people understand that there is always a solution.

Jota Castro

The slogan says it all:

'By young peeps, for young peeps'.

Live magazine might cover what could also be in the pages of i-D (rappers Sway, Pirelli and fashion by up-and-coming talent) but this is the work of 16 to 21 year olds in Lambeth.

Founded in 2001, the readership is estimated at 50,000 in the South London area and beyond. Financed by a combination of local government money and a grant from the European Social Union, it's overseen by a group of mentors across journalism, photography and design. All content and look of the mag, however, is created by the young people themselves.

The action happens in a labyrinthine building in downtown Brixton. Step into the *Live* factory and wha' gwan on the streets of SW9 is emphatically making its way onto the glossy pages. Alongside interviews with stars like Sway, Keisha White and Dizzee Rascal, hard-hitting issues are tackled. Cover lines include 'the real deal about crack' and 'Bully or bullied?'. Dan Dutt-Hemp, 18, is a contributor who also has a place on the corresponding Live Futures programme, where local young people are given courses in the hope of finding a job in the media. He thinks the peer-to-peer approach is key to not sounding preachy. Finding *Live* after coming out of jail and 'jamming into trouble like teenagers do when they've got no distractions', he's got the 'been there, done that' story too. "If someone's thinking about getting into trouble, they might think twice if it's me telling them not to," he says. "It's like you always listen to your friend rather than your mum," interjects Zoë Adams, the 21-year-old designer on *Live*.

Everyone involved in *Live* is grateful for a chance to do something different. Adams and editor Shola Laeje, 21, have both escaped dead end jobs, Dutt-Hemp has "a structure, a reason to get up in the morning", and Mario Akimana, 18, *Live's* Film Editor, has found a home away from home. Originally from the Congo, he came to the UK as an orphan in 2004 and was told about *Live* by his social worker. Now he "gets paid to do what I like. I go to watch the football match and write about what I saw. My proudest moment was when Pirelli, Ty and Killa Kela was talking to me like a normal person. I've been through a lot to get that kind of respect and I hope I can inspire other people". *Live* inspires this concern for the next gen. Outside of *Live*, Akimana teaches sex education in local schools with the Lambeth Youth Council and Dutt-Hemp sees his brothers as key to him straightening himself out. "I had to grow up because they look up to me," he says. Jordan Jarrett-Bryan, the first editor of *Live* and 22-year-old journalist extraordinaire, still helps out *Live's* new recruits. "It helps to physically see someone who has made the *Live* journey and come out the other side," he says.

Where to go next is something Adams is thinking about a lot right now. Twenty two in three weeks, her time is up at *Live*. "It's a bit 'whoah'," she says. "My passion is photography but I want to get a job in design because that's where the money is. Right now, I have money for bills with a little bit leftover for shoes. But I want a maid, a butler." With the opportunities *Live* has given her and buckets of talent, she might just get the mansion too.

Lauren Cochrane

Photography by Zoë Adams.

Hussein Chalayan

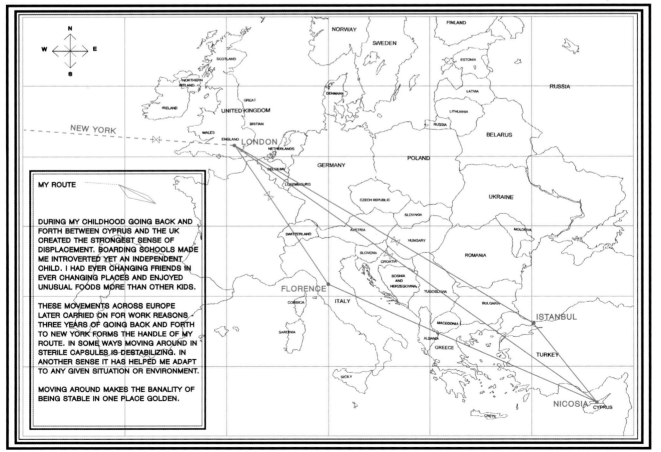

MY ROUTE

DURING MY CHILDHOOD GOING BACK AND FORTH BETWEEN CYPRUS AND THE UK CREATED THE STRONGEST SENSE OF DISPLACEMENT. BOARDING SCHOOLS MADE ME INTROVERTED YET AN INDEPENDENT CHILD. I HAD EVER CHANGING FRIENDS IN EVER CHANGING PLACES AND ENJOYED UNUSUAL FOODS MORE THAN OTHER KIDS.

THESE MOVEMENTS ACROSS EUROPE LATER CARRIED ON FOR WORK REASONS – THREE YEARS OF GOING BACK AND FORTH TO NEW YORK FORMS THE HANDLE OF MY ROUTE. IN SOME WAYS MOVING AROUND IN STERILE CAPSULES IS DESTABILIZING. IN ANOTHER SENSE IT HAS HELPED ME ADAPT TO ANY GIVEN SITUATION OR ENVIRONMENT.

MOVING AROUND MAKES THE BANALITY OF BEING STABLE IN ONE PLACE GOLDEN.

My sister's wedding, July 1968.

As I came to the edge of the field, the summer breeze carried the sweet sounds of children laughing, and of parents talking together; but at that moment as I stopped and listened, I knew with a total certainty that any sort of normal life was no longer possible for me: I would never be able to have a happy family life; no children would laugh and play on my lap. I had crossed over an invisible line into death and darkness and there was now no way back – no point of return.

Some weeks later I went to bed in the large hay loft which had served as a temporary home, whilst we built our experimental antediluvian mud dwelling in a remote spot hidden in the beautiful hills of Devon. This project had been energetically started by me and a group of friends, but when the autumn and the rains really set in, everyone else pulled out and I was the only one left.

I had taken a lot of drugs and fallen asleep. When I woke it was pitch dark. It was the middle of the night and the one source of light, the kerosene lamp, had just gone out. I started to pour more kerosene into the lantern when I became aware of something at the far end of the hay loft. I could feel the presence of something which was extremely powerful and dominant and I could somehow tell that it was observing me and seemed to be drawing closer.

At that moment I knew – I don't know how, but I absolutely knew that I was going to set fire to myself and that I would die.

I knew that the kerosene was spilling and I could observe myself lighting a match to see what was going on. I could see myself making this mistake and I also knew that I was unable to stop what was about to happen. At the same time as this realisation, I became aware of this 'presence of darkness', I can't describe it any other way, that was getting closer to me. I knew in some way that it was involved in what was about to happen.

At that exact moment a thought seemed to form in my mind, perhaps some memory of something that I might have heard from school.

At the time I was a militant atheist and totally against God or anything like that, but I just started to sing a name: the name of Jesus.

As I did so, I could sense the presence of darkness or whatever it was, back off and move away. So I started to sing more and louder! The louder I sang this name the more it went – until suddenly – it was gone. At that point I fell into a very deep and peaceful sleep, in a way that I had not been able to do for years. When I woke up I knew I must leave that place, so I gathered up my few bundles, and left.

I managed to move in with some friends who were deeply into meditation.

I was ill and not well and they seemed happy and stable. I started to meditate and wanted to pursue a more spiritual lifestyle. They were into drugs but in a more creative way. One of them had an old prayer book that he kept by his bed and I remember feeling a pang of jealousy – how lovely it must be to have a really warm relationship with God. In the past I had occasionally read my old copy of the Bible that I had been given at school, but as I was often on drugs when I read it, for the life of me I could not understand it at all.

I began to embrace macrobiotics and was soon practicing Yoga. I intended to join Hare Krishna as this seemed the most direct way possible to meet with God.

I went up to their centre near London and stayed there for a retreat. I very much wanted to join and approached two of them, asking them to put the special sign on my forehead. One of them was going to do so when the other inexplicably stopped him from doing so, saying that for some reason I wasn't yet ready.

Disappointed that the 'offer' of my life to God had been turned down, I returned to my friends in Devon and threw myself into living the Yoga life of a disciple. However, in the relatively unspoilt atmosphere of a small old-fashioned Devon town in the '70s, it didn't seem possible to fully commit myself to what was necessary. I decided to join up with the devotees in London and so moved into the ashram there. Our Guru promised us all sorts of things if we faithfully followed his path.

I decided to have prolonged fasts as that seemed the quickest way to inner realisation. After about a year I was down to below six stone. People started looking at me in a funny way but I wasn't sure why. Again I had some sort of 'visitation' in my room.

I remember my mother coming to visit me and how shocked she was when she saw me. She said if I carried on like that I would probably die very soon.

I was alarmed by the look of pain and fear that I saw on her face as she looked at me.

By this time I was becoming somewhat disillusioned with this Guru and some of the carryings-on. One day he asked us to look deep in our hearts and we would find a name there; I know he expected us all to find his name. After a long period of meditation I found a name. Everyone else found the Guru's name but it was not his name that I found, but the name of Jesus. This really confused me!

By this time I was really ill from the fasting so I decided that the whole 'spiritual' scene was not for me and wanted out, but first I would visit a friend of mine who had somehow become 'religious'. He had been a drug dealer and had written to tell me about all the changes in his life. He invited me to his community in Italy and because my sister was also going to stay nearby, I went along.

It was a really beautiful place and full of young people, who seemed so different to anyone I had met before. I had known Christians at university but they all seemed so dull and boring, so I had just ridiculed, dismissed and argued with them. But there was a sweetness about these people that I couldn't deny, and something beautiful that was obviously happening in their lives. There was a very wonderful lady who was leading the group and who spent, so I was told, a lot of time in prayer.

However I was uncomfortable around them, and I was aware how different my own inner life was to theirs. For example, because they didn't smoke I constantly had to go outside to light up. It was annoying to see how addicted I was to cigarettes.

I could somehow see many inconsistencies in my life when I was around them.

Just after I got there they decided to have a play – we would all act out a scene from the Bible. This was new to me, and I didn't want anything to do with it, but because they insisted, I gave in. The play was about a time when Yeshua (Jesus' Hebrew name) was healing people and there was a huge crowd around him so it was impossible to get near him. So a group of friends climb onto a roof, pull away the tiles, and let this paralysed man down on a stretcher right at Yeshua's feet. Of course He praises their faith and then heals the man.

Someone suggested I was to have the part of the person on the stretcher. Who was I to argue – at least I didn't have to say any stupid Biblical lines!

Anyway I had been on this stretcher for about ten minutes when various pictures of my life started to flash before my eyes. I could see some of the things I had done and the people I had damaged, some of the hurt I had caused and the pain I had created.

I started to cry. I fought against this impulse because it was really embarrassing but I couldn't stop it. In fact it just got worse! I was lying there on this stretcher, silently sobbing to myself. The play carried on around me, and then finished. It must have gone on for about two hours. They gently put me down somewhere and eventually everyone left and I was there on my own, weeping gallons.

The life that appeared before me, my life since leaving art school, was one that had gone into a hopeless spiral downwards. I had completely lost any kind of moral framework. In my travels I had stolen money from people who had let me stay in their house; there had been a trail of broken unhappy relationships, lies, and deceptions.

My relationship with my parents and family was non-existent; I had built up a fantasy world where I could no longer tell what was lying or truth any more – I no longer even knew myself. I felt like I knew things about death that I was not permitted to know. All this was so far from where I had come from.

I had been brought up in a loving and lively prosperous Jewish home. As a child I had even had a beautiful experience of God. I was lying out in a field one evening looking up at the stars. I felt that if I was big enough I could tread on each one and could leap over them. Suddenly it was as if a light bulb had lit up in my mind. "Of course there is a God," I thought. "There has to be." It was just childish thoughts, but it was also so very obvious, so clear and without a doubt.

Later on at boarding school I had been very wild and promiscuous. After my parents' divorce I went to art school and started painting and writing poetry in a serious way. Although I initially resisted the drugs scene, it wasn't long before I was pulled into its wake. Being of a fairly obsessive nature, the amount of drug intake increased until I became emotionally addicted.

I started travelling around and sleeping wherever I could find a bed for a few months. I painted and wrote poetry obsessively and continually. My one aim was to be free. What was freedom? Was it possible to lead a really free life? Free from all the oppression and senselessness all around me. I despised the repressive bourgeois existence of modern living. I would live a life totally free from all of that.

Others of my acquaintance gave up and took normal jobs but I was not going to give up – I was going to be free and find myself fully.

All through this time I was becoming more and more depressed and inwardly dark and gloomy. And yet, at times of deepest darkness, once

or twice I would take refuge in a church and just sit there and cry. Once I had a very intense vision of Christ in the centre of a huge Indian meditation circle. He was in the centre and holding everything together. And now, as I lay on this stretcher, weeping and crying, all this pain, loneliness and grief was at last, in some way spilling out. It was all too much for me! I made up my mind that come nightfall I was going to sneak away and go back to England. About two in the morning I crept out and closed the outside door behind me. I had just started to leave when I heard a voice from an upper room calling to me – it was the lady of prayer – she knew what I was trying to do and talked with me from the window encouraging me to stay.

The next day my friend came to me and we went for a long walk together. He started to tell me about Jesus and all the things that had happened in his life. At first I was sympathetic but our walk went on for miles and miles, and I started to become really angry and full of rage toward him although I wasn't sure what I was angry about.

All of this really was just too claustrophobic for me so I decided that night I was definitely escaping – whether the praying lady was there or not! So I repeated the process that night, but I knew she was watching and saw me, because my friend followed me to the station and begged me to come back to the community and get myself sorted out – no way! On the way back to England I met some Billy Graham workers and started to talk to one of them. Eventually I let him pray with me but nothing happened so I dismissed it as being somewhat irrelevant.

When I got back to England I really had had enough of 'spiritual things'. I felt that I had tried a whole variety of pathways. They were all roughly the same and I would learn from them all and eventually start to live again but now as a 'realised' person, one who was aware and spiritual but totally free.

This was all very well but I had to earn some money – the store of money I had been given at my bar mitzvah was now completely dry. So I ended back at my sister's place, and carried on my lonely life of wandering around London at night and writing poetry. One night I became pretty desperate so I started to cry out to the universe or something to help me. I really cried from my heart. I did not have a fixed point that I was aiming these cries for help toward – but I just reckoned if perhaps something might be there, possibly I might get some kind of answer. I was amazed when a few days later someone came around and said they needed help in finishing some building work on their home in Wales, would I come?

During my stay in Wales I had a dream. In this dream I was standing in front of a shop and there was a girl with me; we were really happy and laughing together.

The dream really affected me as I had come to the point where I felt that I would not, indeed could not, ever be really happy again. When I reached my friends in Devon an American girl was there who later on would become my wife. We came from a similar Jewish background and had had similar experiences. Before long we were wonderfully and devotedly in love, but in a very different way than I had ever been before.

We got married and settled into a new life together. I took up my painting again with even more determination than ever before to become a great painter and completely came away from any drugs.

I had my first London exhibition and started to have work shown in some of London's top galleries. I was about to be taken up by one of the most prestigious of these galleries and to be accepted as one of their resident artists – a hugely exciting thing.

In the meantime we had started to re-explore Judaism. It was a very laid back sort of thing with no hard sell. I felt that perhaps I had not done it justice before and possibly there were things I had missed. So we started to go to the local reform synagogue on a regular basis. We must have seemed a rather odd couple to them. They were all very nice and proper and we sort of descended on them out of the blue!

They were extremely gracious and welcoming and we really enjoyed being with them, it certainly was different anyway.

This synagogue had had difficulties in finding their own building and the local united reform church had kindly offered them the use of their building, as it didn't have a cross or anything on the walls. At the end of one of the services we bought a few books from the bookstand at the back of the church. One of these was the Good News Bible, a modern translation of the New Testament.

My wife and I started to read it and we were totally amazed by what we found. It wasn't really a religious book, like the Hindu or Buddhist books I had read, but it was all about this Jewish Rabbi and the miracles He did. It was more like a history book, very down to earth. This book made two extreme assumptions. I found that it declared openly that we are much more amazing than we realise: we are made in the very image of God. We are loved, chosen, special, and precious in God's sight. It says He loves us with an indescribable love. On the other hand, it also unequivocally states that we are worse than we think: we are sinners each one of us, having strayed far away from God and being intrinsically selfish, self-centred, disobedient and rebellious to God's laws.

I was amazed by the person of Yeshua, Jesus. He seemed to leap off the page into my life. Who was He? Were these conflicting claims true? He said He was the Messiah – was He? Was He the Son of God that He claimed to be? Did He really rise again from the dead? Was it true that there had really been a flood? Had there really been a Garden of Eden? What about Adam and Eve? Also I was disturbed by the whole problem with evil. Now I had actually encountered this. But was there really some spiritual power of evil that was an actual 'being' of some kind?

All these issues threw me into a spin! I had never been so challenged as I was the first time I read the New Testament in a readable English translation.

These questions seemed to fill my waking hours. I was horrified by the idea of becoming a dreaded 'Christian' – the idea seemed totally repulsive to me. Apart from the Jewish concerns, I had ridiculed and despised Christians. Also I had no desire at all to return to my 'spiritual searchings' either; the idea of returning to a new spiritual adventure filled me with horror. I decided to read on, feeling that I could sit on the fence, watch everything from there and definitely not make any sort of unwise jump.

At the same time another strange thing was happening to me. Normally I came down in the morning at 7am, started painting or drawing and carried on until evening, sometimes late into the night. Inspiration is mainly (but not all) a matter of determination and hard work and so at some point the work would start to come, and I would always end the day with something to show for my efforts.

But now suddenly, it was as if this flow of energy was completely blocked – something I had never experienced before. This continued for two weeks; I seemed to be completely paralysed; I couldn't paint or draw, nothing was flowing.

I felt completely empty and it was like I was fighting with someone, or rather that someone was fighting with me. Then gradually it dawned on me, that it was as if God was wrestling with me in some way. At that moment I realised what the issues were about: it was about Yeshua and that He wanted me to make a decision: I had to come off the fence! In the end, I don't remember actually making the decision to follow Yeshua.

It was always a continuous yielding to His presence and His leading. I came off the fence; I gave Him my life – what it was worth!

I couldn't do otherwise. It was now obvious to me that He was who He said He was. He could do with me what He wished, I was now a believer.

But it wasn't as if I had at last found the truth but rather that at last, the truth had at last found me, bundled me up and carried me back home. The healing process started immediately, although much of it took many years of love and understanding before some issues were sorted out.

I immediately tried to somehow make amends for the past damage. I repaired the relationship with my parents that had been so badly severed. I really wanted to lead a better, more God-centred life.

Over the years, the Lord graciously restored all 'the years the locusts had eaten'. It was like a miracle of new life and new birth. The life I thought I would never be able to have again, God gave that back. The happy family life was returned to me as a gift from His hand. I heard again the sounds of childish laughter. The joy I thought had been destroyed forever – it came back. A deep peace replaced the chaos of despair, a hope and a comfort in place of the pain and utter loneliness.

I put my hand in His hand and He has lead me to still waters; "He heals the broken hearted and binds up their wounds".

Of course sometimes there is pain, sometimes great difficulties, that is natural in our lives. It's impossible to live without these things, but it is possible to experience them with Him – and that's what makes it all so different.

David the young shepherd boy put it like this: "He restores my soul, He leads me beside the still waters, and the Lord is my Shepherd so I shall lack nothing."

Stuart Cohen

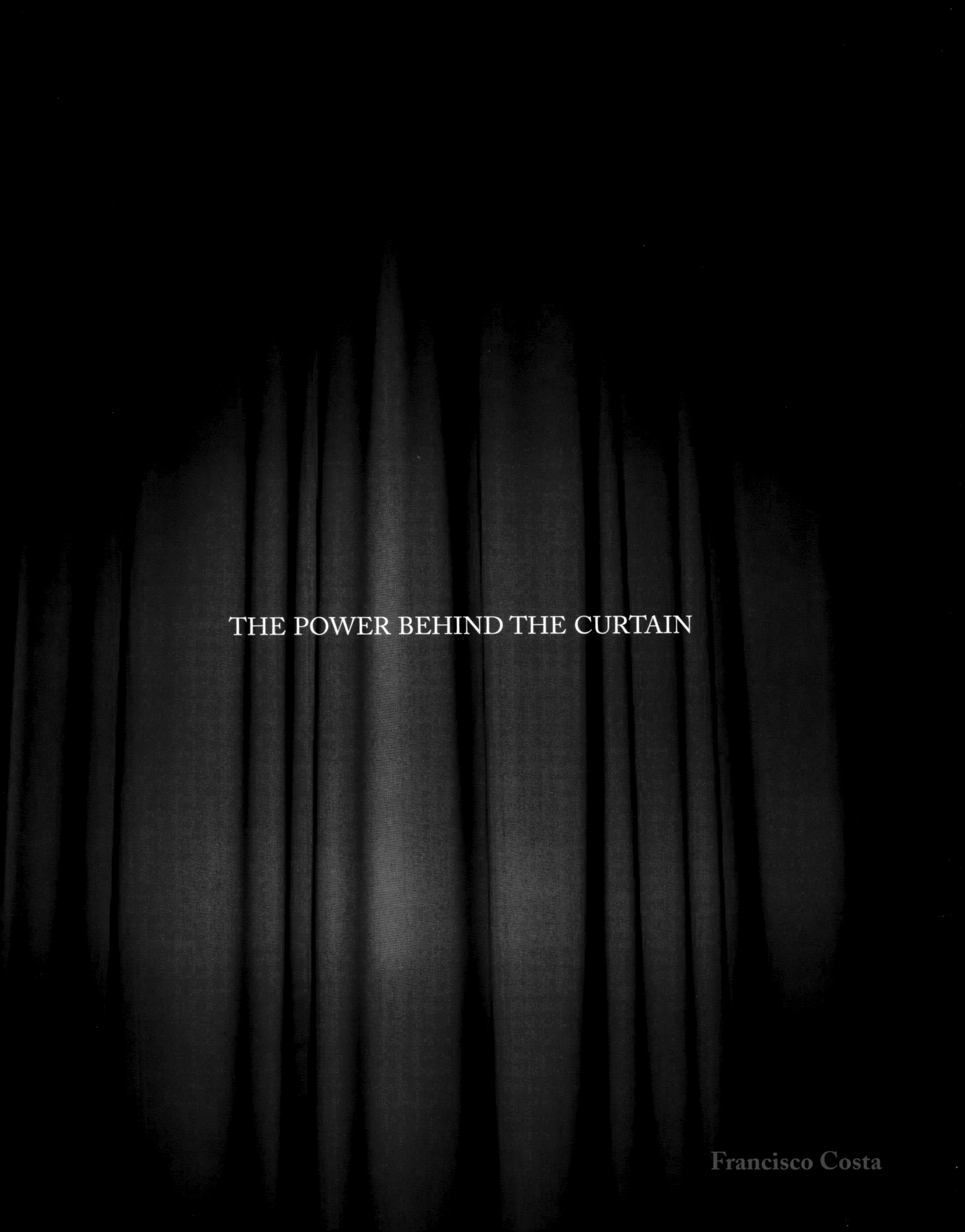

THE POWER BEHIND THE CURTAIN

Francisco Costa

There is almost nothing that can affect you more powerfully for the positive or the negative than the strength of your own mind and how you view the world or your surroundings through your own unique lens.

All we perceive passes through that channel and for some, during certain periods or situations, it can turn into unsettling territory. What to most or even yourself seems or seemed harmless, normal, comfortable, pleasant, can become scary, strange, uncomfortable and very unpleasant.

Just everyday things such as walking down the street, getting on a bus or the tube, crossing a bridge can suddenly turn into an ordeal and you are gripped with an irrational terror. It's hard to breathe, difficult to swallow. Your heart is pounding and things around you seem suddenly slightly off kilter, unfamiliar and even perhaps menacing. It's possible to almost freeze, your brain racing and feeling light headed anxious, as if you could almost implode or die on the spot.

Welcome to the state most commonly known as a panic attack or in some cases phobias, which incidentally affect many more people than most realise and usually those who suffer from them may not initially understand what is happening and often feel that they are the only ones who are experiencing this horrible sensation. And once you've had one of these "attacks" you are petrified that another will strike.

The fear of the fear. It's a terrible cycle and the concern for it happening again is precisely what makes it so inevitable that it will indeed strike once more.

Many who have experienced this will immediately recognise the description.

I first experienced this strange sensation when I was in my teens. The family was away and whilst lying in bed, I was gripped with a sudden fear. I started shaking and my heart was beating, it would not go away and actually became more intense. Not knowing what to do and being into running at that time, I decided to get up in the middle of the night and try to run it off, thinking that the exertion would eventually calm me down.

So in the middle of the night I ran and ran like crazy through the deserted streets of my East London suburban youth.

It did help. Temporarily.

But the cycle had begun. No way did I want to feel that again. At one point I was so numb that I thought I could stick pins through my gums But the fact that you dread it so much is precisely what causes it inevitably to return.

Fear of the fear.

We all go through events and periods of our lives that are stressful and upsetting, and there are different ways to deal with them. If you suppress emotion it finds an uncanny way of getting out somehow. Almost like the cartoon characters that get hit over the head with a mallet and a bump appears. When you push the bump down it pops out somewhere else. I think it's a lot like that with pain of the emotional kind.

For me this cycle would intermittently revisit in different forms. Fear of public speaking could set it off, being in the middle of vast spaces, crowded subways, trains, cars, driving across bridges, large structures, and being on mountains with huge vistas were the common recurring scenarios in which it could arise and can still do so. But some other seemingly totally irrational harmless things such as birds, types of food, insects… the list can become very bizarre, to be honest, can cause a similar reaction.

First the breathing gets erratic and then the rest would follow; you feel very alone and scared. Abject panic takes over and it overwhelms. Often bouts of depression can go hand in hand.

This type of affliction affects millions of people and probably some of your friends or people that you meet have experienced this, you just don't usually realise that they have encountered something of this nature, unless a chance conversation reveals this often embarrasing closely guarded fact.

Some are more prone to this than others and perhaps being sensitive is in some ways a prerequisite to having this disposition.

In my case a mild flirtation (by many standards, during the crazy late '80s) with certain psychoactive amphetamine laced drugs didn't seem to help out too much and perhaps magnified the storm that lurked under the surface. Perhaps? Who knows and far be it for me to preach what anyone should do or not do during their exploratory years.

I guess if you like being slightly out of control then it's cool, but if you prefer to have a firmer grip on the wheel, it may not be your cup of tea.

Anyway all of that notwithstanding, the moral of all this is that it's not an endless cycle that cannot be broken. These paralysing feelings that can sometimes result in individuals being unable to leave their house for fear of what may trigger them outside, in extreme cases, is not a closed case that cannot be conquered. You are not condemned for life.

Understanding what is actually happening and that it's not as critical or harmful as it feels is the first step. Sharing your feelings and learning to relax and calming your mind are further steps and although it can seem an insurmountable task, it is not. You can do whatever you want to do. Or at least try.

The only limiting factor is your own mind and what you tell yourself is possible. It may sound corny but although you're not in control of what happens externally, the way you choose to react to that is entirely within your grasp. For every action there is a reaction and for that you hold the key.

Fraser Cooke

The new generation must be encouraged to remain curious and inspired. Free from our preconceived ideas and open to positive new experiences... don't follow. Find your own path and always be true to yourself.

Maria Cornejo

Joey, Atticus, Jackson, Pfion and Leirden.

José Luis Rial (38), also known as Jacko, was born into a traditional family in Isidro Casanova, located west of Buenos Aires, Argentina. Since 2001 he's been working with enthusiasm at Malba (Museo de Arte Latinoamericano de Buenos Aires), and his story is one to be told. Like many other children in Argentina, Jacko began working at age 14. He started working at a pizza parlour, and then moved to being a bartender, dish-washer, and wall painter. At age 18 his homosexuality was a sensitive subject among family members, which pushed him to move out and start a life of his own. He maintains a bond with his family and supports them economically.

In 1998, while recovering from his partner's death from H.I.V., Jacko's life took a drastic turn when he was diagnosed with the same disease. He had two severe relapses, and doctors had low hopes that he would survive. Regardless of this diagnosis, he had a surprisingly fast recovery and held on to life.

Jacko was hired by the museum's general maintenance department to paint walls. He was soon promoted to the exhibition design and installation department, where he is currently responsible for the cleaning of artworks, sculptures, and frames. Jacko also organises the storage room for the museography department.

Jacko is a sensitive, good-hearted man, who learnt to keep a positive attitude towards life. He is eternally grateful to those who took care of him and support him daily.

Jacko believes that human suffering is linked to the mystery of life, which is beyond us and makes us feel vulnerable, but strong enough to confront adversity with hope and love.

Eduardo Costantini

James (far right) jumping into the River Yealm.

Dear James

"I want you to remember this moment forever," I whisper in your ear as you fearlessly launch yourself off the boat into the crystal depths of the River Yealm. I fumble with the camera and manage to take what non-professionals might consider a 'pretty good shot'.

I love this photo of you, sometimes when I'm bored on the long journey from London to Plymouth I zoom in on your face, taking in the wide-eyed open mouthed expression, the adrenaline is almost palpable. I sit on the side of the boat and watch you resurface, the spikes that you spent ages meticulously grooming this morning are starting to steadily droop and it appears you have most of the estuary in your mouth as you gurgle back up to me; "Aunty Nic, Aunty Nic, did you get it?"

Yeah. I get it. This is what childhood should be about. Sod that, this is what adulthood should be about, launching yourself intrepidly into the unknown, not looking back, concerning yourself only with that very moment.

I wish someone had told me that years ago, but unfortunately life doesn't always work out like that and retrospect is a funny business as you will undoubtedly find out.

It has been two years to this very day that your father had been found in a bus shelter with a broken neck. As soon as I got the phone call, I left my insular microcosmic London life behind and took the longest-ever-train-ride back home to look after you. I was nervous but you were pleased to see me. I'll never forget the way you held onto me when you were told your Daddy would never walk again. You defined bravery. "That's alright," you said to me. "He can still watch me play football". You were eight years old and I was 26 but I think we both knew that in a way we had just lost part of our childhoods. I struggled with my new and sudden matriarchal role but you easily adjusted to your new life, dividing half your time travelling to the spinal unit in Salisbury and the rest of your time back at school. Naturally, we were all worried how this would affect you, but your resilience inspired us all.

I'll always remember our night-time chats when I would crawl into your bed and stay with you until you slept, (you wouldn't sleep on your own) "Is everything going to be alright?" you'd ask. I would always answer with the same reply. "Everything's going to be fine. I promise." Only then would you fall asleep, usually on my arm, cutting off the blood supply and causing intense pins and needles. I would then spend the next hour slowly removing my arm inch by inch, finally succeeding before you'd change position, then I'd have to start all over again. There's probably a lot you don't know about me, and there's probably a lot you don't need to know but for the record and just in case you are reading this sometime in the future and I have turned into some middle-aged, floral frock wearing freak, here is a story.

At 18 I arrived in London with a £20 note in my back pocket and a jar of nutella. The nutella lasted two weeks, the note, two hours. I found myself in Camden. It was de riguer for wannabe-indie-kids back then although in reality the best of everything had already happened. The punk boat had sailed through 20 years previously and all that remained was acidic vomit stains on chintzy pub carpets and brit-pop conquests etched filthily on toilet doors. It was also a place of hope and independence, not quite the land of the free, but pretty damn close.

I found a job that afternoon in the market selling prophylactics to geriatrics and butt-plugs to butchers. I told my mum (your nan), I worked in a bakery. It was the first thing that came to mind – I was eating a Cornish pasty at the time. I got my tongue pierced, (and successfully hid that piercing from your nan for three years), dyed my hair and wore luminous cyber punked PVC.

Yeah, I was a real revolutionary. The first in fact. I sang in a band and wore 50s cocktail dresses. I wrote poetry and took experimenting as a way of life. I lived a dichotomous existence between visits home and my life in London.

I'll leave the rest for you to decide, there's far too much to fit into this abridged version. This is my present to you James. If you are reading this at some point in the future, look into the eyes of the little boy in the picture and don't be frightened. Take the leap. Everything's going to be fine. I promise.

Aunty Nic xxx

Nicki Cotter

No act of kindness, no matter how small, is ever wasted – Aesop

July 2002 I was running fast and far from everything.

One afternoon I was off to a secluded beach. I'd been there many times before in summers past, in company.

The stones, the dust clouds and the sea cliff. I knew them all by heart.

Speed can be numbing.

I was going fast. Invincibly fast. Way too fast...

Danger is addictive, a relief. Scratch an itch.

An enormous sound and the car began veering out of control. The front tyre had struck something sharp.

Fear took control.

I found myself wedged on a miraculous slice of earth somewhere between the mountain and the sea.

Arms aching, temples pounding, body sweating excess adrenaline.

Dead beat.

I could only wait for someone to lend me a hand.

It was nearly comic.

The sun was high in the sky.

A Volkswagen bus slowly winding its way along the dusty road in the distance.

Thank God somebody who can help me, I thought.

A weathered man with elbow perched on the open window pulled up next to me.

"Can you give me a hand?" I whispered.
As he opened the door, I saw he only had one.
Fuck.
A one-handed Greek.

He stared at me just as kindly. "Got a spare?"

This guy was actually going to help me.

I fumbled in the trunk for the tyre and the axle. He taught me how to raise the car, unscrew the bolts, and change the tyres.

With each passage he defied his handicap.

I'd been desperate to get to the most remote place, fast and far from everything.

Instead I'd been taken to the most unexpected place of all. Humanity.

With one hand, Vassily, the fisherman, had changed everything.

He changed me.

He mounted the bus, placed his elbow on the open window and called out to me.

"Now slow down and enjoy the sea."

So I did. :-)

Giorgio de Mitri

Photography by Thierry Ledé.

In October 2003, just before his 18th birthday, my boyfriend Huw found a lump in his right testicle. He had testicular cancer. His treatment included the removal of the affected testicle, followed by about five months of chemotherapy when follow-up examinations found that the cancer had spread.

Looking back, I remember how despite everything, Huw still managed to joke and smile. He was so brave. He is now doing brilliantly and has been in remission for two years.

However, one of the effects of the treatment Huw received, and similarly for other cancer patients, is a reduced fertility. The following story is about my sister-in-law who shares my name, Joanna. I wanted to share her experience with you as I feel it gives encouragement and hope to all sorts of people who question their future…

I was 19, and after a traumatic year which ended in the death of my father, I took a spur of the moment and much deserved break with a trip to Australia. While I was in Sydney I noticed a slight puffiness around my collar bone. I mentioned this to a close friend's mum who told me not to worry, so I put it to the back of my mind, and partied hard until I flew to Melbourne to be with my family for Christmas.

By this point I had started to have a slight tingling in my forearm, which by Christmas had turned into numbness and loss of sensitivity in my fingertips. I told my aunt who I was staying with about this and my puffy collar bone, who also told me not to worry, but took me to the doctor's after Christmas day to get it looked at. They initially thought I had a clot in my thyroid gland, so booked me in to have a CT scan. Although I was worried, my aunt discouraged me from calling my mum, as she was in England and we didn't want her to worry.

So, the next day, I went with my aunt to have the CT scan. I went through the 'whirring donut', and waited… The doctor came into the waiting room and said they needed to check something, and so I had another scan, this time using iodine. I didn't know at this point that this is what they use to check for cancer, and thought that there had been something wrong with the machine!

The next day I went to the doctor to get the results. She quite calmly but frankly told me, 'We've found something we believe could be cancer. We need to do a biopsy to check…'

It all happened really quickly after that. I had a cancerous mass that filled my chest cavity, which was pushing my heart, lungs and other organs to the side.

They told me that it was called Non-Hodgkins Lymphoma, that it was very serious, very unusual and those who get it don't have a very high survival rate. They were very matter-of-fact about it.

The hardest part for me was telling my mum and my family. I wasn't in any pain, and so to say, 'I've got cancer' sounded much worse than I felt, it was almost unbelievable. I wasn't feeling the way you'd imagine feeling when you're that ill. The day before I just had this numb, puffy arm, and now I was telling my family I had cancer.

It was the day before New Year's Eve, and they wanted me to start treatment immediately. I wasn't allowed to go home to England as the mass inside me was putting pressure on my organs and the flight could prove to be lethal. I persuaded them to wait until after New Year's Eve to start the treatment as it struck me that this might be my last. I spent the night calling the people I loved, telling them the news.

I started treatment on New Year's Day. At first I felt really positive, and was ready to get this all out of the way. I stayed in hospital having chemotherapy for a week to start off, with my family coming to visit me every day or as much as they could. After that I had to come in for a day of chemicals, every three weeks. On those days I'd go home to my aunt's house, and throw up every hour for 36 hours. It was so tiring. I was really depressed, and really homesick. It was hard to stay positive all the time. There were times that I questioned everything, I asked myself, 'Why me?' When I lost my hair it made me feel ugly. I felt like a boy. And when I looked in the mirror I could see that I was ill.

However, after five and a half months of treatment the mass in my chest cavity had reduced enough for me to go home. This was a real boost for me. I went to the Royal Marsden Hospital in Sutton, which the hospital in Melbourne had suggested as the best place to go.

Although it had reduced a lot there was still a large mass that didn't seem to be responding as well, so I was given 'high dose chemotherapy', which was ten times stronger than the chemo I had before. They warned me that there was an 80 per cent chance of infertility. I couldn't harvest any of my eggs for the future as this was a lengthy and intrusive process which would have taken too long, and I needed to start treatment immediately. I might never have children… I was put on diamorphine for the pain, although I was so drugged up I can't even remember what the pain was.

A couple of weeks later, to the doctor's amazement I had recovered very quickly

probably because of my age, possibly because of my positivity. The final stage of my treatment was when they thought they could see scar tissue in the scans, and gave me radiotherapy to make sure this was all that it was. Radiotherapy was a bit like lying on a sunbed. They gave me four blue coloured tattoos on my chest which, when I lay on the bed, they would line up with a cross of light to make sure I was in exactly the same position each time. They also lay oddly shaped bits of lead on my body to protect other areas from the radioactivity. That was the last treatment I ever needed.

Two years after finding out I had cancer I was told I was in remission, which is as close to an 'all clear' as any cancer patient can get. My hair grew back curly! My life was rebuilt. During the next year I met my future husband, Tom. A year and a half later to my surprise and delight I was pregnant with my first little miracle! And here in 2006 I have three beautiful girls and an amazing, loving husband, and I am happier than I could have ever imagined!

Joanna Dudderidge

Domenico Dolce and Stefano Gabbana

The love ball.

Alber Elbaz

Still I Rise

You may write me down in history
With your bitter, twisted lies,
You may trod me in the very dirt
But still, like dust, I'll rise.
Does my sassiness upset you?
Why are you beset with gloom?
'Cause I walk like I've got oil wells
Pumping in my living room.
Just like moons and like suns,
With the certainty of tides,
Just like hopes springing high,
Still I'll rise.
Did you want to see me broken?
Bowed head and lowered eyes?
Shoulders falling down like teardrops.
Weakened by my soulful cries.
Does my haughtiness offend you?
Don't you take it awful hard
'Cause I laugh like I've got gold mines
Diggin' in my own back yard.
You may shoot me with your words,
You may cut me with your eyes,
You may kill me with your hatefulness,
But still, like air, I'll rise.
Does my sexiness upset you?
Does it come as a surprise
That I dance like I've got diamonds
At the meeting of my thighs?
Out of the huts of history's shame
I rise
Up from a past that's rooted in pain
I rise
I'm a black ocean, leaping and wide,
Welling and swelling I bear in the tide.
Leaving behind nights of terror and fear
I rise
Into a daybreak that's wondrously clear
I rise
Bringing the gifts that my ancestors gave,
I am the dream and the hope of the slave.
I rise
I rise
I rise.

Maya Angelou

This poem was so important to me when
I was growing up as a kid in Ladbroke Grove.

From left to right Pat McGrath, June Sarpong, Ben Skervin and
Edward, Indochine, New York.

Edward Enninful

Photography by Simon Harris.

Twenty-two year old Ben Drew, more commonly referred to as Plan B, hails from Forest Gate, east London. His vivid accounts of inner-city living are brutal and sometimes feared yet consistantly revered. Armed with an acoustic guitar, the rapper and sometimes singer, has drawn comparisons to the Arctic Monkeys, Johnny Cash and The Streets. But a listen to his debut album, *Who Needs Actions When You Got Words*, firmly places him in his own spot, talking on behalf of a jilted generation.

An honest living as told to Chantelle Fiddy...

"You don't have to go to college or University to do well in life, the University of Life is more important than any of that. My mate from Essex, people would think he had a better chance of doing well in life than me: he had money, he lived in a nice area with no crime, fewer drugs, good schools. His middle class neighbours would say he could do something proper. But then he came to London because his village was boring, he was like a naïve kid. I knew about drugs, I was wise, I'd experienced a lot. Drugs are everywhere but you can't blame drug addiction on other people. Some wankers have it around their kids and make them think it's ok. Then there's people who are just clueless. When you're in your 20s it's down to the individual. At 22, I couldn't talk a Manchester United fan into being an Arsenal fan could I? He learnt late on and now he's a smack head, injecting heroin in his veins and I'm here doing what I'm doing. His mum used to look down on me and thought I was a bad influence, if she had life experience she wouldn't have judged me; but she's had to go through her son becoming a heroin addict for her to realise she too had a lot to learn. The only way of avoiding the pitfalls of London are not coming at all, coming as a man or living it and learning. My kids would have to grow up in the city, they'd have to be streetwise and experience it. For me their grades wouldn't be as important, I just want them to go to school to learn how to read, write and speak properly. You just need motivation to succeed. When you see things happen you feel it. When I write my songs, it's a mixture of my own life and what I've seen in other peoples. I'm an artist so I'm going to always look at the world as an artist and someone who doesn't need a grade to make money or be happy in my work. The darkest time in my life was shit that went on at home and stuff that I talk about in my songs. One of the most personal tracks is 'Couldn't Get Along' about a mate that died. I got through things in my life by accepting them and being honest with myself; everybody lies, I lie, but when things get to a certain point where it's really messed up, the best way is honesty. You've got to be honest with yourself, don't believe your own lies. People see honesty. When I was experimenting with drugs I didn't have to kick the habit because I didn't let it become a habit. You know they're not good. The first pill is wicked, the second time you have a bad come down and the third time to even get high you have to double drop. The more you take you're never going to get that initial high, you're just going to keep pumping your body with shit. Ecstasy is a cool experience but you have to be man enough to accept when the bad times outweigh the good, most people aren't that honest with themselves.

I was man enough to say "I don't think this is cool", I don't order a drink to look cool either. I was honest enough to accept that whenever I smoked weed or sniffed coke, it turned me into a paranoid and dishonest person.

Weed may inspire you, but then you roll another joint in the morning and forget what you were going to do. Just be honest, it's having a negative effect. And all those great ideas, like so many things, they're just lost."

Chantelle Fiddy

It won't always be alright. Things often get worse, break down, disappoint. People fuck up, disappear, die. Nothing is totally reliable. Life is random. However, take some time to read this poetry. It may help. It has always helped me.

Simon Foxton

Desiderata

Go placidly amid the noise and haste,
and remember what peace there may be in silence.
As far as possible without surrender
be on good terms with all persons.
Speak your truth quietly and clearly;
and listen to others,
even the dull and the ignorant;
they too have their story.

Avoid loud and aggressive persons,
they are vexations to the spirit.
If you compare yourself with others,
you may become vain and bitter;
for always there will be greater and lesser persons than yourself.
Enjoy your achievements as well as your plans.

Keep interested in your own career, however humble;
it is a real possession in the changing fortunes of time.
Exercise caution in your business affairs;
for the world is full of trickery.
But let this not blind you to what virtue there is;
many persons strive for high ideals;
and everywhere life is full of heroism.

Be yourself.
Especially, do not feign affection.
Neither be cynical about love;
for in the face of all aridity and disenchantment
it is as perennial as the grass.

Take kindly the counsel of the years,
gracefully surrendering the things of youth.
Nurture strength of spirit to shield you in sudden misfortune.
But do not distress yourself with dark imaginings.
Many fears are born of fatigue and loneliness.
Beyond a wholesome discipline,
be gentle with yourself.

You are a child of the universe,
no less than the trees and the stars;
you have a right to be here.
And whether or not it is clear to you,
no doubt the universe is unfolding as it should.

Therefore be at peace with God,
whatever you conceive Him to be,
and whatever your labors and aspirations,
in the noisy confusion of life keep peace with your soul.

With all its sham, drudgery, and broken dreams,
it is still a beautiful world.
Be cheerful.
Strive to be happy.

Max Ehrmann, Desiderata, Copyright 1952.

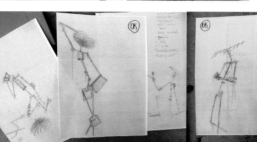

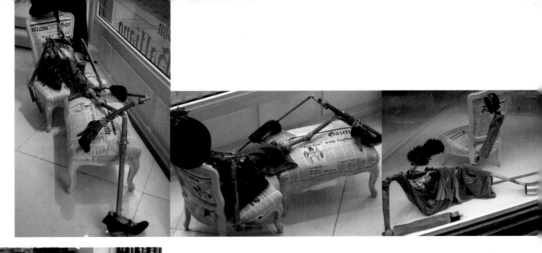

I had become crazy at 13. Because of a tragedy in the family, but more because I chose to. It was then that I discovered the theatre, and thanks to Elisa Palomino, the head of the studio at John Galliano, I am still alive today and not locked up in an institution.

Life is long but some things happen very quickly. The three years before my start at the John Galliano studio had been a slow descent into madness, a long road through the desert that so many from my generation know all too well. I was at the same time rebellious and terrorised by everyone who wanted contact with me. The world today is done in such a way that you get in trouble if you're unable to be categorised and pigeonholed. I didn't do any higher studies because I hated school and because I knew that I could learn everything by myself. The theatre was my life but I was also passionate about art and costume. The marionettes were for me a way to unite all of those things. But I was doing that alone, facing the mirror in my bathroom. To survive I would take any job – waiter, construction worker, sales person, but I could never keep any of them for long. One of the reasons was that I could not stand talking to people. I was paranoid.

One day, or more precisely one evening, after having been fired from McDonald's, I found by chance the address of John Galliano's studio and without really knowing his work except having seen a photo of him as a pirate, I left him my book (actually it was more an unruly pile of drawings, photos and texts than a real book). A few days later, Elisa called me and offered me an internship. The internship has become a part-time job that leaves me enough time to stay in the theatre world. I am free to propose to John anything that takes my fancy. Even in my dreams I couldn't imagine a better job, a job which would be as creative and with so few limits.

Today, everything is much better and the voices talking to me in the night are much calmer, kinder and more insightful. Adrien Beau (25) The photos represent Adrien's work on the summer display for the John Galliano boutique in Paris.

John Galliano

It's not how you start, it's how you finish. It's not where you're from, it's where you're at. It's not where you are, it's where you're going. Everybody gets knocked down, how quick are you going to get up? There's a light at the end of the tunnel. Don't worry, it's not an oncoming train. It's the sun rising on a new day full of endless possibilities. We all have choices to make; should I turn left, right, go straight ahead or just stand still? The temperature is the same whether you dip your toe or dive in head first. At some point you're going to have to get your hair wet. Go on, dive in.

Antony Genn

SPEAK UP...

Мой милый мальчик,
Ты же жизнь моя,
Нет, без тебя - никак!
Люба моя, как же ты так?
Зачем без тебя?
Ведь я же ЛЮБЛЮ!!!!!!!
ЛЮБЛЮ тебя.
Увы, Моя любовь к тебе -
уже больше не секрет.
Целую тебя нежно.
Пожалуйста, ЖИВИ!!!

К.

...DON'T BE AFRAID

As you have the power to lighten someone's life

Katia Gomiashvili

Our ABC for Silva:

Love mummy + Daddy

Apathy is feeling so low that you can not move, you cannot see the wood for the trees and it is ok to feel like this sometimes; remember there is no hot without cold, no up without down. **B**elief is everything. what you believe to be true is true, the truth resides in faith. **C**ourage is being true to you beliefs, telling your truth while respecting the truth of others, but be aware of foolish courage, the 'I can fly!' **D**eath is as certain as life, so start to really live. **E**mpathise by putting yourself in the shoes of others. Know how it is to be them. Remember that we are all one, that you are them so treat others as you would have them treat you. **F**orgive and understand them. **G**ive and never run out of love. keep giving because you can **G** never run out of love. **H**onour yourself, listen to you heart, you already know, you are present, so be present, be here now all ways. **I**nspiration means breath in, take in. let the universe fill you, guide you, with one voice and one song, one verse. **J**oy can not exist with sadness. Both are valid.

Kindness is rooted in intention, it's always the thought that counts. **L**ove is joy expressed, so express your joy. Know what you can know, stay open, keep learning. Love is everything. You are lovable, you deserve love and you are loved, you are our everything. **M**aster all that you can, better to be a master that a guru. **N**o is a great word. Use no as as powerfully as you would Yes. **O**ne step at a time, one by one, one little move every day. Soon you will achieve your goal. **P**ride can be a particularly difficult trap to be proud is OK to be too proud may cause you pain. **Q**uiet, be patient, be still, wait and listen. **R**elease, let go and know that the tightest grip is an open hand. **S**urrender and take the active choice to throw yourself willingly into the arms of chaos. **T**hought first, then word the action. **U**nity reminds you to continuously remove the illusion of seperation. We are all different but not seperate. Honour the difference. **V**oid. Nature abhors a vacuum. So avoid the Void - fill up. **W**onder at our world. Stop and look around you, look up, see the wood for the trees. **X** is a kiss to remind you to keep kissing. **Y**es you can. **Z**zz. Sleep safe and sound little one, good night, sleep tight don't let the bed bugs bite XX

Georgina Goodman and BJ Cunningham

497

The only things that got me through middle school and high school were making art outside of school and taking modern dance classes.

My parents, although supportive of my art interests, wouldn't pay to send me to an art school. My father was a professor of sociology and education at UCLA and thought art school was for dilettantes. I took a year off school. I was sort of aimless. I was frustrated because I wanted to create and express but I didn't have a form for it. All my life I only wanted to be an artist. At some point in my early 20s I worked for Larry Gagosian, who had yet to achieve his art world infamy. He was really moody and mean and would yell at us all the time. I finally quit and worked somewhere else as a framer. Larry was a character we sort of knew because he used to hang around Westwood Village and sell "grey market" art books on the street. Even then he had an interest in high art. I didn't have all the requirements to get into a good college so I started going part-time to a community college in Santa Monica, California where I lived. It cost like $30 for a semester. Those were the days before Ronald Reagan, as governor, hadn't yet taken down the whole school system in California. I waitressed at a tiny Indian restaurant that some friends of mine owned who were engineer grads at UCLA. They went on to become real estate tycoons in Venice, CA. Somehow I managed to get enough credits to transfer to another school. A friend of mine from high school, a percussionist, William Winant, was going to York University in Toronto. They had an interdisciplinary programme there in the arts – music, dance, visual art etc. It was very inexpensive to go to school there. I went but didn't end up liking it that much. While I was there, some friends and I started a noise garage band for our media class, which was taught by George Manupelli, a fluxus filmmaker. We played at the Ann Arbor Film Festival around 1976. I think they pulled the plug on us. Mike Kelley claims he saw us and was inspired to start his own noise band (though he was already a founder of Detroit noise group Destroy All Monsters with artists Jim Shaw, Niagara and Cary Loren). I also made a film there about Patty Hearst but was pretty much left on my own to flounder around. I transferred to Otis Art institute in Los Angeles, probably the cheapest art school ever. A conceptual artist teaching there, John Knight, told me I could petition my way out of school, which I did after a year. After I graduated I decided to move to NY because that was the centre of the art world and I thought if I stayed in LA I would get lost in the dreamy landscape and never do anything. When I moved to NY I had various bad jobs: waitressing graveyard shifts and working for Anina Nosei and Larry Gagosian, who had become a recognised gallerist. At the time, they both had a loft gallery in a non-commercial space. It was really Anina's gallery and I worked for her as a secretary although I had no skills. Larry stayed there when he was in NY and lurked around. They had David Salle's first show. I met Richard Prince when he brought in his watch ad photos. They were in those same metal frames that Larry G. used for his mass art products. I gave Richard a hard time for using them, but they did fit what he was doing. We became friends. Anina didn't really know what to do with his art. She would occasionally show it to clients as a last resort if nothing else interested them. Dan Graham was the first person I met when I moved to NY. He was always immensely supportive. During this time, I sublet different apartments. Every two months, it seemed, I moved. I could never get enough money together for the first and last months' rent. Eventually, I got a settlement from an auto accident that happened in Los Angeles, which allowed me to find a steady apartment. I was going to a lot of music shows. People like Glenn Branca and Rhys Chatham were doing their electric guitar pieces in clubs. Other no-wave bands, like DNA, were playing as well as bands from England like the Slits, the Raincoats, Young Marble Giants, the Fall, PIL etc.

Dan encouraged me to start writing. He guilted me into saying that I had to give back to the community. It somehow made things easier, feeling like I had to do something immediately. I couldn't wait any longer, no more excuses, just do it. The first piece I wrote was short. It was called Male Bonding and Trash Drugs. It was for a magazine called Real Life started by the artist Tom Lawson. It was a description of Rhys Chatham's Guitar Trio piece. Writing is the hardest thing in the world for me to do but I forced myself to do it, like taking medicine. I discovered something I didn't know I could do.

Next, Dan asked if I would participate in a performance piece of his involving an all-girl band. He introduced me to Miranda Stanton. Along with Christine Hahn (the drummer for Glenn Branca's trio The Static, and previously a member of Berlin group Malaria!) we formed a band called CKM. We just played out that once for Dan's mirror piece. We were supposed to interact with the audience in between songs. I was never so nervous in my life, but when it was over I wanted to do it again. Miranda introduced me to Thurston and we started hanging out and subsequently started playing music together. There were difficult years of odd jobs and eating lots of pasta but we never thought about not doing what we were doing. Everything I've ever done has been difficult. Nothing has come easy. I'm not a trained writer, or a trained musician, my singing is limited. Visual art is a more natural thing for me to do. But because I'm known for being in a rock band, it's a challenge to be taken seriously as such. There will always be the snide muso journalist who doesn't get it. To me it's all about the compulsion to create something that drives me away from self-consciousness. Or allows me to use that as a tool and not a deficit. I'm still figuring out how to make it all work.

Kim Gordon

I'm living proof that where there's a will, there's a way.

What I don't want is for people to pity me or think of me as a person who has had her life ruined. That's not how I see it. My mom is always saying, "If life hands you lemons, make lemonade." Which is a great outlook on life, if you can actually see beyond the lemons when you're up to your eyeballs in them! My strength came from my relationship with Christ and from the love and encouragement of my family and friends. In a lot of ways I'm like any fourteen-year-old girl, and in a lot of ways, I'm not. If someone had told me that this is how my life would be, I would have never believed it. It would have seemed too bizarre to be true. Sometimes it still is. I often dream that I have both my arms again, and I wake up expecting the whole shark business to be a nightmare. But it's not. It's my reality now, and I've learned to accept it. I've moved on. I don't pretend to have all the answers to why bad things happen to good people. But I do know that God knows all those answers, and sometimes He lets you know in this life, and sometimes He asks you to wait so that you can have a face-to-face talk about it. What I do know is that I want to use what happened to me as an opportunity to tell people that God is worthy of our trust, and to show them that you can go on and do wonderful things in spite of terrible events that happen. I don't think it does any good to sit around feeling sorry for yourself. I made myself a promise: I'm not going to wallow or walk around moaning, "Woe is me!"

I am excited about some of the opportunities to travel and surf all around the world that have come as a result of my attack and return to surfing. But most of all I am excited about what the future holds. Will I make it to the pro. ranks in surfing? Will my lifelong friend and surf buddy, Alana, be paddling next to me in the years to come as she is now and was during the attack? Will I be able to make a difference, in some small way, in people's lives by sharing my story? What does God have in store for me? I really don't know, but I do know one thing for sure: the adventure has only just started.

Bethany Hamilton

Dear Seb

I never told you what drugs did to my life, did I? I never told you how they affected me. No, personally I never touched them, how could I? They were the reason you got into so much trouble. They were the reason you left. I was eight years old when you went away. Mum and Dad had got to breaking point. They wanted to take you out of the situation you had got yourself into. They wanted to help you. They sent you to Colombia to live with your real Dad. Who knows what happened to you over there? Who knows what situations you faced? You were only eighteen. But somehow you made it through and look at you now; a beautiful wife, dozens of good friends and a job in television that I'm sure hundreds would kill for.

I couldn't help you. I was only a little girl. But I helped someone else and now he's made it too.

Life is a journey, we learn as we go. You learnt and you changed. You worked hard and I'm proud of you.

I think of you always.

Your little sister, Gemma

Gemma Hogan

At sixteen, my son, let's call him David, was doing fine at school. This was more than I had ever hoped for.

His mother and I had separated, by mutual agreement, early on. We had a good working relationship, and were quietly proud of the boy we'd raised together apart, against the odds, though we both imagined there might be some sort of price to pay when he was older, a punishment visited upon us for having parted.

I'd made a new relationship, and David was a big part of the family. My partner and I marvelled at how responsible he was, round at ours of a weekend, and when his heavy homework schedule allowed, during the week. He was an exemplary big brother to his sisters, who adored him. We thought he'd eventually lose interest and turn into a surly teenager, but we could see adulthood ahead, and with no sign of trouble it looked as though he'd got off scot free.

At about this time he revealed, in passing, that he had begun smoking marijuana with his friends. My partner and I were white, liberal and middle class. We made a big show of being understanding. He was a metropolitan youth at a state boys' school, we had to expect this sort of thing. He had African heritage. It was cultural. What right did we have, sipping our own drug of choice, to be anything but accepting, provided it was just an occasional puff?

But then the phone started ringing in the middle of the night. His mother and I had always shared responsibilities, and naturally it was me she turned to at 2am when he'd gone missing and the police couldn't find him. I made a few calls, but before I joined her in a search, he turned up, wild-eyed and jumpy, but persuasive.

It was all OK, a rites of passage thing, we told ourselves.

So it was a bit of a surprise when David, my bright and shining son, suddenly stopped washing or eating or coming round to mine very much. It was tricky explaining things to his lovelorn sisters. It was confusing when the school started writing letters asking where he was, and alarming when his mother and I were carpeted by the head-teacher, who revealed that he'd been AWOL for most of a term. Naturally, David had an answer for everything. It was all a misunderstanding, the school's fault actually, he'd been there nearly all the time, but somehow they hadn't taken the register properly; or Mr. X, the physics teacher, who had it for him anyway, was an idiot who only noticed you were there if you were a thug. Not a good student, like he was, and I was all too keen to believe him.

To my shame I managed to believe him when my wife's wedding ring went missing and he professed to know nothing about it. To my shame I didn't really hear her gentle insistence that she'd seen it on his finger and didn't expect to see it ever again.

His mother was supplying a steady stream of intelligence. He was hanging out with a crowd of undesirables. She was letting them congregate in her house so they weren't out on the street, prey to Dixon of Dock Green. But it was abusive. They drank and swore and even though she asked them not to, they smoked their shit on her sofa. I went round to remonstrate, but the birds had flown the nest.

I talked to friends. Suddenly it seemed that just about everyone smoked, but they managed to do it recreationally, now and again. Why, I asked, did David have to do it all the time?

They all said I should be cool. We'd all done it, gone a bit crazy. I was all too keen to believe it, frightened to face the truth, and perhaps a bit lazy. Wading in, being uncool would take a lot of time and effort.

And then came the disastrous GCSE results, and David's decision to take a gap year, between re-takes and the A levels he wanted to do. He was out of control. What was he going to do with his time off? He was going to chill, he said. In fact he was going to do the opposite. He was going to blaze, a new verb I'd never come across before, a euphemism for getting out of his brain. And that's exactly what it meant for David. I'd now go to help his mother in the dead of night, or on a Sunday afternoon or on a Wednesday at 11am and see him, a boy ablaze. Marijuana was supposed to bliss you out, but it made him into a red-eyed maniac who'd threaten his mother with violence, scream blue murder and flee to the park, shirtless in a rainstorm.

I was watching my beautiful child go down in flames and I felt powerless to do anything about it. His mother was on her knees, threatening to throw him out. I cleared my office at home and got a bed in for him, but he wanted to crash with his friends, the very people who were encouraging him to join them in their express elevator to hell. I played nice cop and then nasty cop, but to no avail. We tried father and son counselling, but it just seemed like chitchat. I'd cling to him after every session, enjoying his sobriety, not wanting him to catch the bus back home.

I could think of nothing but David, and the future he'd thrown away for a lungful of crap. I'd been a duffer at school, but he was a clever child who had every opportunity to live a happy and productive life. I didn't need him to have fame or fortune, but I did want light and joy. Now I lived with the probability that the next time I would see him would be across a courtroom or in a drawer at the morgue.

And then, like a great storm, it blew itself out. He just seemed to emerge from a cocoon, a bit singed but otherwise unharmed. He still reeked, but now, joy of joys it was plain, wholesome nicotine, not the sickly sweet scent of skunk.

Totting it up after the event, I think we lost David for about four years. He went into the pit a child and emerged a graceful young man without qualifications but with hope and humility. We were happy to welcome him back, keen to engineer a new relationship with his sisters.

But when a DVD goes missing or I can't find my watch, it is David I suspect first. I hate myself for thinking it, but I have no choice. The liberal in me still can't argue with legislators who want to soften the law on weed, but the fascist in me wants to kill anyone and everyone who encouraged my own son to chill out and try a little puff.

Ian

I would like to nominate my mate Paolo Hewitt as someone who must be an inspiration to the "next generation of creative thinkers". I will summarise very, very briefly.

Paolo was brought up in care and recounted those days in his book *The Looked After Kid*.

He grew up never knowing who his parents were. Only that he was taken from his mother at a very young age. He spent the rest of his life being brought up in care homes and families until he was old enough to fly the nest. His love of music and football drove him on to achieve his aim of working within those fields. He worked at the NME in his early working life (when the NME really was an important music journal) and has since gone on to write about 15 books on music, fashion and sport. His latest book could see him achieve a lifelong ambition and write the biography of one of his boyhood heroes.

The thing I most admire about Paolo is the fact that a) he's done it all himself b) he's never thought the world owes him a living and doesn't do the self-indulgent stuff and c) he's never sold out. He could quite easily have got involved in writing trashy, high volume, lowest common denominator crap, but it's not him. He's never compromised what he's wanted to do for the quick buck.

"Taken away from mother after two days, still no clue as to who my father is. Placed in care until four years old and then fostered by a woman who made Cruella De Vil seem like a good bet.

Thrown out of foster home at ten and placed back in care. Spent eight years at Burbank children's home. Life lessons learnt.

Don't let the people who have hurt you the most, stop you grabbing life and living every minute, for then they win and you lose.

Also, in the home we never told each other our circumstances, because of that we just got on with life and the situation we were in. It was a good philosophy, stopped you from taking on too much self-pity. I think all children who come through such hurt and pain are the most important children in the world. After I left home I was determined to become a writer, I knew it would be a struggle (still is some days) but I wanted to give it everything I'd got. I was haunted by the thought of never trying and therefore never knowing. God gave me the breaks and I took them. Together with Him, I intend to take many more before I am finished. God bless the child." Paolo

Steve Harris

1984. I am 16. I have the first editions of i-D. My soundtrack is Bauhaus, Bowie and early U2, I've shaved the sides of my head and spiked the rest white.

I walk into the bathroom unannounced. The yellow tiles have spurts of blood on them and the needle still in his arm. I am frozen on the other side of the dream. He was experimenting and now he's falling. He talks about futility. Not knowing what his place is in the world. What future? I see him sink. He lies. He steals. He says only I can save him. But I can't. I watch him take others down with him, all of them losing their chance at brilliance.

I didn't think about the choices he made, but I didn't think much about the choices I was making then either. I didn't play out a chess game considering future steps; I lived in the moment, rife with the emotion of the unknown and the dangerous and the thrilling. "We can be Heroes, just for one day," Bowie sang.

I still find myself instinctively glancing at a man's inner arms in order to check out whether he's clean or not. I lose almost everyone I knew to heroin.

2006. I'm looking at a needle in an arm. I am in a refugee camp on the border with Somalia. The baby will die, despite the drip in his arm. 127,000 people. Thirteen water pumps. Ten years there and no hope of return in sight. The sun burns, the sand shimmers before me. Boys in ragged t-shirts; girls dragging firewood. Huts made of twigs and discarded sacks.

I sit and talk to a group of teenagers. They haven't failed themselves. The world has failed them. In the midst of poverty and death and fear, what strikes me and humbles me is the ability they have to have such clarity. To continue to aspire, and to dream, despite the horror of this camp. "When I grow up, I want to be the president of my country," says one. "We are the future for peace in our country."

I am silenced, I am awed. Would I have such hope, and aspirations, had I been born and raised here in a camp? Would I have that courage? That night in camp, I can't sleep. Lying on my bed with the fan turning through the night, I can almost feel, just minutes away from me, the life of the women lying on rushes on a mud floor, the moonlight flooding through the holes in the roof, sharing a room with 5 others, still hungry. Suddenly all I want to do is crawl back furiously in time, back to shake my 16 year old friends, me, hard. To scream in anger, a shadow looking on as we re-enact those scenes. I want to run and grab my ghosts and shout: what a waste.

"Everything has been figured out, except how to live." Jean Paul Sartre

Hannah Jones

How to get ahead in Fashion.

Most self-help books are rather like naff cosmetic pages in dull women's magazines: 'Disguise your faults and highlight your good points, then you'll get your man'. But what they get wrong is for the creative individual, the reverse is true. To be fucked up is essential. Of course Joan Crawford beat her children, on balance she was an amazing actress. Van Gogh cut his ear off but was a wonderful painter. We know about Kate's chemical problems but that reality is what makes her such an icon. Was Chanel an egomaniac? Why is Karl Lagerfeld so skinny? What people never explain is that creativity is Abnormal expression; Normal expression is working at a bank and having 2.5 children. So there are certain points that it might be good to contemplate:

Be eccentric

Do you really imagine that normal balanced people would come up with unusual ways of presenting themselves? What was the cocktail of dysfunction that spurred Vivienne Westwood to come up with punk? Was it dissatisfaction with the status quo or an egotistical boyfriend and no money?

Be a homosexual

Not completely essential but boy, it helps. Why not turn those parent problems and feelings of rejection into a ballgown? It will have attitude, a point of view and you might look great in it too. And remember having a fashion show is like giving birth – and your legacy.

Be an egomaniac

Do you have a firm idea of what's right and wrong, what's good and bad taste, what you like and what you hate, and find it strange that other people are just 'wrong'? Why don't they understand that it's all about me me me me and not about them them them? Self-belief tinged with an unhealthy amount of manic obsessiveness and a sense of melodrama is crucial to success in fashion. Shy violet? No, precious exotic orchid.

Be suburban

Those glamourous, urbane people in fashion magazines don't have a clue what it's like growing up in Taunton or Coventry. Or maybe that's where they are from in the first place. If you are Goth (or similar), hanging out in a shopping centre on a rainy Tuesday afternoon, realise that your feeling of despondency mixed with anger is in fact fabulous creative energy and use it to get the hell out of there. P.S. Remember the fashion business is completely about re-inventing yourself and in fact we all do it every six months, so you'll fit in just fine.

Be ugly

Ok, you are no oil painting, but with the help of cosmetics and hair dye, you can paint on an interesting New You. (have you noticed that larger girls always have fabulous manicures, or that awkward, strange looking guys look rockstar gorgeous in black eye pencil?) Suppress those ideas of wanting to be pretty or classically handsome; either you are born with it or not.
As Edith Sitwell said, "If you are a greyhound, what is the point of trying to look like a Pekinese?"

Be thick

Ok, it's a sweeping statement, but we are talking about creative expression here, not academic prowess. Was Einstein a fashion God? No. Being clever can get in the way of your muse, you might analyse too much, think that fashion is narcissistic, ephemeral and ecologically unsound without realising that a bit of blind ego, verve and fabulousness can propel you on to the front page of *i-D* and *Vogue*. If you are a secret bookish Balenciaga, keep that all on tap for your memoirs and your retrospective at the V&A.

Au revoir, good luck and smile for the cameras!

Stephen Jones

ME and My Misspent Youth

When I was nineteen I was diagnosed with ME. I couldn't walk.

I photographed the walls of my bedroom, the pills I took, the view from my window and my bed.

I was told that ME was a condition that I would live with all my life.

Over ten years on I would say that it is a MEMORY that I will live with all my life.

I was sick with ME for four years and, for a couple of years after that I was in recovery – cautiously optimistic that I was better – but vigilant in case I relapsed.

I feel very fortunate to have recovered from ME. And now, even though my misspent youth was crazy in a whole different way than what it might have been – I wouldn't change a thing.

Illness can teach you to appreciate very simple things: To take nothing for granted. To live life slower. And to make hay while the sun shines.

Kayt Jones – Topanga – 2006
Photographer, wife, and mother of two beautiful girls.

Kayt Jones

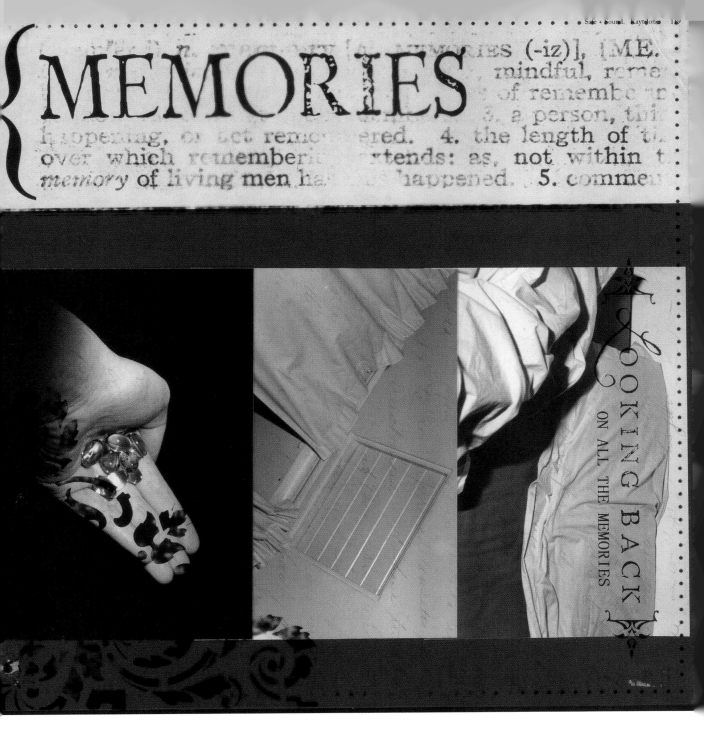

MEMORIES (-iz)], [ME.

mindful, reme
of remember
3. a person, thi
happening, or not remembered. 4. the length of ti
over which remembering extends: as, not within t
memory of living men has happened. 5. commen

LOOKING BACK

ON ALL THE MEMORIES

Stammering

If asked to identify the one little thing that has caused me the most hardship in my life, the one vexation that has brought me most grief, I would have to point, not to a debilitating illness or handicap, but to the consonant that follows ABC.

D, how I hate you.

Of course Bs, Gs and Ss have occasionally wrecked havoc too, but it is Ds that have kept me awake at night, made me weak from anxiety and affected the way in which I see and talk to the world.

I have stammered since I was about five, and it was at school where it hurt the most, obviously. Children are remarkably resourceful when it comes to identifying someone's weak points, but with a stammer the ammunition is handed to them on a plate; with a stammer you are putting the bullets into their hands yourself. I don't remember much from those days, but I remember enough.

Few things are more worrying when you're young than standing in the middle of a playing field with 20 other boys waiting to call out their names, knowing that when your turn comes, your stammer is only going to be exacerbated by the anxiety of getting it right. I also remember standing in the dinner queue, knowing that I was going to have immense difficulty asking for whatever was on the menu that day, the pressure increasing second by second as my school friends swiftly barked their requests before turning away.

Unless you've experienced it yourself, it's difficult to imagine the abject depression of worrying about every single word that comes out of your mouth. Between the ages of about eight and 16 it was utter hell. Every request had to be worked out in advance, every joke required a run-up (and God help you if you fell at the punchline).

The tribulations of teenage angst are bad enough without literally being tongue-tied. Some women say they find a stammer attractive, an indication of sensitivity perhaps, or vulnerability. But no teenage girl ever finds a stammer attractive, at least not the ones I knew at 13.

Just recently I judged a writing competition for young stammerers, and some of the stuff I read was heartbreaking. These children just couldn't talk, couldn't communicate, and were relentlessly bullied by their peers. Just read this: "I would like you to know that you are the only one that I can tell how I actually feel at this moment in time. I have had a stammer for about ten years of my life and at the present time it just seems to be worse than ever. I hate school so much!!! I love going to see my friends but I don't tell them everything I want to I just can't. One minute I think I can so I start to say some words then I just freeze they must think I'm mad. I'm the laughing stock of the whole school well that's what I feel like." Not only did these stories bring back horrific memories from my childhood, it made me think how little we do nowadays to help young people who can't talk properly, and consequently who can't communicate properly. There is still such a terrible stigma surrounding stammering, and one that has hardly been helped by the reductive laddish culture of the previous decade.

As I matured, I began taking my stammering for granted, and it became almost an integral part of my make-up. During my late teenage years, when a different youth cult seemed to invade my life every six months or so, my stammer became a badge of notoriety, a symbol – like an earring or a black leather jacket – of a certain type of 'otherness'. But then I really did grow up, and the stammer (or at least its importance) faded from my life like so many Buzzcocks records. It was never completely debilitating, but seeing that my main hindrance was always the dreaded 'D', obviously one of the worst things for me had been announcing myself on the telephone. It had almost made me reluctant to introduce myself, which, as a journalist, caused all too palpable problems. I mastered it, though, and even grew to conquer public speaking, something I used to abhor.

The first time I ever spoke successfully in public was when a friend asked me to give her away at her wedding, at the Chelsea Psychic Garden in London. Her father was almost pathologically shy, and didn't feel he was up to the task. So I obviously said yes. This was the first time I had been asked to do anything remotely like this, and I was incredibly, almost unbearably nervous.

So I spent a good month collating material, and building a speech around anecdotes and personal observations. With hindsight I don't think the speech was that wonderful, but it was completely, thoroughly researched, so I certainly knew what I was talking about.

When I was actually called upon to say my words – sober, sweating, clutching my speech as though it were the deeds to my house – I took a deep breath, started e-x-t-r-e-m-e-l-y slowly and took extra care to enunciate with care. And everything was going fine until I told my first joke. It wasn't an especially funny joke – I had tailored the material to the crowd – but as I delivered the punchline, the entire crowd fell about laughing. Not only did this give me the confidence to finish the speech, but also taught me a fundamental lesson about captive audiences: they want to enjoy themselves, and they want to laugh.

And that's what I've done ever since: treated every speaking engagement as a wedding speech, assuming that your audience is pleased to see you, and can't wait to hear you. Yes, I still stammer occasionally, but I've learnt to move on, accept it, and treat it with the contempt it deserves.

Dylan Jones

Aimee Mullins is a true inspiration to us all.

Matt Jones

I realise that the brain is an edit machine. I have edited throughout my life stuff that I felt was not helpful or constructive. I learnt that at secondary school after being separated from my mother when she had her first breakdown. I was ten and she had brought up my sister and I without any support from our father, who we never knew. Just the one photo of him in RAF uniform, he had wanted to be a fighter pilot.

As a kid I dreamt I could fly. I am always inspired and intrigued by butterflies. Recently on a transatlantic flight I watched a documentary about the 100 metre butterfly final at the Montreal games in 2005. The world record was broken by Ian Crocker who had suffered from clinical depression yet still managed to win the gold medal.

While studying Commercial Art in Bristol I would meet up with my mother on Saturdays. On 'good days' she was allowed to leave the ward and hospital; we would have lunch and watch a matinee movie in Bristol city centre. Electric treatment or drugs never seemed to fix her nerves permanently and gradually sucked out her energy – my foster parents always thought a career in the air force would give me security. By chance and intuition that plan changed when my mother signed me up to do a commercial art course at the West of England College of Art. Those four years as a student changed my life and was where I met Tricia whose spirit for living became my inspiration – like a butterfly both beautiful and free.

This project made me think of stuff from the past and the swimmer's story illustrated the human ability to rise above the highs and lows, exceeding one's own expectations with coaching and encouragement.

Terry Jones

Caught in the middle – between the love of those who cannot live together

Dearest Mum
You always said it was unfinished business. That
even after all the
years, there was
something that
hadn't gone away,
needed resolving;
something deep in
your soul, where
unrequited love burns
an emptiness
into our spirit.

You had achieved
so much in the
years after
he left, become
so much more.
A rounded, inspirational,
independent woman; but there
was always the never answered
question..why? Why did he go?
Why did he stay away?
Why didn't he love me
enough? Why wasn't
I good enough? And it
stayed with you with
the tenacity and
desperation of an
eighteen year old. It could
bring out the absolute
worst in you, the inappropriate
girly flirting, the kind of
spiteful niggling about
him that corrodes
love.

But underneath
it all he was our Dad
the grand passion
of your life and no later
man was ever really able to
touch him, never able
to live up to your
memories of him.

For years and years
I battled with you
"Let it go Mum,

it's over – move on,
you're bigger than
this… it was thirty-five years
ago" But in the
last analysis you
were so right
and I was so definitely
wrong.

When Dad
finally came to your
funeral after the horrible
letter, the big row of a
few months before, my
friends told me he had
been visibly upset
during the service;
but in true Dad's style
he brushed it off
returning home to his wife with
"well I don't
want a funeral like
that!" But somewhere inside,
an "extraordinary for him"
need to put his affairs,
his papers, his photos,
and his office in order.

He phoned both of us
(my brother and I)
the next morning
"You did your mother
proud" the closest
to a gold medal we
would ever receive
from him, an
acknowledgement that
for once, unconditionally,
we had done something better than
good enough.

Three weeks later he would
be dead himself from
a stroke.

The phone call at
breakfast unusually alone in
our house, a numbness
and out of body,
out of time,

moment that
it's hard to
comprehend now.
In some extraordinary
way I wasn't
surprised, my soul
had got used –
or so I thought – to
the idea of
death over the previous
few months.

It was only later
that the completeness
of it dawned
on me. The joining
up of the circle
that he had fought
so vocally
and definitely
against. It was
over, it had
been over for
him many years
before; but there
was that indefinable
something. That link
that good kids, beautiful
grandchildren and
a future you have
helped to create,
does not allow you
to put down, will
not let you erase.

So almost one year
later I raise a toast
of thanks to you both
from all of us,
the gang you
left behind. The
ones who carry
your genes and all
the best bits of
you into today's
future.

My love and gratitude. xx

This was a totally private letter written to my Mum
approximately one year after her death. It was only later I
realised it was indeed all I wanted to say for Safe+Sound.

In more together times...

Tricia Jones

This is a picture I took of the sun shining from the aeroplane. When I first came to England, from Japan, I had courage and hope. As soon as I came to England, I faced problems. For example, the difference between expectation and reality, language, culture etc. I tried to accept it, as it is with children when they face new things. I tried to be positive and flexible. Through these experiences, I learnt different points of view and a different culture. I had photography and made lots of friends. I'm enjoying living in London now.

Takashi Kamei

Kaws

Nothing can prepare you for the death of a loved one.

There is no set of rules to follow to make things easier, there is no timeframe within which things return to normal. Grief is a deeply personal thing that plays out differently for everyone. It can knock you for six and swallow you whole, it can drop you into a spiral of disbelief and depression, it can turn you against the people who need you and who you need the most.

In January 2006 my mother said to me that she couldn't touch her finger to her thumb properly, we had been moving some furniture the day before and she had at first attributed it to this. However, there was no pain involved at all, it was as though she had a mental block and couldn't physically make herself do it.

Over the next day or two she became quite sleepy and lost more opposability in her hand. After a call to the doctor we were booked for an appointment at the hospital, where she was tested for a possible blood clot as there is a history of this in the family. This showed up clear so they gave her a chest X-Ray as well as a brain scan, the results showed a growth in her chest as well as a further two in her brain.

In some ways she was lucky to have been seen in hospital, her diagnosis was swift. Within a week they had told her it was cancer and that it was incurable; it turned our lives upside down.

In retrospect the grieving process kicked in early, as soon as we heard the word 'terminal'. Sure we masked it with denial and tried to be positive but things were escalating so fast and preventative measures were not proving effective.

My mother died on the 20th June, five months after the first symptom. All sorts of things go through your mind and you have to somehow sort the rational from the irrational, not an easy task when you can't even tell what time of day it is, what day of the week it is, what the point to anything is.

The biggest thing for me, and others I've spoken to who have been in similar situations, is 'what happens next?' This applies to yourself and the person who has died. Well for you, things carry on. They'll never be the same but they will carry on and you will need to find a way to come to terms with what has happened. This ties in to the other part of what happens next. What happens to the person who has died?

No matter what beliefs you already hold, you will question them. This surely has to be the biggest question we face and the most impossible to answer: what happens to someone once they die? Is there some kind of life after death? Is there such a thing as reincarnation? Is it simply the end?

Some strange things happened around the time of my mother's death and I can't honestly explain them rationally (read as scientifically). We had always kept cats when I was younger and during the week approaching my mother's death we had many feline visitors to the house. Probably ten or more cats we had never seen before, all arriving in our garden and just sitting and looking into the house. On a couple of occasions we had the back door open and they would come into the house and sit on our laps, not nervous or anything, as if they had a right to be there.

In the week following my mother's death we had one cat in particular who would be waiting for us on the doorstep in the morning. We would let her in, she'd spend the entire day with us, and then leave in the evening. The day of my mother's funeral was the last time she stayed. It was the crossover of June into July and extremely hot when one day a pair of robins arrived in the garden, my mother's favourite bird. They sat on a bench in the garden and watched myself and my brother for a couple of hours at least. I don't think I'd ever seen a robin in summer before.

Lots of things were happening and I couldn't shake the feeling that my mother was controlling them. It's a strange feeling which I can't really explain, but when certain things happened around me I got a really strong feeling that my mother was in control.

One evening I was sorting through some paperwork and found a note my mother had written for me. It made me cry. I looked out the window and saw the most incredible sunset and was suddenly filled with the feeling that someone was looking out for me.

A year previously my grandmother had died and we had taken a potted rose bush from her garden. On my mother's birthday the bush came into full bloom, again on my brother's birthday (in November!). Finally on Christmas day the bush bloomed once more. At the time it was spooky but also quite comforting, as though she was sending birthday cards and Christmas cards to us all.

Only after my mother's death and the events that occurred did I start to see things in a different way or at least start to genuinely believe some of the ideas I had had after my grandmother's death.

I now have an answer to what happens after someone dies. Now, this is only my personal view but it is one I feel able to embrace. I believe that once a person has died they are manifested in nature, whether this is a conscious decision we are allowed to make or whether it is part of a process is beyond me, but it fits into the experiences I have had.

I take great comfort in my conclusions and for weeks I couldn't look at an animal, a particularly striking cloud formation, a sudden gust of wind happening at an opportune moment in a conversation… without thinking that it was somehow connected to something beyond chance. 2006 was a whirlwind of a year and many things changed, physically, emotionally and spiritually. However, a corner has been turned and things are starting to look up. I will shortly be moving into a wonderful new flat that really couldn't have come at a better time and it feels as though the universe is smiling on me after all I went through last year. Something is missing though, the feeling of being looked after has passed.

The second half of last year felt like a jigsaw puzzle and my mother has been watching over me and helping me fit the pieces together. Now everything seems to be fitting into place it's as though her job here is done.

Ben Kei

I REALLY WANT TO HEAR SOMEONE.
HOW TO GET CLOSER

How to live my one world?

The boxes symbolise a separation between the girls and the world they live in – they feel isolated. They show the inner struggle that they have to find out what they want from life. The boxes covering their heads control the girls' senses.

I love the camera because I can communicate without sound; I only need what's on my mind. Life is not hard just keep going for what you want.

Hyun Jung Kim

This image takes me to a better place each time I see it. Slightly dead peony struggling to be alive and beautiful; modern times can be warped, sometimes cruel. We are living in an uncertain time zone and we never really know what tomorrow brings when it comes, but we can always try for the unexpected journey and the ride may be surprisingly pleasant despite some difficulties along the way... It may all work out to be worth it. Time, speed, beauty, colours, tears, love, sex, layers of life unfold itself each day that we never quite know. Being in England has taught me a little bit about those qualities. Everything is about a memory within. Like a giant flower with its protective petals.

Kirby Koh

Sophia Kokosalaki

Photograph by Benjamin Alexander Huseby.

Nick Knight
Skinhead, 1982.

HOW TO PUBLISH YOUR FIRST

SKINHEAD
NICK KNIGHT

WHEN YOU TURN 14, PHOTOGRAPH YOUR FRIEN
EVERYDAY FOR A YEAR SHOWING EXACTLY WHA
THEY ARE WEARING.
PHOTOGRAPH THEM DANCING, FIGHTING, LARKIN'
AROUND, WITH THEIR PARENTS, WITH THEIR
BOYFRIENDS AND GIRLFRIENDS, AT SCHOOL, AT PARTI
FIRST THING IN THE MORNING, LAST THING AT NIGH
THEN PUT ALL THE PICTURES IN A BOX.
SHUT IT AND DO NOT OPEN IT FOR 10 YEARS
OPEN ON YOUR 24th BIRTHDAY AND YOU WILL
HAVE CREATED A UNIQUE FASHION DOCUMENT
THAT WILL BECOME A CULT BOOK ALL OVER
THE WORLD.

If you first see the world it might not be what you expected, maybe you even have an "electric mother", there are still enough reasons to always look forward and if you have

Helmut Lang

Photography by Helmut Lang.

nothing to lose you might as well get rid of your protective layer and when things dry up a little bit you will be encouraged, supported, loved and respected, and slowly you will be

your own star. – Helmut Lang Dedicated to Marianne Kohn, 60, lives and works in Vienna as manager of the Loos-Bar and La Divina. povera_7@hotmail.com

Image from David's inspirational
film *RIZE* (2005).

David LaChapelle

I first met Charlie as a student of my Dad's. He had come over to help out doing some tests for a shoot later plotted & schemed our ideas & plans for the future. It felt like a special time, everything lay ahead, goals

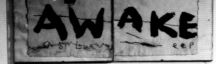

I don't think wrapping the young in cotton wool to protect them is the answer. Its many of the risky things in life that are most rewarding & life-giving. And although advice is valuable and important, I think the best way for young people to learn is through experience, and what goes on around them. In Charlie's death he has given many different gifts and lessons to the hundreds of young people whose lives he touched. For me I grew a new awareness to the fragility of life, and a greater sense of value for each day I wake up alive. And of course, that getting into a car with a drunk driver is definitely not worth risking the pain & destruction it has the potential to cause.

privilege of Charlie's positive energy in their lives. The SafeSound project wants to address how we can

that week. We experimented on Dad's IOx8 badboy with black&white paper that we developed in trays under the
and dreams within reach. Three days later, on fireworks night, Charlie died in a car crash. I hadn't known

bed. It was an exciting period for us both. For different reasons, we had both been holding back our passion for photography for some time. But now,

Charlie was denied the opportunity to fulfil his aims & ambitions, which is a huge

Charlie long, but his death affected me deeply.

The young person I am closest to and care for most is my brother Frank. Later this year he is going to be 13. I would never want anything bad to happen to him, but at the same time I must give him the space to make his own decisions. This summer I watched him standing

at the top of a tall wall trying to build the courage to jump into the sea.

He stood there for a while thinking about it, sussing out the situation. I wasn't sure he was going to do it, then suddenly... he took the plunge.

Tyrone Lebon

tragedy. Not only for Charlie, his family, and his friends, but also everyone else who was yet to have the
Oct'05, we had each turned a corner and were at a similar place: hungry and ready to immerse ourselves. Charlie's

When Tricia invited me to participate in this issue, I had to say "yes", for two reasons.

First of all as Tricia was asking me. She is a person I admire a lot. We met a couple of years ago, when both of us were working on this special project on women. At that time I was about to make another major step in my life as well, and I will always treasure that moment, because I learned a lot. Our paths have been crossing ever since…

Life is beautiful. And it takes courage to embrace it.

I have learned this along the way and it is the other reason for me to join the project. As a kid, I was the youngest of two. Brecht, my elder brother, was and is exceptionally intelligent, something he inherited from my dad, a civil engineer. And there I was, with seemingly no mathematical intelligence at all. This definitely shaped my character. Unfortunately as a teenager it convinced me that I was extremely stupid. And the Belgian scholar system, with its focus on theory, did not help

much either. I started to fight it, I was a rebel. I wanted to prove I wasn't stupid. Despite all this, I pulled myself through university.

It takes time to realise life is a great adventure. There was one moment in my life, a milestone to realise that, a turning point. A "disaster" happened during my final project in University. The printing job went terribly wrong. I was so devastated. I was ready to end my life. I went to my parents' house, ran out into the woods, where I used to go for a walk with my dog Billy. Thank god my dad found me. Good old dad, always there at the right moment.

Like all of us I have faced many challenging moments since then in both my private and corporate life. What seemed so disastrous then was really not so bad. Things for women are not always easy. But I have used that memory, in the woods, ever since. 'Whatever may happen, nothing will ever be as bad as that night'. Life is beautiful.

Drieke Leenknegt

Photography by Wim Van De Genachte and Franky Claeys.

At the age of 18 I was told I had a serious mental illness called schizophrenia and that I would need to take strong drugs for the rest of my life. 21 years later, I now work as a clinical psychologist;

I have not taken any psychiatric medication for over 19 years. I now work with people who hear voices, people who experience strong mood-swings and unusual ideas. I believe that if you go crazy, as I did, with the right support and effort your experiences can be made sense of and you can make a strong recovery. If I am helping someone I am not interested in what diagnosis they have been given, I am interested in who they are, and what they have been through. My personal experience, and that of helping others, has made me realise that while drugs can calm problems down in the short term, taken over a long term period they make someone's health problems worse. I have found people's mental health problems make sense if you creatively and carefully understand their life stories. When I was 11, my mother had a brain haemorrhage. A brain operation saved her life but left her mentally and physically disabled. She eventually made a strong recovery through her own determination and the support of neighbours and friends. However, during my teenage years my mother and I argued constantly and I became less and less interested in my education, spending a lot more time hanging out on street corners. Aged 15 I began smoking cannabis pretty heavily for a couple of years. At 17 I got a girlfriend and tried to focus on getting into advertising. However, a year later my girlfriend had left me and I found myself in a dull career as an office junior in a small business. I began to escape more and more into a fantasy world that became more and more real. At first I felt I was getting messages from God that I was special and that I had a mission. I wondered what my mission could be. What if I was a trainee spy rather than an office junior? What if the packages I was asked to deliver were top secret documents? As the ideas intensified I slept less, I began to hear messages warning me to be careful on the radio and television.

Eventually I ended up in a psychiatric hospital and was forced to take strong drugs that subdued me. My parents were told I had schizophrenia, that drug treatment would need to be lifelong. I disagreed. I believe my breakdown, what they called schizophrenia, was a kind of grief reaction, that my fantasies and paranoia were fuelled by strong emotions that till then had been suppressed. I was upset by my girlfriend leaving me and I no longer felt I had a place in a world that seemed hostile and uncaring. My madness offered me a break from that reality. It also had the clues to my recovery. Like a spy, if I was to recover a meaningful role in society I would have to be creative and careful who I listened to.

I decided not to believe I had a lifelong brain disease instead that I could rebuild my life. One close friend also believed in me and visited me almost daily when I was in hospital. Her friendship made a massive difference. I also knew I had to learn how to express my emotions. I used drama, art and dance to do this. When I came out of hospital I got a lucky break, my first part-time job involved walking each evening in the wooded grounds of Highgate cemetery as a security guard. Although it sounds scary, I think this was actually a very healing activity. On two occasions I had tried to stop taking the medication due to the fact that it made me feel emotionally blocked and too sleepy. I was not given any medical support to do this and I got very high and was re-hospitalised. However, the third time I tried I managed it. I used exercise and breathing exercises to maintain a calm attitude. I also started to avoid smoking cannabis and focused on helping others. After my breakdown I felt I needed to change my approach to life, that to be happy I needed to help others and make a contribution to society. I was unhappy about how I and my fellow patients were treated in psychiatric hospital and how many friends had also written me off. I became determined to try and change this by training to be a psychologist in order to change professional and public attitudes to mental illness. So in the end I found my 'mission impossible' to help transform how we all respond to peoples' mental health problems. In my work I have created lots of self help groups that focus on working towards recovery, growth and healing. I have helped get holistic approaches like Tai Chi into the hospital where I work. I also organise public meetings and campaigns for more holistic approaches to mental health (see www.evolving-minds.co.uk). In 2005 we pushed a bed from Bradford to Manchester in pyjamas, chased by a giant syringe and called it the Great Escape Bed push. We gained national radio, television and press coverage. In August 2006 we did another from Brighton to London to highlight the need for psychiatry to move forward in the way it treats people with mental health problems.

For more information, email me at rufus@rufusmay.freeserve.co.uk

Rufus May

Tracey has succeeded in using her personal
experiences to make confessional artwork that can
provoke and inspire others.

Mary McCartney

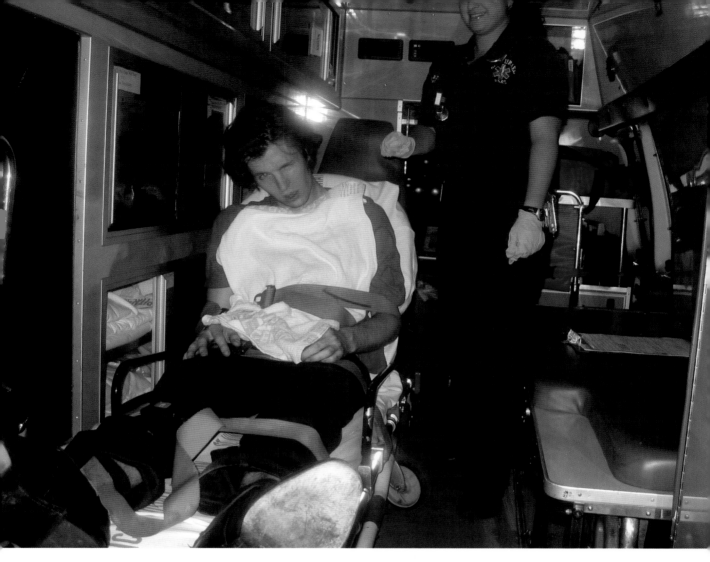

Be yourself.

Ryan McGinley

ALEXANDER McQUEEN

As I have learnt ...

'I am convinced that human nature is basically
gentle, not aggressive. And every one of us has a
responsibility to act as if all our thoughts, words
and deeds matter. For, really, they do. Our lives
have both purpose and meaning.'

HH 14th Dalai Lama

1994-1997. They kept telling me I couldn't do it. My best didn't seem to be good enough. They told me so often I started to believe and my anger and fear blinded me (and them) to any potential I might have had.

1997-2006. Time passes, you make choices, meet people and make memories. Distance makes it easier to rediscover your passion. Friends encourage you to see your potential and everything becomes clear.

2006. I'm not what I thought I'd be, or where I thought I'd be, but I like who and what I am. I've done everything I wanted and more. I'm happy!! I was good enough after all.

Francesca McCarthy

A photo of me teaching at Polardans – a week's course to which I return each year. This shot was taken of a choreography put together by myself and the students in 2004. The course takes place in Tromse, the city I lived in for three years in North Norway.

White is just a colour.

Becoming aware of how ignorantly white my life has been took 40 years. Even with multi-ethnic experiences, my ignorance and sensitivity to how others live in a predominantly white world has been sedated. As a Pakeha (a non-Maori New Zealander), I subconsciously – also consciously – claimed a self-granted superiority, living naïve to colour inheritance, naïve of many aspects of my clumsy ways. By sharing openly the ethnic and cultural differences that separate us, I have, and I am sure you can too, bred a stronger personal self. White is what I continue to be, only now I am aware of how influential colour is to a good white man. Thank you, Asta. "Poipoia kia puawai."

Dani Kiwi Meier

Photography by Marc Ross.

Being of service

Throughout my youth I found that volunteering – doing community service or being socially active with causes in need of attention – was enormously fulfilling. Volunteering helped me come to terms with my own challenges – with a greater sense of perspective. The experience of volunteering shaped my sense of self and self-esteem. By focusing on others, I found a balance within myself.

Through giving service, I learned how to cope better with my problems, simply by realising how small they were relative to other people's struggles. I have been active in a number of human rights issues from the start of my career. By donating my time and my talents – I learned to have a greater compassion towards others. My problems seemed manageable when compared with the global AIDS pandemic or issues of economic development.

When asked why people volunteer the response is

frequently the same – it makes them "feel good" about themselves. Volunteering in my youth helped shape my world view, as well as teaching me valuable lessons about life and the world around me.

Recently I visited Mongolia to begin work on a photo book about the country and culture. While there, I stayed at the Don Bosco Savio Children's Home and Technical School.

My time spent there was the highlight of my journey. The children there were rescued from the streets and sewers of Mongolia's capital – Ulaam Bataar, and are given housing and an education. Although it is a Catholic institution, volunteers come from many different faiths. I was inspired by watching teenage volunteers from abroad building a new school and housing for the 60 plus orphans. That inspiration led to these photographs. It was great to see youth working together across cultural and national differences. Each inspiring the other.

Mongolia has only recently opened its door to the West. The country is in a state of transition from its former

communist government to a democratic one; as well as changing from a nomadic culture to that of an urban industrialised economy.

Due to high unemployment and alcoholism, many children are forced to live on the streets. Natural disasters have also contributed to this. Severe blizzards in recent years have killed many families' entire herd of livestock rendering them bankrupt, and driving them to move to a capital which is not equipped to handle them.

It is astonishing to encounter eight year old children fending for themselves on the street. The children in residence were literally found living in the sewers of the capital.

Ulaam Bataar is the world's coldest capital, therefore in winter, they heat their sewer system to prevent it from freezing. The children range in age from six to 19 years old. They are given an education and are taught a technical skill to prepare them for adulthood and to be self-sufficient. The camaraderie and warmth of the children towards one another is moving, considering their shared history. Although the project is only a few years old, the children are growing fast and need asistance. The project is run by Father John Nguyen Van Ty. They are looking for volunteers from abroad and those interested should contact Father John via his email johntisdb@yahoo.com. Volunteers will be given housing and food, and are needed all year round. The administrators of the project all speak English and they are teaching the children as well. The goal of their project is to create a completely self-sufficient farm and school, giving children practical job experience, an education, a sense of community, and a means towards growth into adulthood.

Thanks to LA's Chrome-n-R Lab for printing and scans.

Shawn Mortensen

I met Peter in my first year of university. He was clever, generous, warm and thoughtful and our common passion for history made us close friends. He worked hard and got a first in classics, which made me sick with envy. He was a troubled soul, however, and despite his clarity in academic thinking he couldn't always understand his own personal difficulties. He spoke a lot to me about his interest in boys instead of girls. He clearly needed to come out at university and express his sexuality. The problem was that he was from a conservative Christian background that encouraged him to repress how he felt and not embrace it in an honest and healthy way. Over the next couple of years Peter seemed to find it continually harder to reconcile his sexuality with what he had been brought up to believe. I saw the severe depression it was causing. I continued to talk to him regularly and would encourage him to come out more openly. He was only ever able to tell people that he had a close emotional dependency about his sexuality. He never found a way of embracing his true sentiments and not hiding them in everyday life. In 2003, a couple of months after his first attempted overdose Peter took his own life.

I would've wanted Peter to have read the following positive experiences. They might have given him the strength he needed to be happy within himself and not to have cared about what other people wanted him to be.

Jo Metson Scott

With thanks to Saeed Taji Farouky and Kieran Mahon.

Emily Mcdonald, 29, actress. At school, I'd always had crushes on boys and girls. I didn't ever really think much about it. I think it wasn't really until I met a girl that I wanted to have a full-on proper relationship with, rather than just a fling, that it occurred to me that was the route I was going down.

With my parents it was very much fine.

I come from a very relaxed, liberal, very eccentric family. They were never fazed by it at all, really. I think I just slipped into conversation that I'd met this girl, and then shortly after I moved in with her, so it just came out that way, rather than any big announcement. In that sense that meant coming out, but it wasn't because I'd suddenly had this dawning that I was only ever going to be with women – it was because I was in love with a woman and I wanted people to know about that.

Julius Scott, 22, drama student. There was no way I was ever going to come out at school. I just thought "I value my life too much".

In college, I made a really, really close friend called Kate, and she was the first person I ever told. We were talking and she was saying "please, please, please tell me you fancy someone" and I went "well, there is kind of a reason why I don't fancy people" and

she whispered to me "is it because you're G-A-Y?" She spelled it out! That's when I burst out crying. It was the first time I'd ever cried about it.

That was very liberating telling her, but also nerve wracking because I thought "there's no going back now". I took a while to adjust to it, but it was more adjusting to the fact that people knew rather than adjusting to being gay. I never hated myself or hated what being gay was, I never wanted to be straight, I just wanted it to be easier in the world to be gay.

Julia Hackel, 23, fashion assistant. It's kind of unfortunate... Just before I split up with my first proper girlfriend, I was going to take her home to meet my parents. I hadn't come out to them at that point and it would have been the way I would have liked to have done it, in a natural way, introducing someone to my parents that I was really proud of. Especially as my mum is kind of conservative, it would have been nice to say 'Ok, I'm gay, but look at the girl I have!! She's pretty, intelligent and polite'.

As it was, my mum asked me when we were alone in the car. She said

'You don't like boys much, do you?'

Considering this was my 'coming out', my mum's reaction was quite weird. She was more concerned that it was because she hadn't been feminine enough as a mother and told me that she had even rung the gay and lesbian switchboard to ask if it had anything to do with the way she had brought me up. I said I didn't think there was any particular reason!

Sander Lak, 23, fashion student. I never really wanted to say the words. In fact I hate the words "I'M GAY", I don't know why, I think I'm just being stubborn.

If you're straight you don't have to turn around and say "Ok, I'm straight".

I don't want to have to explain it. I don't really tell people unless it comes up in conversation. Like when I was having dinner with my family, my sister asked about the hickey I had on my neck and asked who had given it to me, and I said a boy's name. And that's how my parents found out I was into boys. They are very relaxed people so they were like "Oh, ok... can you pass the salt please".

Stevie Westgarth, 25, stylist. My ex-girlfriend was the first person I told; after we split up she had become my best friend.

When I told her, she was really happy, and said she'd always wanted a gay best friend.

We were in a bar and we spent the next hour going through all the boys we knew and who we fancied. Even if you know the people you are telling are going to be fine with it, it still feels like quite a big thing – but it never really is. Most people were actually quite excited by it. My sisters are fine about it now. One of them cried – it was a shock for her – but she wasn't crying because she thought it was a bad thing. It made her so sad to think that I had had to keep it a secret for the whole of my life. I hadn't expected her to think of it in that way. It was nice, really.

Charlie Campbel, 27, photographer. I was prepared for the worst when I told my mom. She just wept. Well, actually, the very first time I told her she was so shocked we didn't speak about it for another four years. It was horrible, I felt very let down and I wanted her to accept me. I brought it up again when I had someone very significant in my life and that's when she wept; she completely broke down. It was completely alien to her. But it was never going to be something that she got used to overnight and it has taken time.

She wept I think because she was disappointed,

she was grieving for the things she wanted for me: marriage and babies. She didn't understand how I could be attracted to someone of the same sex. But it has gotten so much better – I think she just needed time to get used to it, and she has, which has made me so much happier.

David Perez, 24, buying assistant. I came out when I first went to university. I remember in my first week, a friend of mine asked me one evening whether I was gay or not, and I was a bit like "Yeah, I think so, but I'm not really quite sure". And then a couple of days later I met a guy, and then I was sure. I told everybody in the space of about a week, all my friends, although to the majority of people it was like "I've got something to tell you…" "Oh, you're gay." I thought, "You're ruining my moment of drama here!"

And then the same thing happened with my mum, she said "I've known for years."

I think deep down I knew she knew, but acknowledging that someone knows and telling them are two different things.

EXPOSE YOURSELF TO YOUR
DEEPEST FEAR;
AFTER THAT, FEAR HAS
NO POWER, AND THE FEAR
OF FREEDOM SHRINKS AND
VANISHES. YOU ARE FREE

Jim morrison

I LOVED HIM, HE HATED HIM, HE LEFT ME, I MISSED HIM, HE HATED HIMSELF, I THOUGHT I WAS STRONG, I HATED HIM, I REBELLED, HE WANTED TO KILL ME, I RAN AWAY, WE GREW WISE, WE FELL IN LOVE, WE WERE BRAVE, WE SOFTENED, WE PARENTED, WE SURVIVED, ALWAYS "I LOVED", HE WAS STRONGER, HE LOVED ME, HE HAD ME, HE LOVED ME

- Its never to late to change.
- Follow your ♡ and the $ will come
- Don't apologise for who you are
  But always be wise enough to apologise
  when you are wrong
- Never be afraid to tell someone you love them
  You really never know if today is the last time
  you see, speak or smell them
- Whatever it is you do, do it well
- Life is worth fighting for

In memory of my father
27/01/45 — 31-05-06
who taught me all this and more

Nadia Narain

538 safe+sound

Terry is my brother. I think about him every day.

During my childhood he was always around, his presence felt although we knew not to speak of him. It is only now that I realise it was not entirely my parents' decision for him to remain anonymous. It was their other children, me included. Whenever my mother's eyes began to swell with pride at the mention of her living children, I now know it was Terry she thought about. The one that had been forgotten, the one that remained that way because she knew her sadness and total isolation made everyone else around her uncomfortable.

You might say my version of him and who he was, differs from anyone else in my family. But I like that, the more memories and stories of him there are, the more full his short existence seems to be. My sisters and I are all part of him, yet the only people that really knew him were Mum and Dad.

They gave him life but couldn't rescue him from death. It would be wrong for me to suggest that I can understand my parents' pain, knowing that while every day they are living, he is gone. Somewhere that he can't be protected, or feel loved and appreciated. It is for this reason alone that I can only begin to comprehend my parents' guilt. (Irrational but inevitable). They feel it every day as if it were a punishment, never allowing them to remember him for who he was. Their simple question, who would he have become? It is the not knowing that has helped thwart their own lives. The responsibility of birthing a child is a great one; the responsibility of burying your own child is an unforgivable one. How do you cope, stay sane, and keep it together for the children it didn't happen to? My mother and father watched my brother enter the world together, the three of them united. How then do you watch as your child is lowered into the ground and then walk away from him?

It was fate that stole him away, that and his willingness to explore. The fear he didn't yet know, was what ended his life; this is of little consequence to those he left behind, but to me it is huge. Fear was something Terry never really (and thankfully) had time to understand. This is what I hope will give my Mother and Father peace. Terry did not choose to die, in the same way that my parents could have chosen not to go on living when this terrible tragedy happened.

My life began three months later. The birth was completely normal and so was I, though I am constantly reminded through my mother's determined smile that even as the smallest of her babies, I proved to be an awkward delivery. This was my beginning and the start of my mother's recovery.

This is where my story begins…

As a child I would have tested the boundaries of any parents, let alone my own, who had quietly begun to accept their grief.

I fought with my own temper, I worried about living, feared dying and lived in a fragile bubble protected and sealed by my parents capacity to keep on loving me.

I have one defining memory of my father holding me as a small child and saying, 'Erin, you can do anything you want to in life'. This is what I hold onto every day.

As an adult I now look upon my big brother as a small child. I have an overpowering need to protect him by keeping his memory alive. I hope that by writing on this page, it will remind us all of how much life is there to be lived. Terry you have brought such love into our family. Mum, Dad, thanks for going the distance. You are my greatest love…

In loving memory of Terence O'Connor, who died in a traffic accident aged 3 years. (1974-1977).

Erin O'Connor

My survival ABC

Azzedine Alaïa, the great! I will never forget the first time my mother came back home with one of his creations! There were stars in her eyes and guess what, it happened the same to me and to so many women. Thank you, Azzedine!

B like Barrat Martine. Fantastic photographer! For the last 20 years she has been photographing people from Harlem with such humanity and beauty. She has definitely been my teacher in photography. Whenever I don't feel right I just have to look at her images.

C like Maria Callas. The voice … what else to say… you just have to listen to it

D like Dance or Dancer and immediately after I think of Pina Bausch dancers' performance. For the last 15 years I have been following their work and it has become to me like a rendez-vous. I just can't miss a performance or I feel empty. They give you all the human emotion, from the worst to the best, just in a couple of hours…

E like Emotion, the most important thing in life, give it, get it

F like Family, the one you come from, the one you make with your partner or friends, without it you are useless…

G like Ghesquière Nicolas, The designer of the Time. 10 years ago nobody would have thought he would give life again to the fantastic house of Cristobal Balenciaga. Well, he made it and how!!!

H like History. History is the key to the future

I like Irene, my godmother, she taught me so much. Thank you, Irene!

Jun Takahashi, designer of Undercover. His shows are pure emotion, and the man himself, totally charming.

K like Kessel Joseph, French author who is a fantastic storyteller, an adventurer.

L like Louise, my second daughter. A gaze, a smile from her gives me the answer of why I am here

M like «My life without me» this movie by Isabel Coixet has been one of the most impressive movies I have seen for the last couple of years. This is pure and true love.

N like Nudi by Paolo Roversi. This book of nude women is like mother Nature, breathtaking.

O like «ONE» interpreted by Johnny Cash, I could listen to it on and on forever and just get the right feeling from it.

P like Penelope, my first daughter. The minute she appeared was a gift from God, at that moment there was no more doubt.

Q like Questions, millions of questions, always, probably forever, but lately I have undertstood that this is my engine…

R like Rilke ' Letters to a young poet' is one of the most inspirational books.

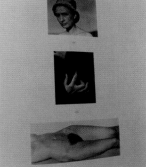

S like Stieglitz Alfred and Smith Eugene, two monsters of photography. I cherish their books like treasures.

T like Tokyo, the city where I became what I am.

U for YOU and because of you, life is beautiful.

Volver by Pedro Almodovar, the movie I must see, absolutely because again Pedro is the master of emotion.

W like Walking, whenever my head is too full of stupidity or stress the only way to get away is to walk, walk fast until the head is empty and ready to get to the next step.

X the unknown…

Y like Yamamoto Yohji, my great master. His vision opened my eyes forever.

Z like Zinedine Zidane, killer on the grass, gentleman in life.

Make your own ABC survival and it will become your motto!

Nathalie Ours

Palazzo d'Arco, Mantova. Still life.

A background of strong family certainties or the total lack of them can both lead to happiness or desperation. Is it a matter of intelligence, of instinct, of chance?

Manuela Pavesi

Here is my contribution, it ain't much but this is all I could come up with. It was in fact kind of a special thing for me... Anyhow, when I went through a real tough patch, and tough in every sense of the word, in my early 20s – broke, recently split up with a long-term boyfriend, and a fucked up family situation... A friend of mine gave me a fortune cookie paper that read:

THIS TOO SHALL PASS

It meant the world to me, and I kept it attached to my computer for another five years or something crazy like that.

Javier Peres

If you're doing a project at college – you need money to make it happen, if you try and do without – the project ends up suffering. Well, I decided long ago, why should my work suffer because I have no money? So donning a black hooded balaclava and leather gloves (with a SWAG bag slung securely over my shoulder), I became a thief. It wasn't intentional, it all happened by mistake – honest!

I was working on a 'Design a Vespa' competition at the time – there were three up for grabs, and I hated the bus. I really needed a zip disk to save my work, and I'd spent my last pennies on my bus pass, so it was either fail my project or steal a disk. So I took the initiative and took one from the shop – £6.50 they were!

I didn't win, and was soon back on public transport, but needless to say this incident opened up a whole can of worms. I shan't go into detail for fear of incriminating myself any further, but in the future, if I needed something I'd take it... for creative purposes only of course. It's not about being selfish, or greedy, it's about self-sufficiency, about keeping your head above the water, about getting what you need to survive.

It all boils down to one very important lesson, as my Nana always says – "shy bairns get nowt!"

For want of a better phrase, if you don't try, you'll never know, and if you don't try, then what's the point?

Images and text from Gareth's college project, *Some of the Things I have Stolen*.

Gareth Pugh

Padlock – when I moved into halls the biggest complaint I had was that our floor didn't have a microwave, it took the entire winter term to get one. This padlock is from the table the microwave sits on, it is used to stop people from stealing the microwave, ironically...

Potpourri – taken from the gents toilets of Liberty's, London. I felt my room needed a little sprucing up, and as the toilets at Liberty's smelled fine, I thought that I could use it more than they could.

A1 cutting board – it was the end of term at my last college, and this big green cutting board was just staring at me. I just kept thinking I need it more than they do, so I rolled it up and left with it under my arm, it has been very useful.

Blue cotton shirt and name badge – this was taken as a reminder of a job I held last October. I worked at the Mitre Hotel, in Tooting London, the job interfered a great deal with college work, the shirt reminds me that I'm here in London to do my degree, and this should be my priority.

My photos are for anyone coping with bereavement. My dad died when I was 12 and within a week of him dying I had collected a box full of his things: a favourite jumper, ties, drawings, photos, his glasses...

I wrote in a notebook about how I was feeling, what the funeral was like, what he was like etc... so this was all in a box in my room.

When given this project I was at first gonna do it about naughty kids, but then when I was lying in my bed one morning I looked at the box on my shelf and thought "there's my project!" So I just laid it all out on my bedroom floor and went and got his favourite CDs from downstairs cos that made it better, he loved his music. The CDs weren't in the box cos they still get played. So I just started taking pictures. Voila!

Millie Robson

Kris Ruhs

Spire*
I will learn how to feel
with all the spires
I will learn how to speak
so no one tires
and I'll create a spark
As none before
I'll spread the light
and gifts in store
I'll dream of a peace
that will not cease
I'll lie there and dream
and receive words
from a beam
of light
and create a maze
a form
unknown before

For the young art student
I would like to dedicate this song and image to young creative people
who may be facing difficulties in their life. To impart that each of you
has something special to give while you are here and that, though it
may be difficult, you must never give up your artistic expression. Life
will always be a mystery but doing art will reveal inner truths, give
context to your experience, and – in my case – give a sense of meaning
to it all. You do not have to show your work to anyone but remember
that many of us have been touched and, in some cases, saved, by works
of art, music, literature etc. Your creative efforts and honesty are vital
and may also help others one day.

Sabisha

I had sent my portfolio to the Fashion
Institute of Technology (FIT in NYC)
when I was 18 years old in hopes of
getting accepted to study – I was so
enamoured with the idea of going there
as this was the Fashion Institute of
Technology. I mean fashion is in their
name! To me it seemed like there was no
higher you could get – these were the
experts right?! So here I am in Kansas
City a small town boy with big city
dreams and I get this letter back from
them saying quote unquote that I lacked
originality, creativity and artistic ability
and would therefore not be able to be
accepted into the school. Needless to say
it was devastating to my 18–year–old
self! I nearly cried for a whole day
feeling that my very life's existence was a
farce as this almighty oz of a school was
telling me that I didn't stand a chance
and who's going to argue with the
experts?!! After sulking around my house
in Kansas City for a week I then decided
to just go to New York and figure it out
myself nothing was going to change if I
didn't change it myself – so I went to
New York to discover that often when
one door closes a whole hallway full of
'em opens!

Jeremy Scott

Peter Saville

Daniel Brown is a designer, programmer and art director, specializing in the fields of digital and interactive design and applied arts.

With a background in research and commercial based programming, internet, mobile, interface, scalable systems and user experience design, Daniel combines this with traditional aesthetics focused creative/artistic direction, working for internationally renowned brands. He has created projects for: Sony PlayStation, MTV, Warp Records / LFO, BBC, Volkswagen, Hi-Res! / TBWA, POP Magazine, Nick Knight, SHOWstudio, Dazed and Confused, Amaze, Saatchi and Saatchi, IDEO / Vodafone, Play-Create, Software As Furniture and Private Commission.

Since 1999, Daniel has been chosen by Internet Business Magazine as one of the top 10 internet designers, one of Creative Review's 'Stars of the New Millennium' and more recently represented the best of British design as one of the exhibitors in the Design Council's 'Great Expectations' show in New York and the British Council's 'Great Brits' show in Milan and Tokyo. He has been acknowledged as a pioneer in the new media field and his original experimental works are now archived in the San Francisco Museum of Modern Art. Currently, Daniel is a new media director for renowned fashion photographer and image maker Nick Knight, and works on independent projects and commissions though his own company Play-Create.

He was chosen as London Design Museum's Designer of the Year in 2004; and since then selected for The Observer's '80 people who will define the next 10 years', Design Week's Hot 50, Debrett's 'People of Today' and invited to Buckingham Palace in celebration of British design.

Key to postcard

A May 4th 2003
   Buys this postcard on holiday because of the co-incidence that his accommodation is visible

B May 5th 2003
   While swimming he is struck by a wave and suffers a broken neck at level C4-6 of his spinal cord

C May 5th 2003
   Taken to Hospital Del Mar and stays there in Intensive Care for 4 weeks before being transferred to St Thomas' Hospital, London

   February 2004
   Daniel is discharged from hospital but suffers permanent paralysis in most of his lower body, is wheelchair-bound and unable to move his legs or fingers

This is Karin and Michelle. I think they were 17 and 15 years at this time. Michelle is literally the girl from next door, or actually across the street. Karin wrote her a note that said "Would you be my girlfriend?" Michelle said "yes". Karin and Michelle were girlfriends for three years. They were really in love and they slept over at each other's houses. Michelle liked to pretend that Karin was a boy when they went out in public, so Karin wore a really tight bodysuit so no one could see her breasts. I'm not sure if this was because their town is a small one or because Michelle really thought Karin could be a boy. I admired Karin because she wanted a girlfriend and she got one. Probably she got the idea that it was a big deal because I was her Aunt's girlfriend.

I always thought how amazing to grow up with a gay Aunt and just get a girlfriend when you're a teenager instead of waiting till you leave home.

It was great to photograph them as this young couple in this bucolic landscape, to see gay adolescents living a somewhat normal life. If you look into their eyes, all you can see is that they see each other and they reflect that they are together. It is beyond brave, because thankfully, they never felt the prejudice of their neighbours. Perhaps they were just lucky.

Collier Schorr

With thanks to 303 Gallery.

Follow your bliss, Alix

I'm not really someone whose advice is trustworthy. I'm not rich or well-respected and I can't tell you how to be successful. But I've lived the way I wanted, more or less, and had a pretty good time doing it without killing anybody, or myself. Though I've come close to both on occasions. Of course, one never looks more stupid than when trying to appear wise, so please forgive my presumption. But I was asked to recall being young and confused, and then offer myself advice from the future. So here it is. Advice to my younger self.

Alix, you will learn that being different is not a disadvantage. Quite the opposite. It's a headstart. So stop wearing your difference as a badge, and start exploiting your potential. Ignore trends and fashions and plunge headlong into whatever you find fascinating. This will involve some loneliness. It's the price you pay for going your own way. Get used to it. It's a good skill to develop. Self-reliance will make you seem more attractive, and eventually win you friends.

I'm not suggesting that you shun others' company, just that you don't crave it, or betray yourself in order to gain their acceptance. If you spend all your time with others, with your boyfriend or girlfriend, if you're always surrounded by people, it's far more difficult to understand and learn about yourself. Especially if you've been branded different from the outset.

Be open to new experiences and avoid narrow-mindedness. Avoid cruelty. It's even more ugly and banal than conformity. You will undoubtedly hurt people along the way, but try to minimise the damage. Because one thing's sure, Alix. What goes around comes around, and you'll be hurt, too.

When it happens, don't whine. I know you will, but I'm telling you anyway.

Try to curb your arrogance. I realise that it's part of your defence system, a by-product of being ridiculed and vilified when you were small. But believe me, it's not only repellent, it's also unproductive. Alix, I want you to cut out the following paragraph and stick it on your wall.

Never worry about anything. Here's the deal with worry, right? There are only two categories of problem: those you can do something about, and those you can't. If a problem falls into the first category, stop worrying and do something about it. If a problem falls into the second category then you cannot do anything about it, so why are you worrying? It's out of your hands. Either way, there's nothing to worry about.

Worry and related states like anxiety, fear, stress, insecurity, denial and so on, these are some of the root emotions of addiction. You're going to flirt with addiction, Alix, and you'll just about get away with it, exactly like you think you can. But don't start preening yet, because you're still going to wake up in your 40s and chew your lip for a month, wondering why you wasted so much of your life getting caned. And you'll also see plenty of casualities along the way, the people who didn't get away with it. Like that guy lying on the floor behind the sofa, at a Christmas party in the early '80s? That's right, his name is Paul and everybody thinks he's drunk. But even now he's turning blue, while you're all smiling and dancing in the same room. Paul has overdosed and tomorrow you're the one who's going to wake up next to him and realise he's dead.

Keep that in mind. You're only this far away from death at anytime, especially when Class As are involved. This is not the Puritan rap, and you know it. Getting wasted now and again is OK, but getting fucked up routinely is just pathetic. Looking at you from the future, Alix, I can see you're going to spend way too much time nursing hangovers. And that massive speed binge in your mid-20s? You should have been doing yoga instead; you would have looked much better in your 40s and saved a lot of money on dental work. Other than that, pretty good. Oh wait, you had a big thing with Ecstasy in your late 30s, I see. Hmmm. We'll put that down to a mid-life crisis. At least you didn't buy a Harley. (But it was close, huh?)

Respect is a big word that's brandished all too easily these days. You would do well to really contemplate it, understand it. If I could be you all over again, Alix – if I could go back and be my cute, young, priapic self – I would seize many missed opportunities to learn from people that you are going to meet along the way, people older and wiser than you. But at the time, I didn't understand – sorry, you didn't understand – the word respect.

Realising your potential will always involve daring and courage. It often means going against the grain. Sometimes you might think you don't have the courage you need, but almost certainly you are wrong. Think about that, Alix: you may be wrong when you doubt yourself, when you shrink and recoil from a challenge.

For instance, you were brave before you could think, before you were self-aware, before you even had a concept of yourself. You had the courage to be born, for a start. The birth trauma is something we have all forgotten, but if you try to imagine it, you realise what a terrifying experience it must have been. Somehow, as a tiny, frail baby, you got through it.

Then you had the courage to clamber onto baby legs and try to walk. You kept falling down. But with a little encouragement, you always got back up, until eventually you succeeded. You had the courage to work through countless mistakes until you could walk, talk, count, sing, feed and dress yourself, read, write, draw and dance. Have you forgotten how frightened you were, learning to ride a bike? If you think you don't have courage, Alix, you're really not paying attention.

Finally, I'll leave you with a few words from the late Joseph Campbell, one of the greatest students of the human condition. "A sacred place… is an absolute necessity for anybody today. You must have a room, or a certain hour or so a day, where you don't know what was in the newspapers that morning, or who your friends are, or what you owe anybody or what anybody owes you. This is a place where you can simply experience and bring forth what you are and might be. The place of creative incubation. At first you may find that nothing happens there. But if you have a sacred place and use it, something will eventually happen."

Alix Sharkey

RAIN PEOPLE IS A
KIND OF PEOPLE
THAT IS MADE OF
RAIN. THEY CANNOT
CRY BECAUSE WHEN
THEY CRY, THEY
CRY THEMSELVES
AWAY. RAIN PEOPLE
IS A MOVIE THAT I SAW
LONG AGO. I DREAM
ABOUT IT SOME TIMES.

Wing Shya

One of my closest friends and my right hand at Jil Sander is Patrick. This year Patrick's boyfriend had two heart operations. They were very risky operations that were really a matter of life or death. I know a lot of people but I don't know anyone like him. His attitude in these difficult circumstances has been quite extraordinary. He's a very exceptional person.

I have to tell his story because I haven't been through this type of situation. Luckily I haven't lost anybody close to me.

My outlook on life is very different from his; he's the sort of person who turns everything around, who always looks at the positive side of a situation.

I know this because he had to be at work on the two days of the operations, but his attitude on both those days was "let's make it a fantastic day". There was not even a doubt in his mind that his boyfriend would not be ok.

It's had such an impact on me. We were working together every day and Patrick was so positive. I would have been so different if I had been in his position. When I asked him how he could be so positive and so strong at such a difficult time he said, "I learnt from my mum." He comes from a medical family so he believes in the hands of doctors. On the day of one of the operations when I asked him, "Are you a bit ok?" He replied, "Of course I'm ok. I believe in love. I believe in the future and I believe in science."

It has just changed my whole way of how to behave and how to look at things. On the one hand I'm thinking, 'My god, you're such a strong person…' If you have people like him around you, it gives you such a good energy. For me this is the essence of feeling safe and sound, the fact that there are always people in this world to get you through things, and people who are there for you… it's the ultimate.

Raf Simons

For starters my friend The-O and I should probably try and explain this picture a little bit.... it depicts a re-enactment of one of The-O's recent performance art pieces (a collaborative piece with his best friend Eka), a playful and passionate remake of R Kelly's epic Hip-Hopera – 'Trapped in the Closet'. Theo used glitter, fake blood and binliner costumes. For a better idea of what inspired him you can search for the R Kelly version on youtube.com – as The-O says, "It's amaaazing!!"

The-O is sixteen and performs regularly at gigs he organises all over London, in my eyes he is everything I didn't have the confidence to be at his age. When I asked him whether or not people had bullied him at school, he replied, "No not at all... well I suppose some people would

call it bullying, but I wouldn't because I just don't care... and I wouldn't let it be that important."

When I started to write this about him, by way of an explanation to him, I said that I wanted to show people how difficult it is to be as self-confident as he is, and not just at his age. I said that I wanted to be realistic about the difficulties bold kids like him have to face, but that I didn't want to portray it as any sort of sob story. He replied, "That's because it isn't a sob story is it?" To which I replied, "No, it's really not."

Matthew Stone

Out of bad, good things can come.

My world fell apart the day I had a bad accident running into a car on my bike. After five years of passionate racing with a dream of becoming a professional cyclist, it was all over. Despite spending three months in hospital I still had the idea that maybe I could start training again. However, as we know, time can make things change. After I returned home I arranged to meet some people that I had become friendly with during my time in hospital and by chance the place we arranged to meet, a local pub, was where all the young art college students went. After a few visits I got to know some of them. Slowly a new world emerged from mixing with these future artists, architects and fashion designers.

The rest, as they say, is history…

Paul Smith

Out of bad, good things can come . . . .

Paul Smith

On the BA Photography degree course at the London College of Printing (now known as London College of Communications) we have a policy of allowing entry to 'mature students' – those who hadn't come straight from school and foundation courses, being older than the general cohort, generally in their mid-twenties. As well as being older than average, having had more experience of life, work, and the world, they helped create a more motivated and mature atmosphere amongst the year. The drawback was often their lack of academic qualifications, a fair trade-off to us because of their visual abilities and positive input, but nevertheless sometimes an issue.

One particular mature student was producing very strong images right from the start of the first term, but I soon became aware that he was struggling with essays and written work generally.

When I had a chance I asked him if there were any particular problems, had written work been difficult for him at school? When he replied that it had been, I asked him if he had ever been tested for dyslexia. It turned out that he had not.

Luckily we have an excellent dyslexia unit, and in no time he was referred, tested, diagnosed, and sorted with our usual and very effective support package. This computer programme which could help students to help themselves had been very successful with other students before, so I felt confident it could help him.

A few weeks later we met up again at the start of the spring term. He asked me what I had done over Christmas. I noticed that he seemed particularly confident and positive which was a great improvement. He told me that he had had a really great Christmas. When I asked further he explained how he had gone home and had a conversation with his father which went like this,

"Dad, you know you always said I was thick and stupid at school? Well, I'm not thick and I'm not stupid, I'm dyslexic." And you know what? He apologised!

Paul D. Smith

Behaviour Guide

(In order to avoid mere survival) Intended for younger generations

1. Although appearance shows quite the reverse, the natural trend of the system is to turn you into a slave. Your mission is to remain erect, and never crawl.

2. When learning, you must know how to make the clear distinction between what is ideology and what is genuine knowledge.

3. Be fully aware of the difference there is between making a compromise and compromising yourself.

4. Whatever happens, Heartbreak hotel is sure to be your dwelling place for one or several stays. This is no reason to overindulge in the pangs of love for too long.

5. Learn how to make simple and excellent meals.

6. Fear no gods, whatever appearance they may have.

7. For girls: all boys are more or less the same. For boys: all girls are different.

8. Keep well away from competitive sport that will only cause wounds that will make you suffer when you are over forty.

9. There is no such thing as good and evil. There is what is right and what is bad, what is consistent and what is wrong.

Jean Touitou

Speed, 2003.

Sam Taylor-Wood

Salli Tomlinson My mother was sent to Farnham Art School at the age of 12, as recommended by her school. As she was accepted at such a young age, by the time it came to do her Diploma for a London art college, she was still too young. The only way to follow the natural process of art college to gallery representation would have been to hang around at Farnham Art College until she was old enough to go there.

Her friends from art school (who were all older) had got their diplomas and had moved up to London. Her life changed direction by marrying at the age of 17 just before my brother Gary was born.

The disappointments of not moving through the London college scene didn't stop her pursuing her own ambitions to paint, it only delayed the attention that she later received.

She fundamentally achieved her ambitions, and has an ongoing relationship with the art world.

Marcus Tomlinson

Growing up, I always felt a bit of an outsider in my little, traditional, Belgium village. In fact, it can take a while before you finally find a real friend…

someone who really understands what you are about, and thus helps you discover and define yourself.

It took me till the age of 22. I moved to Paris and ran into an American guy, Billy. He gave me this book, The Precious Present…

It's about this young boy talking to an old man about what really matters in life. It is a play on words; 'present' as in 'gift' and 'present' as in the 'here and now' we live in.

Billy had already received this book from another friend, and I am supposed to hand it over to someone else one day, someone who I really care about…

Kris Van Assche

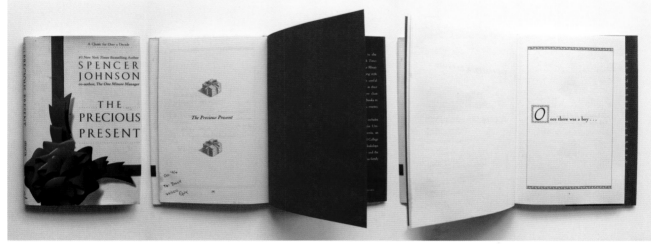

This was taken in East Berlin this summer during the World Cup. There were a bunch of local kids playing at an empty Soviet era sports complex, many in bare feet or sandals. The two smallest kids were taking penalties for hours. Germany had just beaten Argentina in a shoot-out the night before.

Kevin Trageser

TO ALL FUTURE FASHION DESIGNERS:
YOU ARE YOUNG
YOU ARE THE FUTURE!
REACT UPON AND RETHINK THE
FASHION SYSTEM!
TIME TO CHANGE
BE BRAVE
DO BELIEVE IN YOURSELF
BELIEVE IN YOUR POWER
AND CREATIVITY!
IT'S YOUR LIFE
IT'S YOUR GAME
PLAY IT TOUGH, BUT FAIR
BE AN ORIGINAL!
DO REMEMBER:
YOU ARE NOT ALONE!

http://www.waltervanbeirendonck.com/

Walter Van Beirendonck

"Thoughts Circle, Ink Marks, Writing Frees, Paper Always Listens. Nothing To Fear."

Willy Vanderperre

I've chosen Brooke Shields because she has glamorously survived being a kid star.

Francesco Vezzoli

Homage to Francesco Scavullo: Brooke Shields (before & after) (2002).
B/W laserprint on canvas with metallic embroidery Diptych – 61 x 83 cm.

Daughter
Friend
Mother
Lover
Wife
Exile
Immigrant
Milliner
Survivor
Heroine
Cafe owner
Collector
Grandmother
Modernist
Photographer
Traveller
Inspiration

Gertrude 'Trudie' Vogel – Born in Czechoslovakia, moved to London 1942. My grandmother was many things to different people. To me, a complete inspiration. Displaced from her home, she created a new life in another country and achieved so much through so many obstacles.

Julian Vogel

Adventure and travelling, especially on a camel, open your eyes and heart.

Ellen Von Unwerth

Phlip is from Philadelphia, he was a gymnast, he was supposed to go to the Olympics but he got stabbed (the scar you can see), he had to give up gymnastics but he is now a really good breakdancer.

Above: Cast members from David LaChapelle's film, *RIZE*.

Ben Watts

"Look at that sports car in the movie… you see that riverside loft in Wallpaper*? Wow, that's a cool restaurant to take a girl to… And that guy in the movie is probably just in his mid-20s, I suppose I can at least do half as good as them, in about seven or eight years' time? When I am 25…"

I didn't exactly believe in this thought of mine, which I had when I was 16 or 17. But I didn't disbelieve it either. I thought, "OK, it may not be a Ferrari but at least I'll have a Benz. It shouldn't be that difficult… Just work hard in my ART degree and I should be fine." And then slowly, you realise. "Hang on, something's wrong here." Before you know it, you graduate. Welcome to the world of student debt and rejection emails, or the lack of them.

I learn that my mates from high school, who studied Maths, have a starting salary more than three times mine. If I should be so lucky to find an internship that leads to a job, out of my 100 application letters. Panic and paranoia grew, as I couldn't help but compare myself to my friends and then-girlfriend, "Am I going to be the poorest one at the reunion ten years from now?"

Screw a design or creative job. I picked up books about finance and marketing, researching jobs that make big money.

I began to hate the old me: Why spend all that time in a band making music? Why spend four years getting a degree that gives you so little financial prospects? I stopped playing guitar, stopped listening to music. Nor did I bother with unpacking all the art books and cd's from the boxes after I moved house.

Those finance or marketing books were no fun to look at, of course, but I thought that was my only way out. I forced myself into them for a few months.

Unemployed and disheartened, a friend asked me to team up with him to build an advertising portfolio. My first reaction was, "Don't bother me with that". But it was almost Christmas, and I thought, "Well, most companies won't be interviewing people in December anyway." I said "yes" the second time he asked.

We worked very hard, came up with ideas, wrote ads everyday and showed our portfolio to agencies every week. We got some good feedback and encouragement, but no job.

Yet, already I felt that I liked this 'me' more than the one studying books about nothing but money. I wasn't sure.

Some more time went by. An email arrived, recognising me as one of the winners of a competition held by Nick Knight's SHOWstudio five months ago. The prize was an i-D internship.

I had forgotten that I had taken part in it. Five months ago I met up with some friends for coffee, moaning about how hopeless it was pursuing a design career. In that meeting one of my friends asked us to accompany her to SHOWstudio's competition, the theme of which was creativity and identity. I thought, "I'll give it a go too, just for a laugh." That internship became a job.

I just moved house again. Now my problem is, not enough space for my cd's and guitars as I unpack them.

You probably have heard it before, but opportunity does come when and where you least expect it.

It would have been easy if I just told myself, "Oh well, it's not like I am going to win any competition. I never have. Let's go home." But you just have to try, and keep trying. And when the opportunity comes, it may not be exactly what you have applied for all along. But keep an open mind because the path that you haven't thought of may just be the path to what you want.

Now I know, only by doing what one really loves to do, does one have any chance to enjoy going to work everyday. Or at least be able to live with yourself, knowing that the digits in your account are not the only reason you worked your socks off.

Kevin Wong

Clothes just happened
to be the thing for me

In the third year of university, I became fed up with everything. I didn't feel like doing anything. I felt I had no future. So I took the Trans Siberian Railroad and left for Europe. The city I reached was called Rome, and what I remember most about it is the fact that I was annoyed, pissed off. Each and every back street and building had a story or an episode associated with it. In other words, everything had a meaning, and that left me uneasy. The whole town was a museum in itself. It annoyed me.

It is true that everything is created and pronounced because a person, old or young, wants to be understood – he wants his existence to be recognised and remembered. (And a fashion designer is considered the extreme embodiment of this exhibitionistic desire.) But I feel we have accumulated too much creation and meaning already, and that is probably what irritated me back then in Rome. When we talk about environmental issues today, we say we have to be ecological or have a volunteering spirit. But what we should actually do is to dump everything. It might do the Earth even better if we got rid of ourselves. Now, I know I'm being extreme. I realise that there is also "a nostalgia yearning for people who struggle hard to fulfil his mission", as novelist Ango Sakaguchi once said. But those words sound so empty in today's Japan. The fact that there actually were people even in Japan who, although they didn't make much money, lived "well" does not mean much today in a society where market economy prevails and everything is based on capitalism. If you look at the textile industry, for example, the dye works are supposed to treat wastewater before discharging it, but actually, it is quite likely that untreated effluents are poured into the rivers of capitalist China. People won't realise what bad things they are doing until one day they see dead fish floating on water.

As I knew things like this were apt to happen, I purposely chose to place myself in a world they call "Vanity Fair" and make things that are considered unnecessary in life. Fashion is totally unessential when it comes to living, and "Vanity Fair" literally is a place where people show off things that are not fundamental in life. Today, everyone carries around imported brand-name products, hoping to become a "celeb." We often hear the word, short for celebrity, in the world of fashion, but it has no more meaning than being rich in Japan now. It is just one way of labelling people, like the recent trend of dividing people into "winners" and "losers". TV producers know exactly what interests the Japanese audience and attracts them to the "celeb world" trends they make with clever show titles. These people who are making the trend are much smarter than the likes of me.

Fashion, to me, is a desire to be different. In theory, this desire is supposed to accumulate and evolve gradually, but that is not what is happening today. People buy clothes because they see some celebrity wearing them on television or because someone they know has bought it. While repeating itself over and over, *Vogue* is moving in the exact opposite direction from the true meaning of fashion. Everyone is looking for an easy way out, and practically no one has the guts to live without wearing make-up anymore.

When I started making clothes, all I wanted was for women to wear men's clothes. Japanese women back then wore imported feminine clothes in a matter-of-course manner, and I hated that. After graduating from university, I had no drive to do anything, so I went up to my mother and said I'd help her with her store. She became furious. My mother ran a dressmaker's shop by herself in Tokyo's busy Kabukicho district to raise me. She had expected me to finish university and join a big firm, and so it was natural that she became disappointed. She said, however, that if I was

serious I should go to a dressmaking school and learn the basics of cutting at least. That is how I entered Bunka Fashion College. In those days, if there were 100 students, only a few were men and the rest were women. I finished college and started working in my mother's store in Shinjuku. Customers brought clippings from magazines and asked for a dress just like the one in the picture. I kept taking measurements of women's waistless waists, thinking how it would be impossible to make the dress look exactly the same. Having been raised in the neon-lit district of Kabukicho, my schoolboy memories of women in general were of professional temptresses and therefore I made it a rule not to produce any pretty men-pleasers Barbie doll.

And so I ended up making a brand of my own called Y's. My principle for the brand is quite simple. If I liken it to a space, it would contain a bed and about 100 books. It may or may not have a TV set. It won't have to have a bathtub – a shower booth would be quite sufficient enough. It would hold sets of clothes (underwear and outerwear) that would last for three days, plus a bag. Ideally, a million things that the wearer wishes to express would constitute a huge capsule and she the wearer would lie inside it. People praise my clothes as being "simple", but I know the word "simple" also means stupid or goofy though.

We humans are pathetic in the sense that we are all born by coincidence, and we feel the urge to take action to prove that we exist. We desperately show ourselves off or search for a reason for being, and those streets in Rome are one outcome of our struggle. Take me for an example. I was born coincidentally in Tokyo in 1943. When I came to, I was born already. I did not decide to do so myself; I just never had a choice. Leaving behind an achievement is not the only way to prove our existence. We also work hard for someone else, serving and satisfying people around us. And suddenly we realise, we find that we ourselves are fulfilled.

People think I design clothes for the sake of showing myself off, but that is not quite so. Since my childhood, I have always been good at playing alone, and I just enjoyed the time I spent making clothes. I wished to stay in my studio everyday and keep making clothes if I could. I thought it would be a wonderful ideal if I could spend my life without expressing myself verbally using a word.

It could have been anything – clothes just happened to be the thing for me.

The process of making and displaying clothes isn't enough for me, though; I want my clothes to be worn. A piece of clothing isn't complete until a living person – someone who is in love with another or suffering from pain right this moment – wears it.

It needs to be bought at a store and be worn again and again. And that's why I simply feel happy when I see someone wearing pieces of my work that she's bought with her hard-earned money.

My work doesn't (and shouldn't) consist only of creative activities. An evil being called economy makes up a part of the picture. I often say to young novice designers, "Welcome to Hell," because we live in a cauldron where everything that attracts humans boils together. We have to keep on creating while carrying heavy business issues on our shoulders.

I often ask myself if I've ever served anyone near me – even just one person – well in my life. It is a tough question. I ignore the topic and go out for a drink, pretending that it is the fate of a creator to sacrifice himself and those close by in order to please the general public.

Yohji Yamamoto

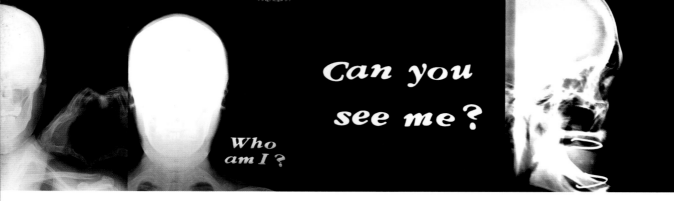

Who am I ?

Can you see me ?

The reasons why I want to do this project are two-fold. Primarily I fully understand how it feels to go through a traumatic experience having suffered from an eating disorder myself. At the time I didn't know how to express what was happening to me. I felt lost but once I started to communicate how I felt through photography, drawing and the written word my life began to have a clearer direction.

I want to communicate to other people who are experiencing what I went through the message "if I can do it then so can you". If I could inspire and give courage to at least one person then I would consider that an achievement. It's important for them to realise that there is help and support available but ultimately the breakthrough is self-initiated.

The concept I have for the Safe+Sound project is centred around the theme of X-Rays. Not only are they great images in and of themselves but for me X-Ray images show the real person. It's beneath the skin and is the framework on which we hang the clothes and accessories. These form the personality that we project to the world. It is the very core of our being.

Michiko Yamamoto

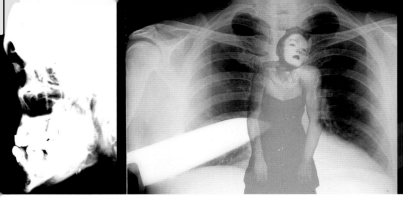

If I can do it,
so can you.

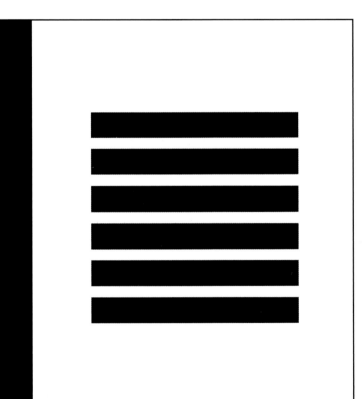

The One is not included by any Limits.

From D.A. Freher's "Paradoxa Emblemata" Manuscript, XVIII Century.
Hexagram "Ch'ien", from "I Ching", The book of Transformation.

Italo Zucchelli

To a Healthy & Happy Life!

biographies

Chidi Achara A photographer who works primarily in the fields of fashion and music, Chidi started taking pictures of friends at school and continues to be inspired by the energy and creativity of youth culture and underground music. He is a regular contributor to i-D as well as having various other editorial and commercial clients in the UK and abroad.

Miguel Adrover Born in Majorca, Miguel moved to New York in 1991 and set up Horn boutique in Manhattan's East Village in 1995. He then founded his own label in 1999. He is known for making elegant clothes from recycled materials which he showed once a year in New York. When his backer withdrew in 2005 he was forced to close his studio. He has now moved to Palma de Mallorca where he has built up a private client base, as well as continuing to create eco-friendly recycled clothes.

Eloise Alemany Born Tokyo, 1974, of French parentage. Eloise remained in Japan until the age of 17. She studied Art History and Visual Arts at Princeton before moving to London, where she worked in fashion communications and publishing. Her six years at i-D saw her working as P.A. to Terry Jones, as well as managing a number of special projects including the magazine's 20th and 25th anniversary exhibitions. In 2006, she moved to Buenos Aires where she has completed numerous projects in the fields of design, publishing, fashion and advertising.

Hilary Alexander Born in New Zealand, Hilary is Fashion Director of *The Daily Telegraph*. She has been named British Fashion Journalist of the Year twice (1998 and 2003). In May 2001, she was awarded the title Visiting Professor by the London Institute. She regularly appears on television, principally on GMTV as well as various documentaries, and previously on BBC2's *Style Challenges*. She is a passionate traveller, long distance walker, gardener and cat lover.

Mark Anthony Mark started as a fashion designer, creating clothes for his own label which helped him when he moved to fashion styling. A long-term Contributing Fashion Editor at i-D, he also contributes to *Zoo*, Japanese *GQ* and *Vision*. He has worked closely with both John Richmond and Japanese designer Takeo Kikuchi, as well as musicians and bands including Franz Ferdinand and Jay-Z and actors including Daniel Craig and Clive Owen.

Ron Arad Born Tel Aviv, 1951. Ron is a designer and architect. In 1981 he co-founded the design and production studio One Off with Caroline Thorman and later, in 1989 Ron Arad Associates architecture and design practice. Alongside his limited edition studio work, Ron designs for many leading international companies including Kartell, Vitra, Moroso, Alessi and Cappellini. He has been the recipient of a number of prestigious awards, and his work has been widely featured in international design books and magazines. He has exhibited in many major museums and galleries throughout the world. Ron is also currently Professor of Design Product at the Royal College of Art. Portrait by John Davis.

Paul Archer Born Dulwich, 1961. Paul has been working as a gardener at one of London's best-loved outdoor spaces, Regent's Park, since the age of 16. He is now in charge of the Inner Circle rose garden and guarantees that the roses bloom well into December!

Giorgio Armani Born Italy, 1934. Armani grew up in the northern Italian town of Piacenza. He spent two years studying medicine at university, but decided to leave to pursue his interest in fashion. He became a Merchandiser at La Rinascente department store in 1957. He then worked as a Fashion Designer for Nino Cerruti for six years and as a freelance designer for five years. In 1975, he founded Giorgio Armani S.p.A. (with his partner Sergio Galeotti), and presented his own women's and men's collections. In 1981 he opened the first of many stores worldwide, Milan's Emporio Armani. Today, he continues to personally oversee both the company's strategic direction and all aspects of design and creativity. The company's product range now includes women's and men's clothing, shoes, bags, watches, eyewear, jewellery, fragrances, cosmetics and home furnishings. It is one of the most famous fashion brands in the world, and has been the subject of a retrospective exhibition at the Guggenheim museums in New York and Bilbao. He has won countless international awards including Italy's highest governmental award in 1986 and the Goodwill Ambassador for the United Nations High Commissioner for Refugees in 2002. In 2006, Emporio Armani became a launch partner in (PRODUCT) RED, the pioneering initiative founded by Bono and Bobby Shriver to fight AIDS in Africa.

Anette Aurell Born in Paris, Anette started photographing for i-D in 1992. Her work has appeared in publications including Italian *Vogue*, *The Face*, *Arena* and *Jane*, and she has shot advertising campaigns for Costume National, Cerruti 1881, Nike, Atsuro Tayama and Nordstrom. She now lives in Chiang Mai in Thailand where, for the past two years, she has been immersed in building a house which, she says, "has been an incredibly tiresome but very rewarding experience".

Claire Badhams Born Birmingham, 1981. Claire studied Art and Visual Culture at the university of the West of England in Bristol. After working for BBC Bristol Magazines for two years, she moved to London to complete a part-time MA in Arts Management whilst working at i-D. Claire now works as an Account Project Manager at *The Guardian*, where she continues to look after a number of high profile projects on guardian.co.uk

Christopher Bailey Born Yorkshire, 1971. Christopher attended London's Royal College Of Art graduating with a Masters in Fashion in 1994. He worked for Donna Karan in New York before he was appointed Senior Designer for Gucci womenswear in Milan in 1996. In May 2001, Christopher joined Burberry. As Creative Director, he is now responsible for the design of all product lines as well as the company's overall image and international advertising. In July 2003, Christopher was made an honorary fellow of the Royal College of Art and was awarded Designer of the Year at the British Fashion Awards in October 2005.

David Bailey Born London's East End, 1938. Bailey is one of the most iconic photographers of his generation. He assisted John French in the late '50s after completing his National Service, then went on to photograph for British, American, French and Italian *Vogue*. His first contribution to i-D was a portrait of Sophie Hicks for the cover of the June 1984 issue. He has directed commercials and documentaries, and in 1987 he won The Golden Lion at Cannes for his *Greenpeace Meltdown* commercial. Bailey was awarded a CBE in 2001.

Caroline Baker A stylist and editor of various magazines and newspapers in Europe and America, Caroline's career was launched at *Nova* magazine in its most influential heyday, and she went on to contribute to i-D, *Elle*, *Vogue*, *Cosmopolitan* and *The Sunday Times*. She is currently the Fashion Director of *The Mail On Sunday's You* magazine and styles many advertising campaigns and brochures as well as freelance work for international publications. Portrait by David Yeo.

William Baker Born Manchester, 1973. William has worked with numerous music industry figures, including PJ Harvey, Shirley Manson and Björk, yet he is best known for his 13-year career as Kylie Minogue's Creative Director and Stylist. He directed her recent *Showgirl Homecoming* world tour and the accompanying documentary *White Diamond* and he is also working on her forthcoming *KylieX2008* tour. In addition to his collaboration with Kylie, William directed a radical new version of the musical phenomenon *RENT* in London's West End. William is currently busy on his recently launched underwear and swimwear line, B*Boy.

Fabien Baron Born Paris, 1959. Fabien studied at Ecole des Arts Appliqués, then trained with his father, an acclaimed graphic artist and art director. In 1982 he moved to New York; where he worked at Barneys as Creative Director. He redesigned Italian *Vogue* under Franca Sozzani (1988), became Creative Director of *Interview* magazine (1990), founded the design studio Baron & Baron, Inc. (1990), redesigned *Harper's Bazaar* under Liz Tilberis (1992), and worked as Editor-in-Chief and Design Director of *Arena Homme Plus* (2000-2002). In 2001, Fabien designed his first residential furniture line with Cappellini and became the Creative Director of French *Vogue* in 2003. He continues to work on a broad range of assignments for a select group of international clients and is now Editorial Director of *Interview* with Glenn O'Brien.

Neil Barrett Born Devon, 1965. Neil graduated from London's Royal College of Art in the late '80s. He was selected by Gucci at his final year show for the position of Senior Menswear Designer, where he worked for the next five years. In 1994 he was appointed Design Director on the Prada Uomo collection, and stayed for eight seasons before leaving to launch his own menswear collection in 1999. In addition to his Neil Barrett label, he was named Puma's Creative Director for a series of fashion, lifestyle and sport collections in 2003. In 2007, he launched his second line, Blackbarrett, dedicated to a younger audience. It is sold exclusively in Japan.

Victoria Bartlett Born in Gloucester, Victoria graduated from the London College of Fashion with a degree in fashion design. She started her career assisting Rhavis of London. After moving to New York, Victoria introduced a collection called BC with Jeffrey Costello in 1989. She then became a stylist and has worked for numerous magazines including Italian and Chinese *Vogue, L'Uomo Vogue, Numéro, Composite* and i-D. She is now the designer of the VPL Collection which launched in 2003.

Marie-Claude Beaud Born France, 1946. After a Masters degree in History of Art and Archeology from the University of Besançon, Marie-Claude taught at the University of Grenoble also working as Assistant Curator at the city's museum alongside Maurice Besset who inspired her with his interest in contemporary culture. In 1976, she became Director of the Grenoble museum and from 1978 to 1984, she was curator of the Toulon Museum. In 1984, Marie-Claude moved to Paris where she became Director of the Cartier Foundation for Contemporary Art and in 1994, she became General Director of the American Center in Paris. Since January, 2000 she has been managing the Mudam in Luxembourg.

Zoe Bedeaux Born in London, Zoe studied in Delphi, Greece. She is currently working on two hand-printed books with artist Benjamin Duarri entitled *Apperture* and *Conceived by Light* and she has just finished styling *Stubborn and Spite* directed by Lou Birks. Zoe is also in the band The Oink Pistons and is the owner of a vintage shop called The House of Harlequin in Brighton.

Vanessa Beecroft Born in Italy, Vanessa now lives in New York. She has earned an international reputation as one of contemporary art's most provocative artists. Her innovative performances present people as visual subjects in museum and gallery settings. Among the venues where her work has been exhibited are Museum of Contemporary Art, San Diego (1999), Museum of Contemporary Art, Sydney (1999), Spiral Wacoal Art Center, Tokyo (1999), the Solomon R Guggenheim Museum in New York (1998), Venice Biennale (1997) and the Institute of Contemporary Art in London (1997). Portrait by Jennifer Livingston.

Clare Bennett Born Dublin, 1984. Clare moved to London at the age of three. Since graduating from London College Of Fashion with a BA in Fashion Photography, she has been working as a freelance photographer. Her clients include Sony and *Time Out*. She is currently working for the picture library Photoshot.

Ben Benoliel Born North of England, 1985. Ben graduated from the London College of Fashion in 2007 with a degree in Fashion Photography. His work has been featured in both *Golf Punk* and *Punk* magazine and is currently working for websites oki-ni.com and stoneisland.co.uk.

Sarah Bentley Sarah is a London-based writer and radio broadcaster with a passion for documenting global culture, grassroots music scenes and anything with a cause. She is inspired by palm trees, travel, children and the amazing people around the world who have helped her with her work.

Antonio Berardi Born Lincolnshire, 1968. Of Sicilian parentage, Antonio studied at Central St Martins while working as John Galliano's assistant. He started his label in 1995 after successfully selling his graduate collection to Liberty and A La Mode. Kylie Minogue modelled for his first official show with Philip Treacy and Manolo Blahnik designing the accessories. By his fourth collection (1997), Berardi had an Italian backer, Givuesse and in 1999 he moved from the London catwalks to Milan. Antonio's diffusion line Berardi was shown in New York in September 2006. He currently shows in Paris and is Creative Director of Wolford.

Orion Best Born London, 1970. Orion's photographic training was gained assisting Craig McDean for two and a half years. He worked as a fashion and portrait photographer for 12 years contributing to i-D, *The Face* and *Interview*. Following a life-changing trip to Japan in 2003 and the birth of his first child Orion decided to move into fine art photography. He is currently working on his first book and a documentary film.

Judy Blame Judy is a stylist, jeweller, designer and art director for both the fashion and music industry. Since the early '80s he has been designing accessories, his DIY origins and punk past have resulted in endlessly scavenged chains, safety pins, rope, string, bottle tops, champagne corks, feathers and buttons, all being re-worked and refined. He has styled, designed and art directed for numerous artists including Neneh Cherry, Björk, Boy George, Iggy Pop and Kylie Minogue, and has collaborated with designers including John Galliano, Philip Treacy and Comme des Garçons. He has also worked on magazines with photographers Nick Knight, Juergen Teller, Mark Lebon and Jean Baptiste Mondino, amongst others. His future is now firmly based in accessory design with a new outlet in Dover Street Market as well as selected shops worldwide.

Sam Bleakley Born Cornwall, 1978. Sam is a professional surfer and freelance writer. He is the reigning English Longboard Surfing Champion and a multiple European Champion. Sam recently edited *The History of British Surfing*. He is currently working on his own book, a collection of travel stories, *Travelling With a Conscience*. Sam lives with his wife Sandy and baby daughter Lola.

Hardy Blechman Born London, 1968. Hardy is Head Designer of Maharishi, the streetwear company he founded in 1995. In 2000, he was named Streetwear Designer of the Year by the British Fashion Council. A second line, MHI, was launched in 2001 and in 2003, he also set up a company producing non-violent toys. Hardy's flagship MHI store, DPMHI, opened in 2004. In his first book, published the same year, Hardy explored the subject of camouflage in great depth. *DPM: Disruptive Pattern Material* won Best Book of 2004 in *Wallpaper*'s Design Awards issue and was one of *The Daily Telegraph*'s Books of the Year 2004.

Moira Bogue Born Brazil, 1960. Moira was Art Editor for i-D from 1981-1987. She then formed a design partnership for a few years working as consultant, art director, designer and photographer. Clients included Conran, Sony Music, Hodder & Stoughton and Amouage. Since 1990, she has studied Japanese Ido shiatsu, reflexology, massage, herbalism and yoga. She now works as a freelance graphic designer on a mixed bag of projects. Moira lives with her husband and two children.

Koto Bolofo Born South Africa, 1959. Photographer Koto was raised in Great Britain after his family was forced to flee South Africa as political refugees. Koto's father, a history teacher, was found to have writings by Karl Marx among his teaching materials and was exiled for his supposed "Communist practices". After nearly 25 years, father and son returned to South Africa. This return was documented in Koto's short film *The Land is White, The Seed is Black*. Along with his short films Koto also shoots both editorial and advertising work. He is currently based in Paris.

Bono Born Dublin, 1960. Paul David Hewson aka Bono met his future band members at school. In 1978, U2 was formed. Acknowledged as one of the best live acts in the world, U2 have sold over 140 million albums and won numerous awards, including 22 Grammies. Bono is also a well-known advocate in the fight against AIDS and extreme poverty in Africa. In 2006, he launched Product (RED) with Bobby Shriver to raise money from businesses to buy drugs for people unable to afford them. He has received a number of awards for his music and activism; these include the Legion d'Honneur from the French Government in 2003 and an honourary British knighthood in 2007. Bono lives in Dublin with his wife Ali and their four children.

Gemma Booth Born Stockport, 1974. Gemma was raised in East Africa, but returned to England in 1981. She studied Graphics at Leeds University and then worked in i-D's art department as an assistant. She became Picture Editor at *The Face*, where her photography was first published, then left to concentrate on photography full-time. She has produced campaigns for clients as varied as American Eagles Outfitters, Clarks, Levi's and many major record labels. Her editorial work includes i-D, *Nylon, Amelia's Magazine* and *125*.

Johnny Borrell Born London, 1980. Johnny is the frontman for Razorlight. After a number of top 20 hits, their debut album *Up All Night* charted at number three in the UK. Their self-titled follow-up album, released in 2006, debuted at number one in the UK album chart and they scored their first UK number one in October that year with the single 'America'.

Mark Borthwick Born Turkey, 1978. Mark's photography regularly appears in magazines including i-D, Italian *Vogue, Interview, Purple, Self Service* and *The New Yorker*. Commercial clients include Sony, Nike, Adidas, Maxmara, Yohji Yamamoto, Hussein Chalayan, Comme des Garçons and Maison Martin Margiela. Mark's work is widely exhibited in museums around the globe. His book *Synthetic Voices* (1998) received the prestigious Art Directors Club (New York) Silver Prize for Book Design and his films include *Will Shine* (2002) and *Cat Power/Speaking for Trees* (2004), while the project *Wycoff Street* documents his personal family life. Mark lives with his wife Maria Cornejo and two children in Brooklyn.

Debbie Bragg Debbie is a photographer who shoots mainly music and travel. In 2003 she set up Everynight Images, a picture library specialising in music, urban lifestyle and global youth culture. Initially this was an archive of her own photographs but now represents the work of more than 20 photographers. Debbie divides her time between running the library, editorial shoots and trips abroad. Her next planned trips are to document the dancehall scene in Japan and beauty queens in Venezuela. Her other passions are interiors and Arsenal. Portrait by Billa.

Véronique Branquinho Born Vilvoorde, Belgium, 1973. Veronique studied Fashion Design at the Royal Academy of Fine Arts in Antwerp. In 1997 she presented her first collection under her own name in Paris. Based in Antwerp, Veronique now designs both men's and women's collections as well as a footwear line. In 2000, she was awarded the first Moët Fashion Award and in 2007 she was chosen as guest editor of *A Magazine*. In March 2008, Véronique held an exhibition of her work at Momu in Antwerp.

Zowie Broach and Brian Kirkby London-based design duo, Zowie Broach and Brian Kirkby started Boudicca in 1997. Zowie and Brian have always been involved in the arts, giving regular talks at the Tate Modern in London, as well as collaborating on projects with artists including Cindy Sherman and film director Mike Figgis. Boudicca is the first independent British fashion house to be invited to become a guest member of Haute Couture in Paris and showed its first Haute Couture collection in January 2007 to rave reviews. Portrait by Tomoko Suwa.

Neville Brody Born in 1957, Neville grew up in North London and studied Fine Arts, before switching to a Graphic Design degree at the London College of Printing. In 1981, he was made Art Director of Fetish Records, which led to him becoming Art Director of *The Face* in the early '80s. In 1986, he set up a design studio with Fwa Richards, which in 1994 became known as Research Studios, whose clients include Katharine Hamnett, The Museum of Modern Art, Camper, Reuters, Giorgio Armani and Jean Paul Gaultier Parfums. This expanded to become Research Publishing, producing experimental multi-media works by young artists. Since then, studios have been opened in Paris and Berlin with plans to also open in New York. The primary focus is on FUSE, the quarterly forum for experimental typography and communications, which brings together speakers from design, architecture, sound, film and web.

Matt Brooke Born West Yorkshire, 1969. Matt was brought up in Ipswich, and studied Graphic Design at Liverpool John Moores University before becoming Art Editor of i-D in 1993. He left in 1995 and went to work for *Elle* and later *Arena*. In 2000, he left for New York and launched *Maxim Fashion*. As an Art Director Matt's clients include Iceberg, Gieves & Hawkes, Motorola, Dunhill and Nike. He has also consulted for publishing and PR companies, including Condé Nast and Hearst. In 2004 he art directed a photo-biography for Luis Figo, and a new book marking Jean-Paul Gaultier's 30th anniversary. Matt's most recent editorial project is a new photography-based music magazine *Sly'n'Chic*.

Richard Buckley Born New York, 1948. Richard grew up in Germany, Taiwan, France and various western states of the USA. After receiving a BA at the University of Maryland, where he also did post-graduate work in film and photography, his first job as a journalist was with *The New York Magazine* in 1979. Magazines Richard has contributed to include *Dutch*, Italian *Vogue, Vanity Fair, WWD* and *W*. He was Editor-in-Chief of *Vogue Hommes International* between 1999 and 2005. He now divides his time between London and Los Angeles, where he looks after his two smooth fox terriers, Angus and India. Portrait by Bruce Springsten.

Terry Burgess (now **Terry Newman**) Born Wimbledon, 1967. Terry has juggled many different jobs in the fashion industry – as a journalist, lecturer, and writer. She was i-D's Shopping Editor for over ten years. As a freelancer she has worked at *Self Service* and *Attitude* and as a TV presenter for Channel 4 fashion programmes *She's Gotta Have It* and *Slave*. Her freelance work has been published in *The Guardian, The Saturday* and *Sunday Times, Time Out, The Big Issue, The Independent* and *Viewpoint*. She also contributed to i-D's *Fashion Now* and *Fashion Now 2* books. Terry lives in Marylebone with her husband Andrew and two boys, Freddie and William.

Danny Burrows Born in 1968, Danny spent his formative years in South America, Africa and the USA. After studying South American history in the US, Danny went on to be a freelance writer specialising in sports and travel. At present he is working as the Editor-in-Chief of *Onboard* snowboarding magazine in Munich as well as photographing and writing social documentary stories for other magazines and newspapers. He is also a copywriter for Nike ACG.

Paul Burston Born Yorkshire, 1965. Paul is a leading gay journalist and author. At present he edits the Gay section of *Time Out* and is a frequent contributor to TV and radio. His books include the novels *Shameless* (2001), *Star People* (2006) and *Lovers & Losers* (2007). In May 2007 he made the *Independent on Sunday's* Pink List of the most influential gay people in Britain. In September 2007 he was nominated for a Stonewall Award for Best Writer alongside Russell T Davies and Val McDemid. Portrait by Gozra Lozano.

Jeff Burton Born California, 1963. Jeff received a BFA in Fine Arts, before taking a Masters in Painting at the California Institute of the Arts in 1989. Since then, his photographic work has appeared in exhibitions around the world, and is included in permanent collections at the Guggenheim and the Museum of Contemporary Art in both Los Angeles and Miami. He has continued to overlap and integrate his multi-part career in art, fashion, pornography and special projects with high-end designers. Jeff contributes regularly to museums and various publications worldwide. His third book *Jeff Burton: The Other Place* was published in 2005, and he is currently working on a project on Carlo Mollino, a project on Gio Ponti's work for the Italian design magazine *Domus* and *Vogue Hommes International*.

Martha Camarillo Born in Texas, Martha is a self-taught photographer. Her work has appeared in numerous publications including i-D, *The New York Times, The Telegraph, Numéro* and *Journal.* Martha was the winner of Le Festival International de Mode et de Photographie à Hyères in 2001 and the 2002 Art Director's Award. Her first book, *Remote Photos,* a collaboration with artist Avena Gallagher, was an in-depth look at the identity of teenage models, this was exhibited at the Léo Scheer Gallery, Paris in 2005. She released a second book *Fletcher Street* earlier last year which was exhibited at the Jack Shainman gallery in New York in 2007. Martha's currently filming a documentary on the urban horsemen of Philadelphia.

Joe Casely-Hayford Born Kent, 1956. Joe studied at Central St Martins. As well as designing his own label for men and women, he has undertaken commissions for film, ballet and the music industry. He has worked as a freelance Creative Director in Italy, designed exhibitions and contributed to i-D, *Arena Homme Plus, The Independent* and *Senken Shimbun.* Joe is presently Creative Director of Gieves & Hawkes and a freelance consultant. Portrait by Dan Annett.

Jota Castro Based in Brussels, Peruvian-born artist Jota studied Political Science and International Relations. In the late '90s, he worked as a diplomat at the United Nations and the European Union. Jota has exhibited extensively: he participated in the Venice Biennale in 2003 and he won the Gwangju Biennale Prize in 2004.

Natascha Chadha Born and raised in Holland, journalist Natascha finished her studies in Chicago. After graduating, she moved to London in 2000 and started her journalism career working as an intern on the i-D book *Learn and Pass It On.* She later moved to Amsterdam to become the in-house copywriter for fashion brand Mexx. In 2006 Natascha wrote the book *It Started with a Kiss: 20 Years of Mexx.*

Hussein Chalayan Born Cyprus, 1970. Hussein graduated from Central St Martins in 1993. He launched his own label in 1994, was awarded the Absolut Design Award in 1995, and named British Designer of the Year in both 1999 and 2000. In 2003 he directed two short films *Temporal Meditations* and *Place to Passage.* In 2004 he directed his third film *Anaesthetics* and in the same year opened his first store in Tokyo. In 2005 Hussein had a ten-year retrospective of his work at the Groninger Museum in the Netherlands and then in Kunsthalle Wolfsburg in Germany. He was also the representative for Turkey in the Venice Biennale and contributed to the i-Dentity exhibition. In June 2006, Hussein received an MBE in recognition of his contribution to fashion.

Jake and Dinos Chapman Born Fulham, 1962 (Dinos) and Cheltenham, 1966 (Jake). The artist brothers have been working together since the early '90s after graduating from London's Royal College of Art. Their first solo installation, *We Are Artists,* featured Letraset stuck to a wall smeared with brown faeces-coloured paint. They followed this with *Disasters of War,* a Goya-inspired piece which was the first to exploit their trademark use of castrated shop-window dummies. Arguably their most ambitious work was *Hell* (1999), an immense tabletop tableau destroyed by the fire that burned down the Momart warehouse in 2004. Solo shows have been at Tate Liverpool (2006), Kunsthaus Bregenz (2005), Kunst Kunst Palast Düsseldorf (2003) and Modern Art Oxford (2003). Portrait by Johnnie Shand Kydd.

Tim Chave Born Leamington Spa, 1977. Tim has collaborated with photographer Barry Edmunds as Tim and Barry – since 2000, documenting the grime scene and working for clients as diverse as P.A.M, *Colors,* Tempa T, Jean-Charles de Castelbajac and the Special Olympics. Since July 2007, Tim and Barry have been developing their online TV station timandbarrytv. Tim also produces music and DJs with Dave Cushway under the name of No Requests.

Rowan Chernin Born in 1969, Rowan started work at i-D in 1991 as Advertising Assistant. He wrote about Swansea clubbing for the first issue of *Loaded* in 1994, then became their Clubs Editor. Today he is the Director of an ongoing surf-art-music-film project, and a fulltime Qualitative Market Researcher.

Neneh Cherry Born Sweden, 1964. Neneh is a singer, songwriter, rapper, DJ and occasional broadcaster. She is the daughter of legendary jazz trumpeter and world music fusion musician Don Cherry. She began performing after leaving school at 14 and moving to London, where she joined the punk band The Cherries. Neneh was then a floating member of Slits, a member of Rip Rig & Panic and Float Up CP. She has had three solo albums and her hits include *Buffalo Stance, Manchild* and *7 Seconds,* a collaboration with Youssou N'Dour. She is currently one of four members of a music group called cirKus which was formed in 2006. Neneh, her husband, Cameron McVey and their two daughters, Tyson and Mabel, now divide their time between Sweden and London.

Donald Christie Born Stirling, 1960. Donald studied Fine Art at Newcastle-upon-Tyne Polytechnic, specialising in film, video and sound. After completing his degree he moved to London and started working as a runner in the pop promo industry. He then decided to concentrate on photography. Initially specialising in reportage and portraiture, before moving into fashion photography in the early '90s. He has since worked for numerous magazines including i-D, *Arena, Glamour* and *Interview.*

Suzanne Clements and Inacio Ribeiro Born in the UK and Brazil respectively, the couple married and set up the Clements Ribeiro label after graduating from Central St Martins. They have shown at London Fashion Week and have collaborated with celebrated artists such as Peter Saville and shoe designers Manolo Blahnik, Jimmy Choo and Christian Louboutin. In 2000, the designers took over as the Creative Directors of Cacharel in Paris, but in 2007 they left the fashion house in order to dedicate themselves fully to personal projects, including their very successful range for Blossom as well as a demi-couture collection for the exclusive e-luxury retailer Couturelab. Their designs have been worn by numerous celebrities including Madonna, Nicole Kidman, Kylie Minogue, Tom Cruise and Mick Jagger.

Lauren Cochrane Born Birmingham, 1977. Lauren moved to London six years later. After completing a degree in English Literature, she has worked as a journalist since 2000. Writing for publications including *The Face, NME, The Guardian, The Observer* and *Vogue,* fashion, music, art and youth culture are favourite subjects. She joined i-D in 2006 as Deputy Editor but left in January 2008 to pursue her freelance career.

Joe Cohen While Joe studied at the Department of Theatre, Film and Television at the University of Bristol, he also ran Student Action for Refugees. He has since been working at various independent television production companies as a Development Researcher. He is currently embarking on an MA in Documentary Direction at the UK National Film and Television School.

Stuart Cohen Born London, 1949. Stuart is an evangelist and artist working on the streets of London. Stuart speaks at various venues, mainly in England and occasionally abroad. He was the Pastor of a Messianic Jewish congregation for ten years. His painting is about landscape and creation, and it often has a biblical theme running through it.

Bethan Cole Born in 1971, Bethan started at i-D in 1993 while at Edinburgh University. She later became Beauty Editor of i-D until 2000. Bethan has subsequently worked at *Nova,* British *Vogue* and latterly *The Sunday Times* as Beauty Director. She is currently freelance and writes about beauty, fashion and music amongst other things.

Nick Compton Born in 1968, Nick is now Features Director at *Wallpaper** magazine. He has previously worked at *Arena* and *Arena Homme Plus* and has written for i-D, *Details, The Observer* and *The Independent on Sunday.* He lives in London Fields and has a three-year old son, Jackson (after Brown rather than Pollock).

Fraser Cooke Born Whitechapel, 1966. Fraser grew up in Ilford. A fascination with skateboarding led to forays into the West End to the infamous South Bank from the age of 12. In 1997 Fraser founded the Hideout (formerly Hit and Run) with Michael Kopelman. He also opened Foot Patrol Sneaker boutique in London, which led to his current position at Nike in Global Brand marketing. During the '90s and into the early '00s, Fraser wrote and compiled articles for *The Face, Arena Homme Plus, Cube* and i-D. He has also hosted various exhibitions including the first group show in the UK for Stash, Futura 2000 and Lee Quinones. Fraser is currently based in Tokyo.

Kieran Cooke Born in London, Kieran started his journalistic career as a newsreader and disc jockey in Chiang Mai while studying in the early '70s. He then went to work for Radio Hong Kong before returning to London and joining the BBC World services radio in 1978. Various foreign reporting assignments followed in Indonesia, Greece, Ireland and Malaysia. Kieran has since been training journalists around the world in various aspects of environmental and business reporting. In 2007, he carried out training and reporting assignments in Georgia, Armenia, Albania and Nigeria. Kieran is married to Gene and has two sons.

Maria Cornejo Born in Chile, designer Maria moved to England with her family when she was a child. Following work as a Creative Consultant for Joseph, Tehen and Jigsaw Maria moved to New York in 1996, setting up her first atelier and store in 1997. She won the Fashion Prize of the 2006 Smithsonian Cooper Hewitt Design Awards and in May 2006, Zero Maria Cornejo opened its second store in New York's West Village. The Zero + Maria Cornejo collection is shown during New York fashion week and is sold in leading stores around the world. Maria now lives with her husband, the photographer Mark Borthwick, and their two children in New York.

Lena Corner Born Kilmarnock, 1970. Lena worked as Assistant Editor of i-D from 1998 until 2000. Following that she worked on the daily features desk of *The Independent* before moving to Australia in 2003 to work as a presenter on an arts-based TV show. She returned just over a year later. She is now one of the editors on *The Independent on Sunday News Review* magazine. Lena has one son called Ronnie and another baby on the way.

Susan Corrigan Born in Minneapolis, Susan is a writer of cultural commentary, criticism, features and fiction. She started writing for i-D in 1991. Susan edited the fiction anthology *Typical Girls* (Sceptre) and contributed to this year's *Riot Grrrl: Revolution Girl Style Now!* (Black Dog Publishing). Current projects include a documentary on the musical inspirations of prominent film directors and writing *The Glam Descend*. Portrait by Andrew Cannon.

Francisco Costa Designer Francisco was born to parents who owned an apparel business in a small Brazilian town Guarani near Rio. In the early '90s he moved to New York and studied at the Fashion Institute of Technology. After graduating, Francisco was recruited as a dress and knitwear designer for Bill Blass. In 1993 he began a five-year collaboration with Oscar de la Renta, and in 1998, Tom Ford asked him to join the Gucci design group as Senior Designer. Since 2002, Francisco has been at Calvin Klein and in 2006 he was named Womenswear Designer of the Year by the CFDA.

Eduardo Costantini Jr. Born Buenos Aires, 1976. Curator Eduardo has been Executive Director of Malba - Fundación Costantini since 2002 and is currently working with MoMA, KW Berlin and the Fassbinder Foundation in bringing a show about the legendary Berlin Alexanderplatz to Latin America. In 2005, he published and edited *BIG Buenos Aires: Portrait of a City*, dedicated to the city of Buenos Aires and in 2006, Eduardo formed a film production company with the Weinstein Company, to develop, produce and finance Latin American films.

Nicki Cotter Born in Plymouth, Nicki's first big break was winning the under 10's story writing competition on BBC1's much loved kid's TV show *Going Live*. At 18, she arrived in London with a £20 note in her back pocket and a jar of Nutella. Nicki is now the Advertising Director of i-D and spends every non-working second finishing a book she started to write many moons ago.

Giannie Couji Born in Martinique, Giannie has lived in London since 1994. She first started working for *Femme* magazine and went on to be one of the Contributing Fashion Editors to i-D. She has also worked for *The Face, Tank* and *L'Officiel*, amongst others. She is currently Fashion Director of *Above* magazine. Giannie has styled a large number of prestigious advertising campaigns for brands such as Chanel, Chopard and Cartier. She has also worked with celebrities, including Uma Thurman and Ralph Fiennes.

Suzy Crabtree Suzy is an ex-teacher and educational psychologist who now walks, trains and boards dogs, and contributes to *The Times*. Suzy's plan for the future is to write for a living and move to the Peak District or the Yorkshire Moors.

BJ Cunningham BJ is a serial entrepreneur. His first business importing classic cars collapsed. He then created DEATH™ Cigarettes. This infamous venture culminated in the European Court of Justice where he took on every Member State of Europe and every major tobacco company. He lost. He then founded and sold an advertising agency and went on to start the highly successful Georgina Goodman shoe brand with his wife.

Sophie Dahl Born London, 1977. Model and author Sophie shot to fame at the age of 18 when she was discovered by fashion maverick Isabella Blow. Her first shoot was for i-D, when she was photographed by Nick Knight and art directed by Alexander McQueen. Sophie has appeared in campaigns for Yves Saint Laurent, Versace, Alexander McQueen and Burberry, amongst others. Her first love, however, has always been writing and in 2003 she published her debut, an illustrated novella entitled *The Man with the Dancing Eyes*. Since then she has contributed to many publications including American *Vogue, The Guardian* and *The Spectator*. Her second novel *Playing with the Grownups* was published in 2007. Sophie lives in England and is a Contributing Editor at *Men's Vogue*.

His Holiness the Dalai Lama Born northeastern Tibet, 1935. His Holiness the 14th Dalai Lama, Tenzin Gyatso, is both the Head of State and the spiritual leader of Tibet. At the age of two he was recognised as the reincarnation of his predecessor, the 13th Dalai Lama, and thus a reincarnation of Avalokiteshvara, the Buddha of Compassion. His Holiness was called upon to assume full political power on November 17, 1950, after some 80,000 Peoples Liberation Army soldiers invaded Tibet. Awarded the 1989 Nobel Peace Prize, he has lived in Dharamsala India (known as Little Lhasa), the seat of the Tibetan Government-in-exile, since 1960.

Fiona Dallanegra Born Kent, 1970. Fiona originally worked as a make-up artist, before studying Journalism at London College of Printing. She started at i-D doing work experience before becoming Assistant to Edward Enninful. Fiona was appointed Fashion Editor of i-D in 1997, a position she held until the early '00s when she was offered the position of Director of Creative Resources for Chanel. She currently lives and works in Paris.

David Davies Born Southampton, 1966. David worked as a freelance writer for various magazines including i-D, *Blitz* and *NME*. He then became a Contributing Editor for i-D while living in New York. Following stints as the Editor of *Mixmag* and *Q*, David is now Managing Director of *Grazia* and *POP*. Since writing this piece in 1998, David has become the proud father of three daughters. He lives in Islington.

Kevin Davies Born in London and raised in Cornwall, Kevin started his professional career as an extra in *Poldark* and ended his formal education with a Fine Art degree from Winchester School of Art. Since then he has been evolving as a photographer and developing as a parent. He has photographed personalities including U2, Kate Winslet, Jenson Button, Paul Smith and Naomi Campbell. Kevin also shoots fashion and beauty stories for a number of leading titles.

Soraya Dayani Born Tehran, 1971. Stylist Soraya studied Fashion and Textile Design in Liverpool in the early '90s, she then returned to London and produced visuals for launch parties and fashion events. After four years working in print design, Soraya began styling. Starting as an assistant in i-D's fashion department, she later became a Contributing Fashion Editor and has collaborated with many of the industry's leading photographers contributing to numerous international titles. Soraya has worked as a consultant for Topshop, Levi's, H&M and other leading brands, as well as teaching at the Royal College of Art.

Fred Dechnik Born Pau, France, 1971. Fred took a Business degree in Bordeaux, before working as a Sales Associate at Hermès in Paris. Three years later, he became department manager at a Gucci boutique in Paris, where he stayed for four years. A position as Menswear Merchandising Director at Yves Saint Laurent followed. Since 2007, Fred has worked as Chief Operational Officer – and founding partner – of The Webster Miami. Fred currently lives between Miami and Paris.

Thomas Degen Born Germany, 1955. Thomas has been a freelance photographer since 1979. In 1980, he started shooting for i-D and *Vogue* and has since worked for numerous European clients. In 2002, Thomas decided to focus his attention mainly on portraiture and advertising. Different projects have seen him travel to Afghanistan, Africa, India, Jamaica, Japan and the USA.

Alessandro Dell'Acqua Born Naples, 1962. After graduating from Accademia di Belli Arti with a degree in Graphic Design, Alessandro was given an exclusive contract to design a line for Genny working alongside Gianni Versace. He designed for many top Italian brands including Iceberg, Les Copains and Mariella Burani, before debuting his own ready-to-wear collection in 1996. Alessandro Dell'Acqua now includes both men's and women's ready-to-wear collections, women's shoes, fragrances and eyewear. In 2003, Alessandro Dell'Acqua joined forces with the Redwall Group, whose brands include the luxury label Borbonese, for which Alessandro also serves as Creative Director. Together, they have opened Alessandro Dell'Acqua stores in New York. Portrait by Juergen Teller.

Ann Demeulemeester Born Belgium, 1959. Ann studied at Antwerp's Royal Academy of Fine Arts from 1978-1981 and founded BVBA 32 with Patrick Robyn in 1985. Her first women's collection was shown for autumn/winter 1987 and first menswear collection in 1996. Awarded the Culture Award in 1996 by the Belgian government, Ann opened her shop in Antwerp in 1999. She then opened a store in Tokyo (2006), Hong Kong (2006) and Seoul (2007). Ann launched her jewellery collection in 2007. Portrait by Willy Vanderperre.

Giorgio de Mitri Born 1965, Giorgio is the Creative Director for Sartoria Comunicazione which is based in Modena, Italy. Sartoria is a tight-knit group of artists, designers, architects and cultural engineers. Sartoria tailors custom-fit concepts, sounds and images with speed and accuracy from designing multimedia communication tools to redefining brand strategy. Giorgio has worked for various brands, exhibitions and film projects around the world, and is also the Creative Director for *CUBE* bookzine. Portrait by Terry Jones.

Peter De Potter Born 1970, Peter studied at the Royal Academy Antwerp from 1988 to 1992. He is an artist and writer; he also spends too much time indoors listening to Manic Street Preachers. Since 2001, Peter has worked with Raf Simons regularly as Consultant Graphic Designer and concept-loving sidekick. He art directed and put together the *Raf Simons Redux* book, published in 2005. His solo art was also splashed across six pages in i-D no251.

Robin Derrick Born 1962, Robin started working with Terry Jones in 1982 whilst still at Central St Martins. After graduating in 1984 he began at *The Face*, soon becoming the magazine's Art Director until he left in 1987. Following time at *Arena* and Italian *Elle*, and five years based in Paris, Robin returned to London in 1993 to become Art Director of *Vogue*. In 2001, he became the Creative Director of *Vogue* and has twice been voted the PPA Magazine Designer of the Year. He is also a Contributing Creative Director to the Giorgio Armani brand and has photographed fashion and beauty stories for numerous magazines including British, Russian and Japanese *Vogue* and *Glamour*. His advertising campaigns include Armani, Levi's, Rimmel and Rolex.

Dolce & Gabbana Domenico Dolce and Stefano Gabbana met in the early '80s at a design office in Milan where they both worked as assistants. Domenico was born in Polizzi Generosa in 1958 and began to work for his father's tailoring business at a very early age. Stefano was born in Milan in 1962 and after studying graphic design he worked for various advertising agencies. After developing a series of projects together, they opened their own studio. In October 1985, the first women's collection was presented in Milan, as part of the Young Talents shows for women's fashion. They showed their first menswear collection in 1990 and launched their first perfume in 1992. In 1993, Madonna chose Dolce & Gabbana to create 1,500 costumes for her *Girlie Show* tour. Portrait by Mariano Vivanco.

Uwe Doll Born Germany, 1969. Classically trained on the trumpet from age nine, Uwe started with his first band at 15, and after a brief time in Berlin, he moved to London in 1996. The following year he formed the band Airport, and after Rei Kawakubo heard one of their demos in 2000, Uwe began to produce and DJ at the Comme des Garçons men's shows. Today, he is a music producer and writer with a sideline in creating music for fashion shows. Airport is currently putting the finishing touches to their first solo album, which will be released later in the year.

Pete Drinkell Born in Melbourne, Pete arrived in London in 1993. He assisted Craig McDean for three years and has been a freelance photographer ever since. He has contributed to magazines including i-D, *Arena* and *Vogue*. His great love at the moment has to be his bicycle and spending as much time on it as possible. Pete lives in London with his wife Clare and their son.

Joanna Dudderidge Born 1985, Joanna grew up in Buckinghamshire. She is now a London-based photographer who graduated from the London College of Fashion in 2008. She worked for a year as First Assistant to fashion photographers Sean and Seng and also assists artist/photographer Alex Prager. In 2007, Joanna was taken on by The Hospital Club in Covent Garden as one of their six mentees – she shot her debut music video and exhibited her photography at the club from December 2007 to January 2008.

Larry Dunstan Born Fulham, 1968. After graduating from Westminster, Larry became an apprentice for photographer Platon. His first commission was for i-D in 1999. Larry's work includes commercial campaigns for Sony Ericsson, Paul Smith and Polydor. He continues to pursue personal projects exploring health, science and perceptions of beauty and has recently exhibited his work in Singapore as well as Europe.

Alber Elbaz Born in Casablanca and raised in Israel, Alber graduated from Shenkar College, the Tel Aviv School of Fashion and Textiles. For seven years in New York, he was the righthand man of Geoffrey Beene. In 1996, he joined Guy Laroche as the Designer for the ready-to-wear collection and in 1998 he took over from Yves Saint Laurent as Artistic Director for the Rive Gauche collections. Since 2001, Alber has been the Artistic Director at Lanvin for the women's ready-to-wear collection. He has received a multitude of awards including the International Fashion Award by the CFDA (2005) and Knight of the Légion d'Honneur (2006). Portrait by David Sims.

Olafur Eliasson Born Copenhagen, 1967. Olafur completed his studies at the Royal Danish Academy of Fine Arts. In 1995, he established Studio Olafur Eliasson in Berlin, a laboratory for spatial research. Olafur then represented Denmark at the 50th Venice Biennial in 2003. Later that year he installed The Weather Project in the Turbine Hall at Tate Modern which was seen by more than two million people. In September 2007, a large exhibition of Olafur's work opened at the San Francisco Museum of Modern Art, which will travel to The Museum of Modern Art in New York and PS1 Contemporary Art Center in 2008. Portrait by Ari Magg.

Tony Elliott Born Reading, 1947. Publisher Tony launched *Time Out* from his mother's flat with £70 in his summer break from university. Today the Time Out Group has an annual turnover of over £40 million and every week sells 90,000 copies of *Time Out* London, 150,000 *Time Out* New York, and 50,000 *Time Out* Chicago alongside an extensive international city guidebook range sold worldwide. Over 25 licenced editions of *Time Out* are published weekly, fortnightly or monthly worldwide. Tony is currently the Chairman of the Time Out Group.

Edward Enninful At the age of 18, British stylist Edward Enninful was appointed Fashion Director of i-D, a position he still holds today. As well as i-D, he is a Contributing Editor for Italian and American *Vogue* and *L'Uomo Vogue*. Edward has worked with numerous photographers including Steven Meisel, Craig McDean, Annie Leibovitz, Paolo Roversi, Mario Sorrenti, Mario Testino and Ellen Von Unwerth. As well as his editorial work, Edward has styled numerous catwalk shows and advertising campaigns including Lanvin, Christian Dior, Alberta Ferretti, Dolce & Gabbana, Emporio Armani, Jil Sander, Calvin Klein, Giorgio Armani, Hogan, Diesel, Alessandro Dell'Acqua and beauty giants Lancôme and M.A.C Cosmetics.

Luther Enninful Born Ghana, 1968. After a brief stint at the Merchant Navy College studying Electronics and Engineering, Luther stepped into the fashion limelight making his modelling debut for i-D in 1991. He started styling for the magazine in 1997 with a shoot for Ralph Lauren. Since then Luther has assisted his brother, Edward, on advertising campaigns for Missoni and Hugo Boss and styled his own shoots. After completing a two year course in Footwear Design and Technology at Cordwainers College he has pursued his passion for shoes. Today Luther is the PR behind IXBALAMKE, a luxury brand of bespoke handmade shoes.

Jason Evans Born Holyhead, 1968. Jason has been contributing to i-D since 1990. Midway through a Fine Art degree at Sheffield Polytechnic Jason spent a summer in London doing work experience with Nick Knight and Simon Foxton. After graduating he teamed up with Brett Dee to shoot a story for i-D set in Irthing Valley. Jason has been teaching photography for several years and is now Senior Lecturer in Photography at the UCCA in Farnham. Portrait by Antony Beckett.

Alberta Ferretti Born Cattolica, Italy, 1950. Alberta grew up helping her dressmaker mother in her atelier. She opened her first shop at the age of 18 and in 1980, her company Aeffe SpA was founded with her brother Massimo. Her first runway collection was shown in Milan in 1983 and Philosophy di Alberta Ferretti was launched in 1984 for the younger generation. Aeffe now has controlling stakes in many brands including Moschino; production and distribution includes Jean Paul Gaultier and Narciso Rodriguez. Philosophy di Alberta Ferretti showed for the first time in New York in 2007, and her childrens line launched at Pitti Bimbo (Florence) in the same year. Alberta Ferretti has boutiques worldwide including Moscow, Paris, Tokyo, New York and London.

Fabrizio Ferri Born Rome, 1952. Fabrizio began taking photographs at an early age as a social-cultural photojournalist. In 1973, he turned to fashion photography and has since been working for major magazines worldwide. In early 1998, he established the non-profit Fondazione Industria and founded the Fabrizio Ferri Università dell'Immagine in Milan. Fabrizio is also a Director of short films including *Aria* (1997) and *Prélude* (1998) starring Alessandra Ferri and Sting. Both of these short films won the Premio RaiSat Show award at the 55th Mostra Internazionale del Cinema in Venice in 1998. In 2000, he directed *Carmen*, which won the Best Live Performance award in Dance Screen 2002, hosted by Monaco Dance Forum.

Chantelle Fiddy After graduating from the London College of Printing (now LCC) with a BA (Hons) degree in Journalism, 25-year-old Chantelle has gone on to write for i-D, *Dummy, Tank, Touch, Blues & Soul, Mixmag* and fmag.com. She also runs a street team for 679 Recordings while dabbling in A&R, blogging, club night Straight Outta Bethnal and mentoring students at *Live* magazine.

Kathryn Flett Born Hertfordshire, 1964. Kathryn started her career in journalism at i-D in 1984, initially as a receptionist. Failing miserably to take messages, she got sacked by Tony Elliot but reinstated the same day by Terry Jones as a Staff Writer and Assistant to Caryn Franklin. She moved to *The Face* in 1997, becoming both Features and Fashion Editor. From 1992 until 1995 she was the Editor of *Arena*, and launched *Arena Homme Plus*. She has worked at *The Observer* since 1995, both as an editor and a writer, and has been the paper's TV critic since 1999. She appears regularly on TV and radio. Kathryn has two sons Jackson and Rider.

Lorenzo Fluxá Born Mallorca, 1947. Lorenzo came from one of the oldest shoemaking families in the world, he studied Business Administration at the University of Deusto in Spain. In 1975, he founded the company Coflusa with his brothers Antonio and Miguel, later going on to market the brand Camper. With Camper now available in more than 20 countries worldwide, Lorenzo describes himself as a "romantic, rural and simple Mediterranean shoemaker". The Camper business is still firmly rooted in Mallorca.

Tom Ford Born in Austin, Texas, Tom spent most of his childhood in Santa Fe, New Mexico. During his teens, he moved to New York and enrolled at New York University, initially attending courses in Art History. He later redirected his studies to concentrate on architecture at Parsons School of Design in New York and Paris. In 1990, Tom moved to Milan to join Gucci as the company's Womenswear Designer. In 1992, he became Design Director and in 1994 he was appointed Creative Director. In January 2000, following the acquisition of Yves Saint Laurent and YSL Beauté by the Gucci Group, Tom also assumed the position of Creative Director of Yves Saint Laurent Rive Gauche and YSL Beauté. In April 2005, exactly one year after his dramatic departure from the Gucci Group, he announced the creation of the Tom Ford brand. In June 2007, Tom Ford International announced a global expansion with four stores opening in the next three years in Milan, London, Los Angeles and Hawaii. Portrait by David Bailey.

Christine Fortune Born London, 1969. Christine is a freelance stylist based between London and Milan. She graduated from Central St Martins in 1994. After a year of work experience at i-D, where she assisted Edward Enninful, Christine went on to work for MTV Europe, and became a freelance stylist for i-D. She has also styled advertising campaigns including Melting Pot, Levi's and Wella. Christine has a boutique in Milan specialising in non-Italian designers.

Simon Foxton Born Berwick-Upon-Tweed, 1961. Simon graduated from Central St Martins in 1983 and became a freelance stylist in 1984. A regular contributor to *Arena Homme Plus* and *GQ Style*, Simon is currently the Consultant Fashion Director of i-D and the Fashion Director of *Fantastic Man*. He is also the Co-Founder of & Son, a creative practice with collaborator Nick Griffiths. Simon lives in Ealing, West London with long-time partner Donald. In his spare time, he enjoys working on his allotment.

Caryn Franklin From Fashion Editor and Co-Editor of i-D in the early '80s, Middlesex-born Caryn is best known for her 12-year tenure at the BBC's *Clothes Show*. She has written for a variety of publications as well as being the author of four books and lecturing in colleges and universities. Caryn has produced many documentaries on designers including Vivienne Westwood, Philip Treacy and Matthew Williamson. Her own shows include *Style Bible*, *The Frock and Roll Years* and *Style Academy*. Caryn now runs a fashion consultancy. She has also been co-chair of Fashion Targets Breast Cancer for ten years and a patron of the Eating Disorders Association for 12 years.

Kevin Ellis Born Poplar, 1952. After leaving school at 16, Kevin worked at a steel stockbroker firm for five years. In 1973, he joined *Time Out* as a Business Manager but left three years later to work for a distribution company. In 1979, he joined a record company before moving to a firm of music business lawyers. Returning to *Time Out*, Kevin became Financial Director from 1985 until 2004. He is now the Commercial Consultant for i-D and runs the 16th Century George Inn in Felpham Village, West Sussex with his wife.

Sean Ellis Born in Brighton, Sean started taking pictures at 11. Trained as a still life photographer, he moved to London from Brighton in 1994. His work with magazines such as i-D, *The Face, Arena Homme Plus, Visionaire, Dazed & Confused* and *Vogue* has often pushed the darker side of fashion photography. He received a Brit award for his All Saints 'Never Ever' video and also directed commercials for Jean Paul Gaultier, Rimmel and EA Games. 'A photograph everyday for a year' was the idea behind his first published book *365 A Year in Fashion* (1999). His short film *Cashback* (2004) received the top award at 14 international film festivals and an Oscar nomination in 2006. A feature length version of *Cashback* (2006) picked up the C.I.C.A.E award at the San Sebastian Film Festival in 2006.

Tracey Emin Born London, 1963. Tracey is an artist who lives and works in London and has exhibited internationally in Holland, Germany, Japan, Australia and America. Her solo shows have included exhibitions at the Stedelijk Museum in Amsterdam, Haus der Kunst in Munich and Modern Art Oxford. In 1999, she was short-listed for the Turner Prize at the Tate Gallery, London. In 2005, her memoir *Strangeland* was published by Hodder & Stoughton and in 2007, Tracey represented Britain at the Venice Biennale. *Twenty Years*, her next major exhibition, will take place during the Edinburgh Festival at the Scottish National Gallery of Modern Art in August 2008. Portrait by Scott Douglas.

Mary Frey Mary lives in New York with her family Mario, Arsun and Gray Sorrenti.

John Galliano Born Gibraltar, 1960. John was christened Juan Carlos Antonio; his mother is Spanish and his father from Gibraltar. When he was six, his family moved to London. He graduated from Central St Martins in 1984 with a first class Honours degree. His graduation collection, inspired by the French Revolution, caught the eye of Joan Burstein of Browns who put it in the boutique's window. John began to show in Paris in 1990. He has received the British Designer of the Year award for an unprecedented four times as well as receiving a CBE from the Queen. He was made Creative Director at Christian Dior, showing his first collection for spring/summer 1997 couture. John also designs the ready-to-wear collection. Between his own label and Dior, John produces 14 collections a year.

Stephen Gan Born in the Philippines, Stephen moved to New York to go to art school. He began his career as a photographer and then worked at *Details* magazine where he stayed for four years. In 1991 he founded Visionaire Publishing with James Kaliardos and Cecilia Dean, and eight years later, *V* magazine. In 1999, while shooting with Mario Testino in Berlin, Stephen met Tobias Schweitzer, a German landscape architect, who founded the Free Space Design company in 1998. Stephen and Tobias have travelled the world together, photographing landscapes and writing down their experiences. Stephen is currently Creative Director of the US *Harper's Bazaar* and is Editor-in-Chief and Creative Director of *V* and *VMan*.

Kate Garner Born Wigan, Lancashire, 1954. Kate is a singer and a photographer. She was one third of '80s avant-garde band, Haysi Fantayzee, the other members being Jeremy Healy and Paul Caplin. However, the group disbanded after releasing two hit singles and an album that went gold. Kate then began a photographic career and has shot many celebrities including Angelina Jolie, Björk and David Bowie. Her work has appeared in many international publications including i-D, American and British *Vogue* and *Harper's Bazaar*. Kate lives in London with her husband David and their daughter Grace.

Laura Genninger Born Long Island, New York, 1964. Laura graduated from Rhode Island School of Design with a BFA in Graphic Design. After a period living in Rotterdam working for Hard Werken, Laura returned to New York in the early '90s to join M&Co. as Art Director. In 1995, she founded STUDIO 191, whilst also becoming the Art Director of *Index* magazine. From 2000-2003, Laura worked as Consulting Art Director for i-D. Other projects include work with Supreme, Stüssy and Union, the art direction of *Richardson* magazine, artists monographs and fashion catalogues. Most recently, Laura has worked as Creative Director for two new American brands by Abercrombie & Fitch.

Sheryl Garratt Sheryl is a freelance journalist and former Editor of *The Face* and *The Observer Magazine*. She now writes about the arts and popular culture in *The Telegraph* and a variety of magazines including *Elle* and *Vanity Fair*. She regularly works with Oxfam and has most recently visited a school for lower caste girls in India and post-tsunami reconstruction projects in Sri Lanka with actress Scarlet Johansson.

Malcolm Garrett Born Cheshire, 1956. Malcolm is Creative Director at AIG (Applied Information Group), based in London. A communications designer with three decades of experience, that includes over 15 years working in interactive media. His company Assorted Images designed for artists including Buzzcocks, Duran Duran, Culture Club, Simple Minds and Peter Gabriel and in 1994 he founded the interactive communications company AMX. Following two years in Toronto he returned to the UK in 2005 to join AIG. Malcolm was a contributor to various early issues of i-D, including designing the i-D cover for issue 5 in 1981. He continues to collaborate with Alex McDowell.

Jake Gavin Jake was brought up in London and Scotland. He has worked as a photojournalist for Reuters and *The Independent* in Sri Lanka, India and Palestine. He has also been an intellectual property barrister, a bit part actor, a film editor and has run a nightclub, a pub, a restaurant and a photography gallery. He divides his time, with his two lurchers, between London and a farm in the Welsh borders. He is currently editing his fifth solo exhibition, and trying, half-heartedly, to resist the urge to buy a Massey Ferguson tractor and another motorbike.

Bob Geldof Born in Dublin, Bob has been an advocate for Africa for over 20 years, mobilising and uniting people around the world and lobbying governments to fight poverty, disease and injustice. Lead singer and songwriter of The Boomtown Rats, he has also written and recorded four successful solo albums. His music awards include Ivor Novellos, Brits and Grammies. In 1984, Bob set up Band Aid to raise funds for the victims of famine in Ethiopia, followed a year later by the Live Aid concerts. In 2004, former UK Prime Minister Tony Blair appointed him to the Commission for Africa. The Commission's report, "Our Common Interest", argued that Africa must drive its own development, but should be assisted by the rich countries, especially the G8. In 2005, he brought together politics and pop with the Live 8 concerts. In 1986, Bob was awarded a knighthood and he has been nominated five times for the Nobel Peace Prize.

Antony Genn Born Sheffield, 1971. One half of the band The Hours, Antony and his partner in crime Martin Slattery started their band after watching Radiohead's gig in Shepherd's Bush in 2004. Martin played any instrument he could get his hands on and Antony joined him on guitar. Rough Trade started managing the band before A&M Records offered them a deal. Their debut album *Narcissus Road* was released in 2007.

Manuela Gherardi (now **Manuela Arcari**) Born in Bologna, Manuela initially studied Law. The encounter with fashion happened unintentionally when she started working in the design studio of a clothing label. Since then, work has become a passion and Manuela designed her first collection in 1992. Mother of two children, she defines Ter Et Bantine as her "third child". She declares that she brought up all "three" with love and care, protecting them without ever failing to apply strict discipline.

Johnny Giunta Born New Jersey, 1967. Johnny has photographed for many publications including i-D, *The Face, Dazed & Confused* and *Spin*. He currently lives in New York and is working on new projects. One is entitled *Buttons 42*, a documentary of found images from World War II, depicting never-before-seen photos of Officers during the war. Portrait by Joseph Tripi.

Susanna Glaser Born Norway, 1972. Writer and DJ Susanna moved to the UK in 1981. She studied at Cambridge University, followed by Cardiff Centre for Journalism. She was the Founding Editor of Cardiff's arts magazine *Finetime*. After moving to London, Susanna freelanced for various publications including i-D, *Dazed & Confused, The Big Issue* and *The Guardian*, before becoming Managing Editor of *Content*. She has DJed regularly at The Big Chill. She is currently Editor of *The Wire* magazine's website and enjoying motherhood with her two-year-old daughter Maia.

Katia Gomiashvili Katia comes from a very artistic family; her father was an actor and her mother a ballerina. This background played a vital role in her decision to join the world of fashion design. She studied at the European University in Geneva, Intercontinental University of Los Angeles and London College of Fashion. She is the Founder and Designer of Emperor Moth, and her company Chic Blesk Krasota was responsible for bringing the highly successful Smile Moscow to Russia in Spring 2007. Portrait by Rankin.

Georgina Goodman Whilst styling for magazines including i-D and *Elle*, Sussex-born Georgina came to realise that what she really wanted to do was create rather than co-ordinate. With this in mind, she enrolled on the prestigious BA course at Cordwainer's College and then completed a Masters degree at the Royal College of Art. Launching her label in 2002, Georgina opened her first store in Mayfair in December 2002 followed by her flagship store on Old Bond Street. She continues to design shoes for major fashion houses. She has been nominated twice as Accessory Designer of the Year.

Kim Gordon Born Rochester, New York, 1953. Kim and Thurston Moore started Sonic Youth with Lee Ranaldo and Richard Edson in 1981 in New York. The band made their first eponymously titled mini-LP released in 1982 by Neutral Records. Kim also continues to make and exhibit art. She is married to Thurston and they have one daughter, Coco.

Amanda Gowing Amanda began her career in fashion as Assistant Fashion Editor at *GQ* where she remained for five years, styling some of their best selling covers. In 1999, she moved to South Africa to help launch the South African Edition of *GQ*, and in 2004 she became Fashion Director of the newly launched South African *Glamour*. Amanda has styled numerous top celebrities including David Beckham and Ewan McGregor and every Miss South Africa for the last 30 years.

Nick Griffiths Born London, 1969. Nick started working for i-D in 1994 as a Contributing Fashion Editor. Projects with Massive Attack and Levi's followed before his move to New York where he joined *Black Book* magazine as Fashion Director. He moved back to London three years later. Since then, he has set up creative practice & Son with Simon Foxton. Together, they have worked on projects for Stone Island, Adidas Originals, Fred Perry, Converse RED and SHOWstudio. Nick is married to Heidi and has two children, Scarlet and Franklin.

Didier Grumbach Born Paris, 1937. Didier is the former head of the Mendès textile company where he worked for 15 years. During this time, he also co-founded Yves Saint Laurent Rive Gauche with Pierre Bergé. Leaving both companies in 1978, he became President of Thierry Mugler and Dean of Studies and Marketing Director at Paris' Institut Français de la Mode. In 1993, Didier wrote the book *Histoires de la Mode*. Since 1998, he has been President of the Fédération Française de la Couture, du Prêt-à-Porter des Couturiers et des Créateurs de Mode and President of the Chambre Syndicale de la Haute Couture.

Mauricio Guillén Born Mexico City, 1971. Mauricio left his hometown in 1991 to study Photography at the Parsons School of Design and Video at Cooper Union, both in NYC. In 1997, he moved to London and worked as a photographer until 2001, shooting for i-D, *Purple, Dazed & Confused* and *W*. He now teaches at the Royal College of Art and had a solo exhibition at Galeria OMR in Mexico City in January 2008.

Henrik Halvarsson Born, raised and likely to retire in Stockholm, Henrik has been a photographer for the last 15 years. He spent a lot of time in London in the mid '90s when he began contributing to i-D. He had his first meeting with Terry Jones in a pub in Charing Cross Road. He is married to Katja and has three children John, Lilly and Leia.

Bethany Hamilton Born Hawaii, 1990. Bethany began her surfing career with her first competition at 11 years old. By 13, she was an accomplished surfer and was well-respected in the surfing world. Her career was interrupted on 31 October 2003 when she was attacked by a 14-foot tiger shark while surfing off Kauai's North Shore and lost her left arm. Bethany is sponsored by the Rip Curl surfwear company. Her book, *Soul Surfer* was released in 2004. She won the 2004 ESPY Award for Best Comeback Athlete and was presented with a special Courage Award by Janet Jackson at the 2004 Teen Choice Awards.

Katharine Hamnett Born in 1947, Katharine led a peripatetic life as a child, following her RAF father to France, Sweden, Romania and England. She studied Fashion at Konstfackskolan Stockholm and did a BA Fashion and Textiles at Central St Martins. Her Katharine Hamnett label was launched in 1979. She was awarded Designer of the Year in 1984 and was the first British designer to take her catwalk show to Paris. Frustrated at the industry's refusal to even attempt to do things ethically and environmentally, Katharine decided to go back into manufacturing herself in 2004. A new line Katharine E Hamnett was launched. In 2007, she accepted the position of Honourary Professor for University of the Arts London. Portrait by Alex Sturrock.

Liz Hancock Born in Lancashire, Liz is now a London-based writer covering a wide range of topics, from beauty and fashion to the environment, wellbeing and lifestyle trends. An ex-Beauty Editor of i-D, she writes for publications including *Vogue, Stella* magazine (*The Sunday Telegraph*), *The Sunday Times Style* and *10*. In 2004, she founded the UK's first glossy environmental style magazine project. Her commercial assignments include work for Prada, The Future Laboratory and Max Factor.

Amanda Harlech Born in 1959, Amanda grew up in London. She first started working for i-D in the mid '80s as a freelance fashion stylist, and went on to contribute regularly to *Harper's Bazaar* and *Vogue*. Closely collaborating with John Galliano for 12 years, Amanda started working for Chanel in 1996 as Karl Lagerfeld's muse. When not in Paris with Lagerfeld, Amanda is at home in Shropshire with her horses, dogs and cats where she enjoys riding, cooking and gardening. Amanda also has two children, Jasset and Tallulah.

Steve Harris Born Hammersmith, 1962. Steve has a passion for tennis and regularly assists with the training of young British hopefuls. For his day job, he deals with the headache of builders, so you don't have to. He did just that for i-D eight years ago after he found the home the magazine is now in. He supports Spurs.

Wichy Hassan Born Libya, 1955. Wichy moved to Rome with his family. After graduating in foreign languages, he began painting, igniting an enthusiasm for the arts that would influence his whole career. He turned to fashion in 1983 when he opened his first retail store Energie, in Rome. The success of Energie led to the creation of a collection in 1989, when Wichy's creative spirit met Renato Rossi's business savvy. From this collaboration began the Sixty Group which now includes the Miss Sixty, Energie and Killah brands, as well as the Sixty hotel in Riccione. In 2006 Wichy won the prestigious Pitti Immagine Uomo Award.

Matthew E. Hawker Born in 1966. Matthew graduated with an MA from Central St Martins. He moved to Sydney in 1990 where he art directed four fashion titles with studio publishers and launched the internationally acclaimed arts magazine *Black+White*. Returning to London in 1994, Matthew first worked with Terry Jones at Instant Design producing advertising material for snowboard brand Fire & Ice. He then spent four years as Art Director at the Hayward Gallery and Royal Festival Hall. In 2000, he joined i-D and is now Production Director. Matthew was recently appointed an Associate Lecturer at the London College of Fashion.

Rick Haylor Born Kent, 1960. Photographer Rick is continually travelling the world. A keen supporter of West Ham United Rick now lives in New York with his wife and two daughters, Molly and Darcy.

Desiree Heiss Born Freiburg, Germany, 1971. Desiree completed her Fashion Studies degree at the University of Applied Arts in Vienna, Austria (1990-1994). Desiree met Ines Kaag as students at the Concours International des Jeunes Createurs de la Mode in Paris, and they went on to become co-designers of the label Bless. Desiree lives and works in Paris.

Gemma Hogan Born Reading, 1983. Gemma graduated from the University of Southampton in 2005 with a BA (Hons) degree in Fashion Studies and French. She began working as Terry and Tricia Jones' assistant at i-D in 2005 and is now heavily involved in i-D's special projects and exhibitions. In her spare time Gemma enjoys running and horseriding, and dreams of one day having her own shoe shop.

Takashi Homma Born Tokyo, 1962. Takashi studied photography at Tokyo's Nihon University. He moved to London in 1991 when he started contributing to i-D. Takashi returned to Tokyo in 1993 and has since participated in group and solo exhibitions across Japan and Europe. In 1999, he received the 24th Ihei Kimura Memorial Photography Award. Takashi lives and works in Tokyo.

Mark Hooper Born 1972, Mark was Assistant Editor of i-D from 2000-2004. He has also worked at *The Face, Arena, Esquire* and was Editor of the Channel 4 website 4music. He is now Editor of *Electric!* magazine and contributes to *The Guardian, Vogue, Wallpaper** and *Condé Nast Traveller*. He is also writing a book, *The Great British Tree Biography*.

Frank Horvat Born Abbazia, Italy (now Opatija, Croatia), 1928. Frank moved to Switzerland at the age of 15. In 1947 he went to Milan to study Art at the Accademia di Brera. On his first trip to Paris in 1950, he met Henri Cartier-Bresson and Robert Capa. In 1954 he moved to London where he worked for *Life* and *Picture Post*, and a year later to Paris where he still lives today. In the late '50s, Frank became a prominent fashion photographer working for *Jardin des Modes*, *Elle*, *Glamour*, *Vogue* and *Harper's Bazaar*. Between 1958 and 1961 he worked as an Associate Photographer for Magnum. Since then Frank has published 18 books of his work and has had countless exhibitions worldwide. In 2006, a retrospective exhibition was held at Espace Landowski, Boulogne-Billancourt, France.

Jane How Jane moved to London aged 18. One of her earliest jobs was styling and doing the hair for an i-D cover. Now Jane, represented by Streeters, is one of the UK's leading international stylists and has acted as Creative Director for Hussein Chalayan. She has also styled shows for Stella McCartney, Pucci and Maison Martin Margiela. As well as overseeing the advertising campaigns for Christian Dior for the past six seasons, Jane is a regular contributor to publications including i-D, *Vogue Italia*, *Self Service*, *Another* and *W*. She frequently collaborates with photographers Mario Sorrenti, Paolo Roversi, Nick Knight and Steven Meisel.

Adam Howe Born 1965, Adam graduated from Central St Martins in 1987. He spent three years assisting Judy Blame, then freelanced as a stylist for i-D, *The Face*, *Arena*, *L'Uomo Vogue*, *Vogue Italia* and *Qvest*. His clients include Nike, Louis Vuitton, Levi's, Speedo and Shiseido. Adam continues to maintain strong Japanese links: he has published three fashion editorials with Nobuyoshi Araki and styled a Takashi Miike movie. Adam is also a sessional lecturer at Kingston University.

Paul Hunwick Born in Kent, Paul worked at i-D for most of the '90s, leaving to edit *Attitude* at the start of 1998. He is currently Editor-in-Chief of *The Burlington Quote Club* and works as a freelance journalist/creative consultant. He also fundraises for his favourite charity, Crusaid SHOP.

Ian A television director, Ian works for the major British broadcasters as well as overseeing broadcasters. He is married and lives in London with his three children.

Marc Jacobs Born New York, 1963. After graduating from the High School of Art and Design in 1981, he entered Parsons School of Design. While there, Marc was named Design Student of the Year. The day after his graduate show Robert Duffy, an Executive with Ruben Thomas, Inc. asked Marc to develop a range. This conversation marked the beginning of what became the partnership Jacobs Duffy Designs Inc. In 1986, Marc designed his first Marc Jacobs collection. In 1997, he joined Louis Vuitton as Artistic Director and later that year the first Marc Jacobs store opened in New York. The Marc Jacobs brand now has numerous stores across North America, Europe and Asia. Marc has also pioneered Louis Vuitton's highly acclaimed collaborations with artists including Richard Prince, Stephen Sprouse and Takashi Murakami.

Liz Johnson-Artur Born in 1964, of Russian and Ghanaian parentage, Liz moved to London in 1992. After graduating from the Royal College of Art with an MA, she started to work as a freelance photographer. In 1996, she was awarded *The Sunday Times Magazine* Prize for Reportage. She currently lives and works in London and Brighton.

Dylan Jones Born in Cambridgeshire, Dylan is the Editor of British *GQ*. He studied Design and Photography at Chelsea School of Art and Central St Martins before becoming Editor of i-D in 1984. He has since been an Editor at *The Face*, *Arena*, *The Observer* and *The Sunday Times*. Dylan has won the British Society of Magazine Editors' Editor of the Year award five times, once for his work on *Arena* (1993), and four times for *GQ*. Published books include his bestselling biography of Jim Morrison (*Dark Star*), a biography of Paul Smith (*True Brit*) and two anthologies of journalism. *iPod, Therefore I Am* was published in 2005, and his most recent book, *Mr Jones' Rules* in 2006. Dylan was the Chairman of the BSME in 2005, and Chairman of Fashion Rocks for the Prince's Trust in 2005.

Hannah Jones Born in Brighton, Hannah graduated from the University of Sussex with a degree in Philosophy and French in 1990. She worked for two of the BBC's social action units and then became the European Manager of Community Service Volunteers Media. She also served as a consultant to Microsoft and Kimberly-Clark on both companies' community affairs programmes. In 1998, Hannah joined Nike Europe as its Director of Government and Community Affairs and she is now the Vice President of Corporate Responsibility based in Oregon, USA.

Kayt Jones Kayt moved from London to LA two years ago. In addition to taking photographs she has also recently directed her first short film *Foxglove* with her husband, actor Jay Rodan. Kayt is a contributing photographer to i-D, the magazine she grew up with, as well as *Harper's Bazaar*, *Blackbook* and *Teen Vogue*. Commercial clients include Levi's, Fendi, Yohji Yamamoto, Y-3 and J Brand. Kayt and Jay live very happily near Topanga with their two beautiful daughters.

Matt Jones Born London, 1976. Photographer Matt has shot editorials for numerous magazines including i-D, *Vogue*, *The New York Times*, *Life Magazine*, *V*, *GQ*, and *Esquire*. His commercial clients include Y-3, Tommy Hilfiger, Nike and Adidas. Celebrity portraits include Louise Bourgeois, Chloë Sevigny, Beyoncé, Cat Power, David Beckham, Damien Hirst, Jake Gyllenhaal and David Lynch. Matt lives in New York and Woodstock with his wife Jicky.

Stephen Jones Born in Cheshire, and schooled in Liverpool, Stephen burst onto the London fashion scene during its explosion of street style in the late '70s. After graduating from Central St Martins he opened his first millinery shop in Covent Garden. Stephen has fulfilled the millinery needs of numerous celebrities including Boy George, Gwen Stefani and the late Princess Diana. He created headdresses for Kylie's *Showgirl* tour and has provided hats for many catwalk shows including Vivienne Westwood, Dior, Jean Paul Gaultier and Rei Kawakubo. His work is represented in permanent collections including the V&A Museum, the Louvre, The Fashion Institute of Technology and the Kyoto Costume Institute of Technology.

Terry Jones Born UK, 1945. Terry now lives in London. He founded i-D in 1980 and continues to work with Tricia and a growing biological and creative family. He began his career in fashion as Art Director of *Vanity Fair* and British *Vogue* in the early '70s. He started his own studio Instant Design after leaving *Vogue* in 1977 and continued working as a Creative Consultant and Art Director for numerous books, exhibitions, magazines, advertising and television projects. Most recently Terry curated and designed the *Smile i-D* and *i-Dentity* exhibitions celebrating i-D's history; cities visited have included Beijing, Buenos Aires, Hong Kong, London, Milan, New York, Paris, Tokyo and Moscow. Tricia and Terry continue to work together on these and other life projects.

Tricia Jones Born London, 1947. Life partner and wife to Terry, natural mum to Kayt and Matt, office mum to i-D crew and since 2004 and 2006 proud "grandma" to two special girls. Infant school teacher from 1968 to 1985. Since 1989, Tricia has produced Instant Design's commercial campaigns including Fire & Ice, Y's and Y-3. She feels very privileged to edit special editions and sections of the magazine when subjects inspire her – other art projects hopefully in the pipeline!

Gabriela Just Born Germany, 1950. Gabriela was Owner and Manager of Germany's leading health club, Just Dance Factory, from 1983-1994. She has produced seven fitness videos and written five books. In 1997, she founded Just Pure, a company producing organic beauty products according to the moon's rhythms. Growing in 2000 to encompass personal treatments, Gabriela opened Germany's first day spa, and in 2005 the first Just Pure retail store opened. The Just Pure Wellness concept is now being put into practice in selected hotels internationally.

Takashi Kamei Born Japan, 1977. Takashi moved to London at 19 to study Fashion Styling and Photography at the London College of Fashion. He now works as a photographer in London and regularly contributes to i-D.

Donna Karan Born Long Island, New York. Following her second year at Parson's School of Design, Donna was hired by Anne Klein for a summer job. After three years as Associate Designer, she was named successor following Klein's death in 1974. Ten years later, she launched the first Donna Karan New York collection which was followed by DKNY in 1988 and menswear in 1991. Social causes are important to Karan, she spearheaded Seventh on Sale benefits with the CFDA to raise funds for AIDS awareness and education and her Urban Zen Initiative was founded in 2007.

KAWS Born New Jersey, 1974. Brian Donnelly aka KAWS started tagging his local neighbourhood aged 12. He graduated from the School of Visual Arts in 1996. KAWS is perhaps best known for his 'subvertising' – the incorporation of his iconic imagery into billboard, bus stop and phone booth advertising. Gallery shows and Diesel collaborations soon followed. Based in Brooklyn, KAWS now produces graffiti inspired toys, T-shirts and artwork. He has also had many successful commercial collaborations with companies including Supreme, Undercover, A Bathing Ape and most recently, Comme des Garçons. In 2006, he established 'OriginalFake', a store and brand in Tokyo.

Ben Kei (real name Kulchstein) Born Suffolk, 1979. Ben moved to Hackney in 1992. Gripped by the sounds of pirate radio he began to experiment with sound and music. At college he studied art, film and photography and went on to graduate in Sonic Arts. After several jobs in both the sound and graphics fields Ben joined i-D in 2005 and continues to pursue music in his spare time.

Hyun Jung Kim Born Korea, 1979. Hyun Jung grew up in Seoul and studied Fashion Design at the University of Korea. She arrived in London in 2004 to study Fashion Photography at University of the Arts. Graduating in 2007, Hyun Jung now lives in Seoul.

Calvin Klein Born in 1942, Calvin graduated from New York City's High School of Art and Design and the Fashion Institute of Technology. He then worked his way up through the ranks in New York's garment centre before creating his own label with childhood friend Barry K Schwartz in 1968. Calvin Klein Inc now includes collections for women, men and the home, plus an extensive range of fragrance and beauty products. Calvin has won six awards for outstanding design from the CFDA and is also a three-time winner of the Coty Award. The Fashion Institute of Technology has recognised him with its President's Award and he has received the President's Medal from the Art Directors' Club for outstanding creative achievement in advertising.

Nick Knight Born London, 1958. Photographer Nick Knight works with leading designers including Yohji Yamamoto, John Galliano and Alexander McQueen. Advertising clients include Christian Dior, Lancôme, Swarovski, Levi's, Calvin Klein and Yves Saint Laurent, and his award-winning editorial has appeared in *W*, British and French *Vogue*, *Dazed & Confused*, *Another*, *Another Man* and i-D. His first book of photographs, *Skinheads*, was published in 1982. He has since produced *Nicknight*, a 12-year retrospective, and *Flora*, a series of flower pictures. Nick's work has been exhibited at many international institutions including the V&A Museum, Saatchi Gallery, The Photographers' Gallery and Tate Modern. Nick launched his award-winning fashion and art broadcasting company SHOWstudio.com in 2000. He lives in London with his wife and three children.

Joerg Koch Born Wuppertal, 1974. Joerg moved to Berlin in 1995. He lives and works as the Editor of *032c* magazine in Berlin, and he is also the Director of the 032c Workshop, a new space next to the German Foreign Office in Berlin. Joerg was responsible for bringing the *Beyond Price* exhibition to Berlin, where it was seen by Angelika Taschen, resulting in the publication of *Smilei-D*. Portrait by Oliver Helbig.

Kirby Koh Born and raised in Singapore, Kirby discovered photography at the age of 17. He studied Graphic Design and Advertising Photography before military service called. Two and a half years later, equipped with a camera and a backpack, he headed for Europe. He completed an MA in Fine Art Photography at Central St Martins, graduating in 1995. Kirby's work has been published in *The Observer*, *The Independent*, *The Sunday Times*, *032c* and i-D. In 2004, he joined Comme des Garçons as a pioneer team member at Dover Street Market. He lives in London.

Sophia Kokosalaki Born in 1972, Sophia studied Greek and English Literature at the University of Athens and then went on to do a Womenswear Masters at Central St Martins. Her first catwalk show was in 1999 at London Fashion Week. In 2003, Sophia won the Best New Designer award at the British Fashion Council Awards and in 2004 she was given the honour of designing the opening ceremony outfits for the Olympics held in Athens. She was appointed as Creative Director of Vionnet in July 2006.

Hiroshi Kutomi Born Japan, 1970. Hiroshi worked as assistant to Kei Ogata before moving to London in 1996. He was Nick Knight's assistant from 1997 to 1999 and since then has been a freelance photographer for i-D, British and Japanese *Vogue*. His advertising clients include Shiseido, Louis Vuitton and Hugo Boss. In 2007, Hiroshi returned to Tokyo, and continues to work from there.

David LaChapelle Born Connecticut, 1969. David trained as a fine artist at North Carolina School of the Arts before moving to New York. Upon his arrival, he enrolled in both the Arts Student League and the School of Visual Arts. Not yet out of high school, David was then offered his first professional job by Andy Warhol to shoot for *Interview* magazine. David's photography has been showcased in numerous galleries and museums. He now also works on music videos, live theatrical events and documentary filmmaking. His short documentary *Krumped* (about a dance craze in California) was an award winner at Sundance. From *Krumped*, he developed *RIZE*, which opened the 2005 Tribeca Film Festival in New York.

Grace Lam Born Hong Kong, 1973. Grace arrived in England at the age of 13 with her twin sister. Her first contact with i-D was in 1996 while studying Graphic Design at Central St Martins where she met Terry Jones. She became i-D's Editorial Assistant and met Edward Enninful, who she then assisted for two years. After living in London for 15 years, she moved to Shanghai to be part of the 2005 launch of *Vogue* China as Fashion Style Editor. Grace is currently based in Hong Kong.

Jessica Landon Born London, 1980. Jessica graduated with a degree in Graphic Design from the University of Brighton in 2003. She then worked in editorial design for publications including *Time Out* and *The World of Interiors*. In 2005, Jessica assisted Terry and Tricia Jones, during i-D's 25th anniversary year. Whilst maintaining her freelance design career, she now works for the leading auction house, Christie's, as Art Director of *Christie's International Magazine*.

Helmut Lang Born Vienna, 1956. Helmut started his fashion label in 1977. He presented his first ready-to-wear collection in Paris in 1986, rejecting the traditional structure of fashion shows and showing men and women together. From 1993 to 1996, Helmut held a professorship at the University of Applied Arts in Vienna. He introduced an underwear collection in 1995, also expanding his business to jeans, eyewear, shoes and accessories. Helmut's was the first fashion house to relocate from Europe to America in 1998 and in the same year, he presented the first ever internet-based fashion show. In 2004, he sold the Helmut Lang trademark to the Prada Group and established HL-art in 2005 to pursue projects both within and outside of fashion. His art projects include *Selective Memory Series* and *Long Island Diaries*.

Ralph Lauren Born 1939, New York. Lauren began his career in 1967 with a tie neckwear line that launched the "wide-tie revolution" and marked the beginning of the Polo label. The following year saw his first menswear collection, and two years later he revolutionised the concept of the retail environment by establishing the first shop-within-a-shop at Bloomingdale's. In 1972, he showed his first womenswear collection. That same year, Polo's original mesh shirt with the polo player logo was introduced in 24 colours and instantly became an American classic. Ralph Lauren is now an internationally renowned fashion brand with numerous collections, stores and concessions across the globe. Lauren has received many awards including the CFDA's Lifetime Achievement Award and it's Humanitarian Leadership Award.

James Lavelle Born Oxford, 1974. James started writing music reviews for i-D in 1992 while still working at Honest Jons record shop. Around that time, he borrowed £1,000 from his boss to start his own label, Mo'Wax. The company went on to become internationally renowned with a roster of respected artists, including DJ Shadow. James now divides his time between his international DJ career, his UNKLE act with singer/producer Richard File, and a brand new independent set-up, Surrender-All, which combines music, fashion and art.

Kate Law Born Sheffield, 1971. After graduating from Camberwell Art College in 1993, Kate began working on numerous UK titles before being sponsored by Hearst Magazines and moving to New York. In 1997, Kate returned to London and became Art Editor of i-D. In 2000 Kate joined British *Vogue,* then went back to i-D in 2002 as Consultant Art Editor. She left i-D in 2006 to work with long-time friend Avril Mair on projects for Chanel. She now works as a freelance art director and as a Consultant for Blunt Management. She is also in the process of developing her label, Veduta. Kate lives in London and has two sons, Pip and Bruno.

Mark Lebon Born London, 1957. Mark has worked for i-D for over two decades, since issue 2. Father of Tyrone and Frank, Mark is single, hairy, not quite available for serious love life partner and heterosexual (so far). Currently rebuilding his studio life and work not far from Notting Hill, which should be ready this year. He is a filmmaker and a lecturer at the London College of Fashion. Photograph by Daniel D'Silva.

Tyrone Lebon Since completing his Masters in Social Anthropology at Edinburgh University, London-born Tyrone worked an assistant to the New York photographer Mario Sorrenti before starting out on his own. At 25 Tyrone is now a photographer and a documentary filmmaker. His first film, made at 18, was about a young Indonesian surfer, Dede Suryana, and is being shown this year at the documentary festivals. He has contributed photographs to i-D, made films for Vivienne Westwood and is a Contributing Editor to website dobedo.co.uk.

Drieke Leenknegt Born Roeselare, Belgium, 1971. Drieke currently lives in Portland, Oregon and is the Global Communications Director for Nike Sport Culture. Her job involves working with editors, artists, stylists and photographers from all over the world. Drieke misses her Belgian friends but loves to travel and meet different people. Her passions in life are people and different cultures, photography, art, and her husband Tom.

Karen Leong Born 1977, Singapore. Karen moved to London in 2000 for her MA in International Journalism. She is currently Managing Editor of i-D and lives in London with her husband and son. She continues to write, and when there are enough hours in the day, goes to the gym, studies French and watches as many dance performances as possible – British choreographer Christopher Wheeldon is her current obsession.

Merryn Leslie Born Australia, 1972. Merryn came across her first copy of i-D at the age of 14. She met Edward Enninful in 1997 and began assisting i-D's Editor-in-Chief, Terry Jones, while styling for the magazine at the same time. She recently swapped a life of frocks and fashion for nappies and sleepless nights, having given birth to her son Levi in March of 2007. Merryn is currently working on the launch of her own label.

Duc Liao Born 1965, Duc arrived in France in 1976 from Cambodia. He started working for *Self Service* in 1995 and has been contributing to i-D since 1998. Duc's commercial clients have included Issey Miyake, Louis Vuitton and Comme des Garçons. He is currently working with Miu Miu on a film for their website and on visuals for Chloé Enfant with *Self Service*. At present, Duc is based in Arizona.

Angel Lopez Born Brooklyn, 1972. Angel's first contact with i-D was when he tried to steal a copy from his local newsagents and got beaten up. He was inspired to try photography by his friend Davide Sorrenti. On a trip to London in 1996, Angel visited the i-D office. He has since contributed to magazines including *Spin, Raygun, Index, Surface* and i-D.

Prof. Wangari Maathai Born Kenya, 1940. Wangari is the daughter of farmers from the highlands of Mount Kenya. She was the first woman in East and Central Africa to earn a PhD which she obtained from the University of Nairobi in 1971. Following positions as Chairman and then Associate Professor of the Department of Veterinary Anatomy and Chairman of the National Council of Women in Kenya, Wangari started the Green Belt Movement, an organisation whose main focus is to help women's groups plant trees to conserve the environment and improve their quality of life. Through the Green Belt Movement she has encouraged women to plant more than 30 million trees and has helped other African countries to start similar schemes. She has addressed the United Nations on several occasions. In 2004, she received the Nobel Peace Prize. Portrait by Mainichi Corporation.

Julien Macdonald Born Merthyr Tydfil, 1972. While studying at the Royal College of Art, Julien worked for designers Karl Lagerfeld, Alexander McQueen and Koji Tatsuno. Karl Lagerfeld was impressed with Julien's craftsmanship and made him Head Designer of knits at Chanel and Lagerfeld's own label from 1996-1998. In 2001, Givenchy invited Julien to become their Creative Director. He designed six collections a year, from Haute Couture to prêt-a-porter. Three years later, Julien returned to London to concentrate on his own label. In November 2007, private investor Jamey Hargreaves announced a plan to promote the Julien Macdonald brand.

Ali Mahdavi Born Tehran, 1974. Ali is an artist living in Paris. He graduated with high honours from Ecole Nationale Supérieure des Beaux-Arts de Paris in 2000, and received a grant from the LVMH group to study at San Francisco Art Institute. Since 1999, he has had numerous joint exhibitions and presented on his own in the Scout Gallery in London and Le Corps Importun, in both Geneva and Paris. Ali has also photographed fashion stories for *Vanity Fair, Vogue Hommes International* and *Tank*. Portrait by Ali Russie.

Avril Mair Born Aberdeen, 1971. Avril started at i-D as work experience while studying English Literature at Edinburgh University. She joined the editorial team in the early '90s and later became the longest standing Editor of the magazine and edited Taschen's *Fashion Now* book with Terry Jones. She left i-D in 2003 to work as a Creative Consultant for Chanel and other luxury brands. Avril is now editing the art biannual *Qvest Edition,* is the Acting Fashion Features Editor at *Elle* and is also writing a book on Chanel.

Michel Mallard Born Mexico City, 1968. Michel studied art in Paris. Now a Creative Director, Curator and Photographer he has worked for numerous magazines including *Vogue Hommes International, L'Officiel, Marie Claire* Japan and *Jalouse*. Through the Michel Mallard Studio, his art direction and design firm, he has conceived several photography books and has curated photography shows including the Centre National de la Photographie in Paris. Michel was Guest Curator at the Rencontres d'Arles, and since 1999, he has been the Artistic Director of Le Festival International de Mode et de Photographie à Hyères.

Maison Martin Margiela Born Limbourg, Belgium, 1959. Martin Margiela studied at Antwerp Academy and assisted Jean Paul Gaultier between 1984 and 1987. He founded Maison Martin Margiela with Jenny Meirens in 1988. The first collection of ready-to-wear for women was presented for spring/summer 1989. Maison Martin Margiela has also participated in numerous exhibitions and projects including the Florence Biennale on Fashion & Art, a book by Mark Borthwick and a solo Maison Martin Margiela exhibition in Rotterdam (1997) and in 2002, Diesel's Renzo Rosso became the majority shareholder of Maison Martin Margiela. In January 2006, Maison Martin Margiela was the invited designer at Pitti Uomo.

Antonio Marras Born Alghero, 1961. Antonio had no formal schooling in fashion, but via his father's fabric store, developed a passion for textiles. An entrepreneur from Rome hired him to create his first collection in 1988. In March 1999, his ready-to-wear collection was shown in Milan for the first time and in June 2002, Antonio presented his first men's collection at Pitti Immagine Uomo. LVMH asked him to become Artistic Director of Kenzo in 2003.

Chris Martin Born in 1977, Chris grew up in Devon. He met Will Champion, Guy Berryman and Jonny Buckland in the mid-'90s and the band Coldplay was born. They recorded a three-track EP and pressed 500 copies, which got them a gig at the In The City music festival in Manchester. Simon Williams signed them to his Fierce Panda label for one single, 'Brothers And Sisters', which in turn led to their deal with Parlophone. Their three successful albums *Parachutes* in 2000, *A Rush of Blood to the Head* in 2002 and *X&Y* in 2005 earned them four Grammies and four Brit awards. Their 2003 international tour was a sell-out. Chris lives in London with his actress wife Gwyneth and two children.

Meg Matthews Born Guernsey, 1966. Meg studied Graphic Communications. In 1993, she became . Betty Boo's PA and then ran her own club and a management company called Flavor, representing bands and record producers. In 1995, she joined Creation Records and set up 2-Active with Fran Cutler and organised events including the launch of Marco Pierre White's Titanic restaurant. She is now an interior designer and has a daughter, Anais, with her ex-husband Noel Gallagher.

Mark Mattock Born Kenilworth, 1961. Mark studied Graphic Design at Central St Martins, then began working with Neville Brody. He became Design Director of *Arena*, but left soon after winning Magazine Designer of The Year to concentrate on photography. He has shot for numerous fashion magazines and campaigns, and has been a regular contributor to i-D over the last few years. Mark is now concentrating on still-life photography, various personal projects and fishing.

Rufus May Rufus works as a psychologist in Bradford. Working with self-help groups and individuals using psychiatric services, he also gives talks about recovery from mental health problems nationally and internationally. Rufus helps run Evolving Minds, a public meeting about different ways to achieve mental wellbeing. He also organises a website and support network for people withdrawing from psychiatric medication. He lives in Hebden Bridge with his partner Rebecca and two sons Gregory and Nathan.

Eamonn J McCabe Born London, 1959. Eamonn started shooting for *Vogue* in 1984. His debut appearance in i-D was during the mid-'80s, when his early covers were a mix of video and photography. In 1989 he won the British Fashion Photographer of the Year award. His first collection of private work, *Ice*, featured a selection of landscapes taken from glaciers in Iceland. In 1990, he moved to New York to continue his fashion photography for American *Vogue*, *Vanity Fair* and *Interview*. He is currently working for various fashion clients from the USA and Europe.

Francesca McCarthy Leaving home at 16 to train at the Northern Ballet School in Manchester, Francesca continued her training at the London Contemporary Dance School. She began teaching in Norway but returned to England to study a BA in Contemporary Dance. Since graduating, Francesca has worked as a freelance teacher of both ballet and contemporary dance at vocational schools and dance companies in London. She is now a Lecturer in ballet for contemporary dancers at the Northern School of Contemporary Dance.

Mary McCartney Born London, 1969. Mary's interest in photography began during her childhood watching her mother, photographer Linda McCartney at work. This inspired Mary to start taking photographs professionally, specialising in portrait and fashion photography. She has photographed numerous musicians, actors and artists including Blondie, Beth Ditto, Liam Neeson and Jude Law. She is a Contributing Photographer to *Harper's Bazaar* and *Interview*. Mary had her first solo exhibition in 2004, *Off Pointe*, a photographic study of the Royal Ballet after hours. *Playing Dress Up*, Mary's latest exhibition, shows a collection of photographs of the world of fashion.

Stella McCartney Born and raised in London, Stella graduated from Central St Martins in 1995. After two collections she was appointed Creative Director of Chloé. 2001 saw the launch of her own fashion house in association with the Gucci group. Her first collection showed in October 2001 in Paris. In addition to her own collections, Stella has designed ranges for both Adidas and H&M. Stella McCartney has three flagship stores in New York, London and Los Angeles selling everything from women's ready-to-wear, accessories and eyewear to fragrances and skincare products. Stella's achievements have been recognised through various awards including the VH1/*Vogue* Fashion and Music Designer of the Year Award in 2000, The *Glamour* Award for Best Designer 2004 and the *Elle* Style Award for Best Designer 2007.

Craig McDean Born near Manchester, Craig began his career in London and now lives in New York. A long-time contributor to i-D, Italian and Japanese *Vogue*, *W* and *Harper's Bazaar*, he has photographed numerous international campaigns including Gucci, Christian Dior, Jil Sander, Calvin Klein and directed commercials for Calvin Klein's Contradiction and Versace's Versus Fragrances. Craig has also released two books *I Love Fast Cars* and *Lifescapes*.

Colin McDowell Colin is the Senior Fashion Writer for *The Sunday Times Style* and the author of 16 books including *McDowell's Directory of Nineteenth Century Fashion*. He is the Founder and Creative Director of Fashion Fringe and is a visiting professor of the Institute of the Arts and The Royal College of Art. Colin also makes a wide variety of television appearances, and has written biographies of leading designers including John Galliano, Manolo Blahnik and Jean Paul Gaultier. His latest TV work, *Fashion Unzipped*, examined US fashion in the '70s.

Jo Metson Scott Jo has spent most of her life in the Midlands, growing up in Nottingham and studying at Birmingham UCE. She moved to London four years ago working as Assistant to Kayt Jones. In 2007, she stopped assisting and has been shooting ever since. She regularly works for *The Guardian*, *The Telegraph* and *Dazed & Confused*, amongst others. Jo is now based in London but spends a lot of time working abroad on documentary projects both in photography and film.

Ryan McGinley Ryan takes colour photographs of his friends and uses photography to break down barriers between public and private spheres of activity. He creates conditions in which his subjects can lose themselves in the moment. Most recently, he has been taking photographs of groups of his friends on long trips around the USA and released a book on this project called *Sun and Health*. Ryan's last solo show in New York featured surreal, colour-saturated images of audience members at Morrissey concerts around the world taken over the course of three years.

Pat McGrath Born Northampton, 1966. After completing a foundation course at art college in Northampton, Pat moved to London to work as a make-up artist. She made her i-D debut at the start of the '90s in a 'plastic' story shot with Craig McDean and stylist Edward Enninful, with whom she went on to collaborate on a hugely successful international level. She now regularly collaborates on major fashion advertising campaigns including Prada, Alberta Ferretti, Calvin Klein and Lanvin, and her editorial work with top photographers like Steven Meisel for Italian and American *Vogue* continually breaks new ground. She is also the Beauty Director of i-D. Her celebrity clients have included Madonna, Jennifer Lopez, Oprah Winfrey and Gwyneth Paltrow. She currently supervises the catwalk make-up for numerous designers including Gucci, Yohji Yamamoto, Christian Dior, Dolce & Gabbana, Versace and John Galliano.

Iain McKell Born Cyprus, 1957. Iain grew up in Dorset. He studied at Exeter College of Art, then moved to London where he spent a year photographing skinheads and new romantics. He contributed to i-D, *The Face* and Italian *Vogue* and won awards for his advertising work on Sony Playstation. He was named Advertising Photographer of the Year in *Campaign* magazine's Creative Future Awards. Iain has also created work for Levi's, Smirnoff, Red Stripe and Dr. Martens. Celebrity portraits include Madonna, Jeremy Irons and Brad Pitt. He is currently working on a new book on travellers in the UK.

Alasdair McLellan Born Doncaster, 1974. Alasdair is a fashion photographer. He moved to London in 1996 after completing his studies in Photography and began to work for i-D and *The Face*. He has since shot for numerous magazines including *Self Service*, *Arena Homme Plus*, French *Vogue* and *L'Uomo Vogue*. Alasdair's advertising campaigns include Zegna, Alexander McQueen, Emporio Armani, Topman and Aquascutum.

Donald Milne Born in 1969, Donald grew up in Scotland. He started taking photographs when his Auntie Claire gave him her old Pentax camera for doing her garden! In 1992, whilst studying at the Royal College of Art, he was commissioned by i-D to photograph the Hispanic gang scene in post-riot Los Angeles. Donald dabbles in film and video and has photographed for numerous publications including *Vogue, Big, Details, New York Times, W,* and *Wired*.

Alexander McQueen Born London, 1969. McQueen was the youngest of six children. Leaving school at 16, he began an apprenticeship in Savile Row. He then moved to the theatrical costumiers Angels and Berman where he mastered six methods of pattern cutting from the 16th Century to the razor-sharp tailoring which has become a McQueen signature. Aged 20, he was employed by the designer Koji Tatsuno and a year later he worked as Romeo Gigli's Design Assistant. In 1994 he completed a Masters degree in Fashion Design at Central St Martins. His degree collection was famously bought in its entirety by Isabella Blow. In 1996, McQueen became Chief Designer at Givenchy where he worked until 2001. He remains Creative Director of Alexander McQueen whose collections include women's and men's ready-to-wear, accessories, eyewear and fragrance. Partnerships have also been formed with Puma and Samsonite and January 2006 heralded the birth of McQ a denim-based ready-to-wear line. McQueen has won British Designer of the Year four times, the International Designer of the Year by the CFDA and earned a CBE.

Cameron McVey Cameron was one of the three founding members of the Buffalo group with the late Ray Petri. An ex-photographer whose editorial work included i-D, *Vogue, The Observer, The Face* and *Interview*. Cameron shot the cover of Madness' album *One Step Beyond*. He has also produced, written songs and helped launch the careers of Neneh Cherry, Massive Attack, Portishead, Michael Stipe, Tricky and Youssou N'Dour. He is a member of the Virgin Souls Group and is also currently one of the four members of a music group called cirKus. Cameron lives between London and Sweden with his wife, Neneh Cherry, and their two daughters, Tyson and Mabel.

Dani Kiwi Meier Born and raised in New Zealand, Dani arrived in Europe in 1998 and became one of Europe's most well-known professional snowboarders. He now owns a very successful locations production company, which caters to clients' advertising needs worldwide. When not travelling, he lives at his villa retreat in Southwest France with his partner Eve. Portrait by Michael Chevas.

Kylie Minogue Born Melbourne, 1968. Kylie released her first single in July 1987. The song became a No. 1 hit in Australia and remained in the top spot for seven weeks. Since then she has released ten studio albums, two live CDs, seven live concert DVDs and the *White Diamond* feature length documentary. She has received countless gold and platinum discs and in 2004 she received a Grammy for 'Come into my World'. She's sold-out six world tours, including the critically acclaimed *Showgirl Homecoming* concert which saw her concluding the original *Showgirl* tour that was cut short due to her illness and has just announced her *KylieX2008* European tour. Kylie has graced the cover of several magazines including *Elle, GQ, Harper's Bazaar, Vogue* and i-D. *Kylie – The Exhibition* opened at the V&A Museum in 2007. Portrait by Mark Mattock.

Paul Mittleman Born New York, 1967. Paul studied Philosophy and Art History before submerging himself in the streetwear fashion world. In 1996, Paul became the Creative Director of Stüssy. He describes himself as a cook, gardener, DJ, artist, designer and cultural critic. Paul now lives in Los Angeles.

Issey Miyake Born Hiroshima, 1938. Issey established the Miyake Design Studio in 1970 and started to show his line at the Paris collections in 1973. His basic tenets for making clothes has always been the idea of creating a garment from "one piece of cloth", and the exploration of the space between the human body and the cloth that covers it. His approach to design has always been to strike a consistent balance between tradition and innovation, handcrafts and new technology. He established the Miyake Issey Foundation in 2004, and opened the 21_21 Design Sight in Tokyo in 2007. Portrait by Yuriko Takagi.

Michel Momy Born France, 1947. Michel started working in fashion photography in 1975. In the early '80s he met Terry Jones and worked with him for British *Vogue* and then i-D. In 1980, Michel moved to New York where he worked for *Mademoiselle*, American *Vogue* and *Harper's Bazaar*. He also studied film at Parsons School of Art, made several short films and painted. Since 1985, he's lived and worked in Paris and he currently shoots for i-D, *Marie Claire* and *Jalouse*. Michel has also photographed campaigns for Kerastase, Citroën, Hermès and Kenzo.

Eddie Monsoon Born Oxford, 1966. Eddie's interest in photography began at the age of 14 when he was given a camera. After college he assisted Mark Lebon and started contributing to the emerging style magazines i-D, *The Face* and *Blitz*. Eddie also worked extensively with musicians including Massive Attack, Neneh Cherry, Boy George, Soul II Soul, Jay Kay and The Verve. His first solo exhibition was in Tokyo and featured a selection of photographs of Massive Attack. Now based in Paris, Eddie is currently planning a book of his archives and concentrating on portraits. Portrait by Brett Walker.

Dennis Morris Born in Jamaica, Dennis had his first picture published aged 11. Spotted waiting for Bob Marley to arrive for a soundcheck in Soho – after bunking off school – Marley became taken with the young photographer and invited him to come along and take pictures on the tour. Dennis' photographs of Marley and The Wailers became famous internationally, appearing on the cover of *Time Out* and *Melody Maker* before he was 17. With a career spanning more than 20 years, and a CV that reads like a who's who of popular culture, Dennis's photographs have become highly collectable. He lives in London with his wife and daughter.

Shawn Mortensen Born in California, a self-taught artist and photographer, Shawn's photographs have appeared in magazines including i-D, *Harper's Bazaar, Vogue, Vanity Fair* and *Interview*. He has exhibited at The Whitney and The Guggenheim museums and has had commercial assignments for companies including Stüssy, Supreme and Coca-Cola. In 2003, he published his first book. He has directed a number of music videos for artists including Tricky, Alice Temple and Bush, and is the recipient of an MTV Music Video Award. In 2007, he published *Out of Mind with Harry Abrams*. He lives in Los Angeles and New York, and is currently at work on his third book *ZAPATISTA!*

Kate Moss Born South London, 1974. Kate was spotted by Storm Model Management's Sarah Doukas at the age of 14. 1992 was the start of her six-year contract with Calvin Klein. Throughout the last decade Kate has appeared in advertising for every major luxury label including Yves Saint Laurent, Longchamp, Donna Karan, Versace, Bulgari, Christian Dior and Chanel. She has also been the face of cosmetics label Rimmel for the past six years. Kate has appeared on countless magazine covers including i-D, British, American, Italian and French *Vogue, W, Another, Dazed & Confused* and *Vanity Fair*. In 2007, she launched her first clothing range with Topshop, her first fragrance *Kate* with Coty and an exclusive haircare range for James Brown London.

Clare Moyle (now **Clare Drinkell**) Born Blackburn, 1970. Clare worked at i-D before leaving in 1999 to work for Boudicca. After working on production for several seasons, she retrained in horticulture. Clare has been working at The Royal Botanic Gardens, Kew as a Botanical Assistant for over five years, specialising in the Orchidaceae plant family. She is writing a book on the revision of Epigeneium, an orchid genera endemic to Asia. Clare lives in London with her husband Pete Drinkell and her new baby boy.

Jeremy Murch Born UK, 1969. Jeremy started taking pictures for i-D in 1993 and now shoots for a wide range of magazines. Recent commissions include *Exit, The New York Times* and *The Observer*. He has undertaken many projects including ones for the BBC and The British Council. Jeremy's advertising clients include Nike, Adidas, Levi's and Hewlett Packard. His photographs have been featured in several group exhibitions and books, including *Surface: Contemporary Photographic Practice* and *JAM* at the Barbican. Jeremy currently lives in Bristol with his wife Jane and two young children, Callum and Esther.

Kostas Murkudis Born Dresden, Germany. Of Greek descent, Kostas studied Chemistry at the University of Berlin before joining the Lette Verein School of Fashion. After graduating, Kostas worked with Helmut Lang for seven years. His own womenswear brand, Kostas Murkudis, debuted in Paris in 1994 and his menswear collection in 1999. He later worked as Creative Director for the Italian brand New York Industrie and launched the brand Haltbar Murkudis in 2003. He also designs for the German label Schiesser. Kostas lives and works in Berlin.

Ravi Naidoo Born Durban, 1964. Ravi is the Founder and Managing Director of Interactive Africa, a Cape Town based media and marketing company. His company project managed the First African in Space Mission and marketed South Africa's bid to host the 2010 Football World Cup. In 1995, Ravi founded the International Design Indaba, a leading design institution that's known for its flagship conference and expo held in Cape Town annually. He also consulted for the Melbourne 2006 Commonwealth Games company, and assisted in their successful campaign.

Raffaello Napoleone Born 1954. Raffaello took a degree in Law at Rome University, followed by studies in Management and Marketing at Stanford University. In 1989, he was made General Manager of Pitti Immagine, a non-profit making company which organises Florentine fashion trade fairs. In 1995, he became Chief Executive Officer, a position which he still holds. Under Raffaello's direction, the company has become an internationally respected producer of innovative events, exhibitions and books.

Nadia Narain Born Hong Kong, 1972. Nadia left home at the age of 16 to travel the world. She spent a few years modelling and assisting on photo shoots. At 23, she trained to become a yoga teacher and has now been teaching for 11 years.

Helmut Newton Born Berlin, 1920. Helmut bought his first camera at the age of 12. At 18 – in a bid to escape the Nazis – he travelled to Singapore then to Australia where he joined the Australian Army and served as a Private for five years. He subsequently opened his first photography studio in Melbourne, and in 1948 he married his wife, June, an actress. In the '50s Helmut moved to Paris. His controversial *White Women*, published in 1976, earned him the title "King of Kink". He received numerous awards for his work including the Grand Prix National de la Ville de Paris and he was appointed both Commandeur de l'Ordre des Arts et des Lettres by the French Minister of Culture. Helmut died aged 83 in Los Angeles on 23 January 2004. Portrait by Alice Springs, Monte Carlo, 1984.

Maryvonne Numata Born France, 1945. Maryvonne studied Art and Advertising Design in Paris and then worked in advertising for a short period. In 1966, she moved to Spain and was a guest painter of the Rodriguez Acosta Fondation in Grenada, later participating in two exhibitions in Paris; *Les Artistes Francais* and *Les Indépendants*. Between 1971 and 1980 Maryvonne lived and worked in London. Returning to Paris in 1981, she started working for Issey Miyake Europe, later becoming the PR Director. In 1999, Maryvonne became PR Director at Yves Saint Laurent Rive Gauche where she stayed until 2001.

Erin O'Connor Born in 1978, the daughter of a furnace builder, Erin grew up in Brown Hills. She was discovered as a model in 1996, and within a few months she had been shot by Richard Avedon for a Versace campaign. In 1999, hairdresser Guido Paulo cut her hair and she truly found her confidence as a model. Erin is also a contributing writer to titles including *Vogue* and *The Times* and is Vice Chairman of the British Fashion Council.

Keiron O'Connor Born Surrey, 1974. Keiron studied Design Photography at The Arts Institute in Bournemouth. He then moved to London and assisted various fashion photographers. During this time he began working for i-D taking portraits and doing small photography projects. Keiron moved to Paris in 2001 and has since contributed to numerous magazines including French, American and German *Vogue*, *Numéro*, *L'Uomo Vogue*, *Jalouse* and French *Elle*. His commercial clients include DKNY and Ramosport.

Jessica Ogden Born Jamaica, 1970. Having worked with NoLoGo (a London eco friendly design collective), Jessica created her own line in 1993. Preferring to use antique and distressed fabrics, she works both on a personal basis making one-off pieces, as well as producing special commissions for stores worldwide. Her work has appeared in installations at London's Barbican Gallery and Design Museum. Jessica Ogden produces a joint label with Fred Perry and continues to collaborate closely with French label A.P.C.

Yoko Ono Born Tokyo, 1933. Yoko is a singer, artist and campaigner. She married John Lennon in 1969 in Gibraltar and they had a son, Sean, in 1975. Yoko has made numerous albums including *Open Your Box* which was released in 2007 and her number one US hits include 'Walking on Thin Ice', 'Everyman... Everywoman...' and 'No, No, No'. She has campaigned for peace and human rights since the '60s and in January 2008 she took out a full-page advertisement in *The New York Times* that simply read "IMAGINE PEACE". She currently lives in New York.

Nathalie Ours Born in France, 1964. After studying Japanese, Nathalie went to Tokyo and worked for Yohji Yamamoto where she became the foreign Press Office Coordinator. After two years, she returned to France and became the European PR Manager at Yohji Yamamoto in Paris. In May 2005, Nathalie left Yohji and founded *On Consulting* in Paris. In September 2007 she opened the Paris branch of *PR Consulting* (New York). Nathalie is also Editor of *A Magazine*.

Khamis Ali Pandu Born 1984. Khamis is currently studying to get his Diploma in Hospitality and Tourism Management in Zanzibar. He works as a ranger at Chumbe Island, an eco-project in Zanzibar when he can. He is particularly interested in environmental issues and specifically the protection of dolphins off the African coast.

Tesh Patel Born London, 1972. After attending university in Sussex in 1990 where he studied Mathematics, Tesh moved backed to London and to follow a career in photography. He assisted photographer Norman Watson until 1998. After a meeting at i-D with Edward Enninful, Tesh began shooting for the magazine allowing him to develop as a photographer. He regularly shoots editorial for Japanese and British *Vogue*, *Harper's Bazaar*, *Flair Magazine* and *V*. He now lives in New York.

Manuela Pavesi Manuela's career began in 1972 as a stylist at Italian *Vogue*. From 1972 until 1992 she looked after Italian *Vogue*'s Haute Couture and ready-to-wear, working with photographers Helmut Newton, David Bailey and Albert Watson. In 1992, Manuela started taking pictures herself for international fashion magazines, often also doubling up as stylist for her photographs. She is currently thinking about a lifestyle photo book.

John Barnes Pearson Born Yorkshire. Aged supermodel, actor, writer, father, husband and enthusiast. Lives in London with his wife Alison and their three children.

Clarice Pecori-Giraldi Born in Florence, Clarice has lived in Rome, Naples, Tokyo, Vienna and Milan. For 15 years, she was a modern art expert, then became the Communications Director at Prada Group. Subsequently, she became Corporate Communications Director at Salvatore Ferragamo. Since July 2006, she has been back in the art world as Managing Director at Christie's Italy.

Tobias Peggs Born Plymouth, 1972. Tobias started writing for i-D's clubs section in the mid-'90s while completing a PhD at the University of Wales. He was running websites, magazines and club nights in Cardiff before moving to London in 1997 where he became Managing Editor of i-D until 2000. Since then he has built and sold dot.coms in England and established software companies in India. He now lives in New York. Portrait by Larnie Nicolson.

Javier Peres Born in Cuba, Javier is a contemporary art dealer. His gallery, Peres Projects, has a base in Los Angeles and in Berlin. He also runs the Asia Song Society with Terence Koh in New York. In 2007, Javier published a limited edition, image-based quarterly called *DADDY*. He opened an off-site project space in Athens occupying a 1500 square metre seven-story building to coincide with the first Athens Biennial. *Art Review* recently included him in the magazine's 100 most influential people in the art world.

Jane Peverley Born Sunderland, 1971. Jane was the Managing Editor of i-D from 2000-2003. She now lives back in the Northeast with her husband Tommy and son Felix. She had their second child in February 2008.

Bianca Pilet Born The Netherlands, 1968. Bianca graduated from the Art Academy Utrecht with a degree in Photography in 1994. She has since contributed to numerous magazines including *The Independent, Rolling Stone, Self Service* and i-D. Bianca has also been involved in various exhibitions which include Le Festival International de Mode et de Photographie à Hyères in 2001, *Photographers of the Netherlands* at the Museum of Photography in The Hague (2002) and more recently *Lucinda Timmerman by Bianca Pilet* at Colette in Paris. Bianca is now based in Amsterdam.

Shannon Plumb Born in Schenectady, Shannon now lives and works in Brooklyn. She is a performer/filmmaker making silent comedies. With over 100 short films under her belt she has had solo exhibitions in New York, Paris, Germany, Austria and at the Aldrich Museum of Contemporary Art in Ridgefield. Her films have also been included in national and international film festivals including, the Rotterdam Film Festival 2007 and the 2006 London Film Festival. An exhibition of her new work was shown at the Sara Meltzer Gallery in February 2008.

Miuccia Prada Born in Milan, Miuccia graduated in Political Science from Milan's Statale University in 1970, at the same time studying mime at the Piccolo Teatro. In 1971, she entered the family business of luggage, set up by her grandfather Mario Prada in 1913. In 1988, she designed the first womenswear collection, Prada Donna. She is now responsible for Miu Miu, Prada Uomo, Prada Sport and Prada Beauty. In 2000, she was given an Honorary Doctorate from the Royal College of Art in London, and recognised for her work in the art world with an award from the New Museum of Contemporary Art in New York.

Gareth Pugh Born in Sunderland, Gareth is a fashion designer who has often been hyped as 'the new Alexander McQueen'. Following his turn at Fashion East in 2004, Gareth received a call from Kylie, asking him to design an outfit for her *Showgirl* tour, showcasing his designs alongside heavyweights John Galliano and Karl Lagerfeld. He was named Young Designer of the Year at the *Elle* Style Awards in 2007, and participated in *Fashion in Motion* at the V&A Museum in the same year. Gareth now lives in London.

Oriana Reich Born New York, 1981. Oriana joined i-D in 2000 as an intern and graduated from Central St Martins in 2002. She is the Co-Founder of Chariots on Fire, a shop in San Francisco, and works on branding and design projects internationally.

Dominique Renson Born 1960. Dominique is an artist based in Paris. For over 20 years, she has looked to her own self, her experience and travels for inspiration. She is currently working on a project called Creatures.

Terry Richardson Born in New York and raised in Hollywood, Terry began photographing his environment while attending Hollywood High School. He has shot campaigns for numerous clients including Gucci, Miu Miu, Levi's, Chloé and Nike, and his work has appeared in magazines such as French, British, Japanese and American *Vogue, GQ, Harper's Bazaar, W* and i-D. He has also photographed an impressive list of celebrities including Daniel Day Lewis, Leonardo DiCaprio, Jay-Z, 50 Cent, Maggie Gyllenhaal, Karl Lagerfeld and Chloë Sevigny. His work has been exhibited in numerous solo and group shows and he has published several books. Terry has recently made the transition from still photography to film with music videos for Primal Scream, Death in Vegas, and Whirlwind Heat. His feature film debut *Son of a Bitch* is currently in development.

Vava Ribeiro Born Rio, 1969. Vava graduated in Graphic Design, then travelled around surfing, before starting as a photographic assistant in New York. After some time as a writer, he returned to photography and regularly contributes to magazines including *Purple, Exit* and *Dazed & Confused*. His commercial clients have included Levi's and Miller, and his work has been exhibited internationally. In 2000, Vava won the prize for photography at Le Festival International de Mode et de Photographie à Hyères. He now lives and works in New York.

Mischa Richter Born in Windsor, UK, Mischa spent his childhood in New York and Provincetown, Massachusetts. He moved back to England in his early 20s and studied Fine Art at the Chelsea College of Art and Middlesex University. He has worked for magazines including i-D, *The Face, Vogue, The New York Times Magazine* and *The Observer Magazine*. His commercial clients include Levi's and Camper and his work has been shown at the Laura Bartlet Gallery in London and the National Portrait Gallery. He is presently working on a solo show in Provincetown. Mischa lives in London and Provincetown with his wife and two children.

Carlo Rivetti Born 1956. Carlo is part of the Rivetti family who have worked in the woollen industry since the mid-18th century. In the late '50s, the family founded one of the leading European clothing manufacturers: the Turin-based GFT Group. In 1993, Carlo and his sister Cristina left the family company to take over the informal clothing branch of the group centred on C.P. Company in Ravarino. It was promptly renamed Sportswear Company, which takes in the brands C.P. Company and Stone Island. Carlo is President of the company and lives in Milan.

Olivier Rizzo After graduating from the Royal Academy of Fine Arts in Antwerp, Olivier assisted various Belgian designers before he started his career as a freelance stylist and creative consultant. He has produced work for numerous magazines including i-D, *Arena Homme Plus, Harper's Bazaar, POP, V, Self Service* and *L'Uomo Vogue*. Olivier has worked with many top photographers including Mert and Marcus, Karl Lagerfeld, Craig McDean, Paolo Roversi, Willy Vanderperre, David Sims and Inez and Vinoodh. Olivier has also worked on several catwalk shows including Prada, Miu Miu, Louis Vuitton and Jil Sander. His advertising campaigns include Lanvin, Jil Sander, Louis Vuitton and Calvin Klein.

Millie Robson 24-year-old Millie is from Kingston-Upon-Thames. She recently graduated with a BA in Fashion Photography from the London College of Fashion and is currently setting up her own photography studio and working on a project photographing pole dancers.

Dame Anita Roddick Born Littlehampton, 1942. Anita worked in the library of the *International Herald Tribune* in Paris, as an English and History teacher, then in the Women's Rights Department of the International Labor Organization. In 1976, she founded The Body Shop. Awarded an OBE in 1988, Anita published her autobiography *Business and Unusual* in 2000 and edited *Take it Personally* (2001), a collection of thought provoking pieces challenging the myths of globalisation and the power of the WTO. Anita passed away in September 2007 at the age of 64. Portrait by Joel Anderson.

Myriam Roehri Born 1965, Strasbourg. Myriam started as a stylist in the '80s, became a photographer's agent in the '90s and has been a photographer since 2006. Recent exhibitions include *Princes et Princesses* at Colette in Paris.

Rose Bakery Rose Carrarini is most famous for setting up Villandry in 1988 with her husband Jean-Charles, a restaurant that went on to inspire many other food places in London. Before that, Rose and Jean-Charles ran a designer knitwear company for nine years. Their next venture, Rose Bakery, opened in Paris in 2002. A London location followed in Dover Street Market in 2004. *Breakfast, Lunch and Tea: The Many Little Meals of Rose Bakery* was released in 2005 by Phaidon.

Paolo Roversi Born Ravenna, 1947. Following an apprenticeship with Nevio Natali, Paolo's first assignment was with Associated Press in 1970 where he was sent to cover Ezra Pound's funeral in Venice. In the mid-'80s Paolo worked with Comme des Garçons, Yohji Yamamoto and Romeo Gigli. His clients include Evian, Kenzo and Woolmark, and his work has been published in numerous books including *Studio, Libretto* and *Images Cerruti.* Paolo photographs for international publications including Italian, American, British, French and Japanese *Vogue, L'Uomo Vogue, Arena Homme Plus, The New York Times Magazine* and i-D. His solo exhibition *Studio* opened in Paris in 2002 and has also been shown in galleries in New York, Lille and Yokohama. His recent group exhibitions include *Clichy sans Clichés* (Paris, 2006), *Yohji Yamamoto Correspondences* at Pitti Immagine (2005) and *Photography & Fashion* (Athens, 2005). He continues to live and work in Paris.

Amber Rowlands Born in Stroud, Amber received a BA in Graphic Design from Camberwell College of Art. In 1997, she began to shoot regularly for i-D. Her work has also appeared in *The Independent, V* and *The Telegraph Magazine.* Her clients include Liberty and Maximo Park. Amber has just come back from a second visit to China where she's been photographing the young super-rich for *Time* magazine.

Kris Ruhs Born New York, 1952. Of German parentage, Kris attended the School of Visual Arts from 1972. That same year he started his first series of sculptures inspired by the wood discarded in the streets next to his studio on lower Broadway. Since graduating in 1975, his work has appeared in several solo and group exhibitions in art galleries internationally including the Romeo Gigli Space in Milan. Kris has been heavily involved in the designing of 10 Corso Como in Milan since it was founded in 1991 by his partner Carla Sozzani. Kris now has studios in both Milan and Paris where he continues to use any material. Portrait by Vanni Burkhart.

Stefan Ruiz Born in San Francisco and now based in New York, photographer Stefan first started shooting for i-D in the early '90s and went on to do advertising campaigns with Terry Jones. In addition to i-D, his work can be seen in such publications as *The New York Times Magazine, The Sunday Telegraph* and Italian *Vogue.* His work has also been shown in the Havana Biennale (Cuba, 2003), PhotoEspaña (Madrid, 2003) and as an award nominee at Rencontres d'Arles 2005. He also had a solo show in 2005 at the Impressions Gallery in the UK. In 2006, the first monograph of his work *People* was published.

Sabisha Born in Johannesburg, South Africa, Sabisha attended the San Francisco Art Institute where she studied painting, sculpture, film, performance and installation, finishing her degree with an emphasis on sound. She now lives in Paris and performs with several projects in Europe and abroad.

Derrick Santini Originally from Scarborough, Derrick started taking pictures aged 13. He went to Harrogate College to do a BTEC in Photography, followed by a BA at The London College of Printing. Derrick's editorial work has appeared in *Flaunt, Tatler, Vice* and i-D. His advertising work includes campaigns for Nike, Reebok, Levi's, Heineken and Avirex. In 2004, Dazed Books published *Persona,* an inspirational collection of Derrick's portraits, with exhibitions in New York, London and Paris. Derrick currently lives in London. Self-portrait with Lily.

Sarah Born near Paris, 1975. Sarah studied History of Art at L'Ecole du Louvre, during which time she assisted at *Purple* magazine. When her mother opened the Parisian concept store Colette in March 1997, she was responsible for exhibitions, the music and bookshop, events and new relations with young designers. Colette stocks an eclectic selection of cosmetics, as well as clothing and accessories by fashion brands including Lanvin, Prada, Dries Van Noten, Raf Simons and Comme des Garçons. There is always an interesting selection of pieces by emerging designers, alongside a selection of books, magazines and music. The store has a small, but influential, exhibition space that displays artwork by young artists. Sarah continues to be the Buyer and Art Director and driving force at Colette. Portrait by Keetja Allard.

Peter Saville Born Manchester, 1955. Peter studied Graphic Design at Manchester Polytechnic from 1975-1978. In 1979, he became a founding partner of the landmark independent record label Factory Records where he created album covers for Joy Division and New Order. Since then, his clients have included Roxy Music, Pulp, the Pompidou Centre, Yohji Yamamoto, Jil Sander, Christian Dior, Givenchy, Alexander McQueen, Stella McCartney and Adidas. In 2003, Peter had a major retrospective staged at London's Design Museum and subsequently in Tokyo and Manchester. He is also Consultant Creative Director to the City Council of Manchester and has an honorary doctorate from his former college Manchester Metropolitan University. Portrait by Anna Blessmann.

Jicky Schnee Born in Scotland, Jicky is an artist and actor. Upcoming films include *The Afterlight* with Rip Torn and *Perestroika* with F. Murray Abraham. Jicky lives in New York and Woodstock.

Stephan Schneider Born Germany, 1969. Stephan graduated from The Royal Academy for Fine Arts in Antwerp and he presented his first collection at Paris Fashion Week the same year. He now presents both a menswear and womenswear collection in Paris each season. The company has grown season by season and is now sold in over 70 places worldwide. In 1996, the first European flagship store opened in Antwerp and a second followed in Tokyo in 2001. Since April 2007, Stephan has been a Professor in the fashion department of The Berlin University of Fine Arts.

Collier Schorr Born in Queens, New York, Collier lives and works in Brooklyn and Schwabisch Gmund in Germany – where the majority of her pictures are taken. She is currently at work on the second volume of her book series *Forest & Fields* as well as exhibitions at Le Corsortium, Dijon and Villa Romana in Florence. Collier has shot for *The New York Times Magazine, L'Uomo Vogue, V Man, Numéro Homme* and *Interview.* She is on the faculty of Yale University where she holds the position of Senior Photography Critic.

Jeremy Scott Born 1974, and raised in Kansas City, Missouri, Jeremy's fashion career began as a student at Pratt University in 1992. Spring 2007 marked the ten year anniversary of the Jeremy Scott brand. In both 1996 and 1997 he won the Venus de la Mode Award for Best Designer of the Year and in 1999 he was recognised by the CFDA and was nominated for the Best Young Designer Award. In Autumn 2001 he moved to Los Angeles. Jeremy has been an i-D cover star appearing alongside Devon Aoki on the front of the July 2007 issue. Portrait by Rony Alwin.

Gilles Rosier Born Paris, 1961. Gilles studied at the Chambre Syndicale de la Couture. Having gained apprenticeships at Balmain, Christian Dior, Guy Paulin and Jean Paul Gaultier, he then became Artistic Director at Leonard. Gilles started his own line in 1992 and was Creative Director at Lacoste until he left to take charge of the womenswear collection at Kenzo in 1999. He left Kenzo in 2002 and is now concentrating on the development of his own line.

Marcus Ross Born Geneva, 1974. Marcus studied Fine Art at Kingston University. Together with two friends, he set up his own studio in Hackney producing paintings and clothes. He joined the i-D fashion department in 1998 working closely with Fiona Dallanegra and Edward Enninful, writing and styling for the magazine. Since leaving i-D in 2003, Marcus has worked as a freelance photographer for *The Sunday Times Style, GQ* and *Esquire,* and his clients include Levi's and Holland Esq. He recently joined *Vice* as European Fashion Director.

Renzo Rosso Born Padua, Italy, 1955. Renzo began making his own clothing after graduating from an industrial textile manufacturing school. In 1978, he joined forces with several other manufacturers in his region to form the Genius Group, which went on to create Katharine Hamnett, Replay, Goldie and Diesel. He became sole owner of Diesel in 1985. The Diesel brand now incorporates apparel, accessories, international talent support initiatives, global fragrance launches and local Diesel Farm wines. Renzo has also built an independent group, Only the Brave, whose brands include Maison Martin Margiela, Sophia Kokosalaki and DSquared. He has an organic farm in the Marostica hills near Vicenza, Italy. Portrait by Corbijn.

Venetia Scott Venetia began her styling career at British *Vogue* and went on to style shoots for numerous magazines including i-D, *The Face*, Italian *Vogue*, *Self Service*, *Another Magazine* and *W*, working with some of the most renowned photographers such as David Sims, Corinne Day, Helmut Newton, Juergen Teller, Mario Sorrenti and Steven Klein. Venetia's advertising clients include Anna Molinari, Calvin Klein, Katharine Hamnett, Marc Jacobs, Margaret Howell and Strenesse. In 1997, Venetia began working at Marc Jacobs as Creative Director of Marc Jacobs and Marc by Marc Jacobs.

Elfie Semotan Born North Austria, 1941. Elfie graduated from the School of Fashion Design Hetzendorf in Vienna. She then lived in Paris for seven years working as a model and also started photographing. Between 1975 and 1985, she shot fashion and advertising campaigns in Vienna, Germany, France and Switzerland. Apart from i-D, Elfie has also photographed for *Vogue*, *Elle*, *Esquire*, *Marie Claire* and *Harper's Bazaar*. Her photography career has led to numerous exhibitions and books. She currently lives and works in Vienna and New York.

Nigel Shafran Born 1964, Nigel started his career as a fashion photographer before crossing over to the art/documentary world. Nigel has exhibited extensively and published numerous books. In 1998, he was commissioned by the V&A to produce a portfolio of photographs of the museum. He also received a commission for Royal Mail Christmas stamps in 2004. In 2007, Nigel had exhibitions at Tate Britain, *How we are: Photographing*, and Aram Gallery, *Accidental Collectors*.

Shambhala Born in Paris, Shambhala worked as a couture model on the European catwalks for seven years after graduating from university. In 1994, she became the assistant of the photographer, Olivier Garros for two years. She began her career in reportage photography by covering the conflicts in Sarajevo. Since arriving in London Shambhala's work has appeared in numerous newspapers and magazines including *The Observer*, *The Sunday Times Magazine*, *Marie Claire* and *The Independent*. Her principal area of work is now in portraiture.

Alix Sharkey Born 1956, Alix is a freelance journalist specialising in pop culture and fashion. He writes regularly for *The Guardian*, *The Observer* and *The Sunday Telegraph*. From 1992 to 1995, he wrote a regular weekly column for *The Independent*. He joined i-D in 1981, became Co-Editor and left in 1989. Since then, he has worked as News Editor for MTV Europe and as a BBC TV presenter; he is currently a Contributing Editor for British *GQ* and *Ocean Drive*. His book about Belgian designer Dries Van Noten, *DVN 1-50*, was a bestseller, and his work has appeared in various anthologies of journalism, including *The Bedside Guardian*, *Beaty Big & Bouncy: An Anthology of Rock Writing* and most recently, *Transculturalism: How The World Is Coming Together*. He lives in Miami Beach and is currently finishing his debut novel, *The Marabout*. Portrait by Ola Mobolade.

Dr. Vandana Shiva Born India, 1952. Vandana is a physicist, ecologist, activist, editor and author of many books. She established Navdanya in India – a movement for biodiversity conservation and farmers' rights. She directs the Research Foundation for Science, Technology and Natural Resource Policy. Her most recent books include *Earth Democracy; Justice, Sustainability, and Peace* and *Manifestos on the Future of Food and Seed*. She has received many prizes including the Global 500 Award of the United Nations Environment Programme in 1993 and the Earth Day International Award of the United Nations for her dedicated commitment to the preservation of the planet as demonstrated by her actions, leadership and by setting an example for the rest of the world. Vandana is currently based in New Delhi.

Wing Shya A Hong Kong-based photographer who works in the field of fashion, film, and art, Wing started his career as a graphic designer. He contributes to numerous international fashion titles including i-D and French *Vogue*. His commercial clients include Louis Vuitton, Lacoste, A Bathing Ape and Nike. Wing is the exclusive Photographer and Graphic Designer on Wong Kar Wai's films including *Happy Together*, *In the Mood for Love*, *Eros* and *2046*. He has also directed music videos for Vanessa Mae and Hong Kong performer Karen Mok. In March 2006, he held an exhibition in Japan.

Irene Silvagni Born in 1941, to Russian parents, Irene worked as a journalist from 1968-1991. She became European Editor for *Rizzoli* magazine and went on to work at US *Mademoiselle*, followed by a position as Deputy Fashion Editor at French *Elle*. Further positions included European Editor at US *Vogue* and Fashion Editor at French *Vogue*. Since 1991, Irene has been Art and Creative Director at Yohji Yamamoto.

Raf Simons Born Neerpelt, Belgium, 1968. Raf graduated in 1991 with a degree in Industrial and Furniture Design, he then worked as a furniture designer for galleries and private interiors. Encouraged by Linda Loppa, Head of the Fashion Department of Antwerp Royal Academy, Raf had a radical change of profession and launched the Raf Simons fashion label in 1995. In November 2003, he won the Swiss Textiles Award which helped further the development of his label. In 2005, he added the Raf by Raf Simons label to his portfolio and, in July 2005, he was named Creative Director of Jil Sander for mens and womenswear. Portrait by Rineke Dijkstra.

David Sims David started working as a photographer in 1989 with his first editorial stories appearing in i-D and *The Face*. After shooting a very influential advertising campaign for Yohji Yamamoto, he received a one-year contract with US *Harper's Bazaar* and shot his first campaign for Calvin Klein. Following a show at Zwemmers Gallery in London in 1994 he was awarded Photographer of the Year (Festival de la Mode) and has since gone on to contribute to a number of exhibitions including the *Exhibition of Contemporary Photography* at the V&A Museum, *Isolated Heroes* with Raf Simons at the Emily Tsingou Gallery and *Roses* at Visionaire. His pictures also appear in permanent collections at Tate Modern and the V&A Museum. David's advertising clients include Jil Sander, Balenciaga, Calvin Klein, Marc Jacobs, Gap, Prada, Rimmel and Burberry, and his work appears in magazines including *Harper's Bazaar*, Italian, American and French *Vogue* and *W*. David lives with his partner Luella Bartley and three children in Cornwall. He is also an avid surfer.

Talvin Singh Born in London, Talvin is a musician. He began studying classical Indian music at the age of 15 and was soon performing classical Tabla recitals and working with artists such as Sun Ra and Courtney Pine. In 1990, he conceived the Tablatronic, an instrument that fuses traditional Indian drumming with sound processing abilities. Talvin has worked with many DJ's and like-minded musicians as well as on his own solo work. His debut release *OK* won the Mercury Music Prize in 1999. Collaborations have included artists such as Madonna, Jay-Z and Blondie, as well as the more traditional artists Jajouka and the late Ustad Nusrat Fateh Ali Khan.

James Sleaford Born Nottingham, 1970. James graduated in Business from Nottingham Trent University in 1993 but was encouraged by his sister Julie to begin menswear styling. In 1997 he shot his first story for i-D featuring Raf Simons' first collection. After i-D, James went to *GQ* from 2001 to 2003. In 2007, James became the Fashion Editor for *GQ* France, which launched in February 2008. He now lives in Paris.

Julie Sleaford Born Nottingham, 1963. Photographer Julie has been shooting editorial for i-D, *Purple Sexe* and *Jane* (New York) and advertising for John Richmond and Harvey Nichols. Then in 2000, her sister encouraged her to go horse riding, and a childhood passion was rekindled. Julie now lives very happily in Essex with her husband, two very spoilt Jack Russells and their horses.

Bob and Roberta Smith Born London, 1963. Patrick Brill is an artist who works under the pseudonym Bob and Roberta Smith. While still an undergradate at the University of Reading, he was awarded the Priz de Rome. Following that, he went on to complete his MA at Goldsmith College. He currently lives and works in London.

Paul Smith Born 1946, Paul's introduction into fashion was working at a local clothing warehouse as a gofer. He took evening classes in the art of tailoring at the local Polytechnic, and opened his first shop in 1970 in Nottingham. This stocked designers such as Kenzo and Margaret Howell alongside early designs of his own. In 1976, Paul showed his first menswear collection in Paris. Within 20 years, he had established over 200 stores worldwide and now has over ten different collections, as well as some home furnishing lines and fragrances. He was awarded a CBE in 1994, and a Knighthood in 2000 in recognition of his services to the British fashion industry. Paul is continually involved in every aspect of the business as both Designer and Chairman. As a result, Paul Smith Limited retains a personal touch often lost in companies of a similar size.

Paul D. Smith Born 1948, Paul studied at London University (1968-1971), graduating with a BSc specialising in Physiology. Following a stint at the Royal College of Surgeons, he went to the Royal College of Art to pursue an MA in Photography. He first met Terry Jones in 1974 when as external examiner Terry awarded him the *Vogue* Scholarship. He currently teaches on the BA Photography degree at London College of Communication (formely London College of Printing).

Franca Soncini Franca has worked in fashion for more than 20 years, starting in the '70s with Elio Fiorucci. She opened her own public relations and advertising agency Franca Soncini in 1979 taking care of the press and art direction for advertising campaigns and fashion shows. To date, clients have included Comme des Garçons, Costume National, Maison Martin Margiela, Bless and Naoki Takizawa.

Francesca Sorrenti Born in New York, Francesca has worked as a fashion designer, creative director, curator and photographer. Her work hs been seen in numerous international magazines and has been shown in many exhibitions. Francesca has also edited a number of photographic books including *Our World in Focus*, *Water Culture*, *Journey in Sight*, *America Off Track* and *Katrina, Personal Objects*. Since 2002, she has worked alongside photographer Jarret Schecter and has also founded SKeGroup (See, Know & Evolve), which brings awareness to social, environmental and artistic issues.

Mario Sorrenti Born Naples, 1971. Mario moved to New York in 1981. He started documenting his life through photography from a young age. At 21, Mario was working on a major advertising campaign for Calvin Klein. He has also worked for clients including Missoni, Ungaro, Jil Sander and Loewe. In 2001, he published a book called *The Machine*, a photographic study of his younger brother and fellow photographer Davide who passed away in 1997. His work has appeared in many other photography publications. Most recently, Mario's work was at the National Portrait Gallery's *Face of Fashion* exhibition in February 2007. His work is also held in the permanent collections of the V&A Museum and New York Public Library.

Vanina Sorrenti Born in Italy, Vanina moved to New York aged nine. The sister of photographer Mario Sorrenti, for the last eight years Vanina has split her time between New York, London and Paris. Her photography has appeared in numerous international publications including i-D, British, French and Japanese *Vogue*, *Vogue Hommes International*, *Numéro* and *V*. Advertising campaigns include Chloé, Martine Sitbon and Tsumori Chisato. Vanina's work has also been shown in various exhibitions including the *Imperfect Beauty* exhibition at the V&A Museum and the *Quatre Jeune Femme Photograph* at the 213 Gallerie. Books she has contributed to include *Women seeing Women*, *Vogue Unseen*, *Porn?*, *Smilei-D*, *Women on Fashion* and *Beauty in Vogue*.

Eugene Souleiman Born Harrow, 1961. Eugene worked closely with Trevor Sorbie for nearly ten years. He became Co-Creative Director for Bumble & Bumble in 1999. Soon after this, he joined Vidal Sassoon as Editorial Director. He was also recently Creative Director for Tecni.Art/L'Oreal Professionnel. Eugene has worked on numerous shows including Alexander McQueen, Dolce & Gabbana, Chanel, Donna Karan, Paul Smith and Lanvin. He is a regular contributor to fashion magazines including i-D, Italian, British and French *Vogue*, *Harper's Bazaar*, *L'Uomo Vogue* and *W*, and has worked with Craig McDean, Paolo Roversi, Irving Penn, Richard Avedon, Mario Testino and Steven Meisel. Eugene recently collaborated with Jake and Dinos Chapman on an art exhibition called *The Art of Chess* where he individually styled the hair of each chess figure.

Stephen Sprouse Born Ohio, 1953. Stephen was a fashion designer, painter and photographer who is credited with pioneering the '80s mix of "uptown sophistication in clothing with a downtown punk and pop sensibility". He moved to New York in the early '70s. After a brief time at the Rhode Island School of Design, Stephen started work as a drawing assistant to Halston. Hanging out with Andy Warhol, going to punk shows and monster-truck rallies, Stephen designed clothes for Debbie Harry, Duran Duran and Billy Idol. In 2000, he met Marc Jacobs for whom he created the iconic graffiti luggage and in 2006 Marc utilised Stephen's 1987 graffiti leopard images which were used for Louis Vuitton handbags, shoes and scarves – they sold out instantly. Stephen died in 2004 in New York aged 50.

Beth Summers Born London, 1962. After studying Fine Art at Central St Martins, Beth started work at i-D in 1983 as Assistant to Caryn Franklin. Three years later she became Fashion Editor herself, leaving in 1992 to have her daughter Eden. Beth then worked as Fashion Editor at *Loaded*, a position she held from the first issue. In 1998 she launched a supplement *Loaded Fashion* as Editor and Fashion Director. However, in January 2000 whilst in Milan for the menswear fashion shows she had a serious scooter accident which left her with brain damage. Beth is making amazing progress and has fought this huge challenge with incredible courage. Her daughter Eden is now a mature and beautiful 15-year-old who lives near to Beth with her grandparents.

Bernard Sumner Born Salford, 1957. Bernard was a guitarist in Joy Division, then the lead singer in Joy Division's reincarnation New Order. With 1983's 'Blue Monday' single – their groundbreaking fusion of black techno, gay disco and killer pop – New Order helped shape the sound of a global clubland community which i-D would go on to cover extensively. They released their seventh studio album, the mega-selling *Republic* in 1993. Bernard now lives in Cheshire with his wife Sarah, and is a keen supporter of Manchester United.

Sølve Sundsbø Born Norway, 1970. Sølve shoots regularly for magazines including i-D, *Pop*, *Dazed & Confused*, *Harper's Bazaar*, *Numéro* and *Visionaire*. His commercial clients include Yves Saint Laurent Parfums, Christian Dior Parfums, Levi's, Nike, Armani and Bally. He has shot covers for bands like Coldplay, The Feeling and Sophie Ellis Bextor. In 1999, he was voted the best newcomer at Le Festival International de Mode et de Photographie à Hyères and has exhibited in numerous exhibitions. Sølve has also worked on films for Nike and Gucci. He lives in London with his wife and three sons.

Matthew Stone Born 1982, Matthew lives and works in London. His romanticised and staged photographic artworks document and celebrate his friends, co-conspirers and collaborators. His artwork references and celebrates not only his immediate community, but also artists ranging from Caravaggio to Warhol and Beuys. His first solo exhibition, *Future Hindsight*, was held at the Union Gallery in London in 2007. Matthew grew up in a house with no mains electricity and a barn owl as a pet. He has squatted in Peckham and more recently camped in the blackout basement of Terence Koh's New York gallery.

Jun Takahashi Born Kiryu, Japan, 1969. Jun entered the Bunka Academy of Fashion and created the Undercover brand in 1988. After graduating in 1991, he presented his first collection for autumn/winter 1994/1995. In the same year, Undercover was established as a company. Jun received the Grand Prize sponsored by the Mainichi newspaper in 2001, and in the following year presented his spring/summer collection in Paris. He continues to show in Paris. Portrait by Keiichi Nitta.

Takahiko Takemoto (Takay) Born Osaka, Japan, 1973. Takay studied Photography at the Visual Arts College in Osaka before moving to London to work as a photographic assistant. His career was launched when he began shooting fashion stories for i-D. Clients now include Armani, H&M, French Connection, Estée Lauder, Motorola, Levi's, Revlon and Shiseido. Takay has exhibited his work in Tokyo, Osaka and London. He is currently based in Europe and divides his time between London, Paris, New York and Japan.

Naoki Takizawa Born Tokyo, 1960. Naoki graduated from Kuwasawa Design Institute and joined the Issey Miyake Design Studio in 1982. Having held many positions within the company, he became the Designer for Issey Miyake Men in 1993, and in 1999, Designer for Issey Miyake Women. He contributed to the *Yanomami Spirit of the Forest* exhibition at the Cartier Foundation for Contemporary Art in 2003. Naoki Takizawa Design Inc. was established in 2006 and in 2007 he was awarded the title Chevalier dans l'Ordre des Arts et des Lettres (Knight in the Order of Arts and Literature) in Paris. Portrait by Daido Moriyama.

Alexi Tan A Chinese director born in the Philippines, Alexi attended the Tisch School of the Arts in New York. He started his career as a stills photographer working for numerous international publications and advertising campaigns. In 2000, he directed his first short film, *17.17.* a 6-minute experimental short, which premiered at the Brooklyn International Film Festival. After moving back to Asia in 2002, Alexi started to direct TV commercials and music videos. His first feature film, *Blood Brothers*, is a Mandarin language film featuring Daniel Wu and Chang Chen. It was the closing film of the 64th Venice Film Festival and was presented at the 32nd Toronto International Film Festival.

Rossella Tarabini Born Carpi, 1967. After attending art school in Modena, Rossella studied Art at the DAMS University in Bologna. Following a period living in London, she moved back to Italy to join the family company Blumarine, and in 1995, she designed her first collection for Anna Molinari. In 2006, Rossella became the Creative Director of Blufin S.p.A. which incorporates the Blumarine, Anna Molinari and Blugirl brands.

Angelika Taschen Angelika was born in Hamburg, Germany, the eldest daughter of bookshop keepers. Growing too tall to fulfil her adulthood ambition to become a ballet dancer she instead practiced as a musical dancer. She then turned her attention to art history and German literature, gaining her doctorate in 1986. Since then she has been working for TASCHEN books, and has published numerous titles on architecture, photography, design, contemporary art, interiors and travel.

Atsuro Tayama Born Kunamoto, 1955. Atsuro graduated from the Bunka Fashion College winning the Pierre Cardin Award. In his 20s, he worked for Yohji Yamamoto and moved to Paris to establish Yohji Europe. On returning to Japan he founded his own company AT in 1982, and launched his AT collection in 1984. Atsuro won the Shiseido Encouragement Award for Best New Designer at the 10th Mainichi Fashion Grand Prix. In 1991, he launched Atsuro Tayama which showed in Paris that same year. He then signed agreements with World Co Ltd as Director of several lines, including INdivi, OZOC and Boycott. In 1999, he launched Atsuro Tayama Green Label and is currently producer of Salotto by Salotto. Portrait by Phoebe Wong Hoi San.

Marcia Taylor Born to the sound of the Bow Bells, Marcia left East London with big dreams of becoming a 'top exec'. After studying advertising, she began working at a marketing company, but soon decided that she loved clothes more. She has worked at i-D since 1996 and is now the Bookings Editor. Marcia is also a freelance stylist.

Sam Taylor-Wood Born London, 1967. Sam graduated from Goldsmiths College in 1990 where her contemporaries included Damien Hirst and Jake Chapman. After college she worked for a brief period at the Royal Opera House as a dresser and in 1991 she began to show her work in group exhibitions alongside her Goldsmith peers. In 1994, Sam produced *Killing Time* in which four people mimed to the sound of Strauss' *Elektra*. In 1997, she received the Illy Café Prize for Most Promising Young Artist at the Venice Biennale and in the following year she was nominated for the Turner Prize. In 2002, Sam became the youngest artist to have a major survey show at the Hayward Gallery (London). There was also a solo exhibition at the Wellington City Art Gallery (New Zealand) that ran until January 2007. Portrait by Johnnie Shand Kydd, courtesy of Jay Jopling/White Cube (London).

Juergen Teller Born Erlangen, Germany, 1964. Juergen discovered photography after an apprenticeship as a violin bow maker was cut short by an allergic reaction to wood shavings. He studied at the Bayerische Staatslehranstalt für Photographie in Munich from 1984 to 1986. Since then, he has been living and working in London. In 2003, he was the recipient of the Citibank Prize for Photography. His work has been featured in numerous books, magazines, exhibitions and on record covers. Juergen has also produced campaigns for Helmut Lang, Katharine Hamnett, Hugo Boss, Miu Miu, Yves Saint Laurent and Marc Jacobs.

Tennekoon Born 1933, Tennekoon was a farmer and inspirational teacher from Sri Lanka. He died in 2005 aged 72.

Wolfgang Tillmans Born Remscheid, Germany, 1968. Wolfgang studied at Bournemouth and Poole College of Art and Design, graduating in 1992. He moved to New York in 1994, but returned to London in 1996. He won the Turner Prize in 2000, and was awarded the Honorary Fellowship at The Arts Institute at Bournemouth the following year. Since 2003, Wolfgang has held the Professorship of Interdisciplinary Art at Städelschule in Frankfurt am Main. He has exhibited extensively across the world, most recently at Maureen Paley in London, the Stedelijk Museum in Amsterdam and the Hamburger Bahnhof Museum für Gegenwart in Berlin. Numerous books containing his work have been published including *Wolfgang Tillmans: Manual*, *Wolfgang Tillmans: Still Life* and *Freedom From the Known*, and his photography has featured in magazines including *Fantastic Man*, *BUTT*, *Esquire*, *Numéro* and i-D. Portrait by Henry Linser.

Marcus Tomlinson Born London, 1961. Marcus initially started out as a graphic designer, and started taking pictures in the mid-'90s. Commissions included work for Christian Lacroix, Issey Miyake, Jamiroquai and Soul II Soul. At the end of 2003, Marcus was invited to exhibit at Mois de la Photo in Paris. He also developed his work with designers including Issey Miyake. In 2007, he was commissioned for the Museum of Modern Art in Luxembourg to create a film based on the work of Gareth Pugh. This will move to the Mode Museum, Antwerp and then to London's Design Museum at the beginning of 2009.

Jean Touitou Born Tunisia, 1951. Jean is the Founder and Designer of A.P.C. A graduate of History and Linguistics from the Sorbonne in Paris, Jean worked for Kenzo in the late '70s and later for Agnes b. He started his Atelier de Production et de Création line in 1987 and launched the first A.P.C. menswear collection in winter 1987, followed by womenswear in 1988. His first shop opened on rue de Fleurus in 1988 and the '90s saw a huge expansion of the brand in Japan. For spring/summer 2008, Jean collaborated with M/M Paris and Bruce Weber. Jean's interests also stretch well beyond fashion. In 1995, he launched a record label and in 2001, sponsored Zoe Cassavetes in a DVD-released film. Portrait by Stephane Gallois.

Guido Torlonia Born Guidalberto Torlonia, after graduating from the University of Rome in 1987 Guido began a career in stage and visual direction. From 1990 till 1993 he assisted Giorgio Strehler at the Piccolo Teatro in Milan where he worked with Peter Brook, the Martha Graham Company and the Royal Shakespeare Company. He has since worked as Theatre Director on several editions of Todifestival and the Festival dei Due Mondi in Spoleto, at Piccolo Eliseo, Teatro Parioli, the Cometa, the Orologio and the Teatro Due in Rome and at San Babila in Milan. He also contributes to the organisation and public relations for gala benefits including Unicef, the Red Cross and cancer research at Teatro Argentina and Teatro Olimpico in Rome.

Oliviero Toscani Born Milan, 1942. Oliviero studied Photography and Graphics at the Kunstgewerbeschule in Zurich. He gained international recognition as the creative force behind campaigns for companies such as Esprit and Fiorucci, and made Benetton one of the most recognisable international brands. He also created and initially edited the magazine *Colors*. As a fashion photographer Oliviero has shot for numerous international publications including *Elle*, *Vogue*, *GQ* and *Harper's Bazaar*. In 1993, he launched Fabrica, the international centre for arts and communication. His work has been exhibited at the Venice Biennale, the Triennale di Milano and in various museums of contemporary art around the world. He now lives in Tuscany and enjoys producing olive oil and breeding horses. Portrait by Orazio Truglio.

Kevin Trageser Photographer Kevin has lived and worked in New York for most of the past decade. He is a contributor to magazines including *Tokion*, *GQ*, *Whitewall* and *Spin*, and his work has been exhibited at the Design Commission (Seattle), the 255 Gallery (New York) and Colette (Paris). Kevin has also published his first book, *Home and Away*, in collaboration with fellow Chinatown Soccer Club members. On days off, he tries to combine his passion for surfing, travel and writing.

Kris Van Assche Born Belgium, 1976. Kris studied Fashion Design at Antwerp Royal Academy of Fine Arts. He moved to Paris in 1998 and established his own brand in 2004. Working with Hedi Slimane at Yves Saint Laurent and then for Dior Homme, Kris began to show his Kris Van Assche collection in January 2005. In 2007, he was Guest Designer at Pitti Immagine and also designed costumes for Bud Blumenthal's Standing Wave dance company. In May 2007, Kris was appointed Artistic Director of Dior Homme, following the departure of Hedi Slimane. Portrait by Gaëtan Bernard.

Philip Treacy Born Ireland, 1967. Since graduating from the Royal College of Art in London 15 years ago, and setting up in the basement of Isabella Blow's house, Philip has built a millinery empire, opening his first store in 1994 in London's Elizabeth Street. He has made hats for the greatest designers of our time – Versace, Karl Lagerfeld, Valentino, Emilio Pucci and Alexander McQueen. Philip's design oeuvre has expanded to include glassware, a chair for Habitat and a sportswear line for Umbro. He has also just completed the interiors for The G Hotel in Galway, West of Ireland. Philip has been awarded British Accessory Designer of the Year five times and in 2002 he won the Moët and Chandon Award for Luxury. In April 2006, he received an honorary doctorate from the National Museum of Ireland.

Robert Triefus Now Executive Vice President of Communications for Giorgio Armani worldwide, based in Milan, Robert started his career as Marketing Manager for the *Today* newspaper and *The Observer*, before he decided to establish his own marketing communications consultancy in 1988. In 1992, he was recruited by The Body Shop, which posted him to New York to oversee communications for its US subsidiary. Robert remained in America for nine years working for Ketchum Public Relations and then as Senior Vice President of Communications for Calvin Klein. He is recognised as a specialist in the area of corporate social responsibility.

Max Vadukul Born in Kenya, Max is a self-taught British photographer first discovered by Yohji Yamamoto in 1984. His work regularly appears in Italian *Vogue, L'Uomo Vogue, Men's Vogue, Harper's Bazaar, Vanity Fair* and *Rolling Stone*. After moving to New York, Max began collaborating with Tina Brown, which led to a three-year contract with *The New Yorker*. This was only the second contract given to a photographer in the magazine's 100 year history (the first was to Richard Avedon). He has published two books *MAX* (2000) and *Crazy Horse* (2001). Max lives in New York with his wife Nicoletta Santoro, the Fashion Editor of Italian *Vogue*, and their two children.

Walter Van Beirendonck Born Brecht, Belgium, 1957. Walter studied Fashion at the Royal Academy of Fine Arts in Antwerp and established his label in 1983. He was one of the legendary Antwerp Six (with Dirk Van Saene, Dries Van Noten, Dirk Bikkembergs, Ann Demeulemeester and Marina Yee) who had their first breakthrough at the British Designer Show in London in 1987. Alongside working on his own collection, Walter is the Artistic Director for Scapa Sports, designs a children's collection and teaches at the Royal Academy of Antwerp. Portrait by Ronald Stoops.

Willy Vanderperre Born Belgium, 1971. Willy studied Fashion Design at the Royal Academy of Fine Arts in Antwerp for two years before changing to the photography department where he studied for four years. He then showed his work at Modo Bruxelea, an exhibition curated by Peter de Potter and Olivier Rizzo. His first published works appeared in *V* and i-D, and he is now a regular contributor to many magazines including *Arena Homme Plus, POP, Another, L'Uomo Vogue, V, The New York Times Magazine, W* and Japanese and Italian *Vogue*. Willy is based in Antwerp, but travels regularly to Paris, London and New York for his assignments.

Inez van Lamsweerde and **Vinoodh Matadin** Inez and Vinoodh met in their hometown of Amsterdam where they started a career as a photography team. Since the early '90s, they have created groundbreaking editorials for such publications as American, French, and Italian *Vogue, V, Visionaire, The New York Times Magazine* and *W,* and have shot numerous advertising campaigns including Balenciaga, Louis Vuitton, Dior Homme, Yohji Yamamoto and Miu Miu. Their photography has also been exhibited in galleries and museums internationally including the Stedelijk Museum in Amsterdam, the Hayward Gallery, London and the Whitney Museum of Contemporary Art in New York. They are represented by Matthew Marks Gallery in New York.

Dries Van Noten Born 1958, Dries started a Fashion Design course at Antwerp's Royal Academy of Fine Arts and was a freelance designer in his spare time. By 1980, he was designing clothing for a Belgian manufacturer, as well as working as a buyer for his father's Antwerp boutiques. Dries launched his own line in 1986, selling to prestigious customers like Barneys New York. In September of that year he opened his first boutique in Antwerp's gallery arcade. He showed his collection at the British Designer Show and it was here that Dries and five of his fellow students from the Academy found international recognition as the "Antwerp Six". Today Dries Van Noten has shops in Antwerp, Paris, Hong Kong and Singapore, and sells in over 400 stores worldwide. Portrait by David Turner.

Donatella Versace Born Reggio Calabria, Italy, 1957. A key figure in establishing the international Versace empire, Donatella worked closely with her brother Gianni even before she had finished her Languages degree at Florence University. In the early '80s, she was responsible for the image of the company; overseeing the art direction of the advertising campaigns and creating identities for the diffusion lines, a concept that was then relatively new. In 1993, Donatella became Head Designer for the Versus range and following the death of Gianni she became Head Designer for the whole company. Today she is Vice President of the board and Creative Director of the highly successful Versace Group.

Francesco Vezzoli Born in Brescia, Italy. Since graduating from Central St Martins with a BA in Fine Art, Francesco has exhibited all over the world. His art includes video installations and petit-point embroideries, mixing heterogeneous languages and genres, bringing together pop icons, art history, political and private issues. Francesco's works have been presented, amongst others, at the 49th, 51st and 52nd Venice Biennial, Performa07, 2006 Whitney Biennial, the 6th Shanghai Biennial and the 6th Istanbul Biennial. He has also had solo exhibitions at numerous galleries including Fondazione Prada, New Museum of Contemporary Art and most recently at the Guggenheim with Cate Blanchett. A book, *The Needleworks of Francesco Vezzoli*, was published in 2002.

Patrick Vieira Born Dakar, Senegal, 1976. Patrick moved to France at the age of eight. He is a French football midfielder who currently plays for Inter Milan. Playing for Arsenal between 1996 and 2005, he won three Premier League titles and four FA Cups, and eventually became club Captain. He spent one season at Juventus, then joined Inter. Patrick made his debut for France in 1997 against The Netherlands and now has 104 caps for his country. He helped France to win both the 1998 World Cup and Euro 2000; he is now the team Captain. Patrick is also one of the founders of the Diambars football academy in Senegal which supports the nation's sporting youth.

Julian Vogel Born in London, Julian spent a year working for fashion PR Jean Bennett after leaving college. At 22, he joined Modus Publicity and became part Owner and Director the following year. Last year, Modus joined forces with beauty PRs Fiona Dowal and Owen Walker to form Modus Dowal Walker. Married to award-winning architect Sally MacKereth, Julian and Sally live in London and Norfolk with their two children Lola and Oscar.

Ellen Von Unwerth Born in Germany, Ellen worked as a model for ten years. Then in 1986, she began taking pictures. Her sensual campaigns for Guess? in the early '90s launched her to international acclaim and she was awarded first prize at the International Festival of Fashion Photography in Barcelona in 1991. Ellen's portfolio includes i-D, *Vanity Fair* and Italian, American and British *Vogue*. She has shot campaigns for Chanel, Alberta Ferretti and Miu Miu, and directed short films for Azzedine Alaïa and Katharine Hamnett, and commercials for Revlon, Cacharel and Lacoste. Her exhibitions include a one-woman show at The Hamilton Gallery (London) and Pobeda Gallery (Moscow). Ellen's photography books include *Snaps* (1994), *Couples* (1999), *Revenge* (2003) and *Omayrah Boyd* (2005).

Matthias Vriens Born and bred in Amsterdam, Matthias is a photographer currently based in Los Angeles. He is represented by The Project in New York where he has had two solo shows. His work for magazines includes *Men's Vogue*, *Numéro*, *Details*, *Elle*, *BUTT*, *Fantastic Man*, *The New York Times* and i-D. He has also worked as Editor-in-Chief/Creative Director of *Dutch* magazine, been Worldwide Creative Director of Giorgio Armani and Senior Art Director at Gucci Group. Matthias is currently creating a new magazine named *bl33n* and is expecting a baby.

Milan Vukmirovic Born France, 1970. Of Yugoslavian parentage, Milan started his career at the French magazine *Jardin Des Modes*. After working at Christian Lacroix, Lanvin, Matsuda, and Emmanuelle Fouks, he went on to become one of the founders of Colette, in Paris, where he was Creative Director and Buyer. At the end of the '90s he joined Tom Ford at the Gucci Group where he became Design Director, and in 2000 he became Creative Director at Jil Sander. In 2005 Milan joined *L'Officiel Hommes* where he is currently Editor-in-Chief. The magazine, now quarterly, has provided him with the opportunity to develop his work as a fashion photographer. His advertising clients include Armani, Neil Barrett, Hugo Boss and Trussardi. Since 2007, Milan has been working on the opening of The Webster, a new fashion space in the art deco area of Miami Beach.

Glenn Waldron Born Devon, 1977. Glenn is a freelance writer and editor. He is currently Contributing Menswear Editor for *The Independent*, Contributing Features Editor for *Fantastic Man* and *10 Magazine* and a former Editor of i-D. Alongside commercial projects for MTV, Uniqlo, Taschen, Virgin and the British Council, Glenn has written for *Vogue*, *Monocle*, *Wallpaper**, *Nylon* and *The Guardian*.

Tim Walker Born England, 1970. Tim graduated from Exeter Art College with a degree in Photography. Following this he worked as Richard Avedon's Assistant. His career took off when he was placed third in *The Independent* Young Photographer of the Year awards. He initially concentrated on documentary and portrait work for UK newspapers which led to editorial work for Italian, British and American *Vogue*, *W*, *Vanity Fair* and *Harper's Bazaar*. Commercial clients include Barneys, Levi's, Comme des Garçons and Yohji Yamamoto. His first solo exhibition took place in 2007 at Kestnergesellschaft, Germany and his first book will be published by teNeues in 2008. He currently lives in London but spends much of his time travelling.

Melanie Ward Maverick stylist Melanie lives in New York where she is Senior Fashion Editor at *Harper's Bazaar*. She has been credited with pioneering the grunge movement working with photographers including Inez and Vinoodh, Mario Sorrenti, Craig McDean, Steven Klein and Larry Clark on numerous editorials and fashion campaigns. A collaborator and muse of Helmut Lang for 13 years, Melanie has also acted as a Design Consultant for Calvin Klein and Jil Sander. More recently, as Creative Director, she designed the Karl Lagerfeld line for Karl Lagerfeld.

Ben Watts Born in London, raised in Australia, and currently living in New York, Ben began his career shooting friends and interesting people he encountered. These images were used for his university projects. Now Ben's photography appears in numerous magazines including i-D, *Harper's Bazaar*, *GQ*, *The New York Times Magazine* and *Rolling Stone* and his commercial clients include Nike, Apple, Polo Ralph Lauren, Bergdorf Goodman and Sony Music. Ben's first book, an urban youth scrapbook called *Big Up* was published in 2003 and his work has been shown in many exhibitions including the Whitney Biennal in Mexico.

Iain R. Webb An ex-Central St Martins School fashion student, Iain graduated in 1980, and 'fell' into writing and styling. Throughout his career he has been Fashion Editor/Director of various publications including *Blitz*, *The Evening Standard*, *Harpers & Queen*, *The Times* and *Elle*. In 1995 and 1996, he won the Fashion Journalist of The Year Award. Iain also moonlights as a photographer. He is currently working on a book about fashion designer Bill Gibb while contributing to *The New York Times Magazine* and *The Independent*. Iain also works as a creative consultant and visiting lecturer. In May 2005, he was honoured with a Professorship at the University of the Arts in London.

Veronica Webb Born Detroit, 1965. Veronica is a model, actress, writer and journalist. The youngest of three daughters, Veronica is of African-American, German and Iroquois descent. In 1965, she moved to New York where she graduated from Parsons School of Design with a major in Animation. Whilst in New York her modelling career took off with high profile campaigns for Nike and Bloomingdale's. Veronica also became a spokesmodel for Revlon and has appeared in several films including *Jungle Fever* and *Malcolm X*. In 1998, her collection of essays *Adventures in the Big City* was published. Veronica has two daughters, Leila and Molly.

Alek Wek Born Sudan, 1977. Model Alek was raised as part of the Dinka tribe. At 14, the civil war forced her to flee to London with her younger sister, where their mother and siblings later joined them. It was in London that Alek was first discovered. Since her first cover for i-D in 1998, Alek has modelled for numerous publications and her past campaigns include Ralph Lauren, Jean Paul Gaultier, Issey Miyake, Moschino and M.A.C Cosmetics. She published her autobiography *ALEK: From Sudanese Refugee to International Supermodel* in 2007. Alek has spoken at the International Black Caucus Foreign Affairs as a member of the panel and has served on the advisory board for the US Committee for Refugees. She now speaks in schools to bring attention to the famine in Southern Sudan. In addition, Alek has worked closely with AIDS awareness benefits, children's charities and Breast Cancer Research. Portrait by Gilles Bensimon.

Vivienne Westwood Born Derbyshire, 1941. At 17, Vivienne moved to London. She began designing in 1971, with her partner Malcolm McLaren. She opened a shop at 430 King's Road which became Worlds End in 1976. In 1981, Vivienne showed her first catwalk presentation at Olympia in London and in 1982, she began to show in Paris. In 1984, she was invited to show her collection in Tokyo alongside Hanae Mori, Calvin Klein, Claude Montana, and Gianfranco Ferre at "the best of five". This was also the year street style and youth culture ceased to play a major part in her world. She now finds inspiration in traditional Savile Row tailoring techniques, British fabrics and 17th and 18th Century art. 1990 heralded her first complete menswear collection and in 1990 and 1992, she was awarded British Designer of the Year. There are now Vivienne Westwood stores across the world, five fragrances and a Vivienne Westwood retrospective exhibition is currently touring the globe. In 2006, she was appointed a Dame for her contribution to British fashion.

Paul Wetherell Paul moved to London in 1992, and was a freelance assistant to fashion photographers David Sims and Cindy Palmano. Paul now shoots both on location and in the studio with a sophisticated understanding of light, pose and printing. His work has appeared in magazines including *Self Service*, *10*, *Acne Paper*, *Fantastic Man*, *W*, *V*, *032C* and i-D. His advertising clients include Yohji Yamamoto, IBM, Daks, Hermès, Bergdorf Goodman, Calvin Klein and Remy Martin.

Patti Wilson Born and raised in New York, Patti spent her early career waitressing and working in a jazz club before finding work as a stylist's assistant. In the early '90s she met Edward Enninful and started working for i-D. During her career as a stylist she has contributed to magazines including Italian, Russian and Japanese *Vogue*, *L'Uomo Vogue*, *Numéro*, *Harper's Bazaar*, *V* and i-D. Photographers Patti has worked with include Steven Meisel, Terry Richardson, Ellen Von Unwerth, Jean Baptiste Mondino, Paolo Roversi and David LaChapelle. Portrait by Ed Robinson.

Kevin Wong Born Hong Kong, 1981. Kevin moved to England to study aged 15. He attended Central St Martins for three years, during which more time was spent making music than doing art. After graduation he won a competition organised by SHOWstudio, in which Terry Jones was one of the jurors, leading to the job of Designer at i-D. Kevin is also working on a series of photographs documenting Chinese creatives in the UK.

Jonathan Worth Born Leicester, 1972. Jonathan began taking portraits for i-D whilst assisting Steve Pyke in the late '90s which continued until he moved to New York in 2000. He now works as a portrait photographer out of both the UK and US. Over the years, Jonathan has built-up one of the most extensive family albums in the history of the world and has three exhibitions of new work showing in the UK through 2008. Jonathan lives with his wife and two children.

Jules Wright Australian-born Jules directed her first main stage production at the Theatre Royal Stratford East in 1979. In 1981, she was appointed Resident Director at the Royal Court Theatre, and soon after became Artistic Director of the Theatre Upstairs. From 1984 to 1986, she was Artistic Director of the Liverpool Playhouse. She then returned to the Royal Court becoming Deputy Artistic Director until 1992. Her career has included productions at the Old Vic, Royal Festival Hall and international work in Europe, Australia and South America. She is also the Creator and Director of one of London's most exciting and prominent artistic buildings, The Wapping Project, which she set up in 1992. Portrait by Thomas Zanon-Larcher.

Michiko Yamamoto Born in Tokyo, Michiko graduated with a BA in Fashion Photography from London College of Fashion in 2007. She is currently working as a fashion and portrait photographer.

Yohji Yamamoto Born Tokyo, 1943. Yohji founded Y's in 1972, and had his first fashion show in Tokyo in 1977. In 1981, he began to show in Paris, and his first menswear collection was also shown there in 1984. Off the catwalk, Yohji has designed costumes for the Opera de Lyon's production of Puccini's *Madame Butterfly* (1990), the Wagner Opera (1993) and Takeshi Kitano's film *Brother* (2000). In 1989, Wim Wenders released a film portrait of Yohji, *Notebook on Cities and Clothes*, and in 2002 his book *Talking to Myself* was published in which he recounts the phases of his life. Yohji became the Creative Director of Y-3 – a collaboration with Adidas – in 2002. The Y-3 collection is now shown during New York fashion week. In 2005, he received the rank of Officer in the National Order of Merit from The French Republic President. Yohji Yamomoto Inc. now includes menswear, womenswear and Y's Red Label and the collaborative lines Y's Mandarina, Y-3 and Y's for Living. Yohji continues to show his men's and women's collections in Paris and has Yohji Yamamoto stores in Antwerp, London, Paris, New York and across Japan. Portrait by Koichi Inakoshi.

Italo Zucchelli Italo grew up near La Spezia, Italy. He graduated in 1988 from the Polimoda School of Fashion Design in Florence and also attended courses for two years at the Architecture University. Italo was Menswear Designer for two years at Jil Sander and a Designer at Romeo Gigli before starting at Calvin Klein in 2000. After close collaboration with Calvin on the design of four men's and two women's collections, he was selected to take over as Menswear Designer in 2003. Italo is now Creative Director of Calvin Klein menswear, and he was nominated for the US Menswear Designer of the Year in 2007.

All biographies and photographs that we were given have been published. A few contributors preferred not to be included in this section.

∫

index

Achara, Chidi 460, 581
Adrover, Miguel 373, 581
Alemany, Eloise 240, 581
Alexander, Hilary 238, 581
Ali Pandu, Khamis 437, 596
Anthony, Mark 126, 581
Aoki, Devon 598
Arad, Ron 238, 581
Archer, Paul 241, 581
Armani, Giorgio 126, 239, 402, 448, 461, 581, 583, 586, 587, 594, 600, 601, 602
Aurell, Anette 247, 581
Badhams, Claire 464, 581
Bailey, Christopher 462, 581
Bailey, David 402, 581, 587, 596
Baker, Caroline 127, 581
Baker, William 185, 581
Baron, Fabien 127, 582
Barrett, Neil 247, 582, 602
Bartlett, Victoria 131, 582
Beaud, Marie-Claude 242, 582
Bedeaux, Zoe 19, 243, 582
Beecroft, Vanessa 128, 582
Bennett, Clare 463, 582
Benoliel, Ben 463, 582
Bentley, Sarah 464, 582
Berardi, Antonio 128, 252, 582
Best, Orion 18, 404, 465, 582
Blame, Judy 19, 128, 403, 582, 590
Bleakley, Sam 467, 582
Blechman, Hardy 130, 582
Bogue, Moira 20, 130, 582
Bolofo, Koto 21, 132, 133, 400, 406, 407
Bono (Hewson, Paul) 409, 420, 581, 583
Booth, Gemma 138, 248, 410, 469, 583
Borrell, Johnny 403, 583
Borthwick, Mark 22, 244, 354, 583, 585, 593
Bragg, Debbie 464, 583
Branquinho, Véronique 248, 469, 583
Broach, Zowie 136, 583
Brody, Neville 249, 411, 468, 583, 593
Brooke, Matt 137
Buckley, Richard 252, 394, 583
Burgess, Terry 138, 583
Burrows, Danny 137, 583
Burston, Paul 24, 137, 583
Burton, Jeff 252, 583
Camarillo, Martha 254, 584
Casely-Hayford, Joe 27, 374, 413, 584
Castro, Jota 470, 584
Cattelan, Maurizio 255
Chadha, Natascha 256, 584
Chalayan, Hussein 139, 159, 257, 375, 473, 583, 584, 590
Chapman, Dinos 24, 584, 600
Chapman, Jake 24, 584, 600
Chave, Tim 258, 584
Chernin, Rowan 140, 584
Cherry, Neneh 68, 582, 594, 595
Christie, Donald 25, 260, 584
Clements, Suzanne 197, 584
Cochrane, Lauren 473, 584, 602, 603
Cohen, Joe 412, 584
Cohen, Stuart 476, 584
Cole, Bethan 140, 584
Compton, Nick 254, 584
Cooke, Fraser 478, 584
Cooke, Kieran 430, 585
Cornejo, Maria 22, 479, 583, 585
Corner, Lena 26, 585
Corrigan, Susan 141, 585
Costa, Francisco 477, 585
Costantini, Eduardo Jr 480, 585
Cotter, Nicki 481, 585
Couji, Giannie 26, 138, 585
Crabtree, Suzy 259, 585
Cunningham, BJ 138, 497, 585
Dahl, Sophie 28, 585
His Holiness the Dalai Lama (Gyatso, Tenzin) 237, 262, 263, 414, 530, 585
Dallanegra, Fiona 28, 124, 265, 585, 597
Davies, David 28, 585
Davies, Kevin 29, 44, 264, 585
Dayani, Soraya 30, 586
De Mitri, Giorgio 482, 586
De Potter, Peter 266, 342, 375, 586, 601
Dechnik, Fred 267, 586
Degen, Thomas 269, 586
Dell'Acqua, Alessandro 145, 586, 587
Demeulemeester, Ann 143, 586, 601
Derrick, Robin 144, 586
Dolce, Domenico 486, 586, 587, 594, 600
Doll, Uwe 268, 415, 586
Drinkell, Clare 586
Drinkell, Pete 272, 586, 595
Dudderidge, Joanna 484, 586
Dunstan, Larry 145, 271, 414, 586

Elbaz, Alber 487, 586
Eliasson, Olafur 416, 586
Elliott, Tony 31, 586
Ellis, Kevin 276, 587
Ellis, Sean 146, 587
Emin, Tracey 273, 376, 418, 528, 587
Enninful, Edward 32, 38, 146, 274, 488, 585, 587, 588, 592, 594, 596, 597, 603
Enninful, Luther 32, 587
Evans, Jason 32, 36, 146, 275, 417, 587
Ferretti, Alberta 148, 587, 594, 602
Ferri, Fabrizio 37, 167, 587
Fiddy, Chantelle 490, 587
Flett, Kathryn 38, 587
Fluxá, Lorenzo 276, 587
Ford, Tom 277,585,587,602
Fortune, Christine 38, 587
Foxton, Simon 32, 146, 148, 276, 491, 587, 589
Franklin, Caryn 39, 125, 148, 277, 419, 587, 587, 600
Frey, Mark 91, 588
Gabbana, Stefano 486, 586, 587, 594, 600
Galliano, John 146, 493, 582, 588, 589, 591, 594, 596
Gan, Stephen 278, 588
Garner, Kate 279, 588
Garratt, Sheryl 421, 588
Garrett, Malcolm 149, 588
Gavin, Jake 284, 588
Geldof, Bob 423, 588
Genn, Antony 494, 588
Genninger, Laura 281, 588
Gherardi, Manuela 149, 588
Giunta, Johnny 150, 588
Glaser, Susanna 40, 588
Gomiashvili, Katia 495, 588
Goodman, Georgina 153, 497, 585, 588
Gordon, Kim 498, 588
Gowing, Amanda 285, 589
Griffiths, Nick 151, 588, 589
Grumbach, Didier 280, 589
Guillén, Mauricio 152, 589
Halvarsson, Henrik 157, 589
Hamilton, Bethany 499, 589
Hamnett, Katharine 424, 583, 589, 597, 598, 601, 602
Hancock, Liz 237, 282, 589
Harlech, Amanda 283, 589
Harris, Steve 283, 502, 589
Hassan, Wichy 154, 589
Hawker, Matthew E. 9, 12, 282, 589
Haylor, Rick 41, 153, 589
Heiss, Desiree 286, 589
Hogan, Gemma 12, 500, 589
Homma, Takashi 287, 589
Hooper, Mark 286, 589
Horvat, Frank 154, 590
How, Jane 40, 155, 590
Howe, Adam 41, 158, 590
Hunwick, Paul 159, 590
Ian 501, 590
Jacobs, Marc 158, 287, 590, 598, 599, 600, 601
Johnson-Artur, Liz 159, 590
Jones, Dylan 44, 506, 590
Jones, Hannah 502, 590
Jones, Kayt 42, 125, 163, 504, 590, 591, 594
Jones, Matt 45, 160, 288, 420, 432, 507, 590, 591
Jones, Stephen 503, 590
Jones, Terry 4, 9, 17, 32, 39, 46, 146, 165, 237, 290, 341, 377, 424, 459, 508, 581, 586, 587, 589, 590, 591, 592, 593, 595, 603
Jones, Tricia 8, 10, 11, 16, 17, 39, 47, 125, 166, 237, 292, 341, 346, 372, 400, 425, 459, 508, 510, 526, 590, 592
Just, Gabriela 291, 590
Kamei, Takashi 512, 590
Karan, Donna 167, 581, 591, 595, 600
Kaws (Donnelly, Brian) 513, 591
Kei, Ben 12, 514, 591
Kim, Hyun Jung 515, 591
Kirkby, Brian 136, 583
Klein, Calvin 167, 299, 585, 587, 591, 594, 595, 597, 598, 599, 601, 602, 603
Knight, Charlotte 32, 50
Knight, Nick 32, 51, 146, 168, 294, 427, 518, 549, 570, 582, 585, 587, 590, 591
Koch, Jörg 300,591
Koh, Kirby 516, 591
Kokosalaki, Sophia 376, 517, 591, 597
Kutomi, Hiroshi 169, 299, 591
LaChapelle, David 170, 523, 569, 591, 603
Lam, Grace 177, 591
Landon, Jessica 428, 591
Lang, Helmut 57, 159, 176, 519, 521, 591, 595, 601, 602
Lauren, Ralph 58, 587, 592
Lavelle, James 58, 177, 592
Law, Kate 12, 592
Lebon, Mark 19, 60, 68, 174, 378, 429, 459, 467, 582, 592, 595
Lebon, Tyrone 525, 592
Leenknegt, Drieke 526, 592
Leong, Karen 12, 301, 592
Leslie, Merryn 177, 592

Liao, Duc 173, 301, 592
Lopez, Angel 64, 180, 592
Maathai, Wangari 430, 431, 592
Macdonald, Julien 181, 300, 592
Mahdavi, Ali 379, 592
Mair, Alix 17, 181, 592, 592
Maison Martin Margiela 183, 303, 583, 590, 592, 597, 599
Mallard, Michel 309, 592
Marras, Antonio 380, 593
Martin, Chris 4, 420, 421, 593
Matadin, Vinoodh 216, 597, 601
Matthews, Meg 181, 593
Mattock, Mark 65, 305, 593, 594
May, Rufus 527, 593
McCabe, Eamonn J. 67, 593
McCarthy, Francesca 531, 593
McCartney, Mary 528, 593
McCartney, Stella 146, 184, 590, 593, 598
McDean, Craig 306, 582, 586, 587, 593, 597, 600, 602
McDowell, Colin 312, 593
McGinley, Ryan 529, 593
McGrath, Pat 69, 488, 593
McKell, Iain 308, 593
McLellan, Alasdair 312, 593
McQueen, Alexander 80, 146, 381, 435, 530, 585, 591, 593, 594, 596, 598, 600, 601
McVey, Cameron 19, 68, 584, 594
Meier, Dani Kiwi 531, 594
Metson Scott, Jo 534, 593
Milne, Donald 70, 594
Minogue, Kylie 185, 581, 582, 584, 590, 594, 596
Mittleman, Paul 181, 594
Miyake, Issey 39, 186, 592, 594, 600, 601, 603
Momy, Michel 69, 187, 330, 594
Monsoon, Eddie 188, 594
Moore, Thurston 498, 589
Morris, Dennis 70, 190, 401, 594
Mortensen, Shawn 310, 382, 533, 594
Moss, Kate 189, 503, 594
Moyle, Clare 191, 594
Murch, Jeremy 72, 151, 594
Murkudis, Kostas 192, 594
Naidoo, Ravi 313, 595
Napoleone, Raffaello 314, 595
Narain, Nadia 315, 538, 595
Newton, Helmut 189, 595, 596, 598
Numata, Maryvonne 385,595
O'Connor, Erin 43, 146, 539, 595
O'Connor, Keiron 384, 595
Ogden, Jessica 318, 595
Ono, Yoko 437, 595
Ours, Nathalie 384, 541, 595
Patel, Tesh 319, 595
Pavesi, Manuela 542, 595
Pearson, Graham Arthur 194
Pearson, John Barnes 12, 194, 595
Pecori-Giraldi, Clarice 320, 595
Peggs, Tobias 193, 595
Peres, Javier 542, 595
Peverley, Jane 319, 596
Pilet, Bianca 317, 596
Plumb, Shannon 320, 596
Prada, Miuccia 192, 318, 582, 589, 592, 594, 596, 597, 598, 599, 602
Pugh, Gareth 542, 596, 601
Reich, Oriana 328, 596
Renson, Dominique 387, 596
Ribeiro, Inacio 197, 584
Ribeiro, Vava 322, 596
Richardson, Terry 195, 324, 596, 603
Richter, Mischa 326, 389, 596
Rivetti, Carlo 327, 386, 596
Rizzo, Olivier 353, 596, 601
Robson, Millie 544, 596
Roddick, Dame Anita 328, 437, 596
Roehri, Myriam 187, 330, 596
Rose Bakery 405, 596
Rosier, Gilles 331, 597
Ross, Markus 531, 597
Rosso, Renzo 12, 331, 436, 593, 597
Roversi, Paolo 73, 155, 196, 332, 541, 587, 590, 597, 600, 603
Rowlands, Amber 74, 197, 333, 597
Ruhs, Kris 335, 388, 438, 546, 597
Ruiz, Stefan 77, 198, 597
Sabisha 547, 597
Sander, Jil 207, 554, 587, 594, 597, 597, 599, 602, 603
Santini, Derrick 78, 199, 337, 597
Sarah 337, 200, 597
Saville, Peter 201, 440, 548, 584, 597
Schnee, Jicky 288, 338, 590, 597
Schneider, Stephan 338, 597
Schorr, Collier 550, 597
Scott, Jeremy 547, 597
Scott, Venitia 340, 598
Semotan, Elfie 83, 176, 202, 598
Shafran, Nigel 205, 598
Shambhala 339, 598
Sharkey, Alix 203, 551, 598
Shiva, Dr Vandana 441, 598

Shya, Wing 553, 598
Silvagni, Irene 341, 598
Simons, Raf 84, 342, 390, 554, 586, 598, 599
Sims, David 87, 207, 586, 597, 598, 599, 603
Singh, Talvin 85, 208, 598
Sleaford, James 84, 598
Sleaford, Julie 84, 598
Smith, Bob and Roberta (Brill, Patrick) 389, 598
Smith, Paul 208, 338, 363, 391, 442, 556, 557, 585, 586, 590, 599, 600
Smith, Paul D. 558, 599
Soncini, Franca 208, 599
Sorrenti, Francesca 90, 344, 599
Sorrenti, Mario 91, 587, 588, 590, 592, 598, 599, 602
Sorrenti, Vanina 92, 210, 344, 599
Souleiman, Eugene 146, 209, 599
Sprouse, Stephen 138, 346, 590, 599
Stone, Matthew 555, 599
Summers, Beth 32, 93, 210, 599
Sumner, Bernard 93, 599
Sundsbø, Sølve 94, 599
Suu Kyi, Aung San 431
Takahashi, Jun 392, 540, 599
Takahiko, Takemoto (Takay) 41, 213, 599
Takizawa, Naoki 212, 599, 600
Tan, Alexi 212, 600
Tarabini, Rossella 211, 600
Taschen, Angelika 346, 591, 600
Tayama, Atsuro 211, 581, 600
Taylor, Marcia 213, 347, 442, 600
Taylor-Wood, Sam 559, 600
Teller, Juergen 57, 96, 214, 350, 582, 598, 600
Tennekoon 443, 600
Tillmans, Wolfgang 98, 349, 445, 600
Tomlinson, Marcus 454, 560, 600
Torlonia, Guido 211, 600
Toscani, Oliviero 48, 101, 600
Touitou, Jean 588
Trageser, Kevin 561, 600
Treacy, Philip 95, 582, 588, 601
Triefus, Robert 343, 601
Vadukul, Max 104, 352, 601
Van Assche, Kris 561, 601
Van Beirendonck, Walter 562, 601
Van Lamsweerde, Inez 216, 597, 601
Van Noten, Dries 393, 446, 598, 601
Vanderperre, Willy 353, 563, 586, 597, 601
Versace, Donatella 102, 601
Vezzoli, Francesco 394, 564, 601
Vieira, Patrick 447, 601
Vogel, Julian 566, 601
Von Unwerth, Ellen 102, 218, 357, 396, 567, 587, 601
Vriens, Matthias 394, 602
Vukmirovic, Milan 354, 602
Waldron, Glenn 220, 602
Walker, Tim 220, 602
Ward, Melanie 107, 602
Watts, Ben 569, 602
Webb, Iain R. 358, 602
Webb, Veronica 103, 602
Wek, Alek 103, 602
Westwood, Vivienne 138, 159, 358, 503, 588, 590, 592, 602
Wetherell, Paul 106, 359, 602
Wilson, Patti 109, 359, 602
Wong, Kevin 570, 603
Worth, Jonathan 108, 603
Wright, Jules 358, 603
Yamamoto, Michiko 572, 603
Yamamoto, Yohji 541, 571, 583, 590, 591, 594, 596, 597, 598, 599, 600, 601, 602, 603
Zucchelli, Italo 573, 603

Helping change young lives.

Prince's Trust

Every day we meet more young people who believe they'll never get anything right. They're wrong, ironically.

If nothing succeeds like success, then nothing fails like failure. Which is what a lot of young people think they are – failures. If they can't keep up at school, they're told they're failing. If they leave without any qualifications, then they've failed. They don't just 'not' get a job, they fail to get a job. And they don't get 'into' trouble, they fail to stay out of it. At first, they blame everyone else – their teachers, parents, the kids they hang around with. Then they start blaming themselves. They're natural born failures, apparently. And if there's anything to feel positive about, they fail to see it. But we do see it. The Prince's Trust believes that every young person has potential. Whether they're falling behind at school, leaving care, finding it impossible to find employment or in trouble with the law, we believe, with the right support, every young person has the ability to change their life. So we offer them support and training. We offer guidance and sometimes even financial assistance to set up their own business. We help them get the skills they need for a sense of purpose. Most importantly, we help them get their self-confidence back. We help them realise their potential. For more information call 0800 842 842. Or visit princes-trust.org.uk

Registered charity, number 1079675, incorporated by Royal Charter.

To stay informed about upcoming TASCHEN titles, please request our magazine at www.taschen.com/magazine or write to TASCHEN, Hohenzollernring 53, D-50672 Cologne, Germany, contact@taschen.com, Fax: +49-221-254919. We will be happy to send you a free copy of our magazine which is filled with information about all of our books.

Editor **Tricia Jones**

Creative Director **Terry Jones**

Design and Production **Matthew Hawker**

Managing Editor **Karen Leong**

Assistant Editor **Gemma Hogan**

Advertising Director **Chris Doherty**

Editorial Assistant **Nicola Pozzani**

Production Assistant **Ben Kei**

Associate Publisher **Angelo Careddu**

Financial Director **Suzanne Doyle**

Biographies edited by **Gemma Hogan, Karen Leong, Lauren Cochrane** and **Tricia Jones**

Special editorial consultant **John Pearson**

Editorial co-ordination **Simone Philippi**

Production co-ordination **Ute Wachendorf**

Printed in Hong Kong
ISBN 978-3-8365-0666-3